WHAT EVERY AMERICAN SHOULD KNOW ABOUT AMERICAN HISTORY

200 Events that Shaped the Nation

Dr. Alan Axelrod and Charles Phillips

BOB ADAMS, INC.

PUBLISHERS

Holbrook, Massachusetts

Published by Bob Adams, Inc.
260 Center Street, Holbrook, MA 02343
Printed in the United States of America

ISBN: 1-55850-309-9 (paperback)
J   I   H   G   F   E   D   C   B

ISBN: 1-55850-152-5 (hardcover)
J   I   H   G   F   E   D

Library of Congress Cataloging-in-Publication Data
Axelrod, Alan, 1952-
    What every American should know about American history : 200 events
that shaped the nation / Alan Axelrod and Charles Phillips.
        p.   cm.
    Includes index.
    ISBN 1-55850-309-9 (pbk.) : $9.95
    ISBN 1-55850-152-5 (hc.) : $15.00
    1. United States—History—Miscellanea. I. Phillips, Charles, 1948- . II. Title.
E178.A96   1993
97300dc20   93-21301
                                                                    CIP

INTERIOR ILLUSTRATIONS by Joanna Hudgens.

REAR COVER PHOTOGRAPHS courtesy of U.S. Library of Congress.

FRONT COVER PHOTOGRAPHS courtesy of U.S. Library of Congress, with the exception of the photo in the lower right-hand corner, which is used by permission of George Holliday and with the assistance of the law offices of James Jordan.

This book is available at quantity discounts for bulk purchases.
For information, call 1-800-872-5627.

To Ian and Tammi

ACKNOWLEDGMENTS

Books, too, have histories. This one began with an idea from Bob Adams. Our able, courageous, and long-suffering agent, Bert Holtje then sold Bob on the notion that we were the ones to write it. Charles Phillips imagined the shape and structure of the narrative, and both he and Alan Axelrod plunged into the research and writing of the book. Without the work of innumerable students of history, many of whom are listed in our bibliography, that plunge would have been more difficult and less satisfying. From these and the many others we read, we not only gathered the facts, but the shape of American history itself, which is after all the collective construction of its writers. Candace Floyd helped with the research and drafting of a number of the entries. Brandon Toropov, an editor most writers would kill for, proved sensitive to language as well as deadlines; he had an imagination to match that of his writers, and his intelligence even more than his professional diligence made work on the project a great pleasure. He was assisted by Chris Ciaschini and by the able, thorough, and, most importantly, artful copyediting of Kate Layzer, worthy descendant of the William Lloyd Garrison who played a major role in the history on some of these pages. Our partner in Zenda, Inc., Patricia Hogan, was with us in the beginning, helping choose events, then interpret them, then write them, then make them better, becoming the true "unsung" hero of our history. Finally, neither of us could have written a word of this book if we had never met Sherman Paul. More than teaching us American history, he taught us to think about American history; more than our mentor, he was the midwife of our collaboration, which started in his classes more years ago than we care to document. All these deserve the credit, none of the blame, and our gratitude for the way this book's history reads.

INTRODUCTION

Most Americans, unlike most historians, are unconvinced that by knowing the past we avoid repeating it. Indeed, the very idea of America grows from an attempt to escape the past, to start over and make things new. This is why American intellectuals have so often talked about a usable past, the one we need to create from the dustbin of dry historical facts in order to get on with the business of reinventing ourselves. That this has led too often to a mindless celebration of our history, rather than a sober-eyed review, does not necessarily change the value of their insight. For a usable past does not have to degenerate into a hodgepodge of homilies for restless and distracted youths to avoid like the plague. Instead, American history can be retold as the colorful story it truly is. Colorful stories are never painless—that's part of their fascination. Yes, Americans should know the basic events of their own history recounted here, but more importantly, they should want to know them, because knowing them truly matters.

We have chosen 200 events by which to narrate the story of what Thomas Jefferson, back at the beginning of the American republic over two centuries ago, called the American right to pursue happiness. Some of the events are interesting because they involve great personalities, personalities that, rightly or wrongly, have been credited with shaping our history. Other events seemed to us to reveal the broader social realities that lay at the root of our lives as citizens and private individuals. They are not the only 200 events we could have chosen, nor are they the 200 events someone else might have chosen, but all are events any American should know about and appreciate to understand fully his or her own pursuit of happiness, the foundation of that elusive American dream so often celebrated in our literature and so seldom fulfilled in our history.

At the turn of the last century, a historian named Frederick Jackson Turner came up with a theory about America that had a profound effect on the way historians told the American tale. Noticing in the 1890 census that white occupation had become evenly distributed on both sides of an abstract "line" once used to divide settled from unsettled regions, Turner produced the "frontier thesis." According to Turner, the history of America was the story of white settlement of the wilderness, the building of a civilization by individuals whose rugged hardiness and freedom-loving values were formed on the isolated frontier, which was just then closing. The frontier itself had a political beginning, when King George had declared the Proclamation Line, a boundary set at the Appalachian Mountains beyond which he would not allow his subjects to go. Then came the American Revolution, and the frontier had been on the move ever since.

As a metaphor for understanding our past, Turner's thesis was both powerful and dangerous: powerful because it explained so much, dangerous because it masked the extent to which American "settlement" of the subcontinent was an invasion and occupation of other peoples' land, fueled by almost instinctual greed and a racist ideology gussied up as "Manifest Destiny." Lost to it were the millions of Indians who happened to live in the wilderness and were dismissed as savages; lost too were the rich cultures of other European colonizers like the Spanish and the French, of American immigrant groups such as the Irish, the Italians, the Germans, the Jews, and any number of East Europeans; and lost were the major contributions to American history of the African-Americans originally brought to the country in bondage.

Other histories at least tried to account for those groups in discourses that concentrated on the perfection of America's centuries-old experiment in self-government. By such accounts America was mankind's last great hope. Having finally freed itself of the curse of slavery that had stained its past, it welcomed the huddled masses of the world longing to be free into a melting pot that transformed them into true citizens of a new world. But this kind of story obscured the extent to which America was the result of the conflict—not merely the amalgamation—of many cultures, a conflict that failed to rip the country apart only because the system, nearly alone in the history of mankind, had at least in theory developed a method of protecting its minority populations.

For us, neither the frontier thesis nor the melting pot theory upon which most American popular history has been based was complete enough to explain the American story. Like all historians, when we looked at events in our past we saw them in the fullness of time and rushed to understand their beginnings in their ends or their ends in their beginnings, believing that the pregnant event engendered the future. But instead of a steady progress—or even, God forbid, a lamentable decline and fall—we chose to understand the events recounted in this book as things that happened in the pursuit of happiness. For it was in that moment when Thomas Jefferson, writing the Declaration of Independence, decided not to use the three basic inalienable rights that the great philosopher John Locke had said were natural to mankind—life, liberty, and property—but to substitute for "property" the "pursuit of happiness," that America was truly born.

The pursuit of happiness does not necessarily lead anywhere, and yet it represents a common thread to string together the events that make up the American past. From the very first event recounted here the reader will recognize that we are concerned not merely with describing or listing an occurrence but with using the event as a jumping-off point, an opportunity to describe the milieu in which the event occurred. Discrete actions, after all, are only sign-posts of their times, never taking place in isolation from other events or actions. Handy guides to the past, perhaps, they are much more fascinating in context, however imperfectly we may capture it in the tricky game of language called narrative. Confident these events shaped all our lives, we have attempted to serve them up in a popular history that will be enjoyable to read even as it explains how things turned out the way they did.

— *Alan Axelrod and Charles Phillips*

TABLE OF CONTENTS

Leif Ericson Explores Vinland (A.D. 1000)

The event: Around A. D. 1000 Norse captain Leif Ericson, out of Greenland, struck land in present-day Newfoundland, establishing a village he called Vinland, the first European colony in North America.

LONG BEFORE THE Vikings arrived in what would come to be called America, bands of hunters and gatherers from central Asia had entered the area from Siberia across a land bridge into Alaska, which rising oceans fed by melting glaciers would later wash away, creating the Bering Strait. Certainly by 10,000 B.C., and perhaps as much as tens of thousands of years earlier, these people spread across two continents, slaughtering wooly mammoth and establishing many and varied cultures. Some, like the Eskimos and Inuits in the North, continued to hunt and gather in small tribal bands; others, like the Olmecs and the Chavin in Central and South America, developed complex societies. By the time Europeans first discovered their "New World," millions of those they eventually called "Indians" had occupied the land for so long that they must be considered a native and indigenous population.

The first European to set eyes on the Americas was probably a Norseman named Bjarni Herjulfsson in A.D. 986. Herjulfsson evidently sighted land but did not go ashore. A decade later, Ericson, some say, spent a winter in rough Viking huts thrown up in the area he named after its abundant grapes or berries. He returned home in the spring, abandoning the rude settlement that, a few years later, would serve as home base for Thorfinn Karlsevni, another Greenlander some claim was Ericson's brother. Thorfinn passed two years in Vinland, exploring the Newfoundland coast and battling local tribes of unfriendly Eskimos, whom the Vikings called skrelings, old Norse for "wretches" or "dwarfs." Thorfinn was killed in an encounter with the Native Americans, and continued hostilities discouraged the Norsemen from further settlement. The Viking explorations, which seemed to Norsemen to have resulted in the discovery of a new land, apparently struck the Native Americans as an attempt to invade their homeland. What neither Viking nor Eskimo could know, of course, was that it was only the first attack of the European "invasion."

Columbus Reaches the Shores of the New World (1492)

The event: On October 12, 1492, after seventy grueling days at sea, sailors in the employ of Christopher Columbus sighted land, marking the end of the "Great Navigator's" first voyage to America and the seminal moment in the "opening" of the New World by the Old.

BORN TO A FAMILY of weavers in or near Genoa about August 25, 1451, Columbus went to sea before the 1470s, and by the second half of that decade was making his home in Portugal. In 1484 Columbus approached Portugal's King João II, seeking his sponsorship of a western voyage to the island Marco Polo called "Cipangu" (Japan). The king turned him down.

He then attempted to interest Don Enrique de Guzmán, Duke of Medina Sidonia, in sponsoring his voyage, but was rebuffed. He turned next to Don Luis de la Cerda, Count of Medina Celi, who arranged for an audience with Queen Isabella (circa May 1, 1486). Although the first meeting proved inconclusive, an influential court official named Luis de Santangel at last convinced the Spanish crown to sponsor the voyage, which was financed by a combination of royal and private funds. Appointed Admiral of the Ocean Sea, Viceroy, and governor of whatever lands he might discover, Christopher Columbus set sail from Palos on August 3, 1492, in three modest vessels called the *Niña* (commanded by Vincente Yáñez Pinzón), the *Pinta* (Martín Alonso Pinzón), and Columbus's flagship, the *Santa Maria*. With a crew of ninety, Columbus enjoyed favorable winds during the first leg of the voyage, but from September 20 to 30, unfavorable winds and doldrums slowed progress and caused crew members to doubt their commander. Indeed, as it became clear to Columbus that he had grossly miscalculated transoceanic distances, he began to keep two logbooks: one with fictitious computations of distance, for the benefit of the crew, and another accurate, but secret, log. Just two days before the Bahaman island the natives called Guanahani (probably Watlings Island) was sighted on October 12, the crews of the three vessels verged on mutiny.

After landing on Guanahani, claiming it in the name of Spain and christening it San Salvador, Columbus explored the Bahamas, Cuba, and Hispañola (Santo Domingo), establishing a post called La Navidad. There the *Santa Maria* was wrecked in a storm on Christmas Day, 1492. Columbus set sail for Spain on January 16, 1493. He left a garrison at La Navidad, which, as soon as the Admiral was safely departed, set about pillaging goods and raping women. The Indians retaliated, so that, when Columbus returned to La Navidad late in 1493, no whites were alive. From the Canaries (February 15), he dispatched a letter to his patron Luis de Santangel describing the voyage. It was immediately printed and, in effect, published worldwide. Two papal bulls (*Inter Caetera* and *Inter Caetera II*) issued in 1493 and the Treaty of Tordesillas (June 7, 1494) effectively divided possession of the newly discovered lands between Spain and Portugal.

It soon became apparent to men such as the mariner Amerigo Vespucci that Columbus had not (as he had thought) discovered a shortcut to the riches of the Orient. On his second voyage in 1501, Vespucci coined the phrase *Mundus Novus* to denote the vast regions that would soon be named after Amerigo himself. This "New World" Columbus had discovered promised more than spices and silk. It promised a vast colonial empire with untold stores of gold and apparently limitless sources of new "subjects" to mine it. Moreover, the entire enterprise seemed blessed by God, who had not only opened up a treasury of riches to Spain but who offered an immense harvest of native souls ripe for the Christianizing influence of the empire's missionaries.

Amerigo's *Mundus Novus* held the promise of a second chance. Spain, like much of Europe, was dominated by a system of primogeniture, which mandated that the first son in a family inherit all titles and property upon the death of the father, thereby severely limiting opportunities for second, third, and fourth sons. Among the lower classes prospects were even more limited. Spain—and, soon, all of Europe—began to realize how much it needed a *new* world. As early as 1497, for example,

Columbus's countryman, Giovanni Caboto, was establishing claim to the Atlantic seaboard for British paymasters, who called him John Cabot; and soon every great power in the world would be vying for a toehold in the Americas. Columbus's voyages, and the fervor they engendered in Old World imaginations, launched a century and a half of European exploration and colonization in America.

Coronado Searches for the Seven Cities of Gold (1540-42)

The event: In 1540 Francisco Vásquez de Coronado launched an expedition in search of the fabled Seven Cities of Gold, exploring much of the present-day American Southwest before returning empty-handed two years later, in spirit the first "westerner" in American history.

COLUMBUS' FOUR VOYAGES, the last of which ended in 1504, sparked the Spanish phase of the European invasion of the New World. That the Spanish considered their expeditions conquests was evident in the title they gave their explorers, "conquistadors." One such conquistador, Juan Ponce de Leon, became the first European to set foot on what would become the United States. After conquering Puerto Rico, in 1513 Ponce de Leon investigated rumors of a large island north of Cuba that supposedly contained a "fountain of youth." Instead he found and named Florida, "discovering" Mexico shortly afterward. And it was in Mexico that the conquistadors would find the vast riches that fueled their dreams of conquest and plunder.

Cortés's destruction and looting of the wealthy and sophisticated Aztec empire in 1519-1521, followed scarcely a decade later by Pizarro's equally enriching leveling of the Inca civilization in Peru, stimulated expeditions by greedy Spanish adventurers north into the borderlands above Mexico. There was no civilization in this region as elaborate as that of the Aztecs or Incas, but there was a legend of gold, obscure references to Seven Cities of Cibola in a fabled kingdom called Quivera that were carried back by a Franciscan missionary, Fray Marcos de Niza. It was enough for the conquistadors.

A series of expeditions into the borderlands culminated in the 1540-1542 explorations of Coronado, who traveled as far as present-day Kansas, but most extensively in the area now occupied by New Mexico. Coronado found no gold, and he abandoned his last outpost, Tiguex (near modern Albuquerque), on October 20, 1542, returning to Mexico City. Although he returned empty-handed, his expedition had established an important base for further exploration—the captured pueblo of Hawikuh, which he renamed Granada-Cibola—and he had himself explored a vast region, discovering, in the process, the Grand Canyon.

The hardships endured—and inflicted—by Francisco Vásquez de Coronado and his Conquistador band as they roamed the Southwest in 1540-1542 are, perhaps, neither more nor less important than the travail and discoveries of many others among the legions of America's Spanish explorers. DeSoto, for example, was exploring Florida and discovering the Mississippi at about the same time. Yet the motive behind Coronado's expedition, an arduous and hazardous quest undertaken on the basis of the vaguest of tales, reports, and rumors of fabulous wealth, not only typifies Spanish patterns of exploration but serves as one of the prototypes for the elusive American Dream, the gambler's desire for instant wealth—an aim that motivated centuries of westward expansion.

Roanoke Becomes the "Lost Colony" (1590)

The event: In 1590 a shipload of settlers, hoping to join a colony established a few years earlier by Sir Walter Raleigh, arrived at Roanoke Island on present-day North Carolina's Outer Banks to find that the village and its inhabitants had vanished, leaving behind only some rusted debris and the word "Croatoan" carved on a tree trunk.

RALEIGH, THE thirty-one-year-old favorite of England's Elizabeth I, had inherited his royal patent for the land he named "Virginia" after his "virgin" Queen from the hapless Humphrey Gilbert. Gilbert, with the Queen's blessing, had twice attempted to colonize America before he was lost at sea in a storm off Newfoundland in 1583. A small group of explorers in Raleigh's employ plunked down on the island in 1585, where Sir Francis Drake ran across them a year later, starving and eager to book passage back to England. In 1587 Raleigh tried again, sending 107 men, women, and children on a poorly planned expedition to the swampy, inhospitable island surrounded by hostile Indians. Ships Raleigh had stocked with supplies for his colony failed to set sail on time because the Spanish Armada attacked Britain, and when they finally did arrive it was too late.

The inhabitants of Virginia's first settlement, which would become known as the "Lost Colony," left behind some rusted debris and the Indian name for a nearby island carved on a tree: "Croatoan." Some speculated they had starved; they probably fell prey to local Indians. The mystery, and the completeness with which they disappeared, emphasized just how dangerous colonization was. Those pioneers who did survive at later colonies were not so much more determined as luckier, lucky enough at least to experience in the first crucial years of settlement the relative goodwill of the Native Americans.

Jamestown Is Founded (1607)

The event: In May 1607, a group of English settlers under the command of Captain Christopher Newport breached the Chesapeake Bay and sailed thirty miles up the James River to a densely wooded area bordering a swamp, where they founded Jamestown, the first permanent English colony in the New World.

TWO YEARS EARLIER, in September 1605, two groups of London merchants, who had formed joint-stock companies, had combined the investments of a number of small shareholders and petitioned King James I for a charter to establish a colony in Virginia, which at that point encompassed all of North America. A prototype of the modern-day corporation, the Virginia Company of London garnered a grant to southern Virginia, while northern Virginia went to the second of the two corporations, the Plymouth Company. After receiving their charter, the Virginia Company stockholders spent the next year organizing an expedition. They recruited some 120 settlers and provided free passage to America in exchange for a contract, under which the settlers agreed to work for the joint-stock company for seven years. Such an agreement was known as "indentured servitude," and would become popular in the colonies. In December 1606 the prospective colonists boarded the *Susan Constant*, the *Discovery*, and the *Goodspeed* and sailed for Virginia. One hundred and four of them survived the trans-Atlantic voyage, but only thirty-eight made it through their first year in the New World.

First they arrived too late to get crops planted. Then, to make matters worse, the site they picked to settle happened to be in the middle of a malarial swamp. Many of the gentlemen among the group had never worked a day in their lives, nor had their valets, and they resisted the hard labor of carving out a home from the wilderness. Within months half of them were dead; others were deserting to nearby Indian tribes. Then in 1609 came "the starving time," when desperate colonists turned to cannibalism, raiding even the recent graves of fellow colonists and local Indians.

That the colony survived at all was chiefly the doing of Captain John Smith, though his own colorful accounts of his career are suspect. A former crusader and pirate turned gentleman, Smith became the military dictator of the Jamestown Colony, instituting martial law, decreeing that those who did not work would not eat, turning hapless settlers into excellent foragers, and developing a successful trade with Powhatan's Indians. From them Jamestown's residents learned how to plant corn and yams and to become expert woodsmen. Though—as everywhere the European met the Native American—the settlers eventually turned on the Indians, and Smith, who had once enjoyed their respect, earned their hatred and fear, one of the more enduring of American myths sprang up around Smith's and Chief Powhatan's friendship: the legend of Pocahontas.

There is no reliable proof that Pocahontas ever risked her life to save Smith, despite what every schoolchild has learned. The myth may have been based on an initiation ceremony Smith endured to become an honorary member of Powhatan's tribe. The Jamestown settlers did capture a seventeen-year-old Pocahantas on one of their sporadic raids, and during her captivity she caught the eye of settler John Rolfe, who married her and established a permanent peace with the Powhatans. He took his bride with him back to London along with a Virginia tobacco seed that he cross-pollinated with a milder Jamaican strain. Both Pocahantas and tobacco became huge sensations in the motherland, and soon tobacco was planted on almost every square inch of fertile soil in the colony.

As the years passed, the settlers fulfilled their obligations to work for the joint-stock company and got control of their own land. Tobacco attracted more settlers, who saw the riches the Virginia planters were able to earn from its cultivation. At first most of the labor needs for growing the crop were filled by indentured servants, but once the period of indenture was over, the planters had to find new sources of labor. As early as 1619 a few planters purchased that labor from Dutch traders, who kidnapped black Africans in their homeland, transported them to Virginia against their wills, and sold them into slavery.

Henry Hudson Looks for the Northwest Passage (1609)

The event: In 1609, Henry Hudson—an English sea dog in the hire of the Dutch—sailed the *Half Moon* out of Amsterdam for the Atlantic coast in search of the fabled Northwest Passage and discovered instead the river that bears his name, launching Dutch settlement of New York.

HUDSON EXPLORED THE Chesapeake Bay first before heading north and sailing up the Hudson as far as the site of present-day Albany. The lack of tides persuaded him he had failed in his quest, and when he returned two years later to give it another try, his crew mutinied and set him adrift in an open boat on Hudson Bay, where he disappeared into the mists of time. Just then Amsterdam was the busiest and richest city in Europe, and no corner of the world escaped Dutch notice. In 1621 the Dutch West India Company incorporated with an eye to taking over the trans-Atlantic trade, and soon the Dutch instead of the Portuguese were dealing in slaves and sugar. In 1624 the company opened a fur trading post at Albany, then known as Fort Orange, and two years later it established a trading village called New Amsterdam at the mouth of the Hudson.

The first settlers, attracted by the promise of work on the West India Company farms, ignored the Indians who claimed the land, but when Peter Minuit arrived that spring and took over the settlement, he arranged to meet with the heads of the local tribes. For the land he traded some hatchets, cloth, metal pots, maybe even a few bright beads worth about sixty Gilders—at the then-current rate of exchange, 2,400 English cents. Far less strait-laced and much more rowdy than the Puritans, the Dutch attracted to their trading post a different kind of pioneer altogether, and soon taverns vastly outnumbered churches. Inviting all comers, New Amsterdam before long boasted, in addition to the original Dutch settlers, immigrants from all over the world. By 1640 the settlers who strolled Manhattan's Wall Street, so named for the wall the Dutch had built to keep out the Indians, or retired to their rude homes in the nearby villages of Breukelen and Haarlem spoke some eighteen different languages, the beginning of a long tradition of cultural diversity in the city's history.

The First African Slaves Are Sold to Virginia Planters (1619)

The event: In 1619, just twelve years after the founding of Jamestown, Dutch traders imported black slaves for sale to the Virginia tobacco farmers, the first step in the establishment of a "peculiar institution" that would survive for more than two centuries, make a mockery of the American Revolution's promise of equality, blight millions of lives, fuel sectional rivalries into bitter hatreds, and lead the new nation into civil war.

RACIAL BIGOTRY WAS endemic to the white European colonials and their American progeny, as their treatment of the Native American population, which they also on occasion enslaved, amply illustrated. The

English seaman John Hawkins began the modern "traffick in men" in 1562 when he opened a direct slave trade between Guinea and the West Indies. By 1600 the Dutch and the French had entered the business, and by the time Jamestown bought its first twenty slaves, the Spanish and Portuguese held more than a million blacks in bondage in their Caribbean and South American colonies.

For the wealthy planters who bought them, black slaves represented nothing more than a new source of cheap labor, one that, unlike indentured servants who worked only for seven years to repay their passage, would be perpetually under the planters' control. In the early colonial period, few could afford the prohibitive costs of purchasing an African slave, so indentured servitude remained the predominant method by which planters exploited the labor force. But by the end of the seventeenth century, the price of slaves began to fall, and as living conditions improved in the colonies, planters who bought slaves could expect to get a full life-time of work from their chattel. Even at twice the price of indentured servants, African slaves were a bargain.

In South Carolina, especially, slavery fast became essential to the colony's economy. By the 1730s, rice plantations covered the tidal and inland swamps of the Low Country. Indigo thrived in the drier regions of the colony, where rice would not grow. Within a few years of the founding of South Carolina's great rice plantations, black slaves outnumbered the white population. Planters forced the slaves to work under abysmal conditions in swamplands infested by mosquitoes, and black men and women died in alarming numbers from malaria and a wide range of infectious diseases. Many others fell disabled from exhaustion and poor diet, together with disease. The planters simply imported more Africans, finding it cheaper to buy new slaves than to sustain the ones they owned.

South Carolina strictly enforced the slave codes and allowed masters to treat their chattel as they saw fit, without restriction. Often, plantation owners lived in Charleston, leaving the operation of their plantations and the supervision of their slaves to overseers, many of whom—more concerned about the commissions they received on good harvests than with their management of black labor—became widely known for their mistreatment of slaves.

Southerners were not the only Americans to engage in slavery as a means of economic improvement. The New England shipping industry relied on the importation of slaves as a part of its "triangular" trade. The trade took many different forms. In one version traders shipped molasses refined in the West Indies to New England for use in the distillation of rum. They then shipped rum to Africa in trade for slaves, whom they transported to the West Indies. New England slave traders then hawked the Africans on the auction blocks in Charleston, New York, and other busy port cities along the eastern seaboard.

American slavery flourished both as an economic system—allowing a few planters to grow rich from the forced labor of the Africans who cultivated their tobacco, rice, indigo, and later, cotton—and as a system for strict racial control. The casual bigotry of the early European settlers became a virulent racism in the service of the South's regionalist ideology. Planters and traders kept questions of morality and human decency in abeyance during the seventeenth and eighteenth centuries, when the economic benefits of slavery were evident for both the South and North and the balance of sectional interests could serve as the basis for compromise. But westward expansion threatened that balance even as slavery developed into the South's own "peculiar institution," the bleak rockbed of its cherished way of life, and grew increasingly irrelevant economically to the rapidly industrializing North.

Pilgrims Settle at Plymouth (1620)

The event: In 1620, rough seas off the coast of Nantucket evidently forced Captain Christopher Jones of the *Mayflower* to alter his course from the mouth of the Hudson River toward Cape Cod, where he deposited his passengers—including some fifty members of a religious sect who would soon come to be called "Pilgrims"—outside the jurisdiction of Virginia, much to the chagrin of those aboard who were not Pilgrims. The two groups settled their differences by signing a brief statement of self-government drafted by the Pilgrims, which became known as the "Mayflower Compact," the first written constitution in North America.

SOME CLAIMED THE Pilgrims had bribed the good captain to alter his course. The Pilgrims had arranged the nine-month journey with the permission of the Virginia Company and the backing of London merchants, who charged the Plymouth Company—as the Pilgrims' corporation was known—a handsome interest on the funds they advanced the group. The Pilgrims were a sect of the Separatists, themselves a splinter group of the Puritans. The Puritans rejected the wordy ceremoniousness of the Church of England as too "popish" and hoped to cleanse it of all traces of Roman Catholicism. Those Puritans who thought the Anglican Church too corrupt to be purified wanted complete autonomy for their congregations, and the Pilgrims were so extreme in their separatist views that the English authorities banned them outright. Pilgrims who did not go underground fled the country, and a small band hailing from Scrooby, Nottinghamshire settled in Leyden, Holland. There, though their theology was acceptable, their culture was alien, and the group at length opted for a second course—a fresh start in America.

They struck their deal with the London merchants, hoping to establish the Kingdom of God in the English colonies, but they took with them on the voyage a number of men faithful to the Church of England, whom they called "Strangers" and who had very different goals from the otherworldly religious cult: to get rich, to own a bit of land, to live the good life on the earth just as it was. Needless to say, the trip did not go smoothly. With the Pilgrims numbering only some 50 of the 102 passengers on board when Captain Jones—for whatever reason—altered course, some sort of arrangement was necessary to stave off a true mutiny. Signing the compact, in which they vowed to create a "Civil Body Politic" and abide by laws created for the good of the colony as a whole, were some of the most headstrong and determined men in our history: Pilgrims like William Brewster, John Carver, Edward Winslow, and William Bradford; Strangers like ship's cooper John Alden and army captain Miles Standish.

Pilgrim and Stranger alike came ashore at the site of present-day Provincetown at the worst possible time. Winter was setting in, and nearly half the colonists died before a supply ship arrived in the spring of 1621. The Pilgrims viewed as a blessing from God the appearance of Squanto and Samoset, local Indians who had learned English from earlier explorers and who helped the Pilgrims plant crops and build their homes. In the fall of 1621, the Pilgrims and their Native American friends gathered to celebrate the harvest, an event that is commemorated yearly on Thanksgiving.

After the colony's original governor died during the first harsh winter in the New World, the settlers selected William Bradford as his replacement. A wise and equitable citizen ruler, Bradford was also an able chronicler. His *History of Plimmoth Plantation* recounts the separatists' life in Holland and in the New World and was the first instance in which the English settlers were called "Pilgrims." Among the struggles Bradford examined in his book was one between the Pilgrims and the "Particulars." These individuals had paid their own way to the New World and did not believe that they were responsible for contributing to the payments due to the Virginia Company. In addition, the Particulars wanted no part in the colony's work to raise funds to bring over more Pilgrims. To end the quarrel between the two factions and to relieve the colony of its mounting debts, a group of prosperous colonists agreed to assume the debts to the Virginia Company in exchange for greater access to land and control of the fur trade. These men, known as the "Undertakers," agreed to pay the Virginia Company £200 a year for nine years.

As the years passed, more and more Pilgrims and Particulars flocked to the fledgling colony. Towns were created throughout the region of Plymouth. Each town had at least one church congregation, independent of all others and in strong control of the religious and secular lives of the townspeople. Only those individuals who freely professed their conversion were admitted to the congregation. But the Pilgrims, unlike their neighboring Puritans in the Massachusetts Bay Colony, did not forbid the unconverted from participating in the colony's affairs. With the Mayflower Compact as a foundation, the Pilgrims were able to develop the broad enfranchisement necessary for managing a colony that boasted any number of Particulars and Strangers, a toleration that would become the hallmark of American civil life.

Puritans Settle Massachusetts Bay (1630-42)

The event: In 1629, five English ships bursting with Puritan emigres sailed into Massachusetts Bay, the first of many that would bring to Britain's newest colony the twenty thousand-odd settlers who participated in the Great Puritan migration.

MOSTLY ANGLICAN PURITANS, these early arrivals were inspired by the New World success of their more radical fellow countrymen, the Pilgrims, who had established their colony at Plymouth a decade earlier. The first Puritans founded Naumkeag, later called Salem, and by the time John Winthrop arrived a year later, carrying a royal charter for a new joint-stock venture called the Massachusetts Bay Company, eleven more ships had deposited a thousand more Puritan immigrants.

To Boston, which Winthrop founded and named after England's great Puritan city, they came in the thousands every year for twelve years, chased out of their mother country by a king who grew ever more intolerant of their disputatiousness, their rigid morality, their grim industriousness, and their seditious religious ideology. No doubt about it, they were an argumentative lot, constantly fighting among themselves—usually over church matters, sometimes over land. Squabble by squabble, it seemed, they settled New England.

The Puritan Migration was uniquely one of families, and the institution of the family first and foremost provided coherence to Puritan social life. The father, absolute head of the Puritan household, ruled with an iron hand over his children—whose strict obedience was expected even after maturity—and his wife, who was by law his subordinate. Not surprisingly, the Massachusetts Bay Colony's general court ruled early on that land would be granted not to individuals but to groups of families in plots of thirty-six square miles per family. The importance Puritans placed on family also explains why they so quickly saw to educating their children, founding Boston's English High and Latin School—the first secondary school in America—in 1635 and Harvard College the following year.

Puritan notions of family were also reflected in the social hierarchy of New England villages. Each town developed a group of leaders, called "town fathers," who were the heads of certain families, were usually university trained or specially skilled in a craft, and who directed local affairs. But though the sons of the town fathers tended to inherit their power and influence, and though a handful of families monopolized local offices, the basis of local self-government was the town meeting—and the decisions of the town meeting required the unanimous agreement of every townsman. The New England church, too, boasted elements of both the patriarchal family's tyranny and the town meeting's freedom. The law required village inhabitants in every state but Rhode Island to attend church on the Sabbath and to tithe, but church membership was voluntary and each village church conducted its own affairs, answering to no higher secular authority. And while ministers exercised considerable informal influence over both public and private life, they were not permitted to participate in government. In the churches, as in the town meetings, the laity enjoyed ultimate authority. Ecclesiastically, the Puritans were as intolerant as the king they had fled; politically, they were dangerous radicals, as the brethren they had left behind in England proved in 1649 when Puritan champion Oliver Cromwell overthrew King Charles I and had him executed.

The coming of the English Commonwealth would spell the end of the Puritan Migration. Though English Puritans continued to settle in New England for a year or two in search of a better fortune than the tumultuous economy of the Glorious Revolution could offer them, by the time Connecticut, New Haven, Plymouth, and the Massachusetts Bay Colony formed the New England Confederation in 1643 in order to settle border disputes, the absolute dominance of the Puritans had begun to decline. Even today, however, Americans are affected by the strange mixture of social authoritarianism and political democracy that make up the Puritan legacy.

Roger Williams Is Exiled to Rhode Island (1636)

The event: In 1636, the radical religious zealot Roger Williams—whose preachments led Massachusetts Governor Roger Winthrop to banish him from Boston—founded Providence, Rhode Island. The same year, Reverend Thomas Hooker's relatively liberal standards for church membership encouraged him to lead another group into Connecticut and build Hartford. When Anne Hutchinson's radical interpretations of sermons began to draw huge, enthusiastic audiences, Winthrop branded her a heretic and banished her, too, from Boston. In 1638, she joined Williams in Rhode Island, founding Portsmouth the same year New Haven was established.

THE REVEREND ROGER Williams was a minister of the Puritan church in Salem. Williams's belief in the separation of church and state—"forced religion stinks in God's nostrils," he declared—was contrary to the Puritans' avowed goal of creating on earth a theocracy, a godly community led by church members. Also contrary to Puritan orthodoxy was Williams's call for "soul liberty," the freedom to be guided by one's own lights in choosing one's religion. Williams based his belief on his interpretation of Christ's teaching that religious truth and error coexist in all nations. Williams believed that, because there was no way for any one group, including the Puritans, to determine absolutely what was religious truth, all groups should be tolerated.

For his heterodoxy Williams was brought before the Massachusetts General Court, found guilty of heresy, and banished from the colony. He and his followers moved to the area around Narragansett Bay, where they established Providence in 1636. Seven years later, Williams received a royal charter for the new colony of Rhode Island.

As leader of the new colony, Williams insisted on granting absolute religious freedom to all settlers. In addition, he insisted that the white settlers had no right to land in the colonies unless they bought it from the Native Americans.

Because of his friendly relations with the Narragansetts, whom he respected and whose language he learned, Williams was himself freed from abiding by this moral imperative when a tribal council gave him, as a gift, the land on which he founded Providence. Although Williams tempered his views on "soul liberty" in the 1670s when large numbers of Quakers migrated to Rhode Island, the colony was the first in New England to offer religious freedom to its inhabitants. This heritage of tolerance made the area attractive to immigrants of many origins and faiths in the eighteenth, nineteenth, and twentieth centuries.

Williams not only set an early example of the toleration of diverse beliefs that would become an American ideal, he was also far more successful than most colonial authorities in establishing peaceful relations between settlers and Indians. Unlike most orthodox Puritans, he did not regard the Indians as benighted devil worshippers or even agents of the devil, but as human beings to be loved and respected. His *Key into the Language of America*, an account of his travels among the Narragansetts, is the first American study of Indian language and customs.

Marquette and Jolliet Explore the Mississippi (1673)

The event: In 1673, two Canadian Frenchmen—Louis Jolliet and Father Jacques Marquette—set off on a journey down the Mississippi River that would pave the way for French colonization of America between the Appalachian and Rocky Mountains.

FROM THE TIME Champlain founded Quebec in 1608, *coureurs de bois*—as casual with their lives as the most ferocious English sea dogs and almost as good at woodcraft as the Indians—chased furs ever deeper into the wilderness. In their wake came French Catholic missionaries, hunting for souls and undaunted by the dangers of the forest. The hardy explorers and the Jesuits, dubbed "Black Robes" by the Indians, built forts all along the far reaches of the Great Lakes. To these remote outposts came the Indians, with animal hides for sale and strange tales about a great "father" of rivers they called the "Mesippi."

In 1673, the French intendant in Canada, Jean Baptiste Talon, commissioned a fur trader named Louis Jolliet to explore the unknown river described by the Indians. Talon hoped this father of waters might prove to be the fabled passageway to the Pacific. He had reason, however, to worry that the new governor, on his way over from France, might not approve his plan. Louis XIV did not appreciate the exploits of his wandering subjects and wanted his New France, which he had taken over from a trading company, populated by hard-working and docile farmers.

Two years before, the king had rejected another scheme by two different *coureurs* to create a trading company that would service the northern fur supply by sea using the never to-be-discovered Northwest Passage and forbidding all but a privileged few from engaging in the fur trade at all. In good order he sent women to entice the wild trappers into a more settled life, placed a bounty on large families, and urged the Church to excommunicate men who left their farms without permission.

Spurned by their king, the two fur traders—Pierre-Esprit Radisson and Médart Chouart—turned to the English and established the Hudson's Bay Company in 1672. Arriving to take over the governor's chair the next year, the Comte de Frontenac realized the strategic and economic importance of the nascent international competition, and he approved Talon's commissioned expedition without hesitation. In June, Jolliet and a Jesuit priest named Jacques Marquette lowered their two birch-bark canoes into the muddy water of the Mississippi.

Marquette and Jolliet reported many strange sights along the way—fish so large they threatened to rip apart the canoes, huge herds of grazing buffalo, wildly vivid Indian paintings a bit upstream from the mouth of the Missouri—but they never did find the Northwest Passage. Nor did they find any silver or gold (the traditional impetus for European exploration), though not for want of trying. They turned back before they reached modern-day Arkansas, fearful of blundering into Spanish territory and causing an incident that might earn them the ire of their reluctant king.

Marquette lingered behind in the wilderness to convert the natives while Jolliet dashed back to Quebec to report on their expedition. Scarcely two years later the Jesuit was dead, broken by the rugged climate. Jolliet, now a former explorer, grew embittered by the lack of recognition he believed he deserved, and he wandered from one minor government job to another for the rest of his life.

The French crown never could decide what to do with Louisiana. Its original plan to create an agricultural kingdom across the sea resulted in a meager scattering of settlements in Nova Scotia, along the St. Lawrence, and here and there in Louisiana. In contrast, the divines and trappers who traveled up and down the Mississippi filled with missionary zeal or searching for precious metals and the non-existent Northwest Passage explored and mapped one of the greatest river systems in the world, made peace with the majority of the native inhabitants, and came to rule the wilderness. Their activities helped the French pioneers by increasing the trade with the Indians and more firmly establishing claim to the area. For unlike the French crown, they were in Louisiana to stay.

Indian Chief King Philip Goes to War (1675)

The event: On June 11, 1675, an irate Massachusetts settler killed an Indian he found looting his cattle. When the Indians, under the leadership of a Wampanoag chief known to the English settlers as King Philip, sought redress from the local garrison, they were rebuffed, whereupon they sought out the settler and killed him, along with his father and five others. In short order New England found itself engulfed by a massive Indian uprising, which, in proportion to its population, would become the costliest war in American history.

FOR SOME TIME before the killing that sparked the uprising, King Philip had been fomenting unrest among neighboring tribes, especially the Narragansetts and Nipmucks. Called Metacomet by the Indians, Philip was the son of Massasoit and a hereditary chief of his tribe whose haughty bearing would indeed have befitted an English monarch. During the period of 1662-1675, there smoldered within him a mighty resentment of the colonists' unremitting land hunger and rising population, combined with the contemptuous and insulting treatment he received at their hands. Worse, the English desired to consume not only the Indians' land but their souls as well; the high-handed zeal of English missionaries threatened every aspect of Indian cultural identity. By the spring of 1675, colonial authorities were receiving reports of looting and cattle killing in outlying settlements. Soon colonists began deserting these frontier regions, and Indians freely ransacked their abandoned property.

It was a war principally of raids and ambushes, with the Indians repeatedly eluding the militia units sent against them. During the first months of the struggle the poorly organized colonists sustained heavy losses. Only after they managed to forge the United Colonies into an effective intercolonial force were they able to pursue, wear down, and thereby defeat Indian raiding parties.

King Philip's War was a catastrophe for New England's colonists and Indians alike. In the course of 1675–1676, half of the region's towns were badly damaged and twelve destroyed utterly, requiring the work of a generation to rebuild them. The fragile colonial economy suffered devastating blows, both as a result of the direct cost of the war—some £100,000—and because of the disruption of the fur trade with the Indians and the virtual cessation of coastal fishing and the seaborne West Indies trade; the war siphoned off the manpower customarily devoted to these industries. Worse, many of these men never returned to their peacetime trades, for one in sixteen men of military age was killed. Many others, older men, women, and children, were also killed, captured, or starved. As for the Indians, at least three thousand perished—chiefly Wampanoags, Narragansetts, and Nipmucks—and many of those who did not die were deported and sold into slavery.

It is difficult to find much good in this terribly destructive conflict, which caused immense immediate suffering and, in the longer run, badly crippled the colonial economy while demonstrating the fundamental incompatibility of white and Indian civilizations in America. King Philip's War did, however, occasion the first effective union of American colonies.

Nathaniel Bacon Launches His Rebellion (1676)

The event: In the summer of 1675, a detachment of the Virginia militia seeking to revenge the death of three local farmers at the hands of the Nanticoke Indians mistakenly killed a group of friendly Susquehannocks. When Virginia's governor sought to control the all-too-familiar cycle of violence sparked by the killing, he found himself facing an outright rebellion led by Nathaniel Bacon, a rebellion that foreshadowed the American Revolution a century later.

WHEN NANTICOKES, SUSQUEHANNOCKS, and allied tribes in both Maryland and Virginia fell to vengeance raiding against whites after a misunderstanding over a debt unpaid to the Nanticokes led to bloodshed, frontier settlers began to desert their homes. Virginia governor William Berkeley espoused a defensive strategy, claiming that he did not want to further inflame the Indians into the kind of war that was devastating New England; his critics claimed that the governor was protecting the white-Indian fur trade, in which he had invested extensively.

Enter Nathaniel Bacon. A noble brat, cousin to Lady Berkeley herself, Bacon was a fiery demagogue who had been expelled from Cambridge University for "extravagances." Arriving in Virginia with a bride and £1,800 from his father, he bought two plantations on the James River, and Berkeley himself appointed his in-law to the House of Burgesses. When Bacon, while drinking with friends, heard about a group of frontiersmen who had had enough of Berkeley's Indian policies and who were preparing to take matters into their own hands, he quickly took over leadership of the venture. Enlisting the Occaneechi Indians as allies, Bacon attacked the Susquehannocks and a captured stock of fur, then fell to arguing with the Occaneechi over the spoils and attacked them in turn. Though Bacon returned a hero to the English settlements, Berkeley summarily posted him as a traitor on May 26, 1676, and arrested him when he entered Jamestown to take his seat in the House of Burgesses.

Bacon admitted his guilt and Berkeley pardoned him on June 5. Immediately Bacon raised an army of five hundred, led it into Jamestown, and demanded that the burgesses commission him commander of all forces fighting the Indians. The terrified assembly granted the commission, and Bacon set out on another campaign—again against friendly Indians, the Pamunkeys of eastern Virginia.

On July 29, in the meantime, Berkeley managed to repeal Bacon's commission and again proclaimed him a traitor, but failed to raise an army willing to move against him. Indeed, within a week of the governor's latest declaration, a group of Virginia's most substantial planters took an oath to support Bacon, who returned to Jamestown and pushed Berkeley and his meager forces into exile on the Eastern Shore. On September 18, master of all but the eastern shore of Virginia, Bacon burned Jamestown.

At this point, New York's powerful royal governor, Edmund Andros, intervened, threatening to take the Susquehannocks permanently under his colony's jurisdiction. In the wake of Andros's threat the Marylanders backed off, and hostilities between settlers and Indians cooled. Bacon's support rapidly eroded. Berkeley rallied a force against him and retook Jamestown, finally forcing Bacon to a stand in mid-October at Yorktown, where he was cut down not by Berkeley's musket balls but by dysentery.

While Bacon's actions were vicious, even criminal, his rebellion was in part a class struggle, a struggle between the Tidewater establishment and those attempting to make a go on the frontier. Like the War of Independence, it was a conflict between remote and unresponsive royal authority and the unruly, though always imperiled, settler.

William Penn Is Granted a Charter for Pennsylvania (1681)

The event: William Penn, brilliant son of Admiral Sir William Penn, a convert to the Quaker faith, received a charter from Charles II on March 14, 1681, granting proprietorship of present-day Pennsylvania and, the next year, of present-day Delaware as well.

PENN'S COLONY WAS a model of toleration in a singularly intolerant age. Not only were the universally persecuted Quakers welcomed, all religious sects and nationalities were tolerated. Whereas the Chesapeake and New England colonies (with the exception of heterodox Rhode Island) tended toward homogenization, Pennsylvania (as well as New Jersey and New York, to a somewhat lesser degree) became the first colony to manifest the national, cultural, and ethnic diversity that would come to characterize the mature United States.

Penn's policy of official toleration produced fascinating political results, as like-minded groups tended to cluster together in mildly clannish communities. Local representation in central government became a paramount concern and greatly contributed to the foundation of representative democratic government. While rural Pennsylvania fostered tolerant isolation among widely scattered communities, Philadelphia rapidly developed into a cosmopolitan city that brought diverse cultural elements into close proximity. Philadelphia produced a prototype of the modern American political party system, including calculated ticket balancing, skillful compromise, carefully targeted propaganda, and vigorous campaigns to muster voters at election time. To a degree unequalled by any other colony, Pennsylvania was born of the spirit of democracy and, in contrast to more homogeneous regions, dramatically foreshadowed the difficulties and virtues that would emerge as the British colonies developed into the United States.

Salem Puts Accused Witches on Trial (1692)

The event: In February 1692, two young daughters of the Reverend Samuel Parris and a few of their friends were diagnosed by a Salem, Massachusetts, doctor as being under the spell of a witch. The girls named their tormentors, and the town magistrates initiated proceedings against those identified as "witches" on February 29.

FOLLOWING THE INITIAL accusations were months of rampant hysteria, as the Puritan colonists seemed to discover witches everywhere. The Salem outbreak, while the most infamous episode of witch hunting in colonial annals, was not the first. In Massachusetts and Connecticut, more than seventy cases had been tried before 1692, although only eighteen of the accused witches were convicted. The Parris girls' accusations, however, precipitated a full-scale epidemic. More than 140 people were accused in 1692 alone; 107 of them women.

The traditional "witch" in the Puritan colonies was a poor, elderly woman or a man without property. Often described as quarrelsome and disruptive, the witch had made enemies among his or her neighbors. The 1692 frenzy of accusations extended well beyond the traditional definition, however. Before long, men of property and their wives stood among the accused, their primary crime being opposition to the Reverend Parris. The minister and seventy other Salem residents—mostly members of his congregation—presented themselves as corroborative witnesses for those who claimed to be, or who were diagnosed as being, under a witch's spell.

The new royal governor of Massachusetts, Sir William Phips, established the Court of Oyer and Terminer to try the cases. The court's first session met in June with a docket of more than seventy cases. Through that summer and into the fall, fifty of the accused confessed to practicing witchcraft, twenty-six were convicted, and nineteen were executed. The governor, growing increasingly alarmed by the number of convictions, abolished the Court of Oyer and Terminer and declared that the Superior Court of Judicature would hear the remaining cases. From October until the end of the year, this court indicted only twenty-one of the more than fifty individuals accused, the trials resulting in only three convictions, which were overturned the following year. Individuals whose cases remained pending at the beginning of 1693 were pardoned by the governor, and in 1693 witchcraft was no longer regarded as an actionable offense. The epidemic in Salem ended almost as quickly as it had begun, but it has remained in the American consciousness not only as a curiosity of history and folklore but as an object lesson in the dangers of superstition and hysteria engendered by group coercion. In 1953, the playwright Arthur Miller retold the story of the Salem witch trials in *The Crucible*, intended as a powerful allegory condemning the anti-Communist "witch hunting" then under way in the dark era of Senator Joseph McCarthy.

James Oglethorpe Is Granted a Charter for Georgia (1732)

The event: In 1732, entrepreneur, speculator, and utopian dreamer James Oglethorpe secured a royal charter to establish Georgia, the last of the thirteen original colonies.

UNIQUE AMONG THE colonies, Georgia began as a social experiment when several London philanthropists decided to petition the king for a charter for a new colony to be inhabited by people selected from English debtors' prisons, hopeless and useless institutions. The land they wished to secure was south of the Carolinas and north of Spanish-held Florida, and the British government, eager to create a buffer between its Carolina colonies and the Spanish territory, quickly granted the charter to the philanthropists, who agreed in return to manage the colony as trustees for a period of twenty-one years without extracting any profits.

The first colonists to arrive were placed on fifty-acre farms, which they were prohibited from transferring or selling. The trustees also banned liquor and slavery from the colony. Only a few of these first hundred colonists to arrive and settle with James Oglethorpe at Savannah in 1733 were debtors, nor did they long abide by the utopian regulations of the trustees. Envious of the vast acreage and cadres of slaves owned by their neighbors in South Carolina, the Georgia colonists soon found ways to increase their land holdings beyond the fifty-acre limit, and slaves were imported to work the land. By 1752, the philanthropists, realizing that Georgia had become no different from the other southern colonies, abandoned their dream of providing a fresh start for British debtors, and the British government declared Georgia a royal colony.

 Georgia was the first of many visionary utopian experiments attempted in America, efforts founded on the hope that the New World, as if by magic, would transform or eliminate the problems of the Old World. While the Georgia experiment failed, it did demonstrate the enduring equation of America with *hope* and foreshadowed the far greater American social experiment that began in the 1770s and has been under way ever since.

Jonathan Edwards Sparks the Great Awakening (1734)

The event: In 1734, the fire-and-brimstone sermons of American-born Jonathan Edwards sparked a fifteen-year wildfire of religious fervor that spread from Maine to Georgia and was called the Great Awakening.

THE CHARISMATIC EVANGELICAL preachers who fostered the popular religious movement were called "New Lights," and chief among them were two very different men, the demagogical George Whitefield and the sublimely philosophical Jonathan Edwards, both of whom believed they were witnessing and participating in a "wonderful work" of God.

 The "wonderful work" manifested itself in such phenomena as (in the words of Charles Chauncy, a critic of the New Lights) "*swooning away* and *falling to the Ground* . . . bitter *Shriekings* and *Screamings; Convulsion-like Tremblings* and *Agitations, Strugglings* and *Tremblings*." When Edwards delivered to his Enfield, Massachusetts, congregation "Sinners in the Hands of an Angry God," certainly the most famous American sermon ever preached, the result was weeping, "breathing of distress," fits, and fainting, as worshippers seemed to writhe in the very hellfire of which Edwards so eloquently spoke.

 The Great Awakening emerged during a period in which the orthodox religion of the Puritan fathers was rapidly disintegrating. In a period also characterized by the increasing political tensions that foreshadowed the French and Indian War and, ultimately, the War of Independence, people were looking desperately for faith and religious guidance. To those who believed in it, the emotionalism of the Great Awakening seemed evidence of God's presence penetrating the contemporary welter of man-made confusion to inspire one individual after another with the Truth. The word *individual* is important; for the Great Awakening, born in the decline of orthodoxy, was against religious interpretation imposed from external authority. The Great Awakening was founded on an especially American belief that the individual is the ultimate arbiter of truth and that any person can have an intimate, direct, unmediated relation to the Almighty. On principles akin to these, the Declaration of Independence was based, as well as the thought of those philosophers considered most typically American—Ralph Waldo Emerson, Henry David Thoreau, William James, and John Dewey—and the writing of the nation's greatest authors, including Nathaniel Hawthorne, Herman Melville, Walt Whitman, Emily Dickinson, Ernest Hemingway, William Carlos Williams, and Norman Mailer, to mention a few.

The Great Awakening had its dark side, of course, most notably the danger that it verged on the antithesis of individualism—mass hysteria—and fostered demagoguery, cultism, the wholesale abandonment of reason, and, ultimately, fanatic intolerance. Suggesting much that is hopeful and strong in the American character, the Great Awakening also pointed to dangers inherent in a free society that exalts above all else individual conscience and belief. While Americans enjoy a heritage of unparalleled liberties, we also endure the lawlessness, violence, and personal anguish such values engender.

John Peter Zenger Is Acquitted (1735)

The event: In 1735, New York's provincial court ruled in favor of a New York city printer, who was on trial for printing "seditious libels" against that colony's royal governor, a landmark ruling that provided the precedent for the Court's jealous guardianship ever since of freedom of the press.

IN 1733, LEWIS MORRIS, chief justice of the provincial court of New York, ruled against the colony's royal governor, William Cosby, in a salary dispute. Cosby retaliated by suspending Morris, who turned to the colony's sole newspaper, *The New York Gazette*, to publicize the injustice done to him. Unfortunately, the paper was dependent upon the patronage of the royal governor, and its editor refused to print anything critical of Cosby. Undaunted, Morris and a group of like-minded lawyers and merchants hired local printer John Peter Zenger to start an alternative paper, the *New-York Weekly Journal*, which he founded on November 5, 1733.

Zenger's paper published unrelenting attacks on Cosby, accusing him specifically of undermining the provincial court system and of flagrantly violating the laws of the colony as well as the mother country. In 1734, Governor Cosby had Zenger arrested on a charge of "seditious libel," and he was imprisoned without trial for some ten months while his wife, Anna, kept the paper operating. When Zenger was finally brought to trial in 1735, Andrew Hamilton of Philadelphia served as his lawyer, defending his client by arguing that, because all that he had printed was true, Zenger could not be convicted of seditious libel. Although Hamilton's defense was frustrated by the court, which refused to admit into evidence material submitted to prove the truth of the anti-Cosby articles published in the *Journal*, the jury was sufficiently persuaded to acquit Zenger.

The successful defense of John Peter Zenger hardly brought an end to seditious libel prosecutions in colonial America, but it did establish an early and crucial principle of freedom of the press: that true statements cannot be defined as libel. Since a free press would prove vital to the development of democratic ideas in the colonies, the Zenger case may be seen as one cornerstone on which American independence was built. As for Zenger himself, he prospered after his acquittal, becoming public printer for the colonies of New York and New Jersey.

The French and Indian War Begins (1754)

The event: In May of 1754, Lieutenant Colonel George Washington from Virginia arrived at Fort Duquesne, near what would one day become Pittsburgh, under orders from Governor Dinwiddie of Virginia to deliver an ultimatum to certain French "interlopers" in the Ohio Valley—leave, or be evicted. Washington's appearance, and the battle that followed, sparked a conflict that would spread from the American wilderness over vast stretches of Europe, across the high seas to the edge of the Near East, and ensnare every great power in the world. In Europe the fighting came to be known as the Great War for the Empire. The English called it the Seven Years' War. The American colonists called their theater of this first truly world-wide conflict the French and Indian War.

THE LONG, BLOODY, complex war was the culmination of a virtually uninterrupted series of smaller wars among the French and British (and their respective colonists) and variously allied Indian tribes for control over the vast valleys of the St. Lawrence River and the Ohio River. Most of the non-Iroquois tribes sided with the French. These included the Delaware, Shawnee, Abnaki, Ojibwa, Ottawa, and Potawatomi in addition to mission-educated Indians living in the vicinity of Montreal and Quebec. The powerful Iroquois Confederation had its own agenda, using its neutrality to play the Europeans off against each other, even as they sought to dominate all other tribes trading with the two powers. The English, through their high-handed and contemptuous dealings with the Indians, seemed bent on deliberately alienating the tribes.

In this tense climate, the crown authorized Governor Robert Dinwiddie of Virginia to evict the French from territory under his jurisdiction. He commissioned twenty-one-year-old George Washington to carry an ultimatum to Captain Legardeur de Saint-Pierre, commandant of a French outpost in western Pennsylvania. At almost precisely that moment, the Iroquois bid for hegemony collapsed at a huge powwow in Logstown, Virginia, and any authority they might have used to keep other tribes from the warpath vanished.

The passionate and mutual hatred that sprang up between native Indians and American pioneer could be traced back to the French and Indian War. The Indians almost always did most of the dying, but next to them, white settlers—not soldiers—suffered the greatest number of casualties. Indeed, for several years, the Delawares—France's most important Indian allies—raided freely the settlements along the frontier, pushing back the western borders of Pennsylvania, Maryland, and Virginia by a hundred miles. The Delaware were brought to a tenuous peace in September 1758 through the auspices of the Iroquois and the promise of hunting rights in western Pennsylvania, which would remain free of white settlement.

The Treaty of Easton (Pennsylvania) lasted a month, right up until the British managed, on November 25, 1758, to take Fort Duquesne, no longer defended by the Delawares, and rename it Fort Pitt. Ensconced in Fort Pitt, the British built the first of three roads that would traverse western Pennsylvania, and the settlers, blithely ignoring the treaty, pushed west once again.

The pattern of white-Indian promise and betrayal on the frontier was established. Even after the French defeat at Quebec a year later, and the subsequent surrender of Canada, the war in the Ohio Valley dragged on for another four years with considerable loss of life and a horrid cruelty and ferocity on all sides. Nothing seemed to daunt the settlers. Despite continued Indian attacks and a royal proclamation on October 13, 1761, reiterating the terms of the Treaty of Easton, would-be pioneers poured into the troubled West.

By the time it was all over, not only France but Austria, Sweden, a number of small German states, and Spain had taken up arms against England and Frederick the Great's Prussia. Spain entered at a very late stage in the war (January 2, 1762) and was quickly neutralized by British seapower: On February 15, 1762, Martinique fell to the English, followed by St. Lucia and Grenada. On August 12, 1762, Havana yielded to a two-month siege, and Manilla fell on October 5. On November 3 France concluded the secret Treaty of Fontainebleu with Spain, in which it ceded to that country all of its territory west of the Mississippi and the Isle of Orleans in Louisiana. These cessions were by way of compensation for the loss of Spain's Caribbean holdings. By the Treaty of Paris, concluded on February 10, 1763, France ceded all of Louisiana to Spain and the rest of its North American holdings to Great Britain. Spain recovered Cuba, in compensation for the loss of territories in Florida, and France retained Guadeloupe, Martinique, and St. Lucia. The treaty at last ended the French and Indian War in America and the Seven Years' War, the European conflict of which the American struggle was a part. France's New World ambitions came to a decisive and abrupt halt. Until the War of Independence, Great Britain would be the dominant force on the North American continent.

Though for Europe the matter was settled in Paris, it was far from over for the native Indians and the American settlers. As Francis Jennings has often pointed out, the French and Indian War was, from the point of view of the Indians themselves, merely the first in a series of wars waged by the various Algonquin tribes of the Old Northwest—first against Britain and later against the United States. From their great victory over Maj. General Edward Braddock on the meadowlands of Fort Duquesne in 1755, through the vicious border skirmishes of Pontiac's Rebellion and the American Revolution to their final defeat by Mad Anthony Wayne at Fallen Timbers in 1794, the Algonquins' objective was to force the English-speaking aliens to withdraw. The great world-wide conflagrations in which France lost Canada and England was soon to lose its thirteen seaboard colonies were minor concerns in the Algonquins' forty-year struggle to liberate themselves and their lands.

From the settlers' point of view, however, the ouster of the French from North America confirmed England's domination of the continent as far west as the Mississippi, and thus changed the goal of the French and Indian War from establishing control of the Upper Ohio to the opening of the trans-Appalachian West. As a result, during the late seventeenth century in Britain's American colonies, a voracious land hunger unlike any the world had ever seen filled the breasts of the white settlers we would come to call "pioneers." The American West itself had been born in the European struggle for empire.

Pontiac Launches His Rebellion (1763)

The event: On April 27, 1763, an Ottawa war chief called a grand council of the tribes in the vicinity of Detroit and urged them to join his band in an attack upon the nearby fort—one of many coordinated attacks by the tribes of the Old Northwest in a great, year-long Indian uprising—an uprising known as "Pontiac's Rebellion."

THE ACTUAL SPARK for the rebellion was General Jeffrey Amherst's refusal, after Detroit fell into British hands, to continue the French custom of giving presents to the Indians, especially gifts of ammunition, but its inspiration came from the visionary known as the Delaware Prophet.

As the French and Indian War drew to a close, English colonials—ignoring treaties with the Algonquins and the admonitions of their own King—poured over the Appalachians into Kentucky and Ohio. The Delawares had seen it all before, on the other side of the mountains, where their people had been disenfranchised and made "women" to the clever and powerful Iroquois while the whites chopped up their hunting ground into homesteads. Among them there arose a soothsayer, Neolin, who urged a total break with the whites. They blocked the Indians' path to heaven, he argued, calling the whites "dogs clothed in red" who seemed to appear only in a "troubled land." "Drive them out," he demanded. "Make war upon them."

As his words—and those of other Indian revivalists—spread through the Ohio Valley and westward, they found a hearing among many Indians, who were not at all pleased with the Peace of Paris. The Algonquins in particular felt betrayed by the French, who had deserted them, and challenged by the English, who continually ignored the treaty-established boundary of the Appalachians. Pontiac himself was only a local Ottawa war chief in a huge resistance movement that included any number of tribes spread over the vast regions of the Old Northwest. These were mostly Algonquin tribes like the Ottawa, Chippewa,

Potawatomi, Shawnee, Delaware, and even the Sac, but also at least one of the Iroquois "nations," the Seneca, as well as bands of Hurons and a few Erie warriors.

If the border skirmishes of the French and Indian War had been harsh, the frenzy of Pontiac's "rebellion" was horrifying. This time, settlers, not Indians, suffered the greatest number of casualties. Rampaging warriors slaughtered some two thousand settlers but killed only four hundred-odd soldiers. The victims were generally those who had violated the bans against invading Indian territory; and the exuberantly brutal Indians inflicted incredible tortures and mutilations on the captured and practiced ritual cannibalism on the fallen. White survivors were forced to flee, seeking refuge in towns and forts.

The savagery, however, was not confined to one side of the conflict. The British commander-in-chief, Lord Amherst, responded to news of the Indian uprising with orders to extirpate the belligerents, taking no prisoners but putting "to death all that fall into your hands." He even requested one of his colonels "to send the small pox among disaffected tribes of Indians." The plan was abandoned for fear of infecting his own people, but revived later during the siege of Fort Pitt.

Parleys were a common practice in backwoods warfare, and during one such sitdown with the besieging Delaware chiefs, the fort's acting commander— a Swiss mercenary named Simeon Ecuyer—presented the Indians, as a token of his personal esteem, two blankets and a handkerchief infested with the pox from the fort's hospital. Captain William Trent, who provided the blankets, gloated, "I hope they will have the desired effect." The Delawares understood the hidden message behind his taunt and withdrew immediately. But they were, evidently, already infected from handling the blankets, for an epidemic swept through the tribe, killing off the Great Chief Shingas and his brother Pisquetomen, among hundreds of others.

A brutal vigilantism sprung up among the white settlers as well in response to the Indian attacks. A mob from Paxton and Donegal, Pennsylvania, massacred a group of peaceful Conestoga Indians in Lancaster County two months after Pontiac had sued for peace and Lord Amherst had reluctantly accepted. The rage with which they stabbed, hacked, and mutilated the defenseless tribe, innocent of any participation in the uprising, was a measure of how far the border skirmishing had traveled toward racial warfare. That warfare over ever-disputed lands would be marked by a lack of mercy on both sides, with atrocity the rule.

As for Pontiac, although he agreed to peace at Detroit in October 1763, the last of the forces associated with him continued to act independently until they, too, surrendered on November 17, 1764, at the Muskingham River in Ohio territory. For the next two years, Pontiac visited French settlements in Illinois country—it was said for the purpose of stirring up another rebellion—but, on July 24, 1766, he signed a treaty pledging loyalty to the English. He kept his word until 1769, when he was assassinated by a Kaskaskia Indian as he was leaving a store in Cahokia, Illinois. Evidence suggests that the assassin had been hired by an English trader, perhaps fearful of the presence of the legendary chief.

King George used Pontiac's rebellion as an excuse for reasserting his control over the American colonies. By the Royal Proclamation of 1763 he declared the hostilities over and limited white settlement by and large to the territory east of the Appalachians. But the Indians gained no lasting benefit from the hard-fought struggle. If anything, the failure of the Indian alliances to prevail and endure seemed to foreshadow the Indians' ultimate doom before the relentless advance of the frontier. As for the white settlers, the King's decree only pushed them further along the path to a rebellion of their own.

King George III Declares a Proclamation Line (1763)

The event: At the close of the French and Indian War, King George issued the Proclamation of 1763, setting the boundary beyond which English colonials could not settle. This only encouraged American pioneers to flout royal authority and paved the way for revolution.

ALTHOUGH VICTORIOUS IN the long, arduous, and dirty French and Indian War, the English emerged from the struggle acutely aware of the insecurity of their frontiers caused by the volatility of white-Indian relations. By the Treaty of Easton, concluded in October 1758, the English colonies had agreed to prohibit white settlement west of the Allegheny Mountains. English victories in the later years of the French and Indian War, combined with the completion of the Forbes Road (built to transport General Forbes's army to the site of Fort Duquesne—modern Pittsburgh), prompted settlers to violate the treaty almost immediately. The Proclamation of 1763 (October 7) reasserted the Easton treaty, this time backing it with the authority of a royal proclamation. Henceforth, except for a settlement in the upper Ohio, whites were forbidden west of the Appalachians.

The Proclamation of 1763 did much to conciliate potentially hostile Indians after the French and Indian War and during Pontiac's Rebellion, the crisis that immediately followed the war. Like the earlier Easton agreement, however, it was honored more in the breach than in the observance and soon proved impossible to enforce. Indeed, to many frontier settlers it seemed a dare that had to be accepted, almost an invitation to cross into the proscribed territory.

But settlers who crossed the proclamation line were subject to raids from resentful Indians. When, from time to time, such raiding became epidemic along the frontier, settlers looked to royal colonial officials for aid. Since the settlers were in violation of the law, however, assistance was not always forthcoming, a situation that steadily widened the gulf not only between Tidewater civilization and frontier settlements but, more importantly, between the colonial fringes and the mother country. A decade later, in February 1774, when the always-seething boundary question erupted into open resistance on the frontier, the crown proved unable to hold the proclamation line. When colonial governors were instructed to enforce the policy, Pennsylvania defiantly responded by declaring a scalp bounty, attracting a horde of bounty hunters, who raided the Indian borderlands, pushing back Indian settlement.

The Proclamation of 1763 provoked more rebellion than obedience, teaching the American colonials that they could flout royal authority with very little fear of punishment—at least not at the hands of the British. The violations it provoked, and the frictions it created, did much to create the conditions under which full-scale rebellion would develop little more than a decade later.

The proclamation line itself was not a border in the usual, European sense of a demarkation between two sovereign powers, nor a "frontier" in the Old World sense of the word. For political reasons, the King had defined the border as a line behind which he would allow "civilization" to flourish and beyond which "savagery" would be contained. The Native Americans, the savages, he in effect claimed as his private wards, who had the use of his land as a hunting ground as long as his "Royal Will and Pleasure" decreed. Colonials breaching the line would be trespassing in the wilderness. All of which, in time, gave the word "frontier" a new meaning as the advancing edge of white settlement. The proclamation's boundary line was the historical reality behind the great American myth of the Frontier.

Daniel Boone Breaches the Cumberland Gap (1767)

The event: By 1767, Daniel Boone—financed by the flamboyant North Carolina promoter, Judge Richard Henderson—had hacked the first rude road over the Cumberland Gap. A decade later, he founded Boonesborough in present-day Kentucky, an enduring bastion of the American frontier.

BOONE, ONE OF the earliest of the "long-hunters" who crossed the Appalachians in the 1760s, was, by 1775, the captain of the permanent settlers laboring westward to occupy the Bluegrass. The invasion of the American West by white settlers was triggered by a massive immigration of the Scotch-Irish, who were fleeing the bad harvests, high rents, and suppression of Presbyterianism in Northern Ireland's Ulster plantation in the decades just prior to the American Revolution.

By 1770 more than four hundred thousand Scotch-Irish, joined by a few Germans escaping the poverty of the Rhine's Palantine, some Huguenots and Scandinavians, and here and there a Highlander, spread through Pennsylvania and trekked south down the Appalachian trench until they reached the foothills and wooded valleys of the Carolinas. As the better land disappeared, these hardy souls plunged into the gigantic forest that, broken occasionally and dramatically by a marsh or prairie, then covered the entire American subcontinent west to the Mississippi. Armed only with an ax and a flintlock—the spiral-grooved long-barrelled gun first called the Pennsylvania, then the Kentucky rifle—they hacked out the clearings where they settled their wives and children and cattle and pigs, then notched a few logs and slung them together into crude cabins. They killed trees by girdling them, leaving the leafless trunks standing while they farmed the now sunny spots until the soil gave out or they got the itch to move on. Hardship and the constant dangers of the frontier made them stern, violent, clannish, hard-bitten, and fiercely independent. Though semi-literate, overly proud, and excessively cantankerous, they were also honest and direct, often rudely so. Years of brutal warfare had made their hatred of the Indian implacable. Their greatest resources were their endurance and their faculty of prolific reproduction. They lived by their own labor and ingenuity in the deep, forbidding forests of the American interior—filled with wild game and hostile Indians. Their slice of land represented to them not wealth so much as dignity: here, in the wilderness, a poor man could subdue and replenish the earth, and by doing so achieve a certain integrity in his life.

For these pioneers, Daniel Boone became the first of many Western heroes, a deerslayer and Indian fighter whose story was so emblematic of life on the frontier that he became their uncrowned king. Born of a lapsed Quaker in 1734 in southern Pennsylvania, at nineteen he had moved with his family to Yadkin County, North Carolina. He first heard about a place called Kentucky from one of his fellow volunteers under George Washington at Fort Duquesne during the opening battle of the French and Indian War. After the war, he left his home to wander the game-rich wilds of Kentucky for months, sometimes years at a time, seeking enough deerskins to allow him to make ends meet. Plagued by debt like most pioneers, uneasy with the growing number of new neighbors he found each time he returned home, Boone developed the burning conviction that there was a fortune to be made beyond the mountains.

In Kentucky, his legend spread. Though he had been fighting Indians since he was a teenager—during the fierce Yadkin Valley raids from 1758 to

1760, again in the French and Indian War, and in sporadic wilderness encounters—it was a Shawnee siege of Boonesborough at the beginning of the American Revolution that became the most celebrated of his many battles.

After the Revolution, Boone's fame began to grow in a fashion that would become standard for many a western legend: he became a hero in the popular literature read primarily by Easterners. His "press agent" was a Pennsylvania schoolteacher turned land promoter named John Filson, who traveled to Kentucky in 1782 and wrote an inaccurate and romantic piece of western propaganda called *The Discovery, Settlement, and present State of Kentucke*, which included a section subtitled "The Adventures of Col. Daniel Boone."

Though Boone became a successful surveyor, trader, and landowner, he lost everything that he made through his own carelessness and the legal chicanery of land speculators. He packed up his belongings and his family and moved west again, across the Mississippi, with a flood of immigrants now pouring into present-day Missouri. There he died in 1820, just as Missouri was applying for statehood. Once again, he proved the quintessential Westerner. An obsession with land, and what it represented, had brought Boone and his fellow pioneers to the wilderness. But their insatiable lust for it also created the paradox of the frontier character. Having fought for their plot of ground and secured it with incredible toil, many became immediately dissatisfied and went looking for something else, something more, further on. The restlessness of the pioneers, in historian David Lavender's words, was so "bone deep it seemed like a new human instinct."

The Jesuits Are Expelled from New Spain (1767)

The event: In 1767, responding to Jesuit arrogance in the running of frontier missions, the Spanish crown expelled all members of the Society of Jesus from its New World holdings, leaving the more humane Franciscans in charge of the "mission system" by which New Spain conquered the West.

BY THE END of the seventeenth century, Spain, which had opened the New World to Europe and, for a time, had dominated it, was a bankrupt nation unable to defend its American holdings against the incursions of Indians and other European colonists. In 1699, when the French established their first enduring colony in Louisiana, the colonial government in Mexico City decided that it could no longer depend on the royal government in Madrid and, on its own authority, gave the Jesuits permission to build a series of Catholic missions in what is today the American Southwest.

Spain's missionaries made effective empire builders. By persuasion or force, they convinced the Indians of the Southwest to help build missions across a frontier that ultimately stretched from the Pacific Ocean to the Red River Valley. The Church provided each new mission with seed money from a special fund to buy beads, vestments, tools, the necessities of life, and—of course—seeds. Older, established missions were expected to contribute as well, offering whatever they could spare in the way of grain, cuttings, breeding stock, chickens, and wine. A couple of padres would arrive on a spot, throw up a temporary chapel and a few rude log cabins, and launch immediately into proselytizing. They purchased the Indian's faith with a few glass beads, clothing, blankets, and most especially food, and they enforced that faith with a detachment of musket-armed soldiers. Once converted, the Indians were not allowed to leave the mission grounds without permission of the clergy. They spent their days tilling the fields and replacing temporary structures with the distinctive architecture of the Spanish West. Not exactly slaves, the Indians nevertheless provided a stable source of labor and were the economic heart of the mission. Over the years they expanded and developed the compound, and by stages the mission grew into a thriving complex—part multiple dwelling, part workshop, part grain bin, all dominated by the church—which sometimes took half a century to complete.

Best known among the Jesuit missionaries was Father Eusebio Francisco Kino, an extraordinary man by any measure. Trained as an astronomer and mathematician, Kino traveled some twenty thousand miles—often as much as seventy-five miles a day on horseback—and founded twenty-four missions in Mexico and the Southwest during the quarter-century of his missionary work in America. He drew up the most accurate maps of the Spanish frontier empire, proving, among other things, that California was not an island, as many believed. Kino was apparently much beloved by the Indians his missions served, and he was also a benefactor to later generations. At least twenty western cities owe their origins to his work, as does the region's great cattle industry—for it was Kino who first introduced varieties of livestock into the country.

Few New World Jesuit missionaries were as beloved or beneficent as Father Kino. The Jesuits were harsh taskmasters, and, especially in the older portions of the Spanish colonial empire—northern Mexico, Paraguay, and Uruguay—they imposed an iron-cruel military discipline on the Indians. The Spanish government found this less objectionable, however, than the degree of autonomy the Jesuits obnoxiously arrogated to themselves. When, in a sudden and devastating move, the Spanish crown expelled all Jesuits from New Spain, the missions in many parts of the colonial empire fell into rapid decay.

But in the American Southwest, the Franciscans quickly stepped in to fill the vacuum left by the departure of their Jesuit rivals. The mission system reached its apotheosis under the Franciscans in California, who at their peak numbered only thirty-eight souls, all told. The padres were patient colonizers, however, assuming from the start that it would take a decade from the time they arrived in an area until they had pacified the local Indians and got the mission functioning properly.

Best known among the Franciscan missionaries was Father Junipero Serra. When Russian fur traders menaced Spain's hold on Northern California, the enfeebled Madrid government turned to the Church and attached Serra to the expedition of General José de Gálvez, who was charged in 1769 with occupying Alta California. Although Serra suffered from chronic ill health, aggravated by his zeal for self-mortification (flagellation, beating his breast with a stone, burning himself with candles), he founded nine of the twenty-one Franciscan missions that stretched in an unbroken chain from San Diego to Sonoma along a dirt path grandiosely dubbed El Camino Real, the Royal Highway.

For better or worse, the Jesuit and Franciscan missions "settled" much of the Southwest and California, protecting the Indians while subjugating them, coercing religion from them, and destroying their own culture. In California alone, six decades after the first padre had arrived, the missions boasted seventeen thousand Indian converts. These were neophytes who not only labored for the church but also displayed considerable talents—in music, for example, forming choirs and orchestras that performed at the weddings and fiestas of the rancheros and farmers who followed on the heels of the missionaries. Exploitative though they were, the missions became the far-flung nuclei around which the settlements, towns, and cities of the region developed. Historically, culturally, and architecturally, the Spanish missions left their mark on the American West.

The Sons of Liberty Throw the Boston Tea Party (1773)

The event: On December 16, 1773, in the infamous Boston Tea Party, a group of sixty colonists dressed as Indians boarded three British cargo vessels anchored in Boston Harbor and threw overboard 342 tea chests, worth £18,000, to protest Parliament's hated Tea Act.

FROM 1765, WHEN colonists got their first taste of victory as a result of their protest against Parliament's passage of the Stamp Act, until 1773, when the colonists in Massachusetts resorted to destruction of private property to gain their ends, America moved steadily closer to a break with Great Britain, having reached the irreversible conclusion that Parliament had no right to tax or otherwise interfere with the daily activities of the colonies. The colonists saw the passage of the 1773 Tea Act as yet another affront to their rights. This law required that all tea shipped to the colonies be imported by the East India Company, and that only consignees of the company in the colonies could then sell tea to merchants. The legislated monopoly was ruinous for most colonial tea merchants, who were, at one stroke, put out of business.

To the American colonists, who had grown sensitive to almost any Parliamentary action, the granting of a monopoly to a private business was deemed an outrage, and they feared the act was but a prelude to further interference in the affairs of the colonies. In Boston, protesters called on the East India Company's consignees, two of whom were Royal Governor Thomas Hutchinson's sons, to resign their commissions. They refused. At a town meeting, protest leaders called on the colonists to boycott tea, as ships laden with it lodged in Boston Harbor. The ships' captains wanted to leave the harbor to sail to another city, where they could distribute the tea to colonists not bound by the boycott. Governor Hutchinson refused to let them leave.

On the night of December 16, the Boston protesters took action. A group of men dressed as Mohawk Indians, boarded the ships and dumped ninety thousand pounds of tea overboard. The Parliamentary response was almost immediate. By the following spring three new laws had been passed to punish the colony of Massachusetts. The Port Act forbade trade in and out of Boston until the colonists paid for the dumped tea. The Administration of Justice Act allowed the royal governor to move trials of crown officials out of the colony if he believed an impartial jury could not be convened. The Massachusetts Government Act increased the power of the royal governor at the expense of the general assembly. In addition, Parliament strengthened the Quartering Act, which allowed royal governors in all the colonies to seize uninhabited, privately owned buildings as quarters for British troops. Together, these four laws became known as the "Intolerable Acts."

Although three of the laws were directed at Massachusetts alone, citizens from other colonies joined Massachusetts in outrage. Some colonies sent food and supplies to Boston, whose port had been closed. In New Hampshire, colonists removed the royal governor from office after he attempted to disband the legislature and to send a crew of carpenters to Boston to build barracks for British troops. Most momentously, throughout the colonies, protest leaders issued a call for delegates to assemble a Continental Congress. In a dispute over tea a revolution was brewed.

The First Continental Congress Meets (1774)

The event: Delegates from every colony except Georgia met in September 1774 for the First Continental Congress in Philadelphia, where they committed themselves and their people to revolution.

AFTER THE BOSTON Tea Party and Parliament's passage of the "Intolerable Acts", a call for the First Continental Congress circulated through the colonies. Delegates met in Philadelphia in September 1774 and came to the momentous conclusion that Parliament had no authority to legislate for the colonies. Previously, colonial protest had been confined to the issue of taxation without representation; now colonists were unwilling to accept any Parliamentary laws whatsoever.

The more moderate delegates, including Joseph Galloway of Pennsylvania, argued that the colonial system was salvageable and proposed a plan calling for a new American government, led by a royally appointed president general and by a grand council, whose members would be selected by the colonial governments. The colonial government would have the power to veto any Parliamentary act that affected the colonies. The radicals, however, not the moderates, numbered in the majority at the Congress, and Galloway's plan did not gain acceptance.

The delegates passed a resolution listing grievances against Parliament and formed a "Continental Association" to manage boycotts of British goods and enforce an embargo of exports to England. The association would appoint committees in each of the colonies to supervise the protest and to expose violators. In addition, the delegates endorsed a plan proposed by the Massachusetts delegates calling for colonists to defend their rights by taking up arms.

The First Continental Congress crystallized opinion against the British colonial system. As John Adams wrote many years later, "The revolution was complete, in the minds of the people, and the Union of the colonies, before the war commenced."

The American Revolution Begins (1775)

The event: On April 19, 1775, seven hundred British troops—on the march since the night before toward a rebel arsenal at Concord—faced off along the way at Lexington against a small and confused rag-tag force of Massachusetts colonials calling themselves "Minutemen." Someone fired a shot, the British broke ranks and returned fire, and within minutes eight of the colonial militia lay dead on the village green. The American Revolution had begun.

BRITAIN'S GENERAL GAGE, recently installed by the Crown as governor of Massachusetts (replacing Thomas Hutchinson) specifically to discipline the king's unruly New England subjects, had sent his troops to secure the Concord arsenal in hopes of nipping the colonial rebellion in the bud. But the Sons of Liberty, following Gage's arrest of John Hancock and Sam Adams, the patriot ringleaders, were expecting the move, and their messengers—Paul Revere and William Dawes, among others—had warned the "Minutemen" in the area. At Concord they mounted an effective resistance that forced the British to retreat under heavy fire. Hoping to end the rebellion by isolating and punishing the patriots in Boston through a show of force, the British launched a reckless frontal assault at Breed's Hill two months later in an attempt to demonstrate the invincibility of trained troops against part-time militia. The demonstration failed. Not only the Americans' refusal to give way until they exhausted their ammunition, but the outpouring of support from other New England towns and commitments of aid from other colonies compelled the British, after the so-called Battle of Bunker Hill on June 17, to reconsider their assumptions about American strength.

Two days earlier the Continental Congress had commissioned Virginia's George Washington to lead the army, and on July 3, 1775, he took command at Cambridge. Washington's Continental Army, a small but usually dependable regular army of state regiments, provided the hard core of the American resistance, supplemented when necessary and where available by state militia. Always hard pressed for money, the patriots financed the war in part by requisitioning the states and taking out both domestic and foreign loans, but primarily by issuing huge amounts of "printing-press" money. Never adequately equipped, the men got most of their arms and supplies from Europe. Despite popular legend, they did not fight like Indians but mimicked the best European tactics based on the "shock power" of smooth-bore muskets at close range. With numbers that fluctuated from four thousand to ninety thousand troops, the Continental Army was filled out in later years by thousands of French volunteers.

Unable to raise enough men back home, the British hired German mercenaries and counted on aid from the Indians and American Loyalists, who were not all that dependable. Except for the Indians, the British forces were not well acquainted with the American climate or terrain, and they were at the end of a vastly over-extended line of supply that stretched across a great ocean. Though the British Empire on paper hugely outgunned the patriots, it was bogged down in a struggle against a tenacious, politically rabid foe camouflaged by a civilian population at a time when questions of costs and clear purpose were fast eroding support for the war back home.

Even before evacuating Boston, the British tried—and failed—to occupy Charlestown. The Americans had no greater luck in Canada, where the British repulsed two columns that had only recently taken Ticonderoga and Crown Point. General William Howe, replacing Gage, left Boston only to seize New York City and a good part of New Jersey, halted by the Americans at Trenton on December 26 in 1776. General John Burgoyne proposed to lead the idle British troops in Canada overland to join Howe in New York, which his London-based superiors saw as a chance to separate New England from the South, but his army was cut off and captured by Horatio Gates at Saratoga in October 1777—a great American victory. Still, Washington's army languished and dwindled during the harsh winter at Valley Forge.

The French, delighted to further embarrass the country with which they had been at war over colonial possessions for the last century or so, had secretly offered the Americans aid from the start, but with Burgoyne's surrender at Saratoga they came out of the closet. To make sure the English and the patriots reached no reconciliation, they struck an alliance with America in 1778. France's ally, Spain, made no deal with the rebels but provided help nevertheless in the South and West. The Russians formed the League of Armed Neutrality, which the French backed and the Dutch—also enemies of the English at that time—tolerated as an anti-British alliance. The British Empire, which had ruled the Seven Seas for decades, was at war with the whole world. If her enemies did not mount full-fledged sea battles against her, their privateers raided merchant ships, exasperated her navy, and drove up her insurance rates. Any British army in America was likely to have its retreat cut off, if only temporarily, and that is precisely what happened when George Washington, with the help of the French navy, trapped His Majesty's troops at Yorktown.

An encounter at Monmouth in 1778 had proved indecisive, and except for Benedict Arnold's attempt to sell out West Point to the enemy in 1780, no major action developed thereafter in the North. George Rogers Clark had beaten the British bands in the West, saving the infant Kentucky settlements, while the brunt of the war shifted south. There the English had won battles but lost the war, chiefly because they could not hold on to what they captured. A disgusted Lord Cornwallis, now in charge of the British forces, settled in at Yorktown, Virginia, to brood over the indecisiveness of his campaigns, only to have Washington and Rochambeau spring their trap. As the French fleet floated menacingly off the coast, Cornwallis surrendered in October of 1781.

Peace feelers that formally had gotten nowhere suddenly led to earnest negotiation. Suspicious of their French ally—who wanted to reward Spain at American expense—the patriots made a separate peace under the 1783 Treaty of Paris, a diplomatic triumph that granted the United States independence and set its boundaries. A great empire was humbled and a new nation was born.

Thomas Paine Publishes *Common Sense* (1776)

The event: In January, 1776, Thomas Paine published the pamphlet *Common Sense*, a polemic in service to revolution that immediately sold 150,000 copies and turned mass public opinion for the first time toward the cause of independence.

 THOMAS PAINE WAS born in England in 1737, the son of a cor-
set maker. From his Quaker father he imbibed basic princi-
ples of humanitarianism and equality, which the young man
soon developed into a forcefully and persuasively expressed
political philosophy. With the help of Benjamin Franklin,
Paine immigrated to Philadelphia in 1774 and soon became
associated with those who were planning America's independence. *Common Sense* was his eloquent first appearance in print—and the
first pamphlet to advocate American independence.

Published anonymously by a patriot press, *Common Sense* was a brilliant
piece of rabble-rousing propaganda that simply and eloquently stated the reasons
for breaking free of England. In stirringly melodramatic prose, Paine skillfully
appealed to the strong anti-Catholic sentiment in the Colonies by comparing the
English king to the pope, reduced the hereditary succession of kings to comic
absurdity, eviscerated all arguments for reconciliation with the mother country,
outlined the economic benefits of independence, and developed two central
points: the inherent superiority of republican government over hereditary monar-
chy, and the equality of rights among all citizens. Perhaps most important of all,
Paine created a sense in the book of the American Revolution as a *world* event,
an epochal step in the history of mankind.

"These are the times that try men's souls," began the book. "The summer
soldier and sunshine patriot will, in this crisis, shrink from the service of his
country; but he that stands it now, deserves the love and thanks of man and
woman. Tyranny, like hell, is not easily conquered." Such language galvanized
the colonies into a union that made revolution possible and laid the American
struggle for liberty before all the world's nations, giving, as it were, all peoples
everywhere a stake in its outcome. John Adams declared in 1805, "I know not
whether any man in the world has had more influence on its inhabitants or affairs for the last thirty years than Tom Paine."

Adams may have been right, but Paine, the acknowledged star of the great
revolutionary drama, died a lonely and unheralded death. After the American Revolution, he returned to Europe and, defending now the French Revolution, launched

into such heated debate with England's Edmund Burke that he had to flee Britain to escape arrest for seditious libel. In France, he became one of the few foreigners elected to the National Convention, but he eventually fell afoul of the Jacobins and wound up in prison. Released in 1794, he wrote *The Age of Reason*, an exposition of deism, which brought him under attack by the evangelical Christians when he returned to America in 1802. At his funeral seven years later, only six mourners attended to pay tribute to the man who once inspired multitudes to think about the world in new ways and, by doing so, helped give birth to a nation.

Congress Adopts the Declaration of Independence (1776)

The event: On July 4, 1776, the Continental Congress of the English settlements along the Atlantic seacoast, then in rebellion against Great Britain, passed "The Unanimous Declaration of the Thirteen United States of America," a document popularly known as the "Declaration of Independence," which set out, briefly and with supreme eloquence, the fundamental premises of American nationhood.

THREE DAYS BEFORE, Richard Henry Lee, one of Virginia's delegates to Congress, had risen in the sweltering heat of the Philadelphia meeting house to propose a resolution declaring that "these United Colonies are, and of a right ought to be, free and independent States." Lee's draft proposal called for the newly declared nation to form foreign alliances and to prepare a plan for confederation. Congress passed Lee's proposal but, in what would become a time-honored legislative tradition, sent the draft to committee for debate and amendment.

The assembly appointed Massachusetts delegate John Adams, internationally known philosopher Benjamin Franklin, New York conservative Robert Livingston, and Connecticut Yankee Roger Sherman, but fell to wrangling over a fifth member, which Southern delegates argued should be one of their own to achieve balance. At Adams's suggestion, Congress named compromise candidate Thomas Jefferson, a Virginian who had a reputation as a fine writer. To Jefferson fell the task of drafting the Committee's report, a resolution whose language would be acceptable to all the delegates.

Jefferson, whose wife was sick and who longed to be home working on his own state's new constitution, then being drafted in the Virginia House of Burgesses, set to work quickly, producing a powerful and incisive summary of Whig political thought that was much influenced by English philosopher John Locke, among others. "We hold these truths to be self-evident," he wrote, "that all men are created equal, that they are endowed by their Creator with certain unalienable Rights. . . ." Following Locke, he declared that chief among these rights were "Life, Liberty, and Property," but then changed "Property" to "the pursuit of Happiness." And, he wrote, "to secure these rights, Governments are instituted among Men, deriving their just powers from the consent of the governed. . . ."

The promise held in these phrases became the cornerstone of American democracy, but at the time it was the more concrete declarations that concerned the delegates. For years the colonials had based their resistance against England on the belief that they were fighting not the divinely chosen English king, whose loyal subjects they remained, but his ministers and his parliament. Not until the Crown had waged war against the colonies for fourteen months and George III had finally declared the colonies in open rebellion and put them officially outside his protection did the Americans turn against the king. Thomas Paine had crystallized American sentiment in *Common Sense*, published at the beginning of 1776, and Thomas Jefferson set about to document specifically why the former colonials felt that the "royal brute" who occupied the English throne deserved their hatred instead of their allegiance.

Jefferson produced a catalog of George III's tyrannies, among them the slave trade, contending that the King had "waged a cruel war against humane nature" by assaulting a "distant people" and carrying them into slavery in "another hemisphere." This was too much for Jefferson's fellow slaveholders in the South, especially in South Carolina, and certain Yankee traders who had made fortunes from what Jefferson called the "execrable commerce." Together, representatives of these southern and Yankee interests deleted the section. But in making the banishment of the word *slavery* from the declaration the price of their endorsement, the Southerners overlooked the word *equality* and the central role it played in the document. By adopting a declaration of independence that promised the equality of all men, the new American nation ultimately doomed the "peculiar institution" of slavery, although at the immense cost of a bloody civil war decades later that would almost destroy the country.

Congress Adopts the Articles of Confederation (1777)

The event: Beginning with the Second Continental Congress, convened in May 1775, colonial leaders had been grappling with the question of how the several colonies—or states—could join together in a single government. The product of their deliberations came in November 1777 when the Articles of Confederation were submitted to the states for ratification, a process completed in March 1781.

 THE ARTICLES OF CONFEDERATION certified the legal status of the Continental Congress, which had been acting on behalf of the states since May 1775. Within the Congress, the articles gave each state a single vote, though "each state retain[ed] its sovereignty, freedom, and independence, and every Power, Jurisdiction, and right, which is not by this confederation expressly delegated to the United States, in Congress assembled." The balance of powers was clearly in favor of the individual states, and among the crucial powers denied the national government was that of taxation; for the delegates were all too mindful of the trouble Parliament's taxes had brought.

Although the national government, as codified in the Articles of Confederation, proved strong enough to wage and win the War of Independence, events following the war proved the government to be too weak. In Massachusetts, for example, Daniel Shays led an attack by small farmers on the state judicial system, which had been foreclosing on farmers who were unable to pay taxes. In Rhode Island the state government continued to issue paper money that was worthless. Under the Articles of Confederation the federal government could do nothing to aid the Massachusetts state government during Shays' Rebellion or to force Rhode Island to adopt more responsible fiscal policies. A change was needed, and a call was issued for a meeting in Philadelphia in May 1787 to revise the Articles of Confederation.

The delegates took much more drastic steps. Instead of revising the Articles they tossed them aside and started from scratch with debates and deliberations that resulted in the United States Constitution and transformed once and for all a loose confederation of colonies into the United States of America.

Congress Passes the Northwest Ordinance (1787)

The event: One of the most important pieces of legislation passed by Congress under the Articles of Confederation was the Northwest Ordinance, which, approved by Congress on July 13, 1787, specified how territories and states were to be formed from the land gained by the United States as a result of the Revolution.

THE LAW CALLED for the land of what was then considered the Northwest—bounded by the Ohio and Mississippi rivers and the Great Lakes—to be divided into three to five territories. Congress would appoint a governor, a secretary, and three judges to administer each territory. When the adult male population of a territory reached five thousand, elections would be held to form a legislature and to select a nonvoting representative to Congress. A territory could write a constitution and apply for statehood when the adult male population reached sixty thousand. The Northwest Ordinance placed certain restrictions on the constitutions of the new states. Slavery was to be prohibited from the region, religious freedom was to be maintained, trial by jury was to be guaranteed, and education was to be supported by the state governments.

The ordinance was to serve as a model for the transition from territory to statehood in other regions and at later times as the population expanded westward. It was also the first national legislative measure restricting slavery in any way, establishing a precedent that would be reflected in later acts of Congress. In addition the law ensured that, once the pioneers had settled in sufficient numbers to create a state, they would have a voice in Congress equal to that of the original thirteen states. And it was precisely here that America displayed the genius of its revolution-spawned republicanism.

The Northwest Ordinance was, in fact, a document for the political handling of colonized land. The "mother country" east of the Appalachians, understanding the psychology of colonial people, declared that it would treat what it was careful not to call its western colonies not as colonies at all, but in the long run as full partners in a single nation. Alone among the expansive empirical powers of the eighteenth and nineteenth century, the United States established an orderly method for creating a coherent polity with conquered land.

The *Federalist Papers* Are Published (1788)

The event: The writings of Alexander Hamilton, James Madison, and John Jay in defense of the new United States Constitution, writing that had appeared in New York newspapers between October 1787 and April 1788, were collected and published in book form as *The Federalist Papers* later in the year, creating a classic work of American political philisophy in the attempt to promote a stronger federal government.

AFTER THE DELEGATES to the Constitutional Convention in Philadelphia submitted the proposed Constitution to the states for ratification, some states, including Delaware, Pennsylvania, and New Jersey, approved the document almost immediately. In others, however, delegates to the ratification conventions battled over the division of power between the central government and the states. Two factions formed, the Federalists and the Antifederalists. The Federalists, who favored the strong central government called for by the proposed Constitution, were generally men of property, professionals, and merchants. The Antifederalists tended to be small farmers or men who owed substantial debts. Among their chief concerns was that the Constitution would nullify the independence of the states. Even the document's first phrase, "We the people of the United States," caused concern among the Antifederalists and prompted Samuel Adams to remark, "As I enter the Building, I stumble at the Threshold."

The most cogent defense of the Constitution was provided by Alexander Hamilton, James Madison, and John Jay, who together produced the "Federalist Papers" under the collective pen name of Publius. Hamilton wrote fifty-one of the Federalist essays, Madison twenty-nine, and Jay five. Printed in New York newspapers between October 1787 and April 1788, and issued as a book in the spring of 1788, the eighty-five essays had a strong effect on members of New York's ratification convention. The essays brilliantly defended the Constitution, the single most famous defense being Madison's in essay number ten. Madison addressed the Antifederalist concern that the country was too large for an effective central government, arguing that the size of the country was precisely the reason republicanism would flourish: the various needs and interests of citizens spread over a large area would prevent a single special interest from gaining control.

Outside their immediate influence on the New York convention, the articles probably did little to sway the public opinion of the day. But published in book form, they were widely read over time with a growing respect for their acute analysis and masterful interpretation of the Constitution, becoming a touchstone for those who wished to understand well the principles upon which the government of the United States was established.

The U.S. Constitution Is Adopted (1788)

The event: Despite their understandable fears about creating a strong—and, therefore, potentially tyrannical—central government, most of the "Founding Fathers," chief among them Alexander Hamilton, realized that the nation was foundering under the weak Articles of Confederation. To frame a stronger government, a convention at Philadelphia produced a new document, the United States Constitution, which was ratified by the states in 1788.

WHEN DELEGATES FROM all the states except Rhode Island, which strongly opposed the convention, met in Philadelphia in May 1787, they set as their comparatively modest task the revision of the Articles of Confederation, the charter for the central American government that had been approved by the states in 1781. That mission had been set for them by an earlier convention, at Annapolis in 1786, which had been attended by delegates from only five states. Among them was Alexander Hamilton, who was most firmly convinced that only a total reorganization of the American government would save the Union from ultimate disintegration. Believing themselves too small a group to undertake the revisions, the delegates at Annapolis issued a call for a meeting in Philadelphia in May 1787, ostensibly to correct the deficiencies of the Articles of Confederation.

All but two of the delegates agreed that some form of government that divided power between the states and the central government was needed. They agreed on the desirability of a republican form of government, drawing authority from and responsible to the citizens. Finally, they viewed a balance of power among the executive, legislative, and judicial branches of government as extremely important. Operating from these basic premises, the delegates boldly moved beyond their original mandate. Clearly, Hamilton had been right, and an entirely new document outlining an entirely new form of government was required.

By the end of May the delegates had agreed to devise a "national" government. What remained for them to accomplish was to define the powers and limits of that government. The document they composed, the United States Constitution, gave the federal government the power to levy taxes, to regulate interstate and foreign trade, and to raise and maintain an army. The delegates withdrew from the individual states the authority to issue money, to make treaties, and to tax imports and exports. To administer these new powers, the delegates proposed a national legislature composed of two houses—a Senate, to be filled by two delegates elected by each state assembly, and a House of Representatives, to be composed of popularly elected representatives whose numbers were in proportion to the population of the states they represented.

Proportional representation necessitated a means of counting population, which meant that the delegates had to come to immediate terms with the issue of slavery. The southern states, of course, wanted all slaves counted among their populations; the northern states wanted to exclude slaves from the population tallies. The delegates devised the "Three-Fifths Compromise," which stated that, for the purposes of counting populations to determine representation in the lower house of Congress, three-fifths of "all other Persons"—that is, slaves—would be counted. This method of counting slaves was also used to determine the amount of taxes due from the states to the federal government.

In creating an executive branch of government, the delegates called for a president and a vice-president chosen not directly by popular vote but by popularly elected "electors." The number of electors for each state equaled the number of representatives the state sent to Congress. In elections in which no candidate received a majority of votes cast by the Electoral College, the House of Representatives would cast votes—one per state—to make the selection. Besides determining how the president was to be elected, the convention delegates gave to that office broad powers. The president was responsible for executing all laws, was to serve as commander-in-chief of the armed forces, was responsible for overseeing all foreign relations, and was empowered to appoint federal judges and other officials. In addition, the president held veto power over the Congress, although Congress could override a presidential veto by a two-thirds vote in both houses.

Throughout their deliberations, however, the delegates were careful to imbue the Constitution with a system of checks and balances among the three branches of government. While the president was commander-in-chief of the armed forces, only Congress could declare war. While the president could veto any law passed by Congress, Congress could override a veto or even impeach the president. The framers of the document clearly imagined that the judicial branch of government would have some oversight function, though just what that would be was only vaguely defined. Not until a strong-willed Chief Justice decided to declare a law unconstitutional years later did the long-lasting tradition of judicial review become firmly established.

Every state but Rhode Island called a ratifying convention in late 1787 or early 1788, and all but one of those—North Carolina—voted to approve the Constitution. Five states—Delaware, Pennyslvania, New Jersey, Georgia, and Connecticut—ratified it in short order between December 1787 and early January 1788. But in Massachusetts, the Constitution ran into strong, organized opposition from Antifederalists, who wanted a series of amendments, in particular a Bill of Rights. When the Federalists refused to budge, insisting the document be accepted or rejected as it was written, John Adams and John Hancock worked out a compromise in which amendments would be considered by the new Congress, should the Constitution go into effect. That promise was enough for most states, and after Massachusetts ratified the Constitution in February, Maryland, South Carolina, New Hampshire, Virginia, and New York followed suit throughout the spring and summer, all of them but Maryland suggesting amendments for Congress to adopt.

Having boycotted the Constitutional Convention, Rhode Island held out, submitting the document to its town meetings, whose voters—in a state-wide voted on March 24, 1788, that was boycotted by the admittedly outnumbered Federalists—soundly rejected it, 2,708 to 237. When North Carolina's convention was still deadlocked in August, the delegates voted to adjourn without making a decision. Not until Congress actually introduced the Bill of Rights in 1789 did North Carolina and then Rhode Island, in that order, elect conventions that approved the already operating Constitution.

The struggle for ratification produced both a baldfaced scramble for votes and an intricate, high-minded discussion of politics and constitutional theory. For the first time in history, the people of a nation had the liberty to decide on their own form of government, and the debate itself proved a catalyst for the birth of a stable national political system that could weather the strains natural to a federation of states.

George Washington Is Elected the First President (1789)

The event: On April 6, 1789, the U.S. Senate convened to count the ballots cast by members of the Electoral College for the first president of the United States. George Washington was unanimously elected, and John Adams, with thirty-four votes, was named vice-president.

THE ELECTION OF Washington was a surprise to no one in the country. In fact, the framers of the Constitution were certain he would be elected, even as they drafted the document that gave broad powers to the office of the president. With a man like Washington in mind, the authors of the Constitution felt confident entrusting a great deal of authority to the office of chief executive.

Washington, owner of the Mount Vernon plantation in Virginia, served in the Virginia militia during the French and Indian War and as commander-in-chief of the American forces during the Revolution. He also served as a delegate from Virginia to the First and Second Continental Congresses. When he took the presidential oath of office at New York City's Federal Hall, he was perhaps the most loved and best known figure in the country. As president he was exceedingly careful to avoid conflicts with Congress, believing that it was not the duty of the president to propose legislation, nor to campaign for or against any candidate for Congress.

As the first officeholder, Washington set precedents that all future presidents would follow. Among these was the naming of a cabinet, a group of advisers not explicitly mandated by the Constitution. For secretary of the treasury, Washington selected Alexander Hamilton. Thomas Jefferson filled the post of secretary of state. Henry Knox was the first secretary of war. Edmund Randolph was the first attorney general.

During his two terms as president, Washington signed important treaties with England and Spain, approved the bill that created a national bank, issued a proclamation of neutrality to ensure that the United States would not become embroiled in the warfare between England and France, and quelled the so-called Whiskey Rebellion in western Pennsylvania by calling up twelve thousand militiamen against the rebels. Washington set yet another precedent by refusing to run for a third term as president. The Constitution did not limit the number of terms a president could serve, but every president until Franklin D. Roosevelt followed Washington's example. (After Roosevelt's election to four terms, the Constitution was amended to limit the terms a president may serve to two.)

During his presidency, Washington maintained a strong position against the formation of political parties, but two major groups began to develop nevertheless. With his second term the two-party system was born, pitting the Federalists, headed by John Adams and Alexander Hamilton, against the Democratic Republicans, headed by Thomas Jefferson.

George Washington was not only beloved and respected by his countrymen but admired by a world sickened by the tyranny of the old order on the one hand and the excesses of the French Revolution and Napoleon Bonaparte on the other. He provided a strong guiding hand during the nation's most formative years, endowed the office of president with an enduring dignity, and did much to win for the United States the respect and support of the nations of the world. If any one man deserved the epithet popularly accorded him—Father of His Country—it was George Washington.

Congress Frames the Bill of Rights (1791)

The event: In 1791, using as its models the venerable English Magna Carta and a bill of rights George Mason had written for the Virginia constitution, James Madison and a committee framed the first ten amendments to the United States Constitution known as the Bill of Rights.

AS THE VARIOUS states debated ratification of the proposed United States Constitution, it became clear to authors of the document that, in order to secure adoption, they would have to amend to the Constitution a Bill of Rights.

The framers had originally believed that such a bill was unnecessary because the Constitution stipulated that the government was to be one of enumerated powers only. As the framers saw it, this eliminated any danger of the government exceeding the powers explicitly allowed by the Constitution. In the minds of many Americans, however, were fresh memories of the abuses inflicted on them by Parliament. From these memories arose the call for a separate Bill enumerating inalienable rights.

On the promise that a Bill of Rights would be provided, the states ratified the Constitution, and, guided by James Madison, who carefully examined and weighed the bills of rights already incorporated into some state constitutions, the first Congress convened under the new document immediately set to work to fulfill its promise. Madison and Congress produced ten amendments, which collectively prohibit Congress from passing laws that infringe on an individual's civil rights. The Bill of Rights explicitly guarantees: freedom of speech, freedom of the press, and freedom of religion (Amendment I); the right to keep and bear arms (Amendment II); freedom from government-imposed quartering of soldiers (Amendment III); freedom from unreasonable searches and seizures (Amendment IV); freedom from being forced to testify against oneself, and due process of law (Amendment V); the right to trial by an impartial jury (Amendment VI); the right to a jury trial in civil matters involving property valued at $20 or more (Amendment VII); freedom from excessive bail, fines, and cruel and unusual punishment (Amendment VIII); the primacy of the rights of individuals over the rights given by the Constitution to the government (Amendment IX); the reservation for the states of all powers not expressly given the federal government (Amendment X).

Eli Whitney Invents the Cotton Gin (1793)

The event: In 1793, Yale graduate Eli Whitney invented the cotton gin, a device that revolutionized the production of cotton and made it a cash staple of Southern agriculture.

A NATIVE OF Massachusetts, Whitney moved to Georgia after college to work as a tutor. There he grew fascinated with the operations of Southern plantations and quickly identified a major problem shared by cotton planters. The short-staple cotton grown across the lower South had seeds that were difficult to remove from the fibers by hand. Always interested in tools and machinery, Whitney turned his attention to the invention of a machine that would handle the manual work. Cotton farmers fed the bolls of cotton into a cylinder equipped with wire teeth. As the cylinder rotated, the teeth pulled the fibers away from the seeds. Using the gin, fifty times more cotton could be cleaned in a day than could be done previously by hand.

Invaluable aid came to Whitney from Georgia plantation owner Catherine Lidfield Greene. She financed his efforts and made final alterations in the design. Some claim she also initially came up with the idea for a machine capable of stripping seeds from cotton bolls.

Whitney received a patent for his perfected machine, and in 1794 he established a business to manufacture gins. He failed, however, to make his fortune. His invention was a simple contraption, easy to copy, and cotton planters built their own models instead of buying Whitney's. As cotton gins proliferated, more and more farmers found the cultivation of cotton profitable, and cotton production soared.

Fueled by the demand from British and Yankee textile mills for raw fiber, the Southern economy boomed, and what was once a secondary crop became King Cotton. As a result, the South became even more dependent on slave labor, and Southern planters grew rabid in their promotion and adamant in their defense of the region's "peculiar institution."

The XYZ Affair Leads to the Alien and Sedition Acts (1798)

The event: In the summer of 1798, the U.S. Congress, controlled by the Federalist Party, passed the Alien and Sedition Acts. Purportedly a patriotic response to the public outrage over two foreign affairs scandals, the legislation was in fact an attempt by the incumbents to suppress political dissent from the Democratic-Republican party headed by Thomas Jefferson and James Madison.

ALTHOUGH FRANCE HAD rendered valuable aid during the American Revolution, the conservative Federalist government did not support the subsequent revolution there. Indeed, the Federalists recoiled in horror from the French Revolution. In an atmosphere of cooling relations between nations that had been so recently allied, the French Girondist regime sent Edmond Charles Genêt—"Citizen Genêt"—as its minister to the United States, instructing him to secure America's amity and to negotiate a new treaty of commerce.

Upon arrival, Genêt began plotting with privateers to prey on British vessels plying U.S. coastal waters. When he persisted despite warnings from George Washington that he was violating U.S. sovereignty, the president ordered the recall of the French minister. Back in France, however, the Jacobins had replaced the Girondists, and instead of recalling Genêt, the French government sent a new minister to arrest him. Observing strict neutrality, Washington refused to extradite Genêt, who, in one of history's more pleasant ironies, became an American citizen and married the daughter of New York's Governor George Clinton.

The Genêt affair soured French-American relations and deepened official U.S. distrust of the volatile French government. When John Jay concluded a trade treaty with Great Britain on November 19, 1794, U.S.—French relations grew so hostile as to verge on war. The French Directory refused to receive Charles Cotesworth Pinckney as U.S. minister, and President John Adams sent a commission consisting of Pinckney, John Marshall, and Elbridge Gerry to cool things down and conclude a trade treaty with the French. Matters only grew worse, however, when the commissioners arrived in Paris in October 1797 to be told by three of Prime Minister Talleyrand's agents that, before a treaty could even be discussed, the United States would have to loan France $12 million *and* pay Talleyrand a quarter-million-dollar bribe! On April 3, 1798, Adams submitted to Congress the entire correspondence from the commission, designating the three French agents "X," "Y," and "Z," and Congress published the file. The "XYZ Affair" outraged Americans of all political leanings. The nation mobilized for war against France, and, indeed, an undeclared naval war ensued, beginning with the capture of the American schooner *Retaliation* on November 20, 1798, and ending with capture of the French vessel *Le Berceau* on October 12, 1800.

It was the preparation for war with France that spawned the sinister Alien and Sedition Acts. Several of the leading Antifederalists were recent European refugees, and the Federalist-dominated Congress passed four acts deliberately aimed at suppressing republican opposition to Federalist policy. The Naturalization Act (June 18, 1798) changed the residence prerequisite for citizenship from five to fourteen years; the Alien Act (June 25) authorized the president to expel from the United States all aliens regarded as dangerous; the Alien Enemies Act (July 6) authorized the president, in time of war, to arrest, imprison, or deport alien subjects of an enemy power; and the Sedition Act (July 14) prohibited assembly "with intent to oppose any measure . . . of the government" and made it unlawful to "print, utter, or publish . . . any false, scandalous, and malicious writing" against the government. The Sedition Act applied to aliens as well as citizens.

Opposition to the Alien and Sedition Acts came swiftly, culminating in the Kentucky (November 16, 1798, and November 22, 1799) and Virginia resolutions (December 24, 1798), framed by Thomas Jefferson and James Madison, respectively. The resolutions held that the Alien and Sedition Acts were unconstitutional and that, therefore, they were not binding on the states. The second Kentucky resolution, moreover, stated the concept of a state's right to judge infractions of the Constitution and to "nullify" such acts, thereby foreshadowing the Nullification Crisis of the mid-nineteenth century, which would come as an overture to Civil War.

The Sedition Act was repealed in 1801, and the Alien and Naturalization Acts expired the following year. In all, ten persons were convicted under the Sedition Act, but after Thomas Jefferson assumed the presidency he pardoned all ten, and Congress restored to them, with interest, all fines paid.

The Alien and Sedition Acts had attempted to place limits on the constitutional rights to free speech, a free press, and free assembly. Though the response to the acts preserved those liberties hard won in the War of Independence, aspects of the Alien Enemies Act and even of the Sedition Act have periodically resurfaced, especially during times of war.

The Supreme Court Rules on *Marbury v. Madison* (1803)

The event: The case of *Marbury v. Madison*, heard before the Supreme Court in 1803, established the authority of the high court to invalidate federal laws deemed unconstitutional, thereby setting a precedent for Supreme Court action that has remained in force ever since.

THE CASE INVOLVED William Marbury, a justice of the peace for Washington, D.C., appointed by John Adams during the last days of his presidency. When Thomas Jefferson took office, he found that a number of judicial appointments approved and signed by Adams had not been distributed. Jefferson was not pleased with the law that made Marbury's and the other appointments possible, the Judiciary Act of 1801. Enacted in an effort to stem the tide of what Federalist congressmen saw as Jeffersonian radicalism, the law provided for the establishment of six new circuit courts and the appointment of sixteen new federal judges, as well as several attorneys, marshals, and clerks. Adams had filled these positions with conservative Federalists.

President Jefferson had two options. He could distribute the commissions and allow the country to be heavily influenced by the Federalists, or he could withhold the commissions and keep Federalism at bay. He chose the latter.

When William Marbury thus failed to receive his commission, he petitioned the Supreme Court for a writ of mandamus that would order the Secretary of State James Madison to distribute the commissions that had been duly approved and signed. Chief Justice Marshall now found himself in a delicate position. If he issued the requested writ, he would place the court squarely against the president. If he refused to issue the writ, he would weaken the power of the court by seeming to back down before the president.

Marshall rose to the occasion and handled the situation masterfully. Although, he stated, Marbury was entitled to his commission, there was nothing the court could do to force the secretary of state to deliver it. He declared that the clause in the Federal Judiciary Act of 1789 that allowed writs of mandamus to be requested of the Supreme Court was unconstitutional and therefore void. In this ruling, Marshall sacrificed Marbury—who never did get his commission—but he gained extensive authority for the Supreme Court. In refusing to force the hand of the executive, Marshall paved the way for the consolidation of power by the court over any law passed by Congress.

The responsibility for judicial review established in the ruling on *Marbury v. Madison* was not a drastic departure for the Supreme Court. Although such review of legislation was not expressly provided for in the Constitution, the Founding Fathers had expected the courts to have some control over the executive and legislative branches of government. The decision reached in *Marbury v. Madison*, however, formalized that control, and all Courts since 1803 have exercised that power.

Thomas Jefferson Agrees to the Louisiana Purchase (1803)

The event: On May 2, 1803, Thomas Jefferson bought from Napoleon Bonaparte all French holdings west of the Mississippi in a treaty concluding the greatest land deal in history, the "Louisiana Purchase."

FRANCE HAD CEDED the vast territory it called Louisiana to Spain when it lost the French and Indian War. But in a secret treaty on October 1, 1800, Spain returned Louisiana in exchange for certain portions of Tuscany, which Napoleon pledged to conquer, and a guarantee that France would maintain Louisiana as a buffer between American and

Spanish settlements. No sooner was the treaty concluded than Napoleon disappointed his ally by abandoning the war that would have given Spain the Tuscan prize. As the French and Spanish fell to disputing, Spain continued to administer Louisiana, and in October 1802 revoked American traders' right of deposit—their licenses to store goods in New Orleans for loading onto ocean-going vessels—thus effectively closing the Mississippi to American trade.

It was the worst of all possible situations for the United States. Spain had closed off trade, but the idea of a West controlled by Napoleon's France was even more distressing. Even if France, at this time a nominal ally of the United States, did not pose a direct threat, war between France and England would likely result in *English* seizure of the Louisiana Territory. With these thoughts in mind, Jefferson threatened war on France and Spain even as he sent James Monroe to Paris with an offer to purchase the vital port city of New Orleans and Florida. The president was thinking of more than New Orleans, however. A dozen years earlier, in 1790, Captain Robert Gray had become the first American to circumnavigate the globe. When he returned to Boston Harbor, he reported a discovery both the English and the Spanish had failed to make—the existence of a great and navigable western river, which Gray named after his ship, the *Columbia*. Jefferson now reasoned that Gray's discovery gave the United States some claim to territory on the Northwest Coast. Establishing a presence at the mouth of the Mississippi would imply a further claim to the territory *between* that river and the Northwest Coast.

At this point, fate delivered into Jefferson's hands something much less tentative and speculative. Napoleon's army, which had been fighting in the West Indies, was dying there—not from English bullets but from yellow fever and guerilla warfare with islanders. Fearful of becoming bogged down in a pestiferous corner of the world, Napoleon decided to retreat from the Americas, at least for the time being. He still feared English usurpation of the Louisiana Territory, and he also needed money to finance his European wars. The perfect expedient was to sell the territory to the United States. On April 11, 1803, even before Monroe had arrived in Paris to negotiate for the purchase of New Orleans, Napoleon's prime minster, the Duc de Talleyrand, asked the U.S. minister to

France, Robert R. Livingston, how much Jefferson would offer for the whole of Louisiana. Negotiations proceeded after Monroe arrived and were concluded in a treaty signed on May 2, 1803. For sixty million francs—about $15 million— the United States had suddenly acquired about ninety thousand square miles of trans-Mississippi territory.

At four cents an acre, it was quite a bargain—although one that would give any self-respecting real estate attorney fits. For while the Gulf of Mexico was fixed as the southern boundary of the purchase and the Mississippi as the eastern boundary, there was no clear understanding as to whether the purchase included West Florida and Texas! Moreover, the purchase posed constitutional problems, since the Constitution made no provision for the purchase of foreign territory. Despite these questions, the Senate ratified the treaty on October 20, 1803, and the United States took formal possession of the territory on December 20. The United States had been doubled in territorial extent and now stood poised to push its government to the very coast of the Pacific.

For Jefferson it seemed a godsend. By the beginning of the nineteenth century, the "West"—that is, the territory between the Appalachian Mountains and the Mississippi River—was filling up fast. Congress had enacted legislation to protect the Indians against rapacious settlers, but the federal government lacked the muscle to enforce a limit. The answer, it seemed, was to find more space, either for white settlement or for Indian relocation. And that space lay west of the Mississippi. Jefferson had bought the land initially to avoid a war, but now he hoped to place the Indians there and check, at last, the rapid west-ward expansion of his land-hungry fellow citizens. But most Americans, unlike their president, saw in the Louisiana Territory what they had always seen look-ing west—the promise of cheap land, low taxes, and a better life.

Lewis and Clark Launch an Expedition (1804)

The event: In 1803, after Congress approved his recent purchase of Louisiana and made it the United States' newest territory, Thomas Jefferson sent two young men named Lewis and Clark to investigate just how much land he had bought for his $15 million. The expedition he launched led the two explorers to discover a new natural wealth of indescribable variety and abundance about which they would return to tell the world.

WHEN MERIWETHER LEWIS and William Clark departed on their famous journey from St. Louis in 1804, many of the town's residents fully believed they would find the Northwest Passage at last and that St. Louis would be the point of departure to the Pacific and the marvels of the Orient beyond. Lewis, a woodsman and hunter from childhood who at twenty had helped to suppress the Whiskey Rebellion, had most recently been Thomas Jefferson's secretary. Once he persuaded the president to let him lead the already-planned expedition, he recruited his former comrade-in-arms, William Clark, younger brother of the famed Indian fighter and Revolutionary War hero George Rogers Clark. Lewis was twenty-nine, Clark thirty-two, and the adventure of their life lay ahead of them.

They started out with twenty-nine in their party, including a few Frenchmen and a goodly number of Kentuckians. Some, like Simon Kenton, were already well-known frontiersmen. Others, like John Colter, would become famous. Along the way they would pick up an interpreter named Toussant Charbonneau and his wife, Sacajewea, a Shoshoni who would prove invaluable as a guide and who would become an American legend. Only one member of the expedition died en route: Charles Floyd, nephew of one of Kentucky's first explorers, from a ruptured appendix.

The Missouri, which Lewis and Clark followed into the interior, had been charted only as far above St. Louis—itself not much more than a trading center of perhaps two hundred houses—as the Mandan villages in the Dakota region where they would make their winter camp. Their trek westward would take them as far as the Columbia River in modern-day Washington, then charted only at its mouth. The country in between was a blank, populated by myth and imagination: tribes of man-hating Amazons, who amputated their breasts to better draw a bow and arrow; Welsh-speaking Indians descended from an ancient Celtic wanderer; the lost tribes of Israel; even eighteen-inch devils at a place named Les Côtes Brulés.

They found instead peaceful Otos, whom they befriended and gave medals stamped with the likeness of Thomas Jefferson; hostile Teton Sioux, who demanded tribute from all traders and whom they fought, establishing a lasting enmity; Shoshoni, who welcomed with open arms Sacajewea, their little sister kidnapped as a child by the Mandans—in all more than fifty tribes, with whom they made for the most part amicable contact. They found an Eden full of giant, ten-thousand-plus buffalo herds and elk and antelope so innocent of human contact that they tamely approached members of the expedition. They also found a hell blighted with mosquitoes so thick they were forced to breathe them and winters harsher, it seemed, than any could reasonably hope to survive. They got desperately lost, then found their way again; catalogued a dazzling array of new plants and animals; even unearthed the bones of a forty-five-foot dinosaur.

When they returned to St. Louis from their expedition in September of 1806, they were eagerly greeted and grandly entertained. They had traveled nearly 8,000 miles. If they had failed to do the impossible and discover the fabled Northwest Passage, they would nevertheless soon help to make St. Louis one of the nations's great cities. The glowing descriptions they gave of this vast new West provided a boon to the westward migration now becoming a permanent part of American life.

Manuel Lisa Establishes Fort Manuel (1807)

The event: In 1807, a shady St. Louis entrepreneur named Manuel Lisa established a trading post on the Little Bighorn, opening the Louisiana Territory to the fur trade and launching the historical career of the trappers called "mountain men," who were to play a crucial role in the westward migration.

FOR TWO CENTURIES the fur trade had been the only true trade of the North American wilderness, simply because pelts—beaver and fox and mink and martin and otter— were the only items found in the wilderness worth anything at all back in the capitals of Europe and along America's eastern seaboard. Despite much wishful thinking and a good deal of wasted prospecting, the other traditional forms of portable wealth, gold and silver, continued to elude the French *coureurs de bois* and the English trappers who paddled their log canoes into the interior. So they threw up flimsy trading posts, collected pelts from the Indians, moved in with the native women, and settled for servicing the demands of contemporary fashion.

The fashion industry was then fueled by the absolute necessity of beaver hats for gentlemen and fur trim of all kind on collars, cuffs, hems, bonnets, and boots. Alone or in small groups or backed by well-financed corporations, the fur traders ranged first the Old Northwest, then the wilds of the trans-Mississippi and Rocky Mountains, and finally the Pacific Northwest looking for easy money off nature's bounty. The Indians, of course, were their proletariat, and the whites often referred to profitable commerce in animal pelts as "Indian trade."

After the French and Indian War, that trade was exploited by two British giants: the North West Company and the Hudson's Bay Company. Before the Louisiana Purchase, the Americans—blocked from the trade early on by the French and their Indian allies and later by the Canadian monopolies—trapped only casually and part time. But even before Lewis and Clark had returned from their expedition, Americans had started forming corporations themselves and cutting each other's throats for the incredible profits the fur trade would yield.

St. Louis, located on the west bank of the Mississippi just below the mouth of the Missouri, was positioned perfectly to become the raucous capital of the fur trade. By the end of the War of 1812, the new steamboats transported men and supplies into the wilderness and brought back pelts by the ton, nearly $4 million worth of this "brown" gold by 1830. Manuel Lisa had arrived in St. Louis a dozen years before. Born in New Orleans, a Spaniard of vague South American descent, Lisa was a mercenary spy who had dabbled in government contracts and bribes and smuggled contraband goods deep into Spanish territory. A violent and ruthless man, he was also an inspired entrepreneur who could talk almost anybody into almost anything. When Lewis and Clark returned to the city in 1806, Lisa had already begun preparations to send a party of fur trappers into the wilderness, and he hired several members of the Lewis and Clark exploration party, outfitted sixty men, loaded them onto keelboats, and headed up the Missouri in the early spring of 1807. Somewhere on the upper river Lisa found John Colter, who had remained behind to do a little trapping of his own. Lisa hired him on the spot, and together the two made history.

To be honest, Lisa was always something of a scoundrel and he constantly challenged the tolerance of his fellow St. Louis tycoons. As Lisa explained it to the investors in his new and thriving company, the old French and British methods would never work in the American West. The Plains Indians were equestrians. They hunted buffalo and stole horses for a living. Plodding through a prairie swamp to plant traps was beneath them. Instead of reimbursing the Indians—who, after all, were never very stable workers—for bringing in pelts from their tribal hunting grounds, Lisa argued for hiring his own white trappers, paying them to chase the fur wherever they could find it without respect for traditional tribal boundaries, and having them bring their catch back to a central spot—in this case, Fort Manuel on the Little Bighorn—for shipping to St. Louis. No Indians to curry favor with, no string of fortified trading posts to keep up, fewer opportunities to be double-crossed. That Lisa could create such a system and still maintain for years a workable truce on the frontier explains why he had at least a portion of virtually all the fur business out of St. Louis until his shockingly peaceful death in bed at a health spa in 1820.

The men Lisa hired to replace the Indians were men like Colter, men who would soon be known everywhere as "mountain men." The requirements for the profession were not all that different from those of a farm laborer—a strong back, a healthy constitution, the knack for handling tools and weapons. Many, in fact, were ex-farm hands grown bored with the settled life. Perhaps two thousand mountain men roamed the wilderness, essaying a trapper's life, before fickle fashion took a turn to the Far East's silk.

After Lisa's death, another St. Louis entrepreneur named William Ashley took over. Each year, Ashley moved men, supplies, and fur between the mountains and the lower Missouri by pack trains and wagons. To keep in touch with his wandering brigades, he established the annual rendezvous, which soon became the major institution of the American fur trade.

The mountain men were the midwives for a new wave of migration to the American West. Their exploits engaged popular imagination and encouraged others to begin another round of exploration. But the "discovery" of new lands for settlement—and the blazing of paths to those new lands—also gave American pioneers a goal: for even the hardiest of the would-be emigrants did not simply load up their conestogas and head west unless they had someplace to go. Finally, as the fur ran out and fashion changed, the mountain men themselves—looking for new jobs—directly encouraged the westward movement by hiring out as explorers, scouts, and wagon-train masters to groups embarking from the growing new supply towns of western Missouri and eastern Kansas in search of an Eden at trails' end.

Robert Fulton Launches the *Clermont* (1807)

The event: On August 8, 1807, Robert Livingston and Robert Fulton launched a steamboat of Fulton's design on a journey up the Hudson River from New York to Albany, creating a revolution in American trade transportation.

ROBERT FULTON DID not invent the steamboat, but he did design and build the first commercially practical one. Fulton was trained not as an engineer but as a gunsmith, jeweler, and artist. He studied with the great American painter Benjamin West in London but soon abandoned art for engineering, publishing in 1796 a *Treatise on the Improvement of Canal Navigation*.

When the American government proved not to be interested in Fulton's canal schemes, he turned without success to the French. Not one to give up, the next year Fulton submitted to the French admiralty plans for a submarine, the *Nautilus*, which he built in 1800 and improved in 1801. An advanced development of David Bushnell's 1776 vessel, the *Nautilus* worked better than any previous submarine, but once again the French were not buying.

Giving up on the submarine, Fulton turned to bringing innovation to surface vessels. In 1803, backed by financing from Robert Livingston, American minister to France, he built an experimental steamboat that plied the Seine. The next year, the British, seeking to woo him away from the French, invited him to England to continue his steamboat experiments. Unfortunately for Fulton, Lord Nelson's triumph over Napoleon's fleet at Trafalgar convinced the British Admiralty that they were in no need of naval innovation.

Despite these many disappointments, Fulton refused to lose confidence. He returned to the United States with Robert Livingston, who obtained a monopoly of steamboat navigation on New York waters. Using Fulton's designs, the two men commissioned a boat to be built and ordered a steam engine from James Watt's company in England. The vessel was launched on August 9, 1807, and, on August 17, steamed from New York City to Albany in thirty-two hours. At an average of about five miles an hour, this was faster than what one could depend on with a sailing vessel. More important to commercial navigation, steam power made accurate and regular scheduling possible; captain, crew, passengers, and cargo were no longer at the mercy of fickle winds. In 1808 Fulton rebuilt his vessel, lengthening it by a full 149 feet and christening it *The North River Steamboat of Clermont*, which public and press shortened to the familiar *Clermont*.

The partners built other successful Hudson River vessels and also operated ferries between Manhattan and New Jersey and between Manhattan and Long Island. Of course, the voyage of the *Clermont* had ramifications far beyond the local success of Fulton and Livingston. Steam power made large-scale, regular navigation of the nation's rivers and inland waterways possible, thereby promoting trade, national industry, and, ultimately, the westward settlement of the United States.

The War of 1812 Begins

The event: On June 18, 1812, Congress—led by western War Hawks against the opposition of New England Federalists—declared war on England in what some have, with exaggeration, called "the second war for independence."

GENERATIONS OF GRADE schoolers have been taught that the War of 1812 was fought because the British, at war with Napoleon and in need of sailors for the Royal Navy, routinely intercepted and boarded neutral vessels, including those of the United States, and, on the flimsiest of pretexts, "impressed" seamen into His Majesty's service. Certainly this was a major grievance and as good a reason as any to go to war. But the fact is that the U.S. declared war on June 19, 1812, even though Great Britain, on June 16, had agreed to cease interfering with commerce on the high seas effective June 23.

The cause of the War of 1812 is to be found not at sea but on land, specifically American western land. As the population of the United States burgeoned, the hunger for new territory became insatiable, and the juiciest parcel of real estate in 1812 was Spanish Florida, which extended as far west as the Mississippi. In 1812 Spain was allied with Britain against Napoleon; therefore, war with Britain would mean war with Spain, and victory in such a war would mean the acquisition of Florida. Nor did westerners need much coaching to convince them that England deserved a good whipping. To begin with, disruption of commerce on the high seas had not only damaged the coastal economy but brought on a bad depression in the West, whose abundant produce could be exported only if the sea lanes were open. More directly, westerners believed that the English in Canada were arming Indians south of the border and inciting them to harass settlers. The crown officially denied this, but in fact English traders were privately furnishing arms and ammunition, and there could be no doubt, as the white settlement line pushed farther westward, that the Indians were becoming an increasing menace. The young land-hungry westerners in Congress, led by Kentucky's Henry Clay, used all of these issues to try to push war on a reluctant President James Madison. In 1812, in the middle of a presidential election, the "War Hawks" got their way and the United States declared war on England.

America was not prepared to fight any war. Its regular army consisted of only twelve thousand widely scattered troops led by politically appointed and inexperienced officers, and its navy was tiny in comparison to Britain's. The first campaigns were disasters. The British soundly defeated the United States at Detroit, on the Niagara frontier, and in New York. Only the small American navy's surprising victories proffered the slightest ray of hope in the first year of the war. In 1813, although Capt. Oliver Hazard Perry won control of Lake Erie and William Henry Harrison defeated the British and Tecumseh's Indian confederation at the Battle of the Thames, American attempts to invade Canada failed miserably. In 1814, with France collapsing, the British could turn their full attention to the upstart America, and they struck a devastating blow by taking and burning Washington, D.C., as Madison and the War Hawk Congress fled. American fortunes revived later that same year, when the British failed to capture Baltimore. And an American naval victory on Lake Champlain that forced the English army of invasion to retreat into Canada led British diplomats in December to sign a proposed truce at a peace conference in Ghent, Belgium, that had been under way since August.

Americans heard about the Treaty of Ghent at about the same time the news reached them that Andrew Jackson had struck a crushing blow against the British at the Battle of New Orleans. The stunning British defeat, which came after the war ended, provided at least the feel of victory, even though none of the avowed American war aims—defending American commerce, vindicating republican independence—had been achieved. Indeed, on the frontier, westerners might be excused for believing that America had lost, since the treaty forbade all military activity there until the United States had concluded subsequent treaties with the "Indian allies of the English." That left the Indians free to roam the territory at will, while the local American authorities were hamstrung by an international agreement. And the Indians knew it, launching their most destructive raids of the war during the six months it took to bring them to terms.

Still, they were brought to terms, chiefly because the withdrawal of the British from United States territory meant the collapse of various alliances with western Indian tribes, most notably the Sioux, who agreed by treaty to recognize the sovereignty of the United States over the Missouri Territory. Because of the war, the United States secured a stronger claim to the far Northwest, while, in the South, the war with the Red Stick Creeks Indians pushed American settlement to the Spanish border. Indeed, Jackson's victories at Horseshoe Bend and New Orleans provided the West with its greatest hero since Daniel Boone, and westerners were not about to trade that for doubts about whether the Treaty of Ghent represented anything other than a cessation of the hostilities they had forced on the reluctant East. It was only one of many ways in which the War of 1812 helped to bind the West, formerly a hotbed of treason seething with talk of separation, solidly to the rest of the country.

In short, though the Treaty of Ghent returned the two nations to the *status quo antebellum*—literally, "the way things were before the war"—this official result is misleading. In a broad sense the war, bumbling and disastrous as much of it had been, fostered a new patriotism and forged a sense of national identity and national purpose.

Tecumseh Is Slain at the Battle of the Thames (1813)

The event: On October 5, 1813, Tecumseh—Shawnee head of a powerful Indian confederation that had terrified American authorities since 1806—was killed at the Battle of the Thames, effectively ending the native resistance to white settlement in the Old Northwest.

FOLLOWING THE DEFEAT of the Old Northwest Tribes at Fallen Timbers in 1794 and the subsequent Treaty of Greenville, the frontier had remained peaceful enough that an encouraged Thomas Jefferson directed the Indiana Territory's governor, William Henry Harrison, to obtain "legal" title to as much Indian land as possible and endorsed further white expansion into the West. Harrison, who made no effort to ensure that he dealt with legitimate tribal representatives, acquired seventy million acres in less than three years by a series of questionable treaties, resulting in growing dissension among the tribes.

Tecumseh, a persuasive and charismatic Shawnee of remarkable military acumen, realized that, while his tribe could not survive a prolonged peace that ushered in thousands of new settlers, his people were not powerful enough alone to endure a prolonged war. Backed by his brother, Tenskwatawa, a Shawnee prophet claiming inspiration from the Great Spirit and preaching the need for Indians to cleanse themselves of the unclean white race, Tecumseh used the threat of war to buy time while he traveled throughout the Ohio country and beyond, west to the Sioux and south to the land of the Chickasaw, Choctaw, and Creeks, preaching the need for a great Indian confederation stretching from the Great Lakes to the Gulf of Mexico. Only as a unified, sovereign state, Tecumseh reasoned, could the Indians resist displacement and death or absorption and death.

While he was gone, his brother managed to embroil the Ohio Valley tribes that had already joined his alliance into a disastrous battle at Tippecanoe. The Shawnee, Potawatomi, Ottawa, Winnebago, Ojibwa, and Wyandot, angry at Harrison's treaties and defiantly ensconced at the abandoned site of Fort Greenville, where Tecumseh had placed them, were joined by the Sac and Fox before Harrison soundly defeated them. The Prophet was discredited.

When Tecumseh returned from his largely unsuccessful recruiting expedition in the South, he, too, engaged in public rebuke of his brother. After the Battle of Tippecanoe, the Potawatomi, Winnebago, Fox, and Sac, though shaken, remained loyal to Tecumseh. Wyandot followers of the militant chief Roundhead likewise adhered to the cause. But among the Delaware, Miami, and even the Shawnee there were wholesale defections. The alliance began to crumble.

At this crisis point, however, the United States and Great Britain commenced the War of 1812. Tecumseh, who had preached abstinence from contact with whites, now eagerly embraced alliance with the British against the Americans. At first, the alliance went well for the Indians, who did great damage across the frontier. In the course of the war's first year, some four thousand Americans were either killed or captured, while combined British and Indian casualties were about five hundred. Yet even the Indian victories were pyrrhic, and their losses—homes burned, crops destroyed, populations displaced—were terrible. By the second year of the war, the British in the West had experienced a number of reverses, and the Indians' alliance with them began to disintegrate.

As the British evacuated the territory, Tecumseh—who had joined forces with the distrusted whites only when he saw his dream of a grand Indian alliance dying—grew desperate. He persuaded the British to take a stand against the pursuing American army at Moravian Town on the north bank of Thames River. In a battle especially distinguished by the brilliant performance of a Kentucky mounted regiment under Colonel Richard Mentor Johnson, Harrison defeated the combined British and Indian forces on October 5, 1813.

No one knows who actually killed Tecumseh on that day, but with him died the last credible hope of denying the insatiable American appetite for native lands.

Andrew Jackson Defeats the Creek at Horseshoe Bend (1814)

The event: On March 27, 1814, Andrew Jackson cornered a force of 950 Creek Indians at Horseshoe Bend in present-day Alabama, killing some three-fourths of them and bringing to an end the Creek War. It was one of two battles Jackson fought during the War of 1812 that would make him a hero in the American West and set him on the road to the White House.

LIKE THE FRENCH and Indian War and the War of Independence, the War of 1812 involved Native American as well as white American and European combatants. The white man's battles provoked a bitter civil war among the great Creek Indian nation of Alabama, Georgia, and Mississippi Territory, dividing the tribe into factions opposed to the United States and those friendly to it or, at least, neutral in the conflict between the Americans and the British. The friendly faction was generally known as the Lower Creeks or White Sticks, and the hostile faction, the Upper Creeks or Red Sticks. When a White Stick leader called Big Warrior arrested and executed an important Red Stick chief, Little Warrior, the gulf between Whites and Reds widened beyond any hope of bridging.

With American settlement in the South encroaching on their Florida territory, the Spanish eagerly equipped a force of Red Sticks, led by a half-breed
known as Peter McQueen, which attacked settlers at Burnt Corn Creek in present-day Alabama. But the worst catastrophe for the settlers came on August 30,
1813, when William Weatherford (Red Eagle), a half-breed follower of the charismatic Tecumseh, attacked a shabby stockade called Fort Mims, on the lower
Alabama River. Major Daniel Beasley, commanding the fort's garrison of Louisiana militia, ignored the warnings of black slaves, who reported spotting Indians in the tall grass outside the fort. At noon, one thousand Red Sticks attacked,
and when the battle had ended, more than four hundred settlers were dead.

Bad as this was, it was not the low point of the war. That point, when it
came, would not be at the expense of the whites. For this was to be the last Indian attack on a settlement east of the Mississippi. An outraged Tennessee state
legislature authorized $300,000 to outfit a large army under Andrew Jackson,
who marched into Red Stick country with five thousand militiamen, nineteen
companies of white-allied Cherokee warriors, and two hundred White Stick
Creeks. Early in November 1813, a detachment under Colonel John Coffee, including the soon-to-be legendary Davy Crockett, ambushed a large party of Red
Sticks at Talishatchee, killing 186 of them with the loss of 5 dead and 41
wounded. Later in the month, Jackson relieved Talladega, a White Stick fort under siege. Perhaps as many as 290 Red Sticks died in this engagement, with the
loss of 15 whites killed and 85 wounded.

Jackson and his second-in-command, General William Claiborne, fruit-
lessly pursued Red Eagle for the next two months. Plagued by desertions and the
more legitimate but no less crippling departure of short-term volunteers, Jackson
was unable to mount a meaningful offensive until January 1814, when he received eight hundred new troops. Thus reinforced, Jackson engaged the enemy
twice that month, at Emuckfaw and at Enotachopco Creek. As he marched, he
destroyed every Red Stick town in his path.

In March his militiamen were augmented by six hundred regular troops
from the U.S. 39th Infantry. Now, spoiling for a decisive battle, Jackson attacked
at Horseshoe Bend, a peninsula on the Tallapoosa River. After a day-long fight,

in which Jackson's army besieged and bombarded the Red Sticks' elaborately fortified position, approximately 750 of the 900 Red Sticks warriors lay dead. Jackson's losses were comparatively slight: 32 dead and 99 wounded. Among his Cherokee allies, 18 were killed and 36 wounded, while the White Stick Creeks lost 5 dead and 11 wounded. William Weatherford—Red Eagle—appeared in Jackson's camp a few days after the battle and formally surrendered. With deep respect for his adversary, Jackson allowed him to depart unmolested.

But that was the American commander's only act of generosity following the defeat of the Red Sticks. The Treaty of Horseshoe Bend, which followed the battle and brought to an end the so-called Creek War, extorted twenty-three million acres from the Indians—and not from the Red Sticks alone. The friendly White Stick Creeks also lost land. Indeed, the Creek nation as a whole yielded up two-thirds of its tribal lands in a massive cession that pushed the tide of American settlement from the Tennessee River to the Gulf of Mexico.

Work Begins on the Erie Canal (1817)

The event: Begun in 1817 and completed in 1825, the Erie Canal opened up the Great Lakes region to commerce and provided a first crucial link between the East and West.

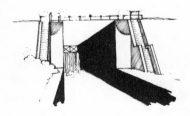

IN OCTOBER 1825, the first boat made the voyage from Buffalo to New York City via the Erie Canal. Originally proposed by Gouverneur Morris in 1800 and approved by the New York legislature in 1817, the canal linked the Hudson River with Lake Erie and, therefore, the West. The canal brought huge savings in shipping costs to manufacturers and others who had previously had to transport goods overland to the Mississippi Valley. It quickly became the chief route for immigrants traveling from the East to the Great Lakes country.

The Erie Canal, which was eight years in construction, was a spectacular engineering achievement. It ran some 363 miles, while the next-longest American canal was only 28 miles. It was also a stunning commercial success, with tolls quickly repaying the $7 million cost of construction. Before long the canal realized $3 million a year in profits. New York City and several smaller cities and towns along the canal—most notably Buffalo, Rochester, and Syracuse—profited significantly.

The success of the Erie Canal triggered a canal-building boom in other states. The Delaware and Hudson Canal, which extended from northeastern Pennsylvania to the Hudson River in southern New York, was completed in 1828. The Mainline Canal—a combination of canals and railroads—was completed in 1834 in Pennsylvania and crossed the mountains to Pittsburgh. Ohio constructed the Ohio and Erie Canal, which ran from the Ohio River to Cleveland, and Indiana built the Wabash and Erie Canal. By 1840, the United States boasted 3,326 miles of canals. Providing crucial links between farmers in the Ohio and Mississippi valleys and the eastern seaboard before the proliferation of the railroad, this network of canals also made possible the commercial development of the West and greatly strengthened the Union by physically connecting it.

The Panic of 1819 Strikes

The event: In 1819, the nation was swept by a financial panic that threatened its economy, brought great hardship to creditors and debtors alike, and badly undermined confidence in the federal government.

THE HARD-WON VICTORY in the War of 1812 boosted American morale and brought prestige to the federal government but had dire consequences for the nation's economy. The government incurred heavy debts during the war. Those debts battered the economy, as did the high protective tariffs passed in 1816 (which brought on commodity inflation), wild speculation in the western lands opened by the war, overextended investments in manufacturing, and the collapse of foreign markets for American goods. On the eve of the War of 1812, constitutional challenges prevented the rechartering of the Bank of the United States. State banks, which were proliferating at this time, offered credit recklessly, and when war broke out, all of the banks (except those in New England) suspended the practice of converting paper bank notes into gold or silver upon demand. The value of paper money therefore dropped. In 1816, in an effort to stabilize the economy, Congress chartered the Second Bank of the United States, which, however, was largely mismanaged. Worse, Congress summarily ordered the resumption of specie payment (conversion of notes to silver and gold), a move that strained the resources of state banks, in many cases, past the point of failure.

Amid bank failures and crisis, investors and debtors alike suffered. The Second Bank of the United States managed to regain a sound footing only by curtailing credit and maintaining a hard line on existing debt payments. The credit of the nation as a whole was thereby preserved, but, as one economist of the time wrote, "The Bank was saved, and the people were ruined." Especially hard hit were the southern and western states, some of which were forced to enact constitutionally controversial legislation for the relief of debtors. While the nation ultimately weathered the Panic of 1819, the crisis brought about a lasting resentment against the Second Bank of the United States, which Missouri's U.S. Senator Thomas Hart Benton called "The Monster." Since early colonial days, the needs of the frontier had often been at odds with the policies of the more established eastern centers of government, leading to dangerous divisions between East and West. The Panic of 1819 deepened regional differences and demonstrated, more than four decades before the Civil War, the potential fragility of the Union.

The Supreme Court Rules on *McCulloch v. Maryland* (1819)

The event: The 1819 Supreme Court decision in *McCulloch v. Maryland* instituted a broad interpretation of the Constitution, strengthened the power of the Congress, and established the legality of the Bank of the United States.

THE CASE INVOLVED the Maryland branch of the Second Bank of the United States, which had refused to abide by a Maryland law that placed an annual tax

of $15,000 on banks chartered outside the state. The state sued the bank's cashier, James McCulloch, for payment. The result of that suit was pertinent beyond the borders of Maryland, since, at the time, five other states had similar laws taxing the Bank of the United States.

The court upheld the legality of the Bank of the United States by referring to Congress's power to make "all laws . . . necessary and proper" to execute its specific powers outlined in the Constitution. Since the power to impose a tax carried with it the power to destroy the taxed entity, the court ruled that the Maryland law was unconstitutional; for a state, of its own authority, could not destroy something created by Congress.

Not only did the ruling strengthen Congress by allowing a broad interpretation of the powers granted to it by the Constitution, it also strengthened the economy and created an atmosphere in which the Second Bank of the United States could flourish. And flourish it did—until it came head to head with Andrew Jackson, who waged a successful campaign to abolish the bank.

Henry Clay Engineers the Missouri Compromise (1820)

The event: In 1818-1819, twenty-two United States senators were from northern states and twenty-two from southern states. This balance, carefully preserved with the admission of each new state since the era of the Revolution, was about to be upset as Missouri petitioned Congress for statehood as a slaveholding state. The impending crisis was averted by the Compromise of 1820.

WHEN MISSOURI SUBMITTED its application for statehood to Congress, Representative James Tallmadge of New York introduced an amendment calling for a ban on the "further introduction of slavery" and for the emancipation of all slaves born in the new state of Missouri once they reached the age of twenty-five. The House of Representatives passed Tallmadge's amendment, but the Senate, where the North-South split was even, saw the matter differently. The senators rejected the amendment and adjourned without reaching a decision on Missouri statehood.

When Congress reconvened, the debate on Missouri's application for admission to the Union resumed in earnest. Northern senators claimed that Congress had the right to ban slavery in new states. Southern senators countered that the new states, like the original thirteen, had the right to determine whether or not to allow slavery within their borders. After protracted and agonizing debate, a two-part compromise was finally reached in March 1820. First, Missouri would be allowed to join the Union as a slave state, but, at the same time, Maine, which had been part of Massachusetts, would be admitted as a free state, thus preserving the delicate slave–free balance in the Senate. Second, a line was drawn across the Louisiana Territory at the latitude of 36 degrees, 30 minutes; henceforth, with the exception of Missouri itself, slavery would not be allowed north of the line, approximately the southern border of the new state.

No one was completely satisfied by the compromise, but it did help to preserve the Union for some thirty years more. Northerners were dissatisfied because the compromise failed to ban slavery from the territories. Southerners were distressed that the law set a precedent for future congressional action regarding slavery. Many political leaders saw the issue in a new light and the sectional debate as a prologue to a disaster yet to come. Jefferson said that the debate over slavery, "like a fire bell in the night, awakened and filled me with terror." John Quincy Adams called the compromise a "title page to a great tragic volume."

The law remained in force until 1854, when Congress passed the Kansas-Nebraska Act, which called for territories to decide for themselves whether or not to allow slavery. The Compromise received another blow in 1857, when the Supreme Court, in its ruling on the Dred Scott case, declared the Missouri Compromise unconstitutional because its ban on slavery in the northern territories sought to deprive individuals of their private property without due process of law.

The Factory System Arrives in New England (1823)

The event: The Merrimack Manufacturing Company, which started business in 1823 in Massachusetts, was the first manufacturing concern to introduce the English factory system into the United States, ushering in a new era in American society.

IN SEPTEMBER 1823, a long-time dream of Patrick Tracey Jackson and Francis Cabot Lowell came to fruition with the opening of the Merrimack Manufacturing Company, a textile mill incorporating the latest in modern machinery and employing thousands of workers.

Lowell and Jackson's vision was rooted in the industrial revolution introduced into the American scene by Samuel Slater and Moses Brown in 1790. An immigrant from England, Slater had worked extensively in English textile mills and had carefully studied mill equipment and operations. Once in America, he sought out Moses Brown, owner of a spinning mill in Rhode Island. The two collaborated on improvements to the company of William Almy and Smith Brown, with Slater providing the technical knowledge and Brown providing the money to finance Slater's innovations. Workers at the new factory not only spun yarn, they also wove cloth, a job that had traditionally been doled out to independent weavers on an uneconomical and inefficient piecemeal basis.

Lowell first became interested in the textile business while vacationing in England. Returning to America, he began working on plans for a new factory that would incorporate all the steps that went into producing cloth. Enlisting the aid of investor Patrick Tracey Jackson, Lowell selected the site of an old paper mill on the Charles River in Waltham, Massachusetts, as the location for his new factory. By 1815, the fully mechanized Boston Manufacturing Company was in operation, with an annual sales volume of $3,000. Over the next seven years, sales grew to $345,000 annually.

Jackson fully realized the potential that lay in the textile business. He established another company, the Merrimack Manufacturing Company, near Chelmsford, and bought four square miles of land on which he erected two mill buildings. The mills opened in September 1823, and three years later, the land around the mills was separated from the town of Chelmsford and renamed Lowell. The company built dormitories and row houses around the mills to house the more than eighteen thousand inhabitants of Lowell. Most of the workers were young girls who earned about $2.50 a week. In the few hours of leisure they had each week, the workers published a literary magazine, entitled the *Lowell Offering*, attended lectures and meetings of sewing clubs, and visited the company's circulating library.

After the creation of Lowell, factories were established throughout New England and the Atlantic states, producing everything from cloth and shoes to clocks and firearms. Though fewer in number, factories were also built in the South, where Virginia manufacturers prospered in the chewing tobacco business and North and South Carolinians engaged in textile manufacture. Ever mindful of the need to hold down costs, factory managers began looking to Irish immigrants to fill jobs at low wages. The availability of jobs opened the floodgates of European immigration, so that, by the 1830s, more than half a million immigrants came to the United States. By the 1850s that number swelled to 2.6 million. Over the next twenty years, as more and more immigrants filled jobs previously held by young New England women, factory owners relinquished their paternalistic responsibilities to care for and house their workers. In some ways, this was a liberating trend for the worker. However, it also widened the gulf between management and labor, as workers came to feel increasingly exploited. This sense of alienation and exploitation led to the later proliferation of labor unions for unskilled and semiskilled factory workers.

James Monroe Announces a New Doctrine (1823)

The event: In 1823, President James Monroe laid the foundation of United States foreign policy with the Monroe Doctrine.

 SINCE 1741, THE western coast of North America—from Alaska to the Oregon country—had been of prime interest to Russia. Vitus Bering had explored the region, and in 1821, the Russian czar claimed for his nation all land and waters north of the 51st parallel. President Monroe issued a warning to the Russians, declaring the American continent off-limits to any nation wishing to establish a colonial empire. In 1824, the United States and Russia signed a treaty whereby Russia relinquished its claims to land south of the 54°40' north latitude—the southern border of modern-day Alaska—and removed restrictions on shipping in the region.

Disputes over European claims in Latin America were another prong of the far-reaching Monroe Doctrine. The various countries from the Rio Grande River south to the Straits of Magellan had gained independence between 1817 and 1822, but the combined forces of Austria, Prussia, France, Russia, and Spain were determined to regain control of Latin and South America for Spain. In addition, France was preparing to send a large army to the region. On this matter, the United States and Great Britain were in agreement. Great Britain saw in the reemergence of Spain as a colonial power a threat to English commercial ties with the new republics. The British foreign minister proposed that the United States join with Great Britain in issuing both a condemnation of any attempt by European nations to regain control of Latin American countries and a pledge to refrain from adding any part of the region to their empires. Secretary of State John Quincy Adams persuaded Monroe that, although the United States might be flattered by a request to act in concert with Great Britain, to do so was not in the best interests of the country. Instead, in his annual message to Congress, Monroe issued a declaration, drafted for him by Adams, on behalf of the United States alone. He stated that the "American continents by the free and independent condition which they have assumed and maintain, are henceforth not to be considered as subjects for future colonization by any European powers." While he pledged that the United States would not oppose the continuation of

European colonies that currently existed, he warned that any interference by a European nation with the affairs of an independent nation in the western hemisphere would be seen as a "manifestation of an unfriendly disposition toward the United States."

While European nations viewed Monroe's declaration as just so much talk, over the coming decades its importance as a policy statement became apparent. Presidents have backed numerous decisions with the force of the Monroe Doctrine, including the building of the Panama Canal, the protection of Cuba in the Spanish-American War, the arbitration of financial disputes between Venezuela and European nations, and the confrontation with the Soviet Union over missile bases it had established in Cuba.

Andrew Jackson Is Elected President (1828)

The event: In 1828 Americans elected as their president Andrew Jackson, a son of the western frontier and an icon of the ascendancy of the "common man" in American politics.

THE ELECTION OF Andrew Jackson to the presidency marked the political coming-of-age of a huge majority of Americans. Whereas all presidents before Jackson had been easterners, born to relatively well-to-do families, Jackson was from the West, a self-made man of modest wealth.

Born in Waxhaw, South Carolina, Jackson fought in the American Revolution, in which most of his immediate family were killed. After the war, Jackson studied law and then decided to move farther west, working as the prosecuting attorney in the western district of North Carolina—present-day Tennessee. When that territory started the process toward statehood, he served as a delegate to the Constitutional Convention and was then elected the state's first congressman. For a brief period he served as U.S. senator, but then returned to Nashville and was elected to the state's Supreme Court, a position he held while building his plantation, The Hermitage.

Jackson's name became a household word during the War of 1812, when he led troops against the Creek Indians in the Mississippi Territory and then, having been commissioned a U.S. Army major general, marched to Louisiana. There he defeated the British at New Orleans, a battle that took place after the Treaty of Ghent was signed but before news of the treaty ending the war had reached Washington, D.C.

Jackson first ran for the presidency in 1824. Although he won more electoral votes than his competitors—Jackson, 99; John Quincy Adams, 84; William H. Crawford, 41; and Henry Clay, 37—no candidate received a majority of votes. The election went to the House of Representatives, where, under the Constitution, each state delegation had one vote. Adams was elected after Clay swung his vote to him. Jackson, believing he had been cheated out of the presidency, charged that Clay and Adams had entered into a "corrupt bargain" and immediately began work on his 1828 campaign, garnering enough support in the South and the Mid-Atlantic region and from expansionists and strict constructionists to be elected handily.

His first day in office was indicative of things to come. After the inauguration, Jackson rode on horseback to the White House, where a private celebration was to be held. Throngs of well-wishers who had lined the streets suddenly appeared at the reception and nearly wrecked the White House as they tried to catch a glimpse of the new president. The common man had made a dramatic entrance onto the national political scene.

Jackson's two terms moved American society toward truer democracy. Many states abandoned property requirements for suffrage. Elected officials began to act more truly as representatives of the people than as their leaders. More and more people took advantage of their right to vote. Soon after his inauguration, Jackson instituted a system of equitable rotation in federal jobs, dismissing many of the political appointees who had held their positions for decades. As the president of the common man, Jackson defeated the plan offered by Clay and Adams for internal improvements because he thought it was biased toward the wealthy. He was a firm believer in the preservation of the Union, and he tried to silence the abolition movement, but the rights of southerners were not paramount to him; when South Carolina issued its nullification ordinance challenging federal authority by prohibiting the collection of tariffs in the state, Jackson declared the state's actions treasonous and prepared to use the army to compel obedience to the national law. Waging a war against the Bank of the United States, he vetoed the bill that rechartered the institution, declaring it a dangerous monopoly that profited the wealthy few.

A man who had built his reputation as an Indian fighter during the War of 1812, Jackson was not, however, an Indian hater. He adopted what was at the time considered an enlightened solution to the Indian problem—removal. Many tribes submitted peacefully to being moved to the West. Others were marched by force, under brutal conditions, along what the Cherokees called the Trail of Tears and other routes to the Indian Territory, now the state of Oklahoma and part of Kansas and Nebraska.

One of Jackson's most enduring legacies was the Democratic Party. Although the political group had been established as the Democratic Republicans during Thomas Jefferson's bid for the presidency, under Jackson it became a highly organized party. In opposition to the Democrats were the Whigs, a political party that attracted supporters of the Bank of the United States and that opposed the tyranny of the man its members called "King Andrew." The Whigs were not as organized as the Democrats in the 1830s, and Jackson's hand-picked successor, Martin Van Buren, won the election of 1836. A less specific but more basic legacy is the populist philosophy of American politics that bears his name, Jacksonian Democracy.

Abolitionists Establish the "Underground Railroad" (1830)

The event: During the 1830s, the long-active secret network of individuals committed to helping escaped slaves find their way north to freedom became more thoroughly organized and acquired the name by which it would be known until the Civil War: the Underground Railroad.

THE NETWORK HAD actually existed since the days of the American Revolution, as evidenced by George Washington's comments on the aid Quakers gave to runaway slaves. By the early nineteenth century, most of the individuals working in the loosely knit network were free blacks living in the North. Harriet Tubman, herself an escaped slave, was among the most active Underground Railroad workers. She is reported to have made nineteen trips into the South, risking her own freedom to help some three hundred slaves flee to the North. White abolitionists also participated in the railroad's activities, but to a lesser degree than free blacks.

The Underground Railroad was most helpful to slaves living in the Upper South. Those in Texas, Louisiana, southern Georgia, Alabama, and Mississippi had little hope of reaching the southernmost "terminal" of the railroad. But even those slaves in the Upper South had extreme difficulty reaching the safety of the railroad's embrace. By the time they had worked their way to sympathetic railroad members, they had already completed the most dangerous part of their escape.

Southern slaveowners raved against the Underground Railroad, which worked to deprive them of their valuable "property." They grew rabid over the Supreme Court's decision of 1842 in *Prigg v. Pennsylvania*, which declared that the states were not required to enforce the Fugitive Slave Act. Northern states also enacted "personal liberty" laws prohibiting state officials from helping southerners recapture their runaway slaves in the North. During the debate in Congress over the admission of California as a state and the establishment of territories in Utah and New Mexico, southern Congressmen pressed for—and won—a stronger Fugitive Slave Law as part of the Compromise of 1850.

Congress Passes the Indian Removal Act (1830)

The event: In 1830, at the urging of the administration of President Andrew Jackson, the U.S. Congress passed the Indian Removal Act authorizing the federal government to push the Choctaw, Chickasaw, Cherokee, Creek, and Seminole living in Georgia, Alabama, Mississippi, and the territory of Florida west of the Mississippi, mainly to an area designated as "Indian Territory" in present-day Oklahoma and parts of Kansas and Nebraska.

THOUGH SEVERAL EARLIER presidents had considered some sort of plan to "remove" the Indians out West, it was John Quincy Adams, responding to an impending constitutional crisis, who laid the foundation of the removal legislation. In 1828, the Georgia state legislature decreed that all Indian residents would come under state jurisdiction within six months, and other southern states planned to follow suit in order to get around federal protection of Indian lands and rights. Not only were southerners after Indian land, they were also alarmed by the continual flight of fugitive slaves into Indian-held tracts. The Seminoles and others customarily refused to return the fugitives, and the federal government was unwilling to compel them to do so. President Adams refused southern demands for the summary removal of the Indians and threatened to call in the army to *protect* tribesmen against the depredations of the state. Facing a divisive showdown between states' rights and federal authority, Adams finally agreed that a plan for removing the eastern tribes to the trans-Mississippi West was the only viable solution to the crisis. It fell to Jackson's administration to enact and implement the plan.

The Removal Act of 1830 was not deliberately evil. It did not sanction seizure of land but authorized a plan of fair land exchanges. But no plan is truly fair unless all parties concerned freely agree to it, and this was certainly not the case with Indian removal. In the face of Indian resistance, Jackson's government, both officially and unofficially, administered the removal policy ruthlessly and in bad faith. When Alabama and Mississippi followed Georgia in passing legislation that abolished tribal government and placed Indians under state jurisdiction, the Indians who were affected protested to the federal government that such state laws violated treaties made with the United States. True, Jackson admitted, but he claimed inability to enforce the treaty provisions on the states. Then, with the bullying illogic regularly employed in negotiating with Indians,

Jackson tried to persuade the tribes to make *new* treaties with this "powerless" federal government agreeing to removal west of the Mississippi.

The Indians continued to protest and the states continued to violate their sovereign rights. Squatters and land speculators waited for neither the state nor federal government to resolve disputed claims but overran Indian lands and, whenever they could, swindled Indians out of their property. The Choctaws were the first tribe to cave in to the unremitting pressure. In 1831 they left Mississippi and western Alabama for the West, suffering through a disastrous winter and the corrupt inefficiencies and callous lack of concern that would characterize the government's handling of Indian affairs throughout the entire nineteenth century. Next followed the Chickasaws, who signed removal treaties in 1832 and 1834.

The Creeks and the Seminoles had a longer and fiercer history of resistance to white encroachments and were more difficult to budge. Following the Creek War (1813-14), both hostile and friendly tribal factions ceded some three-quarters of their land to federal or state governments. But many Creeks clung to what remained and allied themselves with the Seminoles to resist the consequences of the Removal Act. Whites fought two bloody wars with the Seminoles (and allied Creek factions) in 1817-1818 and 1835-1842. The second dislodged most of the remaining Creeks, who left for Indian Territory during 1836, but many of the Seminoles proved impossible to force out of their Florida swampland strongholds. A Third Seminole War was fought as late as 1855-1858, and periodic campaigns followed to flush out the diehards. Some the federal government directly paid to move. Others remain in Florida to this day. One small band refused to make peace with the government until 1934.

When the Cherokees, living primarily in northwestern Georgia and northeastern Alabama (as well as the southeastern corner of Tennessee and the southwestern corner of North Carolina), took their case to the Supreme Court in 1832, the court ruled Georgia's persecution of the Indians unconstitutional. Jackson simply refused to enforce the court's decision. When only two thousand Cherokees had emigrated by 1838, the deadline for removal, Martin Van Buren, Jackson's successor, instituted a vigorous military campaign against the recalcitrant Cherokees. His field commander, General Winfield Scott, constructed what the twentieth century world would call concentration camps, stockades to house Cherokees rounded up in preparation for their removal. Indians were compelled to abandon property, ponies, and other livestock, and the soldiers charged with overseeing the stockades indulged in every manner of abuse, including rape and murder. "I fought through the civil war," one Georgia soldier later recalled, "and have seen men shot to pieces and slaughtered by thousands, but the Cherokee removal was the cruelest work I ever knew."

Except for a very few who managed to hide in the Blue Ridge, the Cherokees were penned into the camps during the long, hot summer. In the fall and winter of 1838-1839, they were marched off to Indian Territory along what they came to call the Trail of Tears. Fifteen thousand followed the twelve-hundred-mile route, cold, sick, and near starvation. Four thousand died along the way before reaching an Indian Territory as barren and alien as their southern homeland had been lush and familiar.

Nat Turner Rebels (1831)

The event: Just before dawn on August 22, 1831, a fanatical black lay preacher, a slave named Nat Turner, began a rampage that resulted in sixty murders and sent bolts of terror throughout the slave-owning South.

THE RIOT STARTED at the home of Turner's master, Joseph Travis, in Southhampton County, Virginia. Turner and his band of rebels first killed every white member of the Travis household. Then, fanning out over the county, they killed every white person they met along the way. As they swept through the region, more and more slaves joined Turner's rebels, and the killing spree lasted until the next morning.

Responding to the revolt, a party of white men routed Turner's band, but the avengers were not content with punishing the rebels alone. The whites went on their own rampage, killing and torturing innocent blacks. Turner himself and about fifty of his rebels were caught in the avengers' net, and twenty were quickly convicted and hanged.

Nat Turner's Rebellion was not the first time slaves had risen against their masters. A 1712 uprising in New York City resulted in the deaths of nine whites and the execution of eighteen slaves, of whom four were burned alive, one was broken on a wheel, and one was kept in chains until he starved to death. In 1739 a group of eighty slaves stole arms and marched toward Spanish Florida, where they planned to join forces with the Spanish against the British. The slaves, however, were recaptured, and forty-four were killed. In 1800, Richmond was the site of a slave rebellion undermined by foul weather. Gabriel Prosser, a blacksmith, and his brother Martin, a preacher, organized slaves for a march to Richmond, where they planned to kill the city's white inhabitants (except the Quakers, Methodists, and French). The conspiracy disintegrated when storms washed out the roads to Richmond on the night of the planned attack. In 1822, Denmark Vesey conspired to incite a slave rebellion in South Carolina. Vesey had bought his own freedom using money won in a lottery, but he was outraged by slavery and, over a five-year period, formulated plans for a revolt. Some of his followers informed on him, however, and he was executed along with thirty-seven slaves; some thirty others were sold out of the area.

Although slave rebellions were sporadic and usually abortive, southerners lived in continual fear of a universal uprising. For the potential for rebellion always seethed under the placid surface of plantation life, which perpetuated a system of intolerable injustice.

Black Hawk Goes to War (1832)

The event: In 1832, Sac and Fox Chief Black Hawk led his four hundred starving warriors, with their wives and children, back across the Mississippi River from Iowa to the tribe's village in Illinois from which he had been banned the summer before, sparking a campaign against him by the Illinois militia in which Black Hawk's "British Band" was destroyed.

WHEN BLACK HAWK returned from the winter hunt of 1830-1831 to discover Saukenuk—the tribe's main village at the mouth of the Rock River in Illinois—overrun by white squatters, he threatened war. A spurious treaty signed a quarter century before by a few drunken warriors and never recognized by Black Hawk or his fellow chiefs had ceded all the Sac and Fox lands in Illinois to the United States. As a matter of expediency, William Henry Harrison deigned to allow the tribe to remain on those lands until the area was needed for settlement. Black Hawk had accepted Harrison's compromise, believing the Americans had given up their claims.

But after the War of 1812, when Black Hawk—following his tribe's traditional predilection for doing business with the more reliable British—had fought with Tecumseh, a veritable flood of settlers had moved onto Sac and Fox land, ravaging their villages and even plowing up sacred burying grounds. Black Hawk protested to the U.S. Indian agents at Rock Island, who told him that they were powerless and that his only recourse was to move west, across the Mississippi. Only the year before, Black Hawk had returned from a hunt to find that a white family had settled in his very own lodge. Through an interpreter he told them to leave, explaining that there was plenty of unsettled land available. They ignored his demand and were soon followed by more whites. Then the U.S. General Land Office made the invasion official by announcing that the area including Black Hawk's village would be offered up for public sale.

This year of 1832, a rush of miners to the Galena lead fields had brought illegal squatters in its wake, and they destroyed or appropriated the Indians' homes, harvested for themselves the Indian corn, ripped down fences, trampled unused crops, and beat those Sac and Fox in the village who protested. Quick footwork by government officials helped to avert violence that summer and fall, and Black Hawk reluctantly retired to Iowa. But when the winter hunt proved fruitless, he led his hungry, homeless "British Band" back across the Mississippi, looking for food regardless of the consequences. The Americans responded with some hysteria, calling to the colors some fifteen hundred volunteers—they had hoped for twice that number—to supplement General Henry Atkinson's two hundred regular troops.

Black Hawk won the first encounter, further incensing the Americans, and was promptly betrayed by the English and the Winnebagos, both of whom promised aid and failed to deliver. He was also betrayed by a member of his own tribe, an ambitious young chief named Keokuk who had been the one to alert the local Indian agent to Black Hawk's approach and who persuaded a number of the of Sac and Fox to stay out of the fight. The band was relentlessly hunted down as they fled north along the Rock River into Wisconsin and massacred when they tried to recross the Mississippi into Iowa.

Black Hawk had done well to escape to the north, by which he avoided the slaughter. But the Winnebagos among whom he had sought refuge proved treacherous again, and in exchange for a reward, turned the chief over to white authorities. After holding him for a year, federal officials decided neither to try nor execute him but rather to exhibit him. He was, accordingly, packed off on a tour of the United States, where he was greeted in some places with hatred and in others almost as a hero. Black Hawk, leader of yet another desperate Indian resistance against the tide of white settlement, died of natural causes in 1838.

The Nullification Crisis Occurs (1832-1833)

The event: The Nullification Crisis of 1832-1833 put President Andrew Jackson, the Constitution of the United States, and the authority of the central government to a severe test. At issue was whether a state could nullify within its own borders a law passed by the United States Congress.

WHEN ANDREW JACKSON became president in March 1829, the nation was embroiled in arguments over slavery, protective tariffs, and the price of western lands. Northern states feared that low prices set on western lands would bankrupt the treasury, and they advocated tariffs to protect their industries. In addition, abolition fever was spreading rapidly throughout the North. Southerners, who were engaged in the production of raw materials, favored low tariffs and low prices on western lands and were outraged by northerners' advocacy of the abolition of slavery. In 1832, Congress passed a new tariff that southerners thought excessive. Radicals in the South Carolina legislature combined their hatred of abolition with their resentment of the new tariff and resolved that the state would not yield to the tariff. On November 24, 1832, a special convention called by the state legislature passed the Ordinance of Nullification, which prohibited the collection of duties after February 1, 1833. In addition, the legislature called for raising and arming a military force.

South Carolinians did not realize how determined President Jackson was to compel their compliance with federal law. They reasoned that Jackson had backed the state of Georgia when it refused to acquiesce to the Supreme Court's decision in *Worcester v. Georgia*, which held that the state had no jurisdiction over the actions of Native Americans on their own land. (The state had convicted a Cherokee Indian of a murder that took place on Cherokee land, and even after the Supreme Court's ruling, the state executed the murderer.) But Jackson's action in that instance of "nullification" had been motivated by his desire to compel the Cherokees to "remove" to Indian Territory. The matter of South Carolina's attempting to nullify a law of Congress was different, and Jackson prepared to take military measures against the state, issuing a "Proclamation to the People of South Carolina" in which he declared that "disunion by armed force is treason," even as he pleaded with Congress to reconsider the tariff.

The South Carolina radicals, led by staunch states' rightist John C. Calhoun, backed down ten days before nullification was scheduled to begin. When a compromise tariff passed Congress in March 1833, the state legislature repealed the Nullification Ordinance altogether. While the ultimate crisis was averted, sectional tensions continued to mount. Radicals in South Carolina and elsewhere in the South came to see that only secession from the Union would protect their way of life. Twenty-eight years after the nullification episode, the southern states would, in fact, secede.

Cyrus McCormick Invents a Reaper; John Deere Invents a Steel Plow (1834)

The event: In 1834, Cyrus McCormick patented a new reaper, which, along with the steel plow perfected by John Deere two years later, made possible the agricultural settlement of America's great western prairies.

CYRUS MCCORMICK GREW up on a farm in Rockbridge County, Virginia, where he experienced firsthand the toil involved in agriculture. At an early age he began tinkering in his father's workshop with ideas for a mechanical reaper. Others had tried before to develop such a device, but none had proved successful. Finally, in 1831, when he was twenty-two, McCormick came up with a practical prototype of a horse-drawn reaper, which included a cutting bar, a reel, divider, guards over reciprocating knives, and a platform on which the grain could be deposited after being cut; the works were driven by a gear wheel. After three more years of work, McCormick felt that his invention was ready for a public demonstration. He showed it at neighboring farms and then patented it in June 1834.

Always a perfectionist, McCormick continued to refine the reaper during the late 1830s, contracted with a few manufacturers to produce the device to his specifications, and marketed a handful during the early 1840s. Even with limited production, demand mounted, and McCormick opened up his own factory in Chicago, in the midst of the grain belt. Despite protracted patent litigation, decided in favor of Obed Hussey (who had patented a reaper in 1833), McCormick exercised his mechanical genius and business acumen first to create a reaper market and then to dominate it as it became increasingly competitive. Few inventors have been so skilled at production, marketing, and distribution.

McCormick's reaper revolutionized agriculture. In 1830 it took twenty hours to harvest an acre of wheat; in 1895, with the fully perfected reaper, it took less than an hour. McCormick's invention made large-scale farming possible at a time when the opening Midwest and West offered huge tracts of land.

Of course, there existed another daunting problem of midwestern land not solved by the reaper. While the acreage was plentiful, the prairie soil was hard and clumpy; it tended to clog the plow and was therefore all but impossible to till. At about the same time that McCormick was developing his reaper, however, John Deere, an Illinois blacksmith, was experimenting with a steel plow shapely and sturdy enough to break the stubborn prairie soil. He perfected his design in 1836, and the following year went into partnership with Major Leonard Andrus in Grand Detour, Illinois, to produce the plow in quantity. Deere sold his interest in the partnership to Andrus in 1847 and moved to Moline, Illinois, on the Mississippi River, where he began John Deere and Company and produced enough plows to supply the needs of ever-growing numbers of immigrants homesteading on the prairies.

Between them, McCormick and Deere had invented modern agriculture, setting the stage for twentieth-century "agribusiness" but, more immediately, providing the technology American settlers needed to make a go of it on the Great Plains.

William McGuffey Publishes His First *Reader* (1836)

The event: William Holmes McGuffey, a professor at Miami University in Oxford, Ohio, completed a series of graded readers for publication by a Cincinnati publishing company in 1836. The books would prove highly influential on the American educational system and were destined to endure well into the succeeding century.

INCORPORATING THE VALUES, beliefs, and lifestyles of "Western people," the McGuffey readers influenced generations of American teachers and students. The books included stories on a variety of topics and were instrumental in teaching religion, morality, and ethics to the nation's public school students.

After the publication of *Eclectic First Reader* and *Eclectic Second Reader* in 1836, McGuffey produced a third and fourth *Reader* the following year. McGuffey's brother Alexander then assumed the role of author of the series, producing the *Fifth Reader* in 1844, a spelling book in 1846, and a *Sixth Reader* in 1857. Through their various editions, the readers have been published by seven different companies. Beginning with the 1857 editions, "McGuffey's" became part of the series titles.

More than 122 million McGuffey readers had been sold by 1920, and some school districts still used the books in their classrooms into the 1970s.

Texans Defend the Alamo (1836)

The event: Faced with a rebellion in what was then the Mexican state of Texas, Mexican troops besieged and stormed the Alamo between February 23 and March 6, 1836, touching off a full-scale revolution that wrested the territory from Mexico and set it on the path to American statehood.

IN 1819 CONGRESS ratified the Adams-Onis Treaty with Spain, establishing the United States' border with Mexico. Although the line drawn excluded from the United States the region called Texas, within a few months of its ratification Americans, led by Stephen F. Austin, settled in the region. By 1830, twenty thousand Americans were living there along with about two thousand slaves.

Various administrations tried unsuccessfully to buy Texas from Mexico as more Americans, eager for land where cotton flourished, swarmed to the area. The settlers not only felt no political loyalty to Mexico, they differed in other important ways from the Mexican people. Most of the settlers were Protestant, while Mexico was overwhelmingly Catholic. Few of the settlers spoke any Spanish at all. In addition, the settlers were products of the plantation culture of the South, now subject to Mexican laws banning slavery. As the Mexican government instituted more controls over the settlers in Texas, they began to seek independence. American volunteers descended on the region and engaged in skirmishes with the Mexican troops. In January 1836, the Mexican president, Antonio Lopez de Santa Anna, led his forces north to put down the Texas rebellion. In February the troops reached San Antonio, where an American force under Colonel William B. Travis was stationed in an old mission called the Alamo. The tiny garrison, numbering only 187 men, held off the

Mexican troops, more than five thousand of them, for ten days. At last, on March 6, the Mexicans stormed the mission, killed everyone inside, and burned the corpses. Slain within the mission's walls were the legendary frontiersmen Davy Crockett and Jim Bowie.

Texas had declared its independence four days before the battle, and after it, a new determination for freedom from the hated Mexican regime filled the American forces, now led by the gritty and able Sam Houston under the battle cry, "Remember the Alamo!" During a major battle on April 21, Houston's forces defeated the Mexican troops and drove them out of Texas. In the first elections in the new republic of Texas, the settlers made Houston president and indicated in a plebiscite about a month later that they would favor annexation to the United States, thereby setting the stage for American domination of the Southwest.

Ralph Waldo Emerson Delivers the "American Scholar" Speech (1837)

The event: On August 31, 1837, Ralph Waldo Emerson, at the time just beginning to make a name for himself as America's leading innovative philosophical essayist, poet, and moral thinker, gave a speech at the Harvard chapter of the Phi Beta Kappa Society entitled "The American Scholar." Oliver Wendell Holmes, Sr., called it "our intellectual Declaration of Independence."

THOSE WHO HEARD Emerson's address, Holmes said, "went out from it as if a prophet had been proclaiming to them 'thus saith the Lord.'" The poet James Russell Lowell remembered it "as an event without any former parallel in our literary annals." Without question the speech made an extraordinary impression.

What was it that so moved those who heard Emerson's speech and the many more who later read it?

Despite their swagger and patriotic pride, the citizens of the still-youthful American republic bowed to the Old World and its traditions when it came to intellectual and aesthetic matters. Politically independent, the United States was still the cultural vassal of Europe. In "The American Scholar," Emerson called upon the students, thinkers, writers, moralists, and artists of the nation to strike out on new intellectual paths as boldly as the founding fathers had ventured a new course in politics. Far from being inferior to the scholar of the Old World, Emerson declared, the American scholar enjoyed the advantage of freedom from the blindness and limitations of an outworn past. The American scholar need take nothing at second hand but was in a position to open up the very frontiers of knowledge, just as the nation's pioneers explored the geographical frontiers beyond the Appalachians, the Mississippi, and the Rockies. Whereas Americans had tended to follow Europeans, Emerson enjoined them to lead. As they had pioneered political freedom, their hopeful and exciting mission now was to pioneer intellectual, moral, and aesthetic freedom, to open up a New World of the mind.

The young intellectuals of the United States rallied round Emerson's speech. America's rising generation of great writers, including Henry David Thoreau, Walt Whitman, Herman Melville, and Nathaniel Hawthorne, all took inspiration from it as they began their careers, writing their best books during the 1840s and 1850s in a period of this nation's literary and cultural history that came to be known as the American Renaissance.

Marcus Whitman Crosses the Continent on the Oregon Trail (1843)

The event: In 1843, Marcus Whitman led what came to be called the Great Migration from Independence, Missouri, to the Williamette Valley in Oregon.

WHITMAN TRAVELED ON the Oregon Trail, stretching some two thousand miles from Missouri to Oregon country. Parts of the trail were blazed in 1812 by Robert Stuart, an agent of fur entrepreneur John Jacob Astor, and for some thirty years thereafter it was a principal route of fur men and other traders. By the end of the 1830s, however, the nation was in the first throes of what would come to be called "Oregon fever," lured by stories that it was an agricultural paradise ripe for settlement—stories in large part circulated by a small group of hearty missionaries. The first organized pioneer band set out along the Oregon Trail in 1841 and was followed by a larger group the next year. But it was Whitman's Great Migration two years later—an epic journey undertaken by two hundred families in 120 wagons and driving two thousand head of cattle—that kicked off similar treks each year until 1869, when the transcontinental railroad was completed.

It took men like Marcus Whitman, zealous, single-minded, willfully authoritarian, and Oregon's most important early missionary, to lead settlers along the grueling trail, where they were subject to every misery and danger known to humankind: starvation, thirst, freezing cold, burning heat, disease, accident, and Indian attack. But the very qualities of character that contributed to survival on the trail—zeal, unthinking self-confidence, and unbending will—could create disaster at trail's end. Whitman was a missionary and physician among the Cayuse Indians in the vicinity of Walla Walla. He tirelessly ministered to the physical and spiritual welfare of the Indians, but he also alienated and enraged them by insisting that they sever themselves completely from their former beliefs. When a measles epidemic swept the mission, killing half the Indians there, including the daughter of Tiloukaikt, an influential chief, some of the Indians blamed their unyielding missionary. On November 29, 1847, Tiloukaikt, Tomahas, and other Cayuse Indians attacked the mission, killing Whitman, his wife, and several others.

James Fenimore Cooper Publishes *The Deerslayer* (1841)

The event: In 1841, America's best-known novelist, James Fenimore Cooper, published *The Deerslayer*, last and most idyllic of the five "Leatherstocking Tales," which bequeathed to American literature and culture its most enduring image of the vanishing frontier and frontiersman.

 JAMES FENIMORE COOPER grew up in Cooperstown, New York, an area his own father had "developed" from wilderness. After attending Yale University for two years, Cooper served in the navy, then married Susan De Lancey, a woman from an influential and wealthy New York family. It was she who challenged him to become a writer. Cooper, who had just finished reading a popular English novel, turned to Susan, and remarked, "I believe I could write a better story myself." She told him, in effect, to prove it, and, in short order, Cooper produced his first novel, *Precaution* (1820), a pale but moderately successful imitation of then-current British fiction.

In this modest, almost accidental beginning, Cooper had suddenly found his vocation. Whereas his first story imitated English writing, his next, *The Spy* (1821), used American subject matter exclusively. The story of a spy in the Revolutionary War, the book was an immediate success. In 1822 the Coopers moved to New York City, where he became a full-time professional writer and a leader of the city's intellectuals. From 1826 to 1833, Cooper lived abroad in England, France, Switzerland, and Italy. The experience gave him a sharp critical perspective on his own country, a perspective he would develop in some of his later nonfiction, especially a work of social analysis called *The American Democrat*.

Cooper became a prolific author, popular not only in the United States but throughout the world; his novels often ranked with those of Sir Walter Scott. While Cooper wrote in many fictional genres—he is, for example, given credit for creating the sea story—by far his most important and best known works are tales of the American wilderness. Of these, his finest novels are the five "Leatherstocking Tales," which include *The Pioneers* (1823), *The Last of the Mohicans* (1826), *The Prairie* (1827), *The Pathfinder* (1840), and *The Deerslayer* (1841). Taken together, the "Leatherstocking" novels present a vivid, epic picture of America's vanishing wilderness. Their focus is broad, sweeping, mythical in its dimensions, and yet personal, as Cooper develops the character of the novels' central figure, a backwoodsman whose given name is Natty Bumppo but who is better known as Leatherstocking, the Pathfinder, the Deerslayer, or Hawkeye. In Hawkeye Cooper presented the ideal of the American frontiersman: knowing but innocent, brave, self-reliant, perfectly at one with nature. He is cast among a host of characters, including the noble Indians Chingachgook and Uncas, and various white characters who act either to exploit and despoil the American land or to help preserve it. Cooper created a drama of American evolution even as the momentous changes were taking place. His novels not only told Americans about themselves but conveyed unforgettable images of colonial America and the early republic throughout the world.

Dan Emmett Stages a New Minstrel Show (1843)

The event: In 1843, fiddler Dan Emmett and his Virginia Minstrels opened at the Bowery Theater in the first minstrel show, a uniquely American and immensely popular form of entertainment throughout the nineteenth century.

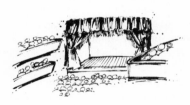

IN 1829, AN entertainer named Thomas "Daddy" Rice appeared in a play called *The Rifle.* Cast as a comic black field hand, Rice inserted into the show a song and dance he had learned from a crippled African American stableboy he had seen in Louisville, Cincinnati, or Pittsburgh (the story varies). It was called "Jim Crow," and it became a national sensation. Rice made "Jim Crow" into a separate act and toured with it for the next thirty years, until his death in 1860. Building on the success of "Jim Crow," a backwoodsman of Irish descent named Dan Emmett gathered some friends together in New York City and planned a show. Calling themselves the Virginia Minstrels, fiddler Emmett and his cast—a banjo player, tambourine player, and a performer who used animal bones as a rhythm instrument—blackened their faces with burnt cork, mounted the stage of the Bowery Theater, sat down in a semicircle, and presented a show they called "The Essence of Old Virginny," trading comic dialogue, singing songs, and ending with a "walk-around." Among the tunes Emmett wrote for the show were "Old Dan Tucker" and "Dixie."

In the hands of Dan Emmett and, shortly after him, Edwin P. Christy (The

Christy Minstrels), then a host of others, the minstrel show became an unprecedented popular phenomenon, enduring through the end of the nineteenth century, when it gradually gave way to vaudeville. It was the first American form of mass commercial entertainment.

Although the minstrel show was inspired by white perceptions of how slaves entertained themselves on the plantation, the minstrel show was by no means a product of folklore. A progenitor of modern mass entertainment, it was as calculated for commercial success as any Broadway musical, movie, or television program is today.

The minstrel show presented a racial stereotype that was, by modern standards, offensive: the minstrel "darky" was pictured not as person bearing the yoke of slavery with strength and dignity but as a well-adjusted, simple-minded, fun-loving caricature. But it is a mistake to assume that the popular appeal of the minstrel show was based simply on racism. At mid-century the United States was rapidly changing, undergoing a transformation from a country of contented yeoman farmers to one of urban industrial workers, many of whom were freshly arrived immigrants from all over the world. Moreover, the union between North and South was clearly beginning to crumble in the two decades before the Civil War. Facing new pressures, American audiences yearned for the bucolic stability of a mythological sunny South where even the slaves were happy. The minstrel show was the first in a long line of popular entertainments peculiar to America that self-consciously catered to national sentiment, particularly to nostalgia for an idealized rural past. It was also the vehicle through which a huge number of popular songs reached the public in the days before the phonograph and radio. "Polly Wolly Doodle," "Buffalo Girls," "The Old Folks at Home," and many, many more were originally written for the minstrel show.

Samuel F. B. Morse Invents the Telegraph (1844)

The event: On May 24, 1844, Samuel F.B. Morse transmitted the first message across a telegraph line connecting Washington, D.C. to Baltimore: "What hath God wrought!" Within a decade, twenty-three thousand miles of telegraph line crossed the nation, touching and transforming virtually every aspect of American life.

MORSE LED THREE remarkable lives. The son of a prominent clergyman, Morse was born in Charlestown, Massachusetts, in 1791, was educated at Yale University, and traveled to Europe to study the history of painting in the grand tradition. He quickly became an accomplished artist, but returning to the United States found little demand for his work. He went back to Europe in 1829, hoping that artistic recognition there would boost his career at home.

That did not happen, but two encounters in Europe did launch Morse on two new lives. While visiting Rome he was struck and knocked to the ground by a soldier because he did not kneel before a passing Catholic procession. When Morse returned to the United States, he wrote a series of widely published articles arguing that the Catholic church aimed to subvert American democracy by sending Catholic immigrants to dominate the thinly settled western frontier. Morse's influential articles gave rise to anti-immigration and nativism movements that would be influential well into the twentieth century.

The second encounter, which gave rise to Morse's third life, was a chance shipboard meeting, on the voyage back to the United States, with a scientist named Thomas Jackson. As a result of their conversations, Morse hit upon the idea of using electrical current as a medium through which communication might be transmitted. He abandoned his artistic career and set about inventing the telegraph as well as devising a coded system of "dots" and "dashes" for transmitting language with the device.

Morse had not only the imagination to invent the telegraph but the vision to realize how his invention would revolutionize life in the nineteenth century. Moreover, he was able to convey that vision to Congress, which subsidized the construction of the first telegraph line, from Washington to Baltimore. Space, seemingly limitless in its vastness, had always been America's greatest resource and its heaviest burden—for a far-flung nation was difficult to unify and govern. As the nation's expansion-minded politicians saw it, Morse's invention, in a single stroke, lifted that burden and delivered to the United States an unqualified blessing.

Frederick Douglass Publishes His Biography (1845)

The event: Frederick Douglass, an escaped Maryland slave, published his auto-biography, *Narrative of the Life of Frederick Douglass*, in 1845, fueling the abolitionist movement and launching his own career as an antislavery leader and reformer.

A GRIPPING ACCOUNT, *The Narrative* was the work of a slave who had escaped to freedom in 1838, having learned to read and write while a house servant. In 1841, while attending a convention of the Massachusetts Antislavery Society at Nantucket, he delivered a speech so passionate that he was immediately engaged as a "lecturing agent" of the society, spreading the gospel of not only emancipation but full equality.

Douglass's autobiography was read widely and fanned the flames of the abolition movement, which was growing rapidly, in large part due to the efforts of William Lloyd Garrison of Massachusetts. Through his newspaper, *The Liberator*, Garrison argued for the immediate abolition of slavery, even if the Union had to be destroyed in the process. In contrast to Garrison, Douglass was determined to achieve freedom for slaves by working within the Constitution, and he broke with Garrison on this point.

From his position with the Antislavery Society, Douglass went on to become the editor of an important abolitionist newspaper and an adviser to radical abolitionist John Brown, whose raid on the U.S. arsenal at Harpers Ferry was a prelude to the Civil War. During that war, Douglass was instrumental in raising African-American regiments.

Douglass wrote two additional autobiographies: *My Bondage and My Freedom*, published in 1855, and *The Life and Times of Frederick Douglass*, published in 1881. After the Civil War and the emancipation of slaves, he continued to press for black rights by attacking Jim Crow laws and the practice of lynching. In the 1870s he moved to Washington, D.C., where he edited an influential black newspaper, producing editorials and other writings that stand as classics in the literature of civil rights.

The United States Annexes Texas (1845)

The event: After much dispute and delay, largely over the issue of slavery, the United States formally approved the annexation of Texas on February 28, 1845, an action endorsed by the Congress of the Republic of Texas on June 23.

THE ALAMO HAD served as a rallying cry against Mexico for a full-scale rebellion headed by Sam Houston, a former congressman and governor of Tennessee. When Houston was elected president of the new republic of Texas, most of its citizens favored immediate annexation by the United States.

The question of annexation, however, was not as simple as the Texans had hoped. It was clouded by the issue of slavery and the certainty of war with Mexico, should the government accede to the request for annexation. Presidents Andrew Jackson and Martin Van Buren refused to act on the matter. President John Tyler, however, was ready to take action, and his secretaries of state, first Abel P. Upshur and then John C. Calhoun, initiated the process. Calhoun, a strong advocate of states' rights and slavery, alienated many northerners and westerners, however, and the annexation of Texas became a hot issue. In June 1844, the Senate rejected a bill proposing annexation.

The senators and the presidential hopefuls of 1844, Martin Van Buren and Henry Clay, both of whom declared their opposition to annexation, had misread public opinion. For at stake was the issue of westward expansion. Americans had come to the conviction that the whole American continent should be theirs. When the Democrats met at their convention in May 1844, Van Buren was passed over for the presidential nomination in favor of James K. Polk, who had announced his intention of annexing Texas. Polk defeated Clay, who had tried to downplay his earlier pronouncements against annexation. President Tyler, in preparing to leave office, saw Polk's election as a mandate for national expansion. He instructed Congress to consider a joint resolution on the Texas question, and a few days before the end of his term, Congress approved the resolution, which called for Texas to be admitted as a state, to retain title to its public lands, and to retain responsibility for all debts incurred as an independent republic. In December 1845, Texas was formally admitted to the Union.

Mexico quickly broke diplomatic ties to the United States, and almost immediately Texans and Mexicans were fighting over the location of the border. Texans claimed the Rio Grande as its proper boundary, while Mexicans claimed the Nueces River. Minor skirmishes soon escalated to full-scale battles, and on May 13, 1846, the United States declared war on Mexico.

John O'Sullivan Writes about "Manifest Destiny" (1845)

The event: In 1845, John L. O'Sullivan, editor of the *New York Post*, first used the words "manifest destiny" to describe the American's restlessness and passion for new land.

"IT IS OUR manifest destiny," he wrote, "to overspread and to possess the whole of the continent which Providence has given us for the development of the great experiment of liberty and federated self-government entrusted to us." O'Sullivan's rhetoric was high-minded, but what it described was something less abstract, something almost visceral. The hungering for riches, the longing to possess land, the search for a good life—in short, the peculiar American transformation of the profit motive into a passion—had been going on since Thomas Jefferson substituted the phrase "pursuit of happiness" for "property" in John Locke's trinity of natural rights.

The acquisition of land was central to an American's understanding of life, liberty, and the pursuit of happiness, and "land" became the central concept in the ideology of the westward movement. From the beginning the leaders of the American republic had been determined to avoid the fate of Europe, with its small elites addicted to luxury and its huge, murderously miserable majorities of people without property. Not just a Thomas Jefferson, who idealized the independent and hardworking farmer and became the patron saint of the West, but also a John Adams, who declared bluntly that "power always followed property," understood what happened when populations grew, as in the Old World, out of balance with the supply of land.

Cheap credit and a small plot of land *somewhere* was ever the dream of the West's common man whose political ideal was Mr. Jefferson's Democracy. And even the privileged class in America, at least before the Civil War, argued that its "experiment" in government depended on the prosperity of individual property holders and thought widely distributed land ownership the best safeguard against dangerous concentrations of power.

It is hardly surprising, then, that Americans developed what Drew McCoy has called "a vision of expansion across space—the American continent—as a necessary alternative to the development through time that was generally thought to bring both political corruption and social decay." It was a vision of innocence as well as of manifest destiny, and one could hear the romantic longing for the lost purity of Eden in Horace Greeley's battle cry of expansion: "Go West, young man, and grow up with the land."

There was something of the missionary's zeal for domination as well as the settler's longing for security wrapped up in this vision of the West as a potential social Eden. And it was no accident that the senior U.S. senator from Missouri, Thomas Hart Benton, who for thirty years was Congress's most vociferous advocate of free land for the homesteader and America's national spokesman for the West, also talked loftily of the holy Anglo-Saxon mission to civilize the continent. It was he who adopted O'Sullivan's phrase and made it the clarion call of western expansion.

For the truth was, the American establishment in many ways had begun to suspect that it could not long survive politically without the West. From 1841 to 1846, nearly five million people, mostly German and Irish immigrants, had packed into the eastern cities, creating just the kinds of problems the founding fathers had feared. During the same period, out of twenty million Americans, only some tens of thousands had moved to the Pacific coast. It must have been clear to America's leaders that if a manifest destiny did not exist, they would have to invent one.

The Knickerbocker Base Ball Club Writes the Rules of the Game (1845)

The event: In 1845, a gang of young men in Manhattan organized the Knickerbocker Base Ball Club and wrote down the rules of the game children in England and America had played for years under names like "rounder," "one o'cat," "base," and of course, "baseball."

TWENTY YEARS AFTER the Knickerbockers played their first game, baseball was more popular in America than cricket. Metropolitan New York was the baseball capital of the world, boasting dozens of Manhattan and Brooklyn clubs whose doings were followed by a strange breed of promoters called "sportswriters" and by a growing number of fans. With the help of their adoring press, the club games—at first local entertainments and occasions for civic pride—had become the "national pastime." The need of these small businesses to attract paying crowds led them to look far and wide for first-rate players, and the remarkable success of the undefeated Cincinnati Red Stockings' national tour during the 1869 season widened the growing economic gap between club owners and the game's players.

In 1876, owners formed the National League of Professional Base Ball Clubs, essentially a small cartel that either ran rival leagues out of business or swallowed them whole by incorporation. The sport of baseball had become a profession just as its popularity created the great sports boom of the late nineteenth century.

The National League operated precisely like the Gilded Age monopoly it was. Controlling the market by granting franchises, the League kept its workers in line with labor practices that reduced the players to virtual chattel, chiefly through the infamous "reserve rule," but also with blacklists, fines, salary limits, pay reductions, and, if all else failed, the use of Pinkerton spies. A Players League, formed in 1890 by unionized players, failed to break the monopoly when their own financial backers sold them out to the National League, which ruled professional baseball virtually unchallenged for decades.

Only the American League, formed in 1901, managed to survive by appealing to immigrant and working-class fans. Where the National League charged fifty cents, refused to sell alcohol, and never played on Sundays, American League clubs charged a quarter, sold beer, and made the Sunday game an institution. The Negro Leagues, organized in the 1920s, succeeded for similar reasons. Though a few blacks played in the major leagues before the color line hardened in the Jim Crow 1880s, baseball was never an integrated sport, and the majors were not much interested in poor black spectators. Growing out of loosely structured touring teams, the Negro Leagues reached their peak of popularity at the end of World War II, offering its fans a chance to see some of history's finest ball players—among them, Satchel Paige.

The whiff of scandal pervaded baseball from its early days, beginning with "fixed" games in 1865. Despite the outrage of its commissioners and the disingenuous moralizing of sportswriters, betting scandals continued: in 1877, when the St. Louis Browns got themselves booted out of the National League for throwing games; in 1919, when gangsters in New York and Boston bribed the "Black Sox" to take a dive during the World Series; in 1989, when Pete Rose was banished from the sport for placing bets on his own team. Like most public figures, ballplayers have often behaved badly outside the spotlight, and the especially close link between the development of the press and baseball's history has only heightened the contrast between the private lives and the mythic stature of baseball heros.

Because baseball isolated individual achievement and enshrined the craft of its players at precisely the time industrial America crushed true craft production, there has always been an aura of nostalgia about the game. Despite baseball's urban roots, its values were rural, and fans sought an imagined past in the game. Hence, perhaps, the endless fascination with individual player statistics and the unending debates about an essentially childlike game played and viewed with great seriousness. This nostalgia may also account for the fact that fans, despite the incredible revenues realized by franchises with the arrival of television and the decline of the minor leagues in its wake, have always hated the fact that players actually made money. They prefer to believe that baseball is still a sport of innocence—and on that enduring, logically indefensible belief rests much of the game's legendary appeal to Americans.

The United States Declares War on Mexico (1846)

The event: On May 13, 1846, the United States, no longer able to contain the rapacious land hunger of its citizens for territory belonging to Mexico, declared war on its southern neighbor.

SCARCELY FIVE YEARS had passed since the first of the wagon trains began leaving for the West. In 1841, a group of young hard cases under the leadership of twenty-one-year-old John Bidwell set out from Sapling Grove in eastern Kansas for the coast. Each year the number of prairie schooners increased, sailing on wild rumors about the golden valleys of California and the black soil of Oregon and following madly inaccurate maps that made the trip look easy.

They came by steamboat to the little towns of Missouri, jamming the holds and decks with cows and chickens and farm implements and household goods, half of which they would abandon in some Godforsaken wasteland on the way. When enough of them had arrived to make a group feel safe, they hired a mountain man, a Tom Fitzpatrick or a Kit Carson, to guide them, and took off in their ordinary ten-by-four-foot farm wagons when the prairie grass was high enough to feed their oxen or their mules.

They waited to pick a captain till they had traveled together for a while, quarreling about firewood, butting in line, and conducting scheming, backbiting elections that left the losers disgruntled and bitter. It hardly mattered, however, since most of them paid little attention to their elected leaders anyway, often deposing them, sometimes breaking away from the main train entirely to travel on their own. And for two thousand miles they lumbered along on the Santa Fe or Oregon trails, shouting and bellowing and braying through swirls of dust at the breakneck speed of twelve to twenty miles a day. A train of fifty wagons stretched a mile or so, and when the terrain permitted, the individual wagons traveled in two parallel lines.

Occasionally a band of Kansas or Pawnees would ride alongside or hang around the camp at night, begging, sometimes stealing, here and there killing a poor straggler. But for the most part during that first decade, the pioneers were safe enough from everything but an early winter and their own stupidity. Shooting accidents killed more of them than Indians did. Bored children often fell from the wagons and were run over. Some groups got lost. Some starved. A few, like the ill-fated Donner party trapped in the frozen Rockies, turned to cannibalism.

For twenty years, Mexico had dreaded the coming of the Anglos. Mexican newspapers decried the "fanatical intolerance" of the American pioneers for nonwhites and called the U.S. a parasite that "devour[ed] Mexico's entrails." The Texas revolution had proved Mexico's point, and now the wagon trains threatened what was left of their land in North America. With Texas now about to join the Union, Mexicans were certain that the expansionist colossus hungered for New Mexico and California.

In the mid-1840s, Mexican newspapers began to call for a preventive war against the United States. The cry was music to the ears of American westerners, who wanted nothing more than an excuse to gobble up the rest of the continent. The Mexicans had been right: Americans were determined to take their land, regardless. At the moment Congress drafted the declaration of war, John C. Frémont—who had been asked to leave California by the U.S. government for stirring up sedition—was rushing back after having heard that war was imminent to declare the Mexican province a free republic; a man named Lansford Hastings was headed east with big plans to lure thousands of immigrants to the West Coast; a party of Mormons was making its way across Iowa toward the Missouri River and the desert beyond; and another Mormon group under Sam Brannan was on the high seas bound for San Francisco. General Zachary Taylor was already roughing up Mexican settlers along the Rio Grande; the brushfire combat along the border flamed into war.

The Mexican War made a number of American reputations, including those of Zachary Taylor and General Winfield Scott, Brigadier General Stephen Kearny, Commodores Stockton and Perry, Army Scout Kit Carson, Colonel Alexander Doniphan, and even Captain Frémont, though he faced a court-martial for his undisciplined glory-hunting. The Americans threatened to make short work of the matter before President James Polk made the mistake of listening to Santa Anna, in exile in Cuba, when the old autocrat began talking peace. Once he returned to power with America's help, Santa Anna immediately revitalized the army. As Taylor and Scott launched the attack on Mexico proper, Kearny marched out of Fort Leavenworth, Kansas, to secure New Mexico and head for California. Led by Kit Carson, Kearny arrived near San Diego to find Commodore Stockton and Frémont already engaged with the hard-riding *vaqueros*, who charged armed with no more than a lance and a lariat, lassoing their enemies at full gallop, jerking them from their mounts, and stabbing them with their spears. Meanwhile, Doniphan led his troop of Missouri regulars, after dividing from Kearny in Santa Fe, on an incredible march through the desert to reinforce U.S. troops south of the border; Commodore Perry took Vera Cruz by sea. In the long run, Mexico had neither the means nor the will to win, and despite some grumbling on the home front, it was quite a splendid little affair for the aggressive empire builders of the American West.

By the terms of the treaty that ended hostilities, the victors acquired, at a price of $15 million and by paying off the claims of westerners against the Mexican government, all of modern California, Nevada, and Utah, most of New Mexico and Arizona, and a good deal of Colorado. Five years later, the Americans would buy the rest of the current-day continental United States from Mexico in the $10 million Gadsden Purchase.

By then, of course, the troops had long ago returned home to heroes' welcomes and parades everywhere. But after the giant barbecues thrown by cities like Nashville, and the grand torch-light marches of a Charleston, South Carolina, the excitement died down, and many of the men who had marched with

Taylor and Scott, Frémont and Doniphan, headed west themselves to the land they had helped conquer.

The Mormons Migrate to Utah (1847-1848)

The event: In March, 1830, Joseph Smith, Jr., published *The Book of Mormon*, the bible of the religion he would found the following month—a religion persecuted like no other in American history.

ACCORDING TO THE *Book of Mormon*, in 1820 a fifteen-year-old boy named Joseph Smith, Jr., was visited by God the Father and Jesus Christ near his family's farm in upstate New York. Three years later, an angel named Moroni told Smith to dig in a certain place on a hill near his home. He unearthed thin golden plates bound together by wire rings. The plates bore a history written by Moroni's father, Mormon, telling of an ancient struggle between two tribes, one good, the other evil, that lived in the New World long before the days of Columbus. Moroni, the sole survivor from among the good tribe, buried the plates. Whoever dug them up again was commanded to restore into the world the true Church of Christ.

Ten years later, in April 1830, Smith would found the Church of Jesus Christ of Latter-Day Saints. Starting with six members, he made converts rapidly, and the Saints (as they called themselves) soon numbered in the thousands. But everywhere Smith took them, his people were met with hostility and persecution. He moved from New York to Kirtland, Ohio, then to northwestern Missouri, then to Illinois, where the flock built a lovely village they called Nauvoo (from the Hebrew word connoting a beautiful and restful place). By 1844, Nauvoo was the largest town in Illinois, with fifteen thousand residents—half the total number of Mormons at the time. The town prospered, and its neighbors grew to resent its prosperity and the arrogant disdain with which Nauvoo's citizens treated outsiders, whom they called "gentiles."

Worse trouble was to come. In 1843, Smith informed church elders that he had received a revelation in which God had given permission for certain Mormons to take more than one wife. Polygamy had obvious advantages for the growth of the Mormonism, but the issue split the church bitterly. Some believers denounced Smith not only to other Mormons but to the gentiles as well, using a newly founded opposition newspaper called the *Nauvoo Expositor*. Smith sent the Nauvoo marshal to destroy the paper's presses, and, in response, the owners of the paper brought in outside authorities to arrest Smith, who was jailed in Carthage, Illinois, on charges of having violated the U.S. Constitution. On June 27, 1844, Smith and his brother were lynched by a mob of two hundred anti-Mormons, who stormed the jail. Mobs were also bent on destroying Nauvoo, but they did not make good their threats. Still, to Brigham Young, a former house painter, carpenter, and glazier who had assumed leadership of the church after Smith's murder, the message was clear. The Mormons would not only have to leave Nauvoo, they would have to find a place of settlement remote from gentile neighbors, a land no one else would ever covet.

Young had read various accounts of western exploration, including that of John C. Frémont, from which he concluded that the ideal spot was on the shores of the Great Salt Lake in the present-day state of Utah. During the winter of 1845-1846, all of Nauvoo turned to building wagons and the other necessities of travel. Young approached the 1,400-mile overland mass migration as a great general might prepare for titanic battle. He himself set off first with a pioneer party to build an Iowa rendezvous point and staging area for the immigrants. When all had gathered there—it was called Camp of Israel—in the spring of 1846, Young began to deploy the Saints westward in manageable groups of a few hundred at a time.

Throughout the balance of the 1840s and 1850s, the Saints poured into the Salt Lake valley. Brigham Young supervised the planning and construction of a city unprecedented by any frontier town, boasting a central Temple Square of ten acres (originally it was to have been forty!), with broad boulevards, and neat, spacious houses, each with its own garden. Young himself designed a remarkable irrigation system at a time when systematic irrigation was unknown in

American agriculture. By 1865, 277 irrigation canals had been dug, irrigating 154,000 square miles of previously arid land. Young constructed his government with equal precision, presiding as president over a "Theo-Democracy," which included separate legislative bodies to administer church and secular affairs and a carefully worked-out system of popular representation.

The migration had been made with remarkably little loss of life, and the settlement grew wealthy enough to finance would-be immigrants from all over the United States and the world.

Female Suffragists Hold a Conference at Seneca Falls (1848)

The event: During July 19 and 20, 1848, 240 women and men met at Seneca Falls, New York, at the first public political meeting on women's rights. Using the Declaration of Independence as a model, the delegates prepared the "Seneca Falls Declaration of Sentiments," a catalog of the various mistreatments women had suffered at the hands of men.

THE CONVENTION DECLARED that men had oppressed women by withholding from them the right to vote, the right to hold property, and access to the educational and employment opportunities available to men.

The Seneca Falls Convention was followed two weeks later by a larger meeting in Rochester, and thereafter annual meetings were held.

Seneca Falls organizers included Elizabeth Cady Stanton and Lucretia Mott. Stanton, who was born in Johnstown, New York, became involved in the abolition movement after graduating from Emma Willard Academy. While attending the World Antislavery Convention in London in 1840, Stanton met Lucretia Mott, the most outspoken and prolific female abolitionist in the United States. Reared in a Quaker family, Mott abhorred slavery and made it a lifetime practice to boycott goods produced through slave labor. In 1833 she founded the Philadelphia Female Anti-Slavery

Society. When, on the basis of her sex, she was denied a seat at the World Anti-slavery Convention in London, Mott used her considerable oratorical skills to spread the doctrine of equality of the sexes.

After their collaboration at the Seneca Falls Convention, Mott and Stanton continued their work on abolition and women's suffrage. Meanwhile, Susan B. Anthony, a Seneca Falls delegate and friend of Stanton's, set about creating grassroots women's rights organizations throughout New York. Through extensive lobbying she succeeded in persuading state legislators to pass the Married Women's Property Act in 1860, which secured for married women the right to hold property, the right to earn and keep wages, and the right to petition for custody of children in the event of divorce.

After the Civil War, Mott was elected to chair the American Equal Rights Association, and Stanton and Anthony worked to link women's suffrage with black male suffrage. When the 14th and 15th Amendments failed to address women's rights, Mott's American Equal Rights Association split into two factions. The New-York based National Woman Suffrage Association, founded by Stanton and Anthony accepted only women to its ranks and opposed the 15th Amendment. The American Woman Suffrage Association, centered in Boston and created by Lucy Stone and Julia Ward Howe, included men and supported black suffrage. These organizations and the Seneca Falls Convention not only formed the basis of the women's suffrage movement, which labored into the twentieth century to secure the vote, but were the precursors of later women's movements that worked toward achieving the legal and social equality of the sexes.

The California Gold Rush Begins (1849)

The event: On Monday, January 24, 1848, James Marshall, an employee of Northern California rancher John Sutter, found gold in Sutter's millrace, setting in motion events that would lead to the great California Gold Rush.

FOR CENTURIES SPAIN had looked for gold in the American West, but it fell to a bankrupt German merchant fleeing his creditors in the Fatherland to realize at

last the dreams of the conquistadors. Johann August Sutter arrived in California in 1838 having twice tried his luck with the Santa Fe trade and having twice gone bust. Determined, like most Westerners, to start over and get rich, he built an extensive ranching enterprise in the future state of California's as yet unsettled, incredibly fertile central valley.

One might think that James Marshall's discovery of gold at Sutter's mill on the American River would have been the answer to Sutter's dream; instead, it ruined him. The United States, which was ceded all of California shortly afterward as a result of the Mexican War, refused to recognize Sutter's claim to the land around the mill, which he had leased from the Indians for a bit of food and a few items of clothing. Within six weeks, Sutter's entire staff had abandoned his stores, farms, ranches, and mills to join every local inhabitant except the sick and the lame looking for gold in the American River's south fork.

But it was a loud-mouthed, big, and burly Mormon elder named Sam Brannan who truly sparked the gold rush. Brannan had sailed a shipload of Latter-Day Saints around Cape Horn to a little northern California seaport called Yerba Buena ("good herb") hoping to establish a colony in the town—which was renamed San Francisco the following year. But Brannan fell afoul of Brigham Young, who had his own plans for a Mormon empire in the Great Salt Lake Valley of the American Desert. In 1848, Brannan visited Young in Utah, Young excommunicated him, and Brannan returned to run a newspaper he had started in California. On the way back, he stayed over at Sutter's Mill and heard about the gold.

When Brannan reached San Francisco, he discovered that his *California Star* was playing down the discovery of gold as a wild rumor. His clothes still dirty from the trip, his mane of black hair still unwashed, he rushed through the streets of the town waving a quinine bottle full of yellow dust and bellowing, "Gold! Gold! Gold from the American River!" Within a fortnight, San Francisco's population had fallen from several thousand to a few dozen: stores and shops closed as workmen and clerks simply dropped what they were doing and left for the south fork. Houses sat next to deserted fields, empty and locked. Come midsummer, Brannan was supplying some four thousand miners with picks, shovels, and pans from a brand-new store he had built right next to Sutter's Mill.

Perhaps as much as a quarter of a million dollars in gold was taken from California soil in 1848. It arrived in San Francisco in bottles and buckskin bags, old tins and beat-up shoes, and much of it was shipped East around the tip of South America in ships that stopped along the way at ports of call in Hawaii, Mexico, Peru, and Chile. Experienced South American miners set sail up the coast. Crowds clogged the docks of Hawaii, filling to the brim every ship bound for San Francisco. Mexicans by the thousands trekked overland from the mining fields of Sonora or shipped out of Mazatlan. By year's end, the number of miners swelled to some ten thousand, and prices skyrocketed.

Stories of golden nuggets waiting to be gathered by the handful and river beds "paved with gold to the thickness of a hand" reached the rest of the United States in late 1848, after the rush was on. But when President James K. Polk—in an address to Congress in December—gave official sanction to the tales of easy money, it reached historic proportions, becoming known ever after as the California Gold Rush of 1849. The '49ers poured out of Atlantic seaboard cities, midwestern villages, and southern plantations, somewhere between eighty and a hundred thousand of them, abysmally ignorant of the geography they were to traverse and the actual conditions they would encounter. Maybe a fifth arrived by ship from the Far East and Australia, from Latin America and western Europe, but the rest came from virtually every county east of the Rockies. Some simply hitched up their farm wagons and headed west. Others, aiming for speed, made complicated travel plans by sea and land across lower Mexico and the Isthmus of Panama. Those on the Eastern Seaboard clambered aboard sleek clippers, jury-rigged hulks, coastal freighters, fishing smacks, even river steamers for the thirteen-thousand-mile voyage around the Horn.

San Francisco was suddenly a major seaport, with more ships ashore than were anchored in most of the world's other harbors. Some of the deserted boats were run aground and leased as stores and hotels; others quickly disappeared under the ambitious land-fill programs of rapacious real-estate promoters. Each day, thirty new houses sprang up to meet the needs of a population that would exceed 50,000 by the time the rush began to sputter. These newcomers, mostly young men and a few prostitutes, were virtually all heavily armed, hard-drinking, hopeless gamblers. They filled the city's more than 500 bars and 1,000 betting dens and made San Francisco a wide-open town where life was cheap but eggs went for six dollars a dozen. (That was still better than the three dollars *apiece* they brought at the diggings.)

Out in the gold fields, a few '49ers grew rich, but most of them simply grew disillusioned. When they realized that their high hopes for quick fortunes and the good life were doomed, they looked for somebody to blame. They settled on "foreigners"—Indians, South Americans, Frenchmen, Mexicans, the Chinese. The first three were subjected to various restrictions, even mob violence, but the Chinese and Mexicans were the favorite scapegoats. The Chinese, many of whom had fled a series of famines in China in the 1840s, still clung to their centuries-old culture, with its traditional dress and the clannish fraternal organizations called "tongs." And the Mexicans had, even worse, the audacity to go to war with the United States. In 1850, the infant California legislature passed a series of special taxes that forbade the Chinese from working any mining district before the "Americans" had abandoned it; persecution of Mexicans became so harsh that in the early 1850s they simply ceased their annual migrations north.

The truth was, of course, that fortunes didn't lie around on the ground waiting for someone to pick them up, and by 1852—when gold production soared to an annual high of $81 million—most of the "placer," or surface, gold was gone and large scale mechanized mining companies had replaced many of the individual prospectors. The ultimate irony was that so few of the great American fortunes launched by the gold rush came from even the large scale mining of gold.

Collis Huntington and Mark Hopkins made their money cornering the market in shovels and blasting powder, taking most of what the '49ers did not throw away at the gaming tables, in the saloons, or on loose women. Teamed with prospector-cum-shopkeeper Charles Crocker and mining-camp grocer Leland Stanford, they would become California's Big Four, flinging railroad tracks across half a continent. John Studebaker used the $8,000 he saved making wheelbarrows for miners to launch his family's modest Indiana wagon works on a decade of expansion that transformed it into America's largest and best known carriage maker. A silk-hatted Bavarian named Levi Strauss changed the way Westerners dressed when he patented the use of copper rivets to reinforce the seams of trousers he made for miners from single bolts of canvas tenting. Philip D. Armour dug ditches for day wages until he saved enough to open a butcher shop in the gold fields, returning, after the rush, to Milwaukee to create America's foremost slaughterhouse. And the immensely successful Wells Fargo organization, founded by two Easterners who visited the West only once, grew from a modest attempt to supply miners using a few mule trains.

The California Gold Rush lasted hardly a decade; it produced a much smaller yield than future strikes in Nevada, the Dakotas, and the Colorado Rockies. But it provided the model for all the gold rushes that followed—and it became a seminal event in American history. By mid-century California's population had swollen to a quarter of a million greedy souls clamoring for statehood, which President Zachery Taylor—eager to avoid the controversy over extending slavery in the territories—proposed to grant directly as a part of the Compromise of 1850. But more importantly, the individual shovel-and-pan enterprise of the California Gold Rush yielded, within a few short years, a consolidated, concentrated heavy industry that put the American West at the forefront of nineteenth-century development.

The West's big mining companies would expose whole stream beds, divert entire rivers, even blast mountains apart to satisfy their thirst for profit. The huge, gaping holes—artificial canyons often 500 feet deep—were testimony to the central role in western migration played by the extractive capitalist (whose credo,to quote historian Patricia Limerick, was "get in, get rich, get out"). The western adventure had a new protagonist, one no longer dressed in the genteel, eighteenth-century garb of the independent property holder. The 49er seeking an overnight fortune had replaced the yeoman farmer looking for a dignified plot of land as the West's cultural icon. Land hunger gave way to the lust for profit.

Congress Reaches the Compromise of 1850

The event: Threatened by mounting regional tensions over whether new territories should be admitted with or without slavery, Congress, in 1850, hammered out a compromise that staved off civil war for one more decade.

THE DISCOVERY OF gold in California in 1848 brought to a boil long-simmering sectional differences over slavery. More than eighty thousand people from the eastern states and territories flooded into California during 1849 alone, making the establishment of a territorial government an urgent necessity. The question of whether territories and new states would be slave-holding or free had been settled—the nation thought—by the Missouri Compromise of 1820, which prohibited slavery in all parts of the Louisiana Purchase north of the latitude of 36 degrees, 30 minutes. Then, in 1846, David Wilmot, congressman from Pennsylvania, introduced an amendment to a bill appropriating $2 million to facilitate negotiations with Mexico for "territorial adjustments" as a way of bringing an end to the Mexican War. His amendment—the Wilmot Proviso, as it came to be called—would have prohibited slavery in any land acquired by the United States as a result of the war. In opposition to the proviso, South Carolina senator John C. Calhoun proposed four resolutions, during February 19 and 20, 1847, that articulated the South's position with regard to slavery. Calhoun proposed that the territories were the common and joint property of the states; that Congress, as agent for the states, had no right to make laws discriminating between the states and depriving any state of its full and equal right in any territory acquired by the United States; that the enactment of any national law pertaining to slavery would be a violation of the Constitution and states' rights; that the people had the right to form their state governments as they chose, the Constitution imposing no conditions for the admission of a state except that its government should be republican. Calhoun warned that failure to maintain a balance between the interests of the South and those of the North would result in "political revolution, anarchy, civil war, and widespread disaster," threatening that "if trampled upon," the South would resist.

During the next three years, various compromises on the issue of slavery in new territories and states were proposed, including an extension of the line drawn by the Missouri Compromise across the full breadth of the continent. But the atmosphere in the Congress and in the country itself had changed since 1820, when the Missouri Compromise had been hammered out. Most Northerners were no longer willing to allow slavery to extend into any territory, no matter whether it lay above or below the compromise line. Faced with a widening gulf of irreconcilable positions, Senator Lewis Cass of Michigan proposed that territories should be organized without mention of slavery. Then, when the territory wrote its own constitution in preparation for admission to statehood, the citizens of the territory would decide for themselves whether to be free or slave. Called "popular sovereignty," the concept held great appeal for President Zachary Taylor, who was faced with the decision of what to do about California. He proposed that popular sovereignty be allowed to run its course and that California should be admitted directly as a state. The controversy of whether slavery would be allowed in California would be avoided, since no territorial government would be set up and since the state of California would determine the issue for itself.

Southern states were horrified by Taylor's proposal. They reasoned that since not only California but also New Mexico would doubtless organize themselves as free states, the balance of slave versus free states as represented in the Senate would be destroyed. Some compensation was required, and the venerable Henry Clay, who had been among the framers of the Missouri Compromise, worked with Senator Daniel Webster to devise a plan that would satisfy the South. California would be admitted to the Union as a free state. Other territories in the Southwest would be organized without mention of slavery. The slave trade in the District of Columbia would be abolished, but the federal government would pass a strong fugitive slave law to prevent escaped slaves from being declared free.

The final leg of the complicated compromise called for the federal government's assumption of debts Texas incurred before it was annexed to the United States.

The Compromise of 1850 was subjected to excruciatingly protracted negotiation and debate. The compromise pleased no one absolutely, but it offered North and South sufficient concessions to preserve the union for another tense decade as extremists on both sides slid exorably toward civil war. Ardent abolitionists saw the new Fugitive Slave Law as caving in to southern pressures. With the admission of California as a free state, and the likely admission of New Mexico and Utah as free states in the future, southern states' rights fanatics saw looming the certain end of any power they had in Congress.

Harriet Beecher Stowe Publishes *Uncle Tom's Cabin* (1852)

The event: In 1852, a novel entitled *Uncle Tom's Cabin, or Life Among the Lowly*, was published. It was to do more than any other piece of writing, whether political treatise or newspaper editorial, to promote popular support for abolition.

WRITTEN BY HARRIET Beecher Stowe, a homemaker in Brunswick, Maine, the novel told the story of Tom, Eliza, and Eva, slaves under the supervision of Simon Legree, the evil plantation overseer from New England. Stowe reported later that she had been moved to write the book after the passage of the Fugitive Slave Act, a bill included as part of the Compromise of 1850, giving slave owners the right to pursue slaves who had run away to free states or territories.

First published serially in the *National Era*, the book publication of *Uncle Tom's Cabin* was an immediate commercial success, selling ten thousand copies in one week and three hundred thousand nationally within a year. Translated into dozens of languages—it sold two million copies worldwide during its first year—the novel was also adapted for the New York stage, where it was performed eighteen times a week. The publication of an anti-slavery book by a woman had another important result, in that it created a legitimate place for women in the abolition movement.

Southerners were outraged by *Uncle Tom's Cabin* and its immediate popularity. They claimed that Stowe had no knowledge of slavery as it existed in the South and that she had exaggerated the mistreatment of slaves. Northerners, on the other hand, discounted southern criticism as biased, and thousands of people who had been undecided over the issue flocked to the abolition movement. When Abraham Lincoln met Mrs. Stowe, he reportedly called her "the little lady who wrote the book that made this big war!"

Congress Passes the Kansas-Nebraska Act (1854)

The event: In 1854, Congress passed the Kansas-Nebraska Act, throwing the decision of whether to allow slavery into territories seeking statehood back to the respective territories. The move caused border warfare to erupt in Kansas and brought yet closer the likelihood of armed conflict.

IN 1850 CONGRESS had averted disaster by shuffling once more to delay the national showdown over slavery. But the Compromise of 1850 was a last-ditch effort. It more or less gutted the Missouri Compromise, which had kept the country together for thirty years, and made the coming battle seem to many to be inevitable. When the territories of Nebraska and Kansas applied for statehood in 1854, Congress collectively threw up its hands, officially repealed the Missouri Compromise, and passed the Kansas-Nebraska Act, which left the question of slavery up to the "popular sovereignty" of the settlers in the two territories.

The act spawned the Republican party and led U.S. Senator David P. Atchison of Missouri, who had already broken with his hoary and respected fellow Senator Thomas H. Benton over slavery, to swear that he would let the territory "sink in hell" before allowing it to be organized as a free-soil state. Nebraskans, clearly, would opt for freedom, but Kansas was up for grabs. Abolitionists in the North organized the Emigrant Aid Society and financed free settlers in Kansas. New England authors like William Cullen Bryant and John Greenleaf Whittier mounted one of history's great propaganda campaigns, quickly aided by newspaperman Horace Greeley and correspondents sent by Eastern papers to report on the Kansas-Missouri "situation."

In response, fearing and hating the "Yankee slave-stealers" and egged on by Atchison, thousands of pro-slavery Missourians, mainly from the tobacco- and hemp-growing western counties, flooded into Kansas to vote illegally and then return home to their farms. Overwhelming the Kansas settlers, the majority of whom were probably free-soilers, they elected a territorial legislature that immediately legalized slavery and won official recognition from the federal government. Free-soilers poured in from Iowa to settle the land, formed their own legislature, set their capital up at Lawrence, and petitioned Congress for admission as a free state. Open warfare broke out along the Kansas-Missouri border.

Atchison resigned his seat in the Senate to lead the fight, organized a posse of Missourians, and—in the guise of answering a U.S. marshal's summons—raided Lawrence. Called afterward "border ruffians" by Horace Greeley, the posse set fire to a hotel and a few houses, chopped up a printing press, arrested several free-state leaders, and killed three others in the process. A monomaniacal abolitionist named John Brown retaliated by murdering five pro-slavery settlers on the Pottawatimie Creek, then mutilating their bodies. Ideologically motivated assassination had begun.

By the time the federal government could join with the governments of Missouri and Kansas to bring the guerilla fighting in "Bleeding Kansas" more or less to an end in 1858, two hundred people were dead and $2 million worth of property had gone up in smoke.

The Republican Party Is Founded (1854)

The event: With the dissolution of the old Whig Party, the Republican Party was established in 1854.

AFTER THE PASSAGE of the Kansas-Nebraska Act, the Whig Party lost favor among northern and western voters. Northerners were incensed when Whigs in

Congress acquiesced to Senator Stephen Douglas's proposal to repeal the part of the Missouri Compromise that banned slavery north of the 36°30' line. Instead of that artificial boundary, Douglas proposed that popular sovereignty be allowed to run its course in the new territories to be established in the West. In the place of the discredited Whig Party, the Republican Party, which had been established in a series of political meetings in the upper Midwest, rapidly developed. Early members of the party included former Free-Soilers, Conscience Whigs, and Anti-Nebraska Democrats, all of whom were united in their opposition to the expansion of slavery into the territories. Before long, the party spread from the states of the Old Northwest Territory to New England. In the congressional elections of 1854, the new party won more than a hundred seats in the House of Representatives. By the time of the next presidential election, the party was ready with a candidate, John C. Frémont, and a slogan, "Free soil, free speech, and Frémont." Although Frémont lost the election to Democrat James Buchanan, the party made a good showing, carrying eleven of sixteen northern states.

The most important contest for the Republicans in 1858 was in Illinois, where Senator Stephen A. Douglas was running for re-election against the Republicans' candidate, Abraham Lincoln. A former member of the Illinois state legislature and United States congressman, Lincoln challenged Douglas to a series of debates that captured the attention of the national press. The strategies of the protagonists were to exaggerate the differences between them. Douglas tried to portray Lincoln as a radical abolitionist; Lincoln tried to portray Douglas as favoring slavery. In reality, the candidates were more similar than dissimilar. Both favored banning slavery in the territories, but neither thought it possible to abolish slavery by political action. Douglas ultimately won the election, in part because of his stance—known as the "Freeport Doctrine"—on the Dred Scott decision. In explaining his position on the Supreme Court ruling, Douglas maintained that a territory could exclude slavery before it became a state by declining to enact the laws that were required for slavery to exist.

Although the Republicans lost the Senate seat for Illinois, elsewhere they made great gains. The North swung heavily to the Republican Party, further discomfiting the South, where radicals soon claimed that if a Republican were elected president in 1860 they would secede from the Union. That Republican, of course, would be Abraham Lincoln, and secession, followed by war, would indeed come.

Frederick Law Olmsted Designs Central Park (1856)

The event: In 1856, the thirty-four-year-old landscape architect Frederick Law Olmsted was hired by the city of New York to supervise the clearing of more than a hundred acres of swampy, hog-infested, shanty-blighted land at what was then the north end of the city. The project was the origin of one of the world's greatest city parks.

THE YEAR AFTER Olmsted commenced the clearing and drainage project, the city leaders announced a design competition for a new Central Park to occupy the site. In collaboration with prominent architect Calvert Vaux, Olmsted entered the contest with a design that incorporated a formal mall area lined by elm trees and acres of more rough, "natural" landscapes, planted with several million trees, shrubs, and plants. The Olmsted-Vaux design was selected from among thirty-three entries.

Although Olmsted was a student and advocate of the Romantic, or picturesque, school of design, which emphasized informal and natural settings, the "natural" look was the product of meticulous design. "Every foot of the park's surface," Olmsted later wrote, "every tree and bush, as well as every arch, roadway, and walk has been fixed where it is with a purpose." Olmsted's work, not only in Central Park but in Brooklyn, with Prospect Park, and Chicago, with Washington and Jackson parks, was instrumental in bringing about park movements in many of America's cities and a national park movement, culminating in the creation of the first national park, Yellowstone, and the National Park System. It is difficult for New Yorkers to imagine their city without Central Park; indeed, Manhattan would present a brutal, unrelieved urban landscape without it. More importantly, it is difficult to imagine the American scene without the influence of Olmsted. For without well-planned, graceful parks, it, too, would be a far harsher place in which to live.

Albert Bierstadt Paints the West (1858)

The event: In 1858, Albert Bierstadt joined General Frederick W. Lander in an expedition to survey a wagon road from Fort Laramie to the Pacific, a journey that would provide the great mythologizer of the American West the first taste of the subject matter he spent a lifetime painting.

ALTHOUGH HE WAS born in Germany in 1830, Albert Bierstadt grew up in America, having immigrated with his parents to New Bedford, Massachusetts, when he was only a year old. By age twenty, Bierstadt was teaching art and exhibiting his own crayon landscapes. Like many would-be American artists, Bierstadt was unable to find satisfactory training in the States, so in 1853 he left for Düsseldorf, Germany, to study at the city's famous academy, which specialized in teaching landscape painting in the grandest of grand traditions. Returning to the United States in 1857, he painted scenes of New England's White Mountains and then, in 1858, returned from the Lander expedition with studies for his first great Rocky Mountain landscapes, which caused an instant sensation.

It was not just that Bierstadt was such an accomplished technician, but that he managed to imbue his paintings, gigantic canvases that were always based on firsthand observation, with his sublime imagination, creating a nearly religious aura, the sense that these western landscapes were nothing less than paradise on earth, God's country. It is no accident that the height of Bierstadt's enormous popularity coincided with the post-Civil War years of westward expansion, the period that saw the Homestead Act and the completion of the transcontinental railroad. Bierstadt helped create the mythology that drew European immigrants as well as eastern settlers and eastern money to the West. His art contributed as much to westward expansion as any trail or railroad.

At the height of his fame, Albert Bierstadt was the most highly paid artist in the world. He built a castle-like studio in Irvington, New York, overlooking the lordly Hudson River, where he transformed the on-site sketches made during various western journeys into finished paintings. But as Bierstadt's fortunes rose with the tide of westward movement, so they declined by the close of the 1880s, when the last of the cheap, arable public lands had been spoken for and the romance of the western paradise had dimmed.

As if to herald the artist's decline, his Irvington studio burned in 1882 (some think the financially faltering Bierstadt set the blaze deliberately). The American Committee for the 1889 Paris Exposition rejected his entry, *The Last of the Buffalo*, as too old-fashioned, and, four years later, his *Landing of Columbus* was turned down for display at the World's Columbian Exposition in Chicago. Bierstadt died in 1902, poor and forgotten. Today his titanic canvases, which rarely reach the marketplace, fetch record-breaking prices.

The Supreme Court Hands Down the Dred Scott Decision (1857)

The event: In 1857, at the height of the bloodletting in Kansas occasioned by the Kansas-Nebraska Act, the U.S. Supreme Court entered the controversy by addressing the question of Congress's power over slavery in the territories, the question at issue in the Dred Scott case.

A ST. LOUIS SLAVE, Dred Scott had been trying to win his freedom through the courts. Scott had belonged to John Emerson, an Army surgeon, who was stationed first in Illinois, then in the Wisconsin Territory, and finally in Missouri. Scott accompanied Emerson to each new station until the surgeon's death in 1846. Scott then sued Emerson's widow for his freedom, claiming that he was a citizen of Missouri and free by virtue of his travels with Emerson in Illinois, where slavery was banned by the Northwest Ordinance, and in the Wisconsin Territory, where slavery was banned by the Missouri Compromise. When the state court decided against him, he and his lawyers appealed to the Supreme Court.

Sentiment among the justices was almost evenly split. Antislavery judges John McLean of Ohio and Benjamin R. Curtis of Massachusetts believed that Scott should be freed because of the Missouri Compromise, which stipulated that slavery could not exist north of the 36°30' latitude. Southern justices hoped that the court's ruling would nullify the Missouri Compromise.

Chief Justice Roger B. Taney ruled first that neither free blacks nor enslaved blacks were citizens and so could not sue in federal courts. The justice also ruled that the Illinois law banning slavery had no force over Scott and his owners after he returned to Missouri, where slavery was allowed. In addition, the Court ruled that the Wisconsin Territory laws had no force either, because the Missouri Compromise that outlawed slavery in the territory was unconstitutional. The Court based its ruling on the Fifth Amendment, which prohibits the government from depriving an individual of property and liberty without due process of law. The justices saw any law that deprived an individual of property solely because the owner had taken his property into a different territory as a violation of the Fifth Amendment.

Politically, the Dred Scott decision had an immediate impact. Republicans, struggling to get their new political party on sound footing, viewed the ruling as an attempt by southern justices to destroy them. Northern and western Democrats saw the ruling as an attack on the policy of popular sovereignty. Northern abolitionists saw the ruling as an attempt by the Supreme Court, a majority of whose justices were from the South, to extend slavery. To the utter amazement of the abolitionists, the court had invoked the Bill of Rights in a ruling that denied freedom to a black slave. For the southern slaveowners, the decision implied that slavery was safe—and according to their reading should be protected—everywhere in the nation.

In short, the Dred Scott decision changed the terms of the national debate on slavery and made the Civil War inevitable. From an argument over how the West should be settled, it became a battle over the nature of property itself.

William Smith Strikes Oil Near Titusville, Pennsylvania (1859)

The event: On August 27, 1859, Edwin L. Drake and the drilling expert he had hired, William Smith, struck oil near Titusville, Pennsylvania, touching off an oil boom that created the American oil industry.

OIL, IN THE form of animal tallow and whale oil, had been used in America since colonial days for lubricating wagon axles, for medicine, and for illumination by burning the material in oil lamps. So-called rock oil, a kerosene product distilled from surface shale rocks, was also used for illumination. In early nineteenth-century America the preferred illuminating oil was from whales, but, by mid-century, that mammal was being hunted if not to extinction, at least to scarcity—and the price of whale oil was becoming prohibitive.

At about this time, John Austin, a New York businessman, learned of a new Austrian lamp that burned kerosene cleanly and effectively. Austin perfected the Austrian prototype and marketed it in the United States, thereby creating a greater need for kerosene refined from shale oil. Various oil companies went into business during the late 1850s, among them the Pennsylvania Rock Oil Company of Connecticut, which was founded by George H. Bissell, a New York attorney, and James Townsend, a businessman from New Haven. Learning that large amounts of oil were floating on water near Titusville, Pennsylvania, the two men secured a sample and took it to Professor Benjamin Silliman of Yale University, who declared that it would make a very good illuminating substance. Bissell and Townsend purchased some Titusville property, set up their company, and hired Edwin Drake to find the oil. Acting on the advice of William Smith, Drake sunk a well and, at a depth of sixty-nine feet, struck oil. Drake's Titusville well was the first time that oil was drilled for and tapped at its source.

An oil boom followed hard upon Drake's discovery, and cheap petroleum products quickly ousted expensive whale oil as the illuminant of choice. Titusville and other Pennsylvania towns sprouted dozens, then hundreds of wells. By 1884, drilling had gone nationwide. Entrepreneurs rushed to grab their pieces of the action, most notably and most successfully John D. Rockefeller, who realized that gaining maximum profits from the new industry meant controlling not only exploration and drilling, but also refining and transporting the product.

Rich as the oil industry became from developing lighting, heating, lubricating, and other products, the rapid emergence of the automobile as a pervasive feature of American life early in the twentieth century made it far richer. Soon, however, American demand for oil outstripped the nation's own supplies, and the United States was forced to turn more and more to imported oil, with all of its economic and political complications.

John Brown Raids Harpers Ferry (1859)

The event: On October 16, 1859, the radical abolitionist John Brown led a raid with twenty-one followers against Harpers Ferry, Virginia, in an effort to obtain arms for a slave rebellion, an action that catapulted him into martyrdom and finally crystallized sentiment in the South that secession from the Union was inevitable.

BROWN BEGAN PLANNING his attack in 1857, after moving to Boston from Kansas, where he had served as self-appointed "captain" of violent anti-slavery forces. (In 1856, with a band of six men, including four of his sons, Brown had raided the proslavery settlement on Pottawatomie Creek and had murdered five settlers. After the Pottawatomie Massacre, fighting spread, and more than two hundred people were killed by the end of the year.) In Boston, Brown became associated with six noted abolitionists, Samuel

Gridley Howe, Thomas Wentworth Higginson, Theodore Parker, Franklin Sanborn, George L. Stearns, and Gerrit Smith, who raised funds for Brown, bought guns, and supplied his family with a house. Brown developed his plans to take the federal arsenal at Harpers Ferry and use the guns and ammunition to arm slaves for a rebellion. From his headquarters on a rented farm, his band of guerilla fighters invaded Harpers Ferry, captured the federal arsenal, and cut telegraph wires. Some of the fighters spread throughout the area to raid plantations, take owners hostage, and free the slaves. On the morning of October 17, federal troops commanded by Colonel Robert E. Lee rushed to Harpers Ferry from Fredericksburg and Fort Monroe, and the following day they retook the arsenal, killing ten of Brown's men and taking Brown prisoner.

The state of Virginia charged Brown with treason, conspiracy, and murder. During his trial and after his conviction and execution by hanging, abolitionists made him a symbol of their efforts. On the day of Brown's execution, December 2, 1859, Ralph Waldo Emerson and William Lloyd Garrison memorialized him at a large gathering of abolitionists in Boston. While northern abolitionists took up the martyrdom of Brown as the new standard of their cause, southerners reacted to the raid with exaggerated alarm. For northerner and southerner alike, Brown's bloody raid—a harbinger of the horrific conflict to come—only served to strengthen the acrimonious forces already trying to tear the country apart. Discussion of compromise grew less and less common amid the acid talk that turned readily to violence. A collision course had been set, and fewer people than ever held any hope that the course might change.

The Pony Express Opens for Service (1860)

The event: On April 3, 1860, a lone rider carrying forty-nine letters and some special-edition newspapers, galloped out of St. Joseph, Missouri, astride a fresh mount on the inaugural ride of the Pony Express.

THE YEAR 1857 promised to be a great one for the western overland freighting firm of Russell, Majors & Waddell. It had government contracts for transporting

some five million pounds of goods, and it built up a fleet of wagons from five hundred to eight hundred. Then the so-called Mormon War exploded in the Southwest, and contracts were let for the transportation of an additional three million pounds of goods. Russell, Majors & Waddell paid premium prices for wagons and the men to drive them—but in this bonanza on top of bonanza, it would be well worth the risk.

What the firm hadn't reckoned on was Mormon sabotage—responsible for the destruction of three entire wagon trains—a crippling winter, and the vagaries of the War Department, which, claiming to have exhausted its appropriations, summarily defaulted on payment of contracts. Facing collapse, William H. Russell turned from slow freighting to express coaching as the company's salvation, proposing to carry passengers and mail in competition with the long-established Butterfield Overland Mail. To make the enterprise work, Russell had to demonstrate that his proposed "Central Route" was faster than Butterfield's "Southern Route." Russell, always a gambler and afflicted with a flair for high drama, proposed to deliver mail from St. Joseph, Missouri, western terminus of rail and stagecoach lines, to Sacramento, California, in ten days. The distance involved was just forty-four miles shy of an even two thousand, and that through the toughest country the continent had to offer. This service would carry mail only—no passengers—and, indeed, there would be no coaches. Just ponies, a relay of them stretching across the continent, and a lone rider on each: the Pony Express.

Johnny Fry would carry his load on the Pony Express's initial run some seventy-five miles to the first "home station," where another rider would relieve him. There were twenty-five such stations along the route. Since the horses were run at full gallop, they had to be changed more frequently than the riders—about every fifteen miles. One hundred sixty-five "relay stations" were set up for this purpose. Russell had purchased five hundred horses and had eighty riders continuously en route, forty westbound, forty eastbound. The riders had answered ads calling for "daring young men, preferably orphans."

The average Pony Express rider was nineteen (though Buffalo Bill Cody was only fifteen when he joined up, and one rider, David Jay, was thirteen), wiry (none weighing over 135 pounds), and capable of surviving long, hard rides and great danger. Pay was high—$50 to $150 a month plus room and board—in an age when a common laborer earned a dollar a day. The riders frequently performed prodigies of endurance. Buffalo Bill reached his home station at the end of his seventy-six-mile route only to find that his relief had been killed. Cody remounted and rode another eighty-five miles, then turned around and made the return trip—a total of 322 miles of riding in one day. Bob Haslan took a Paiute arrow through the arm and another through the jaw, but rode on for 120 miles in eight hours, ten minutes, using thirteen horses. In the nineteen months—and 650,000 miles—of its brief existence, the Pony Express lost only one mail.

The enterprise commanded the awe of the nation, becoming, like many other western endeavors, instantly legendary. But it was never profitable. The charge for delivery was five dollars per half-ounce (soon lowered to two dollars), but each letter *cost* the company sixteen dollars to deliver. Then, on October 24, 1861, a telegraph line from the East was joined to one from the West, and communication became a matter of seconds rather than days. The Pony Express was out of business—and would have been, even without the telegraph. For Russell, Majors & Waddell were galloping rapidly into bankruptcy, and Russell himself was about to be tried, convicted, and jailed for embezzling government funds in another desperate effort to save his firm from extinction.

The Civil War Breaks Out (1861)

The event: At 4:30 a.m. on April 12, 1861, a hot-headed South Carolina rebel fired on Fort Sumter, beginning four years of bloodshed and bitterness called the Civil War.

WHILE THE GENTRY of Charleston watched from that city's fashionable Battery, Confederate artillery bombarded the fort until Sumter commandant Major Robert Anderson, his ammunition exhausted, surrendered. He and his garrison were permitted to withdraw with full military honors. The first shot can be dated precisely, and so too the first battle, but the war really began decades earlier, as economic, social, political, and geographical differences between the people of the North and those of the South heated to a boil. With each new state added to the Union, bitter debate ensued over whether the state would be admitted with or without slavery. Political compromises in 1820 (the Missouri Compromise) and 1850 only postponed the inevitable armed conflict. But nobody dreamed just how horrible and costly the war would be: at least a half-million battle deaths, many more lives shattered by disfiguring wounds inflicted by the weapons of an industrial age, untold poverty, misery, anguish, illness, and, finally, the martyr's death of the Union's leader, Abraham Lincoln, the victim (absurdly enough) of an egomaniacal actor.

Although the population and industrial might of the North far outweighed the technology and numbers of men the South could muster, the cream of the U.S. Army officer corps felt allegiance to the southern states, and the Confederate forces were, in the main, more ably commanded than those of the North, especially early in the war. The Confederates stunned Union loyalists with victories at Bull Run (Manassas; July 21, 1861), the so-called Seven Days (during the Peninsular Campaign of Union commander George B. McClellan), the Second Battle of Bull Run (Second Manassas; August 29-30, 1862), Fredericksburg (December 13, 1862), and Chancellorsville (May 2-4, 1863).

It was not until Antietam (Sharpsburg), on September 17, 1862, that the Union was able to claim something approaching a victory—albeit one purchased at tremendous cost. The outcome of the battle gave the Union military effort sufficient credibility to enable Lincoln to issue, from what he felt was a position of strength, the preliminary Emancipation Proclamation, which brought the slavery issue to the fore of the conflict. For the Union, the Civil War now took on an added moral dimension, officially becoming more than a struggle to save the Union. It was now a crusade to abolish slavery. After General Robert E. Lee invaded Pennsylvania, Union forces under General George G. Meade turned back the Confederate army at Gettysburg (July 1-3, 1863), also at great cost. Gettysburg is usually cited as the turning point of the war in favor of the Union. Not only was an invading army repulsed and northern morale lifted, the southern defeat discouraged both England and France from supporting the Confederate cause.

Still, the war ground on. Union General Ulysses S. Grant scored important triumphs in the war's western theater, at Shiloh (April 6-7, 1862), Vicksburg (under siege from October 1862 to July 4, 1863), and Chattanooga (November 23-25, 1863). Union control of the lower Mississippi began with the victory of Admiral David Farragut, who captured New Orleans in April 1862. In 1864, after a series of mediocre commanding generals, Lincoln finally appointed Grant as the Union's general-in-chief. Slowly, inexorably, he forced Lee's army back toward the Confederate capital of Richmond, fighting the bitter Wilderness Campaign through May and June of 1864. Grant's chief lieutenant, General William Tecumseh Sherman, advanced, in the meantime, through Tennessee and Georgia to Atlanta, which he captured, occupied, and finally burned (September-November 1864) before continuing on his infamously destructive "march to the sea." Sherman, a brilliant strategist, introduced a concept that would become a terrifying hallmark of modern warfare. He called it "total war," by which he meant taking the battle not just to the opposing army but to the civilian population as well, reducing their will and their means to support the fight.

Yet the will of the South was not easy to break, and the bloody conflict refused to end. General Philip Sheridan defeated Confederate general George E. Pickett at Five Forts (April 1, 1865), and Grant took heavily fortified Petersburg after a long campaign that stretched from June 1864 to April 2, 1865, when Grant at last took Richmond. A week later, at Appomattox Courthouse, General Robert E. Lee surrendered his Army of Northern Virginia to General Grant, effectively ending the Civil War.

Healing the wounds of war and reuniting the nation were staggering tasks that would require the wise and charitable judgment and strong leadership of Abraham Lincoln. His assassination on April 14, 1865, was the crowning tragedy of this nightmarish conflict. The unpopular Andrew Johnson was thrust into office, and the process of Reconstruction became a vindictive and opportunistic struggle that greatly prolonged the sufferings of the South, retarding well into the twentieth century the region's economic recovery and, even worse, breeding a vicious and virulent strain of racism that has proven nearly as great a curse to the United States as slavery itself.

Congress Passes the Homestead Act (1862)

The event: On May 20, 1862, Abraham Lincoln signed into law the Homestead Act, authorizing any citizen (or immigrant who intended to become a citizen) to select any surveyed but unclaimed parcel of public land up to 160 acres, settle it, improve it, and, by living on it for five years, gain title to it.

WITH THE NATION in the midst of civil war, Lincoln hoped that rapid settlement of the West would strengthen what was left of the Union by creating an unbroken link between East and West. The Homestead Act was also formulated to encourage orderly settlement by families, instead of the abusive exploitation by land speculators, large ranchers, and others. Alternatively to living on the land for five years, a homesteader could "preempt" the land after six months' residence by purchasing it at the price of $1.25 per acre. The homesteader could also exercise preemption to augment his basic 160-acre claim, though few settlers could ante up the $50 for the minimum purchase of forty acres the government required. Another option for adding to the original grant was to make a "timber claim" by planting ten acres of timber-producing trees. This entitled the homesteader to an additional 160 acres.

The timber-claim incentive was important on the largely unforested western prairies, the hard-packed soil of which was not naturally conducive to the growth of trees. Indeed, had it not been for John Deere's recently developed steel plow, the stubborn prairie soil would have been largely worthless for farming, and the Homestead Act might have had few takers. As it was, the homesteaders soon earned a nickname that reflected the major element they had to contend with. They were called sodbusters.

One thing the hard earth did offer the sodbuster was a building material to substitute for the scarce lumber. Usually, the first sod structure a homesteader built was little more than a hole in the ground, called a dugout. A rectangle was laid out on a rising slope of land, and sod was excavated to a depth of about six feet. Next, using "bricks" cut from the sod, walls were raised to a height of two or three feet, and the structure was roofed over with boards or thatch and more sod. Later, as the family became more settled, they would build a more substantial house above ground, complete with windows, but still using sod for bricks. Soddies, as the houses were called, were filthy and suffered plagues of vermin, especially bedbugs, but they were warm and secure against the brutal forces of a prairie winter.

Although the Homestead Act was formulated expressly to avert the kinds of speculative abuses to which western land grants had traditionally been subject, the unscrupulous found ingenious loopholes in the law nevertheless. The law carefully specified that homesteaders could only secure their claim by constructing a house at least twelve by twelve, with windows. Some speculators perfected multiple claims by building such a house *on wheels*, so that it could be trundled from claim to claim. Others, noting that the language of the act's twelve-by-twelve provision failed to specify feet or inches, set miniature houses—twelve by twelve *inches* in plan, but complete with the requisite windows—on each of their claims. Individuals perpetrated such abuses, to be sure, but the greatest culprits were railroads and mining companies, which claimed and preempted land by means of "dummy entrymen" hired to file as if they were legitimate homesteaders.

Despite the hardships of prairie life and the abuses to which the law was subject, the Homestead Act opened the West to millions. The sodbuster was not really a new breed of westerner—after all, the farmer and his family had been following the solitary trapper, the bachelor soldier, and the trailblazer onto newly "opened" lands since Daniel Boone crossed the Appalachians into Kentucky. This time, however, they came with the official blessing of an American government touting the pioneer homestead as the cultural glue of a civilization stretching across the entire continent.

Abraham Lincoln Issues the Emancipation Proclamation (1863)

The event: On September 23, 1862, President Abraham Lincoln issued the Emancipation Proclamation—a dry, legalistic, timid little document that changed the course of the Civil War.

SLAVERY IS SUCH a manifest evil that it is difficult to sympathize with Abraham Lincoln's caution and delay in issuing the Emancipation Proclamation. Lincoln's letter to *New York Tribune* editor Horace Greeley, written on August 22, 1862, just before the president was ready to announce the Proclamation, might well have troubled his admirers. "If I could save the Union without freeing *any* slave I would do it, and if I could save it by freeing *all* the slaves I would do it; and if I could save it by freeing some and leaving others alone I would also do that."

That Lincoln personally hated slavery is beyond doubt, but as president, he was bound to abide by the Constitution, which protected slavery in slave states. He was also fearful that emancipation would alienate northern Democrats and send the four slave-holding border states into the embrace of the Confederacy. Lincoln therefore began cautiously. If he dared not simply free the slaves, he could seize them as enemy property—contraband of war—and refuse to return them to their owners. In August 1861, Congress made the contraband policy official, passing an act that conferred contraband status on all slaves who had been used in support of the Confederate war effort. In March of the next year, Congress passed legislation forbidding Army officers from returning any fugitive slaves. With these two acts, the Union moved closer to emancipation.

It was a series of Union defeats during the first half of 1862 that at last moved Lincoln's hand. Emancipation, which many northerners had come to see as a moral imperative, now appeared to be a military necessity as well. The South had to be deprived of as much of its labor force as possible. In July 1862, Congress passed a new and stronger confiscation act, which freed slaves who had belonged to owners engaged in rebellion, and a militia act, authorizing the president to use freed slaves in the army, as laborers or even soldiers.

Lincoln was now on the verge of declaring emancipation outright and was held back only by Secretary of State William H. Seward, who convinced the president that the Emancipation Proclamation would ring hollow in the absence of a Union military victory. When the Union declared a victory in the bloody and inconclusive Battle of Antietam, fought on September 17, 1862, Lincoln at once issued his "preliminary" proclamation, warning that the slaves living in states still in rebellion on January 1, 1863, would be declared "forever free." When the deadline passed, Lincoln issued the "final" proclamation, which explicitly committed the armed forces of the United States to liberate the slaves. Sweeping as the Emancipation Proclamation was, it nevertheless did not apply to slaves in the border states or to those in areas of the Confederacy presently under the control of the Union Army—for these areas were not "in rebellion" against the United States.

When the war was over, however, all the carnage needed to be "about" something, and the proclamation ensured that for most people it would be about slavery. And because the war was officially about slavery, the limitations of the Emancipation Proclamation itself could be overcome by the Thirteenth Amendment to the Constitution, which was passed by the Senate on April 8, 1864, and (after a struggle) by the House on January 31, 1865. By December 18, 1865, three-quarters of the states reunified by the war's end ratified the measure, which outlawed slavery throughout the nation forever.

John Wilkes Booth Assassinates Abraham Lincoln (1865)

The event: On April 14, 1865, an egomaniacal actor named John Wilkes Booth, embittered by the South's defeat in the Civil War, shot and killed President Abraham Lincoln. It was the first assassination of an American President.

IF A CABAL OF Baltimore conspirators had had their way, Abraham Lincoln would never have survived his inaugural train ride from Springfield, Illinois, to Washington in 1861. The nation's first private detective, Allan J. Pinkerton and his agents foiled this early assassination conspiracy, but throughout the war, security surrounding the president was appallingly lax as office seekers and other parasites routinely crowded the halls of the White House itself.

Late in 1864, matinee idol John Wilkes Booth, scion of America's most famous theatrical family, hatched a plot to kidnap Lincoln with the intention of exchanging him for Confederate prisoners of war. He gathered about him two friends from his Maryland boyhood, Michael O'Laughlin and Sam Arnold, in addition to George A. Atzerodt, David Herold, and John Surratt.

The plot was foiled when Lincoln failed to attend the theater that evening. Booth's black mood was deepened by the mounting din of celebration throughout Washington. Richmond fell, then Robert E. Lee surrendered. The curtain was ringing down on the great drama, and John Wilkes Booth had yet to play his part. There was no longer any point to kidnapping Lincoln in order to force a prisoner exchange, for the war was practically over. All that remained was assassination.

Booth sent Mrs. Surratt to Lloyd at the Surrattsville tavern her late husband had owned with a message to have the "guns" ready. (At her subsequent trial, Mrs. Surratt claimed the word was "things," not "guns.") In the two or three days prior to Good Friday, April 14, the day set for the assassination, Booth began drinking heavily. Of his original band, only Herold, and Atzerodt were left. They were joined by a former Confederate soldier who called himself Lewis Paine, but whose real name was Louis Thornton Powell. Atzerodt was assigned to kill Vice-President Andrew Johnson. Paine and Herold would do in Secretary of State William H. Seward, who was convalescing from serious injuries sustained in a carriage accident. Booth would kill Lincoln.

Atzerodt backed out and didn't try to kill Johnson. While Herold held his horse, Paine attacked Seward, failing to kill him but making a bloody mess: Seward was clubbed and stabbed; his son Augustus was injured, as was his daughter Fanny; a State Department messenger named Hansell was stabbed, along with one Sergeant Robinson, a male nurse.

In the meantime, John Wilkes Booth entered the president's box at Ford's Theater about ten p.m. of that Good Friday evening. By coincidence, the lock on the door of the box had been broken only a few days earlier; nobody bothered to report it, let alone fix it. Nor had Booth met with any challenge from the men who should have been guarding the president. He leveled his derringer between Lincoln's left ear and spine. He squeezed the trigger.

Few among the 1,675 members of the audience heard the shot. Even Mary Todd Lincoln, seated next to her husband, and Major Henry Rathbone, seated in the presidential box with his fiancée, were not much startled by the dull report of the derringer. Booth, who was very familiar with the script of the evening's comedy, *Our American Cousin*, had timed his shot to coincide with the play's biggest laugh—just after Harry Hawk, playing Mr. Trenchard, said, "Wal, I guess I know enough to turn you inside out, you sockdologizing old mantrap!"

Booth delivered his own line—"Sic semper tyrannis!"—just after he leapt from the box onto the stage. As he jumped, he caught his right spur in the Treasury Regiment flag that festooned the box. His left foot took the full shock of his fall, breaking just above the instep. Booth limped into the wings, fell, recovered, and lopingly ran offstage. That he slipped out of the city so easily became a scandal to the forces guarding Washington.

The conspirators retrieved the weapons they had deposited at the tavern and rode on in search of a doctor to treat the actor's broken leg. Dr. Samuel A. Mudd, who had introduced Booth to John Surratt on December 23, 1864, was, like many Marylanders, loyal neither to the North or South. At his subsequent trial, Mudd claimed not even to have recognized Booth when, acting (he said) only as a good samaritan, he splinted his broken leg at four o'clock on the morning of April 15.

Booth and Herold did not cross the Potomac until April 22. (Ferryman George Atzerodt was supposed to meet them on the 21st, but failed to.) Two days later, Booth and Herold made it over the Rappahannock, about twenty miles below Fredericksburg, Virginia.

All this time, a large, if motley, assortment of soldiers, policemen, and hired investigators were combing the countryside in pursuit of the conspirators. A detachment dispatched by General Lafayette C. Baker, controversial head of a small band of federal agents grandiosely dubbed the National Detective Police, and under the direct command of Baker's cousin Luther and Lieutenant Colonel Everton Conger, tracked Booth and Herold to the Garrett family's Virginia tobacco barn after midnight on April 26. After William Garrett parleyed with the two conspirators, Herold gave himself up, but Booth refused to surrender, whereupon the troopers set fire to the shed. Silhouetted against the flames was a man with crutch and carbine. Someone—the soldier who claimed credit was Sergeant Boston Corbett—fired a shot that passed through the actor's neck. Others say Booth shot himself.

They dragged him out of the burning structure and laid him on the porch of the Garrett house. Booth was paralyzed.

"I thought I did for the best," he gasped out. Then he asked someone to lift his hands for him, so that he might look at them. This was done. He gazed at his hands.

"Useless, useless."

These were his last words.

If Booth had meant Lincoln's death as an act of vengeance on behalf of the South, it hardly served to help the post war situation of southern whites. Lincoln's continued leadership would have most likely promised a policy of healing. With Lincoln gone, radical Republicans in Congress took over the process of Reconstruction, pushing much faster for enfranchisement of recently freed slaves than Lincoln would have. Booth's act not only deprived the entire nation of a great man, it condemned the South to a very hard, slow road of postwar recovery. Southern whites stubbornly resisted social change imposed by Congressional fiat, and radical Republicans saw only evidence of further sedition in the white resistance.

The Fourteenth Amendment Is Ratified (1866)

The event: In 1866, a Congress determined to carry through its plan for "Reconstruction" following the Civil War—a plan bitterly opposed by the defeated South—passed the Fourteenth Amendment. In time, the article would play a revolutionary role in American society far beyond its immediate extension of the franchise to former African-American slaves.

FIVE DAYS AFTER General Robert E. Lee surrendered at Appomattox Court House, President Abraham Lincoln was assassinated while attending a performance of *Our American Cousin* at Ford's Theater in Washington, D.C. With his death, Andrew Johnson came to office determined to treat the recently defeated Confederacy as mildly as Lincoln had apparently intended. The radical Republicans who controlled Congress, however, were wary of the new president, a Democrat (the Democratic party had been considered a vehicle of sedition throughout the war) and a southerner himself.

When Johnson proposed readmitting the rebel states to full partnership in the Union as soon as they had ratified the Thirteenth Amendment abolishing slavery and elected congressional representatives, Congress balked. Members refused to seat the predictably all-white slates of newly elected southern senators and representatives. Instead, the House and the Senate formed a Joint Committee on Reconstruction and named Senator William P. Fessenden of Maine to head it. While the committee conducted public hearings, many of which focused on the mistreatment of blacks in the South, Congress passed a bill to extend the Freedmen's Bureau and passed a Civil Rights Act, which stated that blacks were citizens of the United States and that no state could restrict their rights to testify in court or to own property. Johnson vetoed both measures, but Congress overrode the vetoes. April 9, 1866, the date on which Congress overrode the veto of the Civil Rights Act, marked a shift in the direction of Reconstruction. Congress had wrestled control of the process from the president.

Two months after the Civil Rights Bill became law, Congress passed and submitted to the states the Fourteenth Amendment to the Constitution. The five-part amendment defined American citizenship as including everyone "born or naturalized in the United States." It barred the states from passing laws "which shall abridge the privileges or immunities of citizens of the United States." The third part of the amendment stipulated that if states prohibited any part of their population from voting, then their representation in Congress would be proportionally decreased. The last two sections of the amendment dealt with southerners exclusively, among other things prohibiting former Confederates from holding state or federal offices unless pardoned by Congress.

The only southern state to ratify the amendment was Tennessee. Angered by the South's recalcitrance, Congress then passed a series of Reconstruction Acts. The first, enacted on March 2, 1867, put all of the South except Tennessee under military government, with a major general in charge of each state. The only way a state could shed military rule was by ratifying a new state constitution that included provisions for the black enfranchisement and for the disenfranchisement of ex-Confederates. Congressional approval of the new constitution and the state's ratification of the Fourteenth Amendment were required before a state would be readmitted.

Because the first Reconstruction Act was vague as to how the new state constitutions were to be drafted, Congress passed a second act that empowered the military to register voters in the southern states and to supervise the election of delegates to constitutional conventions. Once the constitutions were drafted, a majority of registered voters had to approve them. White southerners figured out a way to defeat the new constitutions: they simply refrained from voting. Congress then decided that approval by a majority of voters was all that was required for ratification, and between June 1868, with the admission of Arkansas, and July 1870, with the admission of Georgia, all the southern states had been brought reluctantly back into the Union.

In July 1868, the Fourteenth Amendment was ratified by the necessary three-fourths of the states. Congress, however, wanted to go beyond the provisions of the amendment, which merely enabled blacks to vote. In the same month, Congress submitted to the states the Fifteenth Amendment, which prohibited the states from denying the vote to anyone on the basis of "race, color, or previous condition of servitude." Approval by the states was secured in March 1870.

By then, many white southerners, reacting to what they considered the oppression of an American government bent on social revolution, had organized secret societies, such as the Ku Klux Klan, the Knights of the White Camelia, and the Pale Faces, to intimidate blacks and keep them away from the polls. Within a few years, these secret societies gave way to public movements, such as the "Mississippi Plan." As part of this movement, whites no longer hid behind masks, nor did they confine their terrorist activities to nighttime. Instead, they openly paraded and captured and killed many militant blacks. Calling themselves "redeemers," they intended to take back their states from the carpetbaggers (exploiting northerners) and get free of the meddlesome federal government's policy of Reconstruction.

The redeemers rewrote their state constitutions, creating laissez-faire tracts suspicious and distrustful of *any* legislative body. They also framed new laws aimed just as surely at disenfranchising blacks as the Reconstruction legislation had aimed at protecting them. Such pieces of legislation were called "Jim Crow" laws, taking their name from the antebellum minstrel show that had given the Confederacy its national anthem, "Dixie." As more and more formerly moderate southerners joined the ranks of militant racists, the redeemer movement gave birth to the Solid South, a bloc of states that for almost a century could be counted on to vote exclusively for Democratic party candidates for national office. This political juggernaut led, eventually, to the defeat of Reconstruction governments at the polls.

The last showdown between North and South came in the 1876 presidential campaigns of Samuel J. Tilden and Rutherford B. Hayes. The redeemers crusaded against the graft and greed of the administration of Ulysses S. Grant and its carpetbag rule—and intimidated blacks in order to keep them from the polls. This tactic swung the South behind Tilden and won the popular vote. The Republicans, however, reversed the electoral tally of the three Southern states they still controlled under the Reconstruction laws and (there is no other word) stole the election. A deadlock resulted, followed by months of tense wrangling during which the nation had no clear president-elect and the threat of civil disunion loomed once again in the background. Hayes assumed office only because he agreed never again to tinker with the peculiar segregated social structures of the South. Even his closest associates called him "Your Fraudulency."

The compromise left the South free to construct its separate and unequal world, a segregated society that unabashedly oppressed its racial—and to a lesser extent its ethnic and religious—minorities until the civil rights upheavals of the 1960s. The Fourteenth and Fifteenth amendments played no small part in the twentieth-century movements for social equality, providing an activist Supreme Court under Chief Justice Earl Warren with the constitutional leverage it needed to at last protect the civil rights and expand the individual freedoms of all Americans.

The James Gang Robs Its First Bank (1866)

The event: In February, 1866, a band of armed men led by an ex-guerilla named Jesse James held up Missouri's Clay County Savings Association for $60,000. Jesse James and his brother, Frank, had launched their civilian careers.

THE CIVIL WAR had been particularly hellish in Missouri. During the war Jesse James rode with the guerilla leader William Quantrill and his most effective and brutal lieutenant, "Bloody Bill" Anderson, as did other James' gang members—Frank James, Cole Younger, Arch Clement. An icy-blooded, blue-eyed, teen-age killer, Jesse was on Anderson's Centralia, Missouri, raid when Bloody Bill gunned down the twenty-four unarmed Union soldiers he had captured on their way home on leave to Iowa. It was one of the war's most famous and most heinous atrocities. After the war, when the irregular Confederate bands began to break up, robbery and murder had become a way of life to them, the only vocation a goodly number would ever know.

Many of them, like Jesse, were teen-agers when the war started. They had lost their innocence in the 1,162 battles or skirmishes fought on Missouri soil, the third-highest number among all the states. It was a savage passage to manhood, from which they returned home, with the 40,000 other Confederate and 110,000 Union veterans the state produced, often physically crippled, always mentally scarred, to find that some 27,000 of their friends and relatives had been killed, that whole counties had been burned out, that railroads, highways, bridges, churches, and courthouses had all, like them, been damaged, often beyond repair.

Those who had suffered at the hands of the guerillas resented the return of the Confederate veterans and voted to keep Radical Republicans in the state house. These in turn fostered an atmosphere of intolerance. Many communities made it clear that former rebels, no matter how penitent, were not welcome. In Jackson County, Radical-leaning grand juries indicted former guerillas for crimes even after President Johnson had granted them immunity. Not a few took to the bush, and before long word of a robbery here, a murder there, began to appear in the newspapers. A general lawlessness, very much like that which had plagued the state during the war, broke out again in Missouri, and it was during this postwar anarchy that the James gang rode onto the scene.

Lawless brutes, robbing, looting, and killing without conscience, they hid behind a facade of romantic terrorism that led to a long-standing tradition of banditry in the area called the Missouri "breaks." Because the James boys' depredations became associated with the state's attempt to throw off Republican shackles, in the backwoods hollows and seedier city saloons Jesse James gradually became something of a folk hero. Ultimately, there was even martyrdom. After Jesse and Frank escaped the disastrous ambush mounted by local citizens during their famous Northfield, Minnesota, raid, Jesse was forced to recruit new gang members to replace Cole Younger, who had been captured and sent to prison for life, and Younger's brothers and Arch Clement, all of whom had been killed. One of those he recruited, Robert Ford, shot Jesse in the back and killed him for reward money at his home in St. Joseph, where he was living under the assumed name of Thomas Howard. That and a few dime novelists were all it took to make the local folk hero into a legend of the West.

Charlie Goodnight Starts a Cattle Drive (1866)

The event: In 1866, former Texas Ranger Charlie Goodnight and veteran cattleman Oliver Loving pioneered a cattle drive to Colorado, establishing one of the more important cattle trails and helping to provide America with its most beloved archetype, the rugged, freedom-loving cowboy.

WHEN TEXANS WENT off to fight the Civil War, many of them let their livestock fend for themselves. By the end of the war, millions of head of cattle ranged free across the state. After Appomattox, with the economy of their native region in shambles and opportunities few and far between, a good many southern young men went west to round up Texas strays, brand them, and drive them to market up north. That was how the trail drive cattle industry began, and if any one man can be said to have started the enterprise, it was Charlie Goodnight.

He was born on a southern Illinois farm in 1836 and came to the Brazos River country of Texas with his family in 1845. There, in a land of longhorns running wild, he learned how to be a cowboy, to gather the animals and drive them to market for local ranchmen. With his stepbrother as partner he gradually amassed a small herd of his own, but, like many other Texans, left ranching to fight for the Confederacy during the Civil War. Mustered out of the Texas Rangers a year before the war ended, Goodnight and his stepbrother found that the herd that occupied their land, numbering 180 head at the outbreak of the war, had grown to five thousand—a figure they supplemented by appropriating cattle on the open range.

At this time, most ranchmen were starting to drive their cattle to Kansas railheads for shipment to eastern markets. With Oliver Loving, an old-time cattleman, Goodnight decided to move in the other direction, pioneering a trail to Colorado, where mining operations and Indian-fighting military outposts were creating a tremendous demand for beef. In 1866, Goodnight and Loving gathered two thousand head of longhorns and, with eighteen riders, followed the

Southern Overland Mail route to the head of the Concho River, where they liberally watered their stock for the long, dry trip across the desert. They lost some four hundred head on the trail—three hundred of thirst, one hundred trampled to death in the stampede that ensued when they reached a waterhole—but the first drive along the Goodnight-Loving Trail netted the partners $12,000 in gold.

The Goodnight-Loving Trail was one of four principal cattle trails, which also included the Chisholm (from Brownsville, Texas, to the Kansas railheads of Dodge City, Ellsworth, Abilene, and Junction City), the Shawnee (from Brownsville to Kansas City, Sedalia, and St. Louis, Missouri), and the Western (from San Antonio, Texas, to Dodge City and then on to Fort Buford, at the fork of the Missouri and Yellowstone rivers, deep in Dakota Territory). Between 1866, when Loving and Goodnight cut their trail, and 1886-1887, when a single terrible winter nearly wiped out the range-cattle industry, almost one hundred million beeves and ten million horses traversed these great trails.

The trail drive industry produced more than beef, of course. It gave birth to the trail drive cowboy, perhaps the single most beloved and celebrated worker in American history. The cowboy is America's knight—noble, brave, pure, and beholden to no one in a country untrammeled by the petty vagaries of politicians, plutocrats, and police. At least, that's the way Americans have always liked to see him. Actually, cowboys were often the poorest of the poor—Confederate veterans dispossessed of family, friends, and all they had owned, loners and misfits who could hold no other job, and, despite Tom Mix and John Wayne stereotypes, African-Americans, Indians, and Mexicans, who occupied the lowest rungs on the nation's socioeconomic ladder. Yet, even when one is apprised of these realities—that the dirty, dangerous, lonely work of cowpunching was, for most men who undertook it, the only available means of making a living—the powerful romance of the cowboy refuses to fade.

America Goes to War with the Indians of the West (1866)

The event: In 1866, when the Teton Sioux, the Northern Cheyenne, and the Northern Arapaho attempted to close the Bozeman Trail and shut off the never-ending flood of white settlers onto their lands, the U.S. cavalry mounted the first of a series of fourteen campaigns, initiating the final stage in four hundred years of incessant warfare with the native inhabitants of the North American continent.

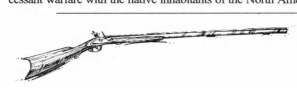

INDIAN WARS ENCOMPASS the entire history of this continent—for American history itself was a European construction—beginning in 1493 with violence between Indians and a garrison Columbus deposited at Hispañola and culminating in the so-called Battle of Wounded Knee, December 29, 1890. But the period 1866 to 1891 saw the most intensive and deliberate set of U.S. military campaigns against the Indians of the West, and it is the conflicts of this period that are most often collectively referred to as the Indian Wars.

Even so, Indian-white conflict in the West did not actually resolve itself into a set of neatly defined wars. For the Indians involved, much of their experience with white contact was one uninterrupted war. For soldiers, Indian "warfare" usually consisted of a great deal of exhausting and fruitless pursuit punctuated by episodes of bloody violence. About 1866, however, the military began labeling its various campaigns and operations, giving the appearance of a series of discrete wars.

Contrary to the claims of some Indian as well as white activists in the twentieth century, it was never the federal government's official policy to practice genocide against the native peoples of the West—though there was no shortage of individual racists and fanatics who advocated just that. If any single approach to the Indian can be identified as the nation's official policy, it was "concentration," the gathering together and installation of Indians on lands "reserved" for them. Theoretically, once consigned to a reservation, Indians became wards of the federal government, which pledged to provide them with rations and other necessary goods. In practice, one of the many tragedies that beset United States Indian policy was the almost universal corruption among the agents entrusted with the administration of the reservations. Many reservation Indians suffered varying degrees of starvation and abuse, which provoked rather than discouraged further warfare. Military action against Indians in the period following the Civil War was almost exclusively undertaken with the purpose of forcing the Indians onto reservations.

From a strictly military point of view, the struggle was not so one-sided as it may seem from our late twentieth-century perspective. The post-Civil War army of the West was small, averaging about twenty thousand officers and men, poorly paid, poorly fed, poorly equipped, poorly trained, and often poorly led. Inadequate as it was, the army was thinly broadcast across a vast frontier, and was up against an enemy whose very culture exalted warfare, warriors, and combat-effective horsemanship. Indian warriors were experts in guerilla tactics, a branch of warfare well suited to much of the western landscape but one the regular army persistently refused to acknowledge, let alone train for.

In addition to tactical advantages, the Indians also possessed the less tangible, but no less significant, advantage of indigenous warriors pitted against "foreign" invaders. Menaced with impoverishment, dispossession, and death, Indians had little choice but to believe in their fight. The army, however, was beset with ambivalence over its mission. Soldiers familiar with Indian acts of brutality—torture, mutilation, and the like—might be able to think of their enemy as beasts to be hunted down. But many soldiers came to respect Indians and to despise the injustice and abuse to which poorly conceived and indifferently, incompetently, or maliciously executed federal policy had subjected them. Ambivalence reigned at the highest levels of government as well. Numerous legislators openly condemned military activity in the West. Yet, for all their physical and spiritual advantages, Indians were fatally handicapped in warfare by the very features of their culture that elevated individual strength, cunning, skill, endurance, courage, and honor. War chiefs were not the equivalents of generals; they did not command their braves so much as they "led" them through charisma and personal influence. Truly coordinated military action was usually impossible. On a larger scale, the exaltation of individual virtue meant that so-called tribes did not often act with unity, and one tribe rarely formed a strategically effective alliance with another. Even if this had not been the case, the fact is that after the Civil War, white population in the West outnumbered Indian population by a factor of ten. Against such odds, no warriors, regardless of skill and commitment, could long prevail.

Congress Impeaches Andrew Johnson (1868)

The event: Andrew Johnson, who became president of the United States upon the assassination of Abraham Lincoln, became a victim of the passions and mistrust that characterized the postwar period of one of the most destructive conflicts in American history. In 1868, radical Republicans initiated impeachment proceedings against Johnson that failed to pass in the Senate by a single vote.

PRESIDENT ANDREW JOHNSON attempted to carry out the conciliatory program of Reconstruction he believed Lincoln had favored at the time of his death. But Johnson, a cantankerous and prickly individual, was no Lincoln. Radical Republicans were suspicious of the new president (a former governor of Tennessee), eager to avenge Lincoln's death at the hands of "another" Southerner, and impatient with foot-dragging on social issues by those but recently in open rebellion. Congress, controlled by the Radicals, rejected Johnson's moderate stance on Reconstruction. Supported by the American public and swayed by social reformers, Congress overrode Johnson's veto of civil rights legislation twice and then proposed the Fourteenth Amendment, which extended full citizenship to blacks and prohibited states from enacting laws abridging that citizenship.

During the 1866 congressional elections, Johnson campaigned against those congressmen who had supported the amendment, but to no avail. the Republicans won large majorities in both houses and quickly passed a series of hard-nosed Reconstruction measures, which Johnson vetoed and which Congress overrode. As a result, there arose a classic example of the periodic struggles over the separation of powers to which the American republic is prone when ideological conflicts are conducted as moral crusades.

Johnson's stubbornness in his dealings with Congress had made him many enemies, and that legislative body was determined to get rid of him—or at least to curb the powers of the presidency. First Congress passed laws that gave it more authority over the army, over amending the Constitution, and over some presidential appointments—including cabinet members. But the radicals did not stop at even these measures. They next passed the Tenure of Office Act of 1867, which required the president to gain the consent of the Senate before removing any Senate-approved appointee from office. In February 1868, in flagrant violation of the new law, Johnson dismissed Secretary of War Edwin M. Stanton. The House of Representatives then invoked the powers granted it by the Constitution to impeach the president. In eleven articles of impeachment, Congress held that Johnson had violated the law. The articles were upheld by the House of Representatives, but fell short of passage in the Senate on May 16, 1868, by a single vote. Johnson was left to serve out his term.

At the end of the Civil War, Americans wanted to believe the four years of carnage had been about something. For the clear majority it was, at least in retrospect, about slavery, and they were consequently impatient with backsliding on black enfranchisement. The radical Republicans, for all their opportunism and vindictiveness, had put their fingers on the moral pulse of America, which is why they were returned to office in numbers sufficient to control Congress. But even in the name of a good cause, trumped-up impeachment was a bad policy. Had the radicals been successful, they would have set a disastrous precedent, paving the way for the future settlement of disagreements between the president and the Congress through impeachment. Congress would have held an awful weapon over the office of the president, and the balance of powers that had been so carefully incorporated into the Constitution would have been disastrously upset.

The Golden Spike Completes the Transcontinental Railroad (1869)

The event: On May 10, 1869, at Promontory Point, Utah, railroad tycoon Leland Stanford—with help from railroad workers—drove the final spike into the first intercontinental railroad.

THE CIVIL WAR made construction of the railroad a top priority; the Union, having been riven north to south, could only be strengthened by a bond running east to west. The Pacific Railway Act and subsequent legislation granted huge tracts of land to the railroads, not only for the right of way but which the railroads could sell in order to finance construction. Generous loan packages were also made available. Yet even with funding and authorization in place, the project did not leap forward. Both the Central Pacific, which was to be built from west to east, and the Union Pacific, building from east to west, faltered. In 1865, after the passage of even more favorable railroad legislation in 1864, Abraham Lincoln called on Oakes Ames, a prominent industrialist, to "take hold of" the transcontinental railroad project.

Take hold Ames did, recruiting investors in a corporation created by Union Pacific vice-president Thomas Durant and named after the company that had financed the French railway system a decade earlier, Credit Mobilier. It was a sweet plan for the investors: Credit Mobilier, run by the directors of the Union Pacific, was paid by the Union Pacific to build the Union Pacific—the directors (who were the principal investors) making a profit on the railroad as well as on the cost of building it. They were, in effect, investing in themselves. The scheme gave rise to elaborately padded construction bills and other corruption culminating in a major scandal, but it did get the transcontinental railroad moving.

Under the leadership of Grenville Mellon Dodge, an Army engineer, the Union Pacific began laying prodigious lengths of track—266 miles in 1866 alone. Through impossible terrain and a hostile climate, and frequently harassed by Indians, the Union Pacific and Central Pacific pushed their track along. Immigrant laborers, especially Irish and Chinese, were hired in unprecedented numbers, and it was largely through dint of their muscle that the project was completed. The graft paid out by the tycoons to government officials and their ilk was enormous. Entire towns, wanting to become stops along the road, in turn paid huge bribes to the tycoons. Thousands of workers died as managers, who cared little for the Irish or the Chinese, cast aside sound construction principles in their rush to lay track and garner bonuses. The great buffalo herds that roamed the plains were decimated by railroaders in order to feed the workers. The government gave away millions of acres of public land to the railroads as plums. Greed, and its handmaiden corruption, more surely than any starry-eyed vision of the future, produced the iron snake that wound its way over mountains, across deserts, and through Indian territory. Yet for all the politicking, profiteering, exploitation, racial hatred, and waste, the line would be a remarkable historical accomplishment.

At Promontory Point, Utah, the eastbound line of the Central Pacific met the westbound rails of the Union Pacific. Workers and executives gathered to savor the final moment, the moment of union, which would be signified by the driving of a golden spike to join the two rail ends.

The ceremony did not go smoothly. Chinese workmen, having suffered much hatred and persecution at the hands of their Caucasian employers and co-workers, were lowering the last rail in place when a photographer hollered, "Shoot!" Whereupon they dropped the five-hundred-pound rail and ran. Next, no less a personage than Leland Stanford—one of California's "Big Four" railroad tycoons—prepared to drive the golden spike, which was wired to a telegraph line, so that each blow would be transmitted across the nation. He swung. He missed.

It took an assist from workers—who had a continent's worth of practice—to drive the golden spike home.

Jay Gould Attempts to Corner the Gold Market (1869)

The event: On September 24, 1869, the New York stock exchange—reacting to events set in motion by the attempts of "robber baron" Jay Gould to corner the market in gold—panicked. By the end of "Black Friday," the market had crashed, and one man had managed to send the entire country into severe depression.

 DESPITE THE STAGGERING amounts of money made by Wall Street's insider traders during the late 1980s, they were pikers compared to the robber barons of the last century, who managed nothing less than the wholesale corruption of American business and government during the Gilded Age.

It all started with the railroads. After the Civil War, the American West offered huge vistas of unlimited wealth. Out there were silver, and gold, and copper; back East the industrial machines needed to mine it lay at hand. Out there were cattle and wheat enough to feed even the millions of new factory workers back East who made those machines. Clearly, all one had to do was connect "out there" with "back East" to make a fortune. And that meant building railroads. And that meant finding the land to lay the tracks across, hiring men desperate enough to break their backs actually laying the tracks, producing enough steel to make the tracks in the first place, and coming up with the money to pay for it all—lots of money.

Just then the weak-minded, morally dubious federal government run by a blushingly naive Ulysses S. Grant was willing to provide the land; the west coast was filled with much-maligned and ostracized Chinese immigrants for whom railroading offered at least a chance to keep from starving; in the East, millions of Irishmen were languishing in the hellish slums of the major cities, eager for work of any kind; and the robber barons had plenty of steel and lots of lucre. "Railroad through" soon became the ubiquitous cry on the lips of crooked capitalist, corrupt politician, exploited laborer, and fast-talking booster alike as, everywhere from the Mississippi to the Pacific, cowcatchers and smokestacks chugged into view and dominated the imagination, the politics, and the livelihood of the postwar generation.

It was in this atmosphere that the robber barons—Jay Gould, Cornelius Vanderbilt, J.P. Morgan, Andrew Carnegie, John D. Rockefeller, and others—made their fortunes. In the name of efficiency, the industrialists among them introduced large-scale, specialized production in the place of earlier, decentralized methods and practiced "vertical integration," controlling not merely the manufacture and sale of a final product but also the raw resources the product required. The financiers among the group set up large trusts and provided loans to the industrialists. While their apologists dubbed them industrial "statesmen" for enhancing and modernizing the American capitalist system, their detractors pointed to their indifference to public welfare and their ostentatious displays of wealth at the expense of their workers—living in huge mansions while their employees languished in urban squalor or bleak company towns, for example. The reigning philosophy was summed up neatly in William Vanderbilt's scornful dismissal, "The public be damned!"

Which seemed to be paterfamilias Cornelius Vanderbilt's attitude exactly when, through bribery and graft, he built the New York Central into the largest single railroad line in America, handing vast wealth to his family, who threw lavish parties at which they had guests dig in a trough for jewels. The comment, too, describes Jay Gould's attitude when he used an unwitting Ulysses S. Grant to manipulate the gold market, urging the president to stop gold sales. This the president did, driving up gold prices until he realized what was going on and then dumped $4 million on the market in one day, precipitating the crash. The railroads—already ripe for disaster from intense competition and a shaky economy—rather than go bankrupt in the wake of the panic, sold out to war profiteer J.P. Morgan. Morgan, who by 1900 owned half of all railroad track in America (his friends owned the rest), set exorbitant rates across the country. It was he who lent Andrew Carnegie the $492 million he needed to start U.S. Steel when the two met at a party and Carnegie scribbled the amount on a piece of paper. With the money, Carnegie ruthlessly set out to control the American steel market and break the back of American industrial unions.

For a generation after the Civil War it hardly mattered who was president. The real "talent," as it were, and certainly the power, lay with the robber barons.

John D. Rockefeller Forms Standard Oil (1870)

The event: In 1870, despite widely fluctuating oil prices, John D. Rockefeller, Henry Flagler, and others created the Standard Oil Company. Over the next ten years, the company came to control 90 percent of the United States oil industry.

IN 1859, DRILLERS struck oil in western Pennsylvania, and the twenty-year-old John D. Rockefeller, then living in Cleveland, Ohio, was determined to enter the oil business. He decided that Cleveland was ideally situated for oil refining and built a refinery there in 1862. To manage the ever-growing corporation, Rockefeller decided to form a trust, and his company was the first and the largest such trust in the country. It controlled all aspects of the oil industry, from extracting the raw materials through pricing and distribution. Rockefeller reaped ever-larger profits, undercutting the competition in—for them—ruinous rate wars he was able to afford by securing preferential rates and rebates from the railroads.

A board of nine trustees ran the trust, managing the operations not only of Standard Oil of Ohio but also of the numerous smaller companies across America that Standard Oil swallowed whole. Rockefeller soon moved the headquarters of the trust from Ohio to New York City, where he employed a massive network of information gatherers and decision makers.

Standard Oil came under attack by reformers, and after Congress passed the Sherman Antitrust Act in 1890, President Theodore Roosevelt ordered his attorney general to bring suit against the trust. It was not until 1911, however, that the Supreme Court, at last responding to the new wave of reform that brought the progressives to power, ordered the trust dissolved into thirty-four companies. The court determined that Standard Oil had operated in such a way as to monopolize and restrain free trade—to put it mildly.

Tammany Hall's "Boss" William Tweed Is Arrested (1871)

The event: In 1871, Tammany Hall's "Boss" Tweed was arrested for failing to audit contractors' bills to the city on projects connected with the Tweed Courthouse, marking the beginning of the end for the organizer of the "Tweed Ring"—which had become a synonym for the corrupt political machines that dominated America's big cities.

TWEED WAS THE prototype of the big city boss. Incipient bosses, like Joel Barrow Sutherland of Philadelphia, and machines, like Tammany Hall, had existed in one form or another since the 1780s. The heyday of the political machine, however, began after the Civil War and stretched up to the Great Depression. Beginning as a city alderman in the 1850s, Tweed had gotten himself appointed chief of the Department of Public Works, a title that conveys no idea of the grip he had on every aspect of city life. Between 1820 and 1870, eight hundred thousand immigrants—most Irish or Italian—arrived in New York, and Tweed won their allegiance by supporting their labor unions and their Roman Catholic Church. In exchange for their votes Tweed would arrange small favors for them, and soon he wielded immense political clout. In the post-Civil War boom of the 1860s, Tweed created a network of city officials, Democratic party workers, and New York contractors, and as the city itself accumulated huge debts, Tweed grew rich from what he called "honest graft"—fraudulent contracts, patronage in high office, kickbacks, false vouchers, and special retainers. He was a Midas-in-reverse: everything he touched diminished in value by the amount of money he took away. And nothing escaped his touch, from the building of the Brooklyn Bridge to the sale of land for Central Park. His enemies called his circle of cronies the "Tweed Ring," and by the time the famous cartoonist Thomas Nast began using it as a model of corruption in *Harper's*, Tweed could afford to offer him $500,000 to withdraw a particular cartoon; Nast refused. The Tweed Ring, which some historians claim permanently besmirched the city's image, was at the height of its power when the Boss was arrested for graft in 1871.

But Tammany Hall had been there before Tweed and it would long outlast him. From the moment it was founded in 1789, as one of several post-Revolution fraternal societies, until the day Mayor Fiorello La Guardia (with the help of Franklin Delano Roosevelt) broke its stranglehold on the New York Democratic party, Tammany Hall was a powerful force in city politics. In the early days, clever men like Aaron Burr and Martin Van Buren had used Tammany and other political clubs to advance their careers. By the time of the Civil War, the clubs not only had pull but had been corrupted by men like James Fisk. (Fisk used Tammany as a conduit for government contracts to dishonest suppliers. They sold the Union shoddy, shopworn blankets and rotten, maggot-ridden meat; Fisk made a fortune.)

Machines like Tammany Hall, though usually without its pedigree, dominated urban politics, and big city bosses dominated the machines. When Tweed left Tammany Hall, Thomas Croker took his place and, along with "Honest" John Kelly, ruled New York throughout its Gilded Age. But there is no reason to single out New York: in Pittsburgh at about the same time it was Chris Magee and Bill Finn who ran the machine; in Philadelphia, "King" Jim McManes; in Boston, "Czar" Martin Lomansey; and in St. Louis—where the political machine, exposed by Lincoln Steffens in *The Shame of the Cities*, was called "The Combine"—the boss was called "Colonel" Ed Butler.

Occasionally, reform movements would topple a boss, but another would soon rise to take his place. Why? Because in the late nineteenth and early twentieth centuries the urban poor—the Irish, Italian, and German immigrants, the unorganized workingmen, and the African-Americans—had no one to turn to but the political mechanics of the big city machines. For a vote, the machine could offer them food when they were hungry, rent and clothing when they were down and out, legal help when they were in trouble, cool jazz to cheer them up, cold beer to help them forget, and now and then a good job to get them on their feet. The machines began to lose ground and big city political bosses some of their power only during the New Deal era, when the federal government took over the social welfare functions that the machines, corrupt as they were, offered to potential voters. But neither machine nor boss ever disappeared entirely from the big city, as anyone who grew up in Tom Pendergast's Kansas City in the 1930s or Richard Daley's Chicago in the 1960s could testify, if they dared.

Montgomery Ward Starts a Mail-order Business (1872)

The event: In 1872, Chicago merchant A. Montgomery Ward began sending copies of a 280-page catalog to thousands of farmers in the Midwest offering them the opportunity to order by mail the goods listed in the publication. Montgomery Ward and Company, the country's first mail-order house, had discovered an entirely new—and incredibly profitable—method of conducting business.

ALTHOUGH WARD'S WAS the first mail-order house, Richard W. Sears' company was most successful at mail-order merchandizing. Sears started his mail-order company, devoted to the distribution of watches, in 1886 and hired as one of his workers A. C. Roebuck, a watch repairman. In 1889, Sears started another company to sell jewelry and watches. From that base, he built Sears, Roebuck and Company, a general mail-order business based, like Montgomery Ward's, in Chicago. Just as Ward had done, Sears advertised his products in catalogs sent to farm families. Among his products were food, clothing, machinery, tools, stoves—anything and everything a farm family might possibly need. In 1900, just six years after his company was incorporated, he sold $10 million worth of merchandise by mail. By 1925, annual sales had grown to $243 million.

Mail-order houses like Sears, Montgomery Ward, the National Cloak and Suit Company, the Chicago Mail Order House, and Spiegel dramatically changed the lives of farm families across the country. Isolated in rural areas and often with limited funds, these families could afford neither the time nor the expense of shopping for goods in cities. But with the improvements to roads and the wide availability of the automobile came a decline in mail-order merchandising. It was to combat the downward trend in their sales that Sears and Montgomery Ward established retail stores throughout the country.

Despite the experience of these two companies, others entered the mail-order business after World War II, and today almost any product available on the market can be purchased through the U.S. Mail.

Joseph Glidden Patents Barbed Wire (1873)

The event: In 1873, Joseph Farwell Glidden, a farmer in De Kalb, Illinois, saw at the De Kalb County Fair an exhibit of barbed wire fencing invented by Henry M. Rose. Glidden improved on Rose's original and applied for a patent on October 27, 1873. The resulting product transformed the landscape—and life in the American West.

GLIDDEN DEVELOPED A design in which the spur wires were held in place by a two-braid length of wire that not only made the fencing very strong but was readily adaptable to mass production. He began manufacturing the wire in De Kalb in 1874, taking a partner the next year, then selling out his interest for $60,000 plus royalties in 1876. The purchaser of Glidden's patent, Washburn & Moen Manufacturing Company, produced 2.84 million pounds of barbed wire in 1876 and 80.5 million by 1880, having rapidly become one of the nation's largest and wealthiest industrial concerns.

Barbed wire was invaluable to the small farmer or homesteader, since it clearly marked off his property from the open range and prevented the free-ranging herds of the cattlemen from trampling his crops. It was also of great use to the cattlemen, who were among the first and biggest consumers of the product. Barbed wire made possible better breeding on Texas ranches because blooded animals could be separated from mongrels and bred exclusively with other blooded stock. Fencing cut labor costs by reducing the number of cowboys required to patrol the range. The wire also promoted the drilling of wells in otherwise unwatered ranges, thereby expanding available pastureland. A rancher who was reluctant to invest in a well on unprotected land, spending money for water anybody's wandering stock might use, would eagerly finance a water project for his own private use. Barbed wire marked off, secured, and tamed the western lands.

Like almost everything else in the West, barbed wire also led to trouble. Cattlemen illegally fenced off public range lands for their exclusive use. The fences damaged stock, and a horse whose tendon had been severed by a barb could be badly lamed. Cowboys attempting to drive their cattle to market through what had formerly been open range were now frustrated. Often they took it upon themselves to cut the fences, triggering violent "fence wars." But the transition away from a free, open range—with all the romance and wildness and freedom it had offered—was an inevitable step in the settlement of the West, a development that, for better or worse, barbed wire had made possible.

Alexander Graham Bell Patents the Telephone (1876)

The event: On March 7, 1876, Alexander Graham Bell received a patent for the telephone, one of the two most important technological advances of the nineteenth century.

BELL WAS BORN in Scotland, the grandson and son of distinguished phoneticians and teachers of speech. Young Bell became a teacher of the deaf, first in England and then in the United States, opening a school for the deaf in Boston in 1872 and becoming professor of speech and vocal physiology at Boston University the next year. At about this time he was also experimenting with two ideas for inventions. One was a so-called harmonic telegraph, a device to transmit multiple telegraph messages simultaneously over a single line. The other was a device to record sound waves graphically, which Bell hoped would accelerate the process of teaching the profoundly deaf to speak. By 1874, the two ideas began to coalesce in Bell's mind. He reasoned that if he could "make a current of electricity vary in intensity precisely as the air varies in density during the production of sound" he could "transmit speech telegraphically."

After two years of work, he applied for a patent on the telephone. Three days after he heard back from the U.S. Patent Office, Bell was experimenting with a version of the device and accidentally spilled battery acid on his lap. In pain, he called to his assistant, Thomas Watson, who was in the next room, stationed at the receiver. Through the device he distinctly heard: "Mr. Watson, come here; I want you."

The invention of the telephone stands with that of the incandescent electric light three years later as the most important technological advance of the late nineteenth century. Although Bell's patent was challenged in numerous lawsuits (other inventors developed telephone devices almost simultaneously), Bell prevailed in the courts and, with the aid of his father-in-law, Gardner G. Hubbard, founded the Bell Telephone Company, which developed into one of the world's largest utilities. Although he had become a very wealthy man, Bell did not rest on his laurels but made other important advances in technology, including the improvement of Edison's phonograph, a vacuum-jacket respirator (forerunner of the life-saving "iron lung"), and many experiments with hydrofoil boats and aviation (a decade before the Wright Brothers). He also used his fortune to finance the careers of promising young scientists and to found the important journal *Science* and the National Geographic Society. He continued to work with the deaf until his death in 1922.

George Armstrong Custer Makes His Last Stand (1876)

The event: On June 25, 1876, the vain and reckless Lieutenant Colonel George Armstrong Custer led his 7th Cavalry against a massive force of some two thousand Sioux and Cheyenne, who annihilated the attacking troops in the Battle of the Little Bighorn.

UNDER THE COMMAND of General Alfred Terry, Custer's 7th Cavalry was part of a three-pronged campaign against the Little Bighorn camps of the Indian alliance headed by Sioux Chief Sitting Bull. On the morning of June 25, Custer's scouts reported sightings of cooking fires in the Little Bighorn valley and the presence of a large war party, numbering in the thousands, nearby. The plan was for Custer to attack on June 26, the day General John Gibbon and Terry were scheduled to reach their position at the mouth of the Little Bighorn, but the glory-hungry Custer decided to act immediately, without securing further reconnaissance. He led his men across the divide between the Rosebud and the Little Bighorn, dispatching Captain Frederick W. Benteen with three troops of cavalry, 125 men, to the south, in order to make sure that the Sioux had not moved into the upper valley of the Little Bighorn. As Custer approached the Little Bighorn River, he spotted about forty warriors and sent Major Marcus A. Reno with another three troops after them. Reno was to pursue the warriors back to their village while Custer, with his remaining five troops, charged the village from the north.

Neither Custer nor his officers had any idea of how many warriors they were going up against. Later estimates put the number at anywhere from fifteen hundred to six thousand. Custer's combined strength was six hundred—and that was divided.

Warriors led by a Hunkpapa chief named Gall surged across the Little Bighorn and pushed the troopers back. As Gall pressed from the south, the Sioux military leader, Crazy Horse, descended from the north. Within an hour, Custer and his men were dead.

The immediate effect of what was destined to become the most famous Indian battle in American history was double-edged. Although Custer was always controversial, he was a popular young military hero. His "massacre" turned public opinion, which customarily wavered between hatred of the Indians and sympathy with their plight, against the Plains tribes. Congress voted more funds for the army of the West. But despite new-found public and political support, that army was badly shaken and demoralized by the horrible end of Custer and his command. In the long run, however, the Battle of the Little Bighorn proved to be the last major military triumph of the Plains Indians in their valiant resistance against the Americans.

The Great Strike of 1877 Occurs

The event: On July, 17, 1877, railroad workers in Martinsburg, West Virginia, went out on strike against the Baltimore & Ohio Railroad, which had cut their wages for the second time in a year, touching off a series of sympathy strikes and work stoppages that would become known as the Great Strike of 1877.

AMERICAN WORKERS EVERYWHERE were reeling under the crushing blows of the most serious and prolonged economic crisis in the country's history. The distress of the industrial workingman in particular had been growing exponentially in the four years of depression since the Panic of 1873. The Panic itself had been caused by wild speculation and a series of ruinous rate wars between railroad tycoons, which benefited no one so much as John D. Rockefeller and his Standard Oil, the first of the big trusts. The corporations made up their losses by shoddy operating practices and wage cut after wage cut. The workers went on strike, only to have their strike broken by hired thugs from the Pinkerton Detective Agency, which had come into its own as a counterespionage organization for the North during the Civil War and had since grown into a privately funded, anti-immigrant, anti-working-class nationwide police force.

By July 1877 the series of wage cuts and abortive strikes resulted in a wave of social insurrection that rocked America from coast to coast. Spreading spontaneously like an electrical charge along two-thirds of the nation's new rail-road tracks, the strike exploded in Philadelphia, Harrisburg, Reading, Scranton, Buffalo, Toledo, Chicago, St. Louis, and San Francisco. The first great industrial conflict in America caught the new president, Rutherford B. Hayes, napping. Without a set policy, and urged on by the hysterics of four state governors, Hayes took the fateful step and sent in federal troops.

In Martinsburg, where it began, the governor of West Virginia at first tried to use his state militia to force the workers—who were simply refusing to let trains through until the B & O rescinded their last pay cut—to restore train service. But the soldiers refused to fire on the strikers, and the governor turned to President Hayes. By the time the first federal troops deployed against strikers since 1830 arrived in West Virginia, the strike had spread to Baltimore. During bloody street battles between workers and the Maryland militia, the outmanned soldiers fired into an attacking crowd, killing ten people. As in Martinsburg, Pittsburgh's local police refused to gun down workers, and state militia brought in from outside the city attracted a militant crowd so ferocious it not only routed the troops but took control of the city before federal troops arrived to impose order.

Down the line from city to city, the strike spread from railroad workers to other industries. Strikers thronged city streets everywhere, doing battle with local policemen, state troopers, and ultimately the U.S. Army. In Chicago, the Workingmen's Party held a demonstration that drew crowds of twenty thousand or more, and in St. Louis the situation grew even more ominous. Suffering none of the bloodshed and little of the property damage that marked the riots in other cities, the St. Louis strike was in many ways more alarming than any of the others to businessmen, property owners, and robber barons. For there the original railroad strike expanded systematically and completely into a general strike. St. Louis, with its huge population of German workers and their proud socialist traditions, became the only American city to be run, if even for a short time, by a workers' council—what we today would call a soviet and what the newspaper editors of 1877, with the Paris Commune fresh in their memories, called "the Commune."

The nationwide struggle seemed to pit all workers against all employers.

This was certainly a pre-revolutionary condition, but the federal troops rushed from city to city, crushing strike after strike, and within a few weeks the Great Strike of 1877 was over. In its wake, many states passed conspiracy laws, beefed up their militias, and built National Guard armories in their major cities. For they, like their employees, had just discovered the power of industrialized workers when they banded together.

"Billy the Kid" Joins in the Lincoln County War (1878)

The event: On February 18, 1878, a party of riders in the employ of James J. Dolan, the "boss" of Lincoln, New Mexico, ambushed an English emigre rancher and Dolan rival named John H. Tunstall, and the Lincoln County War had begun. A nasty affair on all sides, the war would turn one of Tunstall's young hired hands and admirers into a legendary outlaw called Billy the Kid.

ABOUT ALL THAT can be said for certain about Billy the Kid, the most famous of all western gunfighters, is that he didn't kill the twenty-one men a popular ballad credits him with. Out of sixteen documented gunfights, Billy killed four men. In the course of robberies he may have assisted in killing an additional five. This still earns Billy the number-ten spot among the thirty-three most prolific gunfighters of the Old West—though interestingly, Wild Bill Hickok, best known to history and legend as a lawman rather than a criminal, comes in at number five with seven single-handed "kill" notches on his gun handle. Most people know that Billy the Kid was an alias, and a lot of knowledgeable folks will tell you Billy's real name was William Bonney. Actually, it was Henry McCarty, but he was also known as Henry or William or Kid Antrim. He was born in 1859, either in Marion County, Indiana, or in New York City; no one knows for sure. He was raised in Kansas, and after his mother died in 1874, Henry embarked on a career of petty crime that soon escalated to murder, when the seventeen-year-old killed a man in a saloon brawl.

Henry was born in Indiana or New York in 1859, but *Billy* was born in 1878, when he became part of the so-called Lincoln County War. It was a New Mexico feud—known in the West as a range war—in which one set of cattlemen faced off against another in a literally cutthroat contest for a monopoly on lucrative government beef contracts. During this conflict, on April 1, 1878, Billy ambushed and killed the sheriff of Lincoln County and his deputy. A fugitive now, the young man became chiefly a cattle thief and was hunted obsessively by Lincoln County's new sheriff, Pat Garrett, to whom he surrendered in December 1880. Four months later, however, Billy evaded the noose by killing his two jailhouse guards and escaping. Garrett again pursued him, running him to ground at Fort Sumner, New Mexico, on July 14, 1881. Some say Billy had gone to the fort to see his sweetheart. Whatever the motive, the visit proved fatal.

At around midnight, Billy, hungry for a beefsteak, went to the adobe house of his supposed friend Pete Maxwell to cut some meat. He entered Maxwell's darkened room. *"Pedro,"* he reportedly called out, *"quién es son estos hombres afuera?"** —referring to members of Garrett's posse who had been loitering silently outside Maxwell's door.

"That's him," Maxwell said to Garrett, who had entered the house only a few minutes before Billy.

The sheriff fired twice at the dimly visible silhouette. The second shot went wild, but the first had found its mark, and Billy the Kid was dead.

But as they say in any good western, his legend lives on. Like the brothers Frank and Jesse James, Billy the Kid quickly entered western popular lore as the central figure in pseudobiographies, dime novels, songs, movies, and even a ballet by Aaron Copland. In any context but that of the American West, Billy the Kid would have been forgotten, dismissed as a sociopathic killer. Through the sepia filter of western legend, however, he has come through to us as a kind of Robin Hood, an outlaw standing his ground against the forces of a corrupt order.

* "Pedro, who are those men outside?"

Edison Invents the Incandescent Electric Lamp (1879)

The event: On October 21, 1879, Thomas Alva Edison created in his Menlo Park, New Jersey, laboratory a lamp using a carbonized cotton filament that lasted forty hours—the incandescent electric light that wrought sweeping and profound changes in civilized life the world over.

EDISON WAS BORN in Milan, Ohio, in 1847 to a family of less than middling means. Poorly educated and handicapped by a substantial hearing loss from a childhood injury, young Tom Edison embarked on a spectacular ascent that recalls Benjamin Franklin and might have been written by Horatio Alger, creator in his boys' novels of the "rags-to-riches" story that fuels so many American dreams. Edison started his own business, peddling candy and newspapers to railroad passengers, and, while working on the trains, became fascinated with telegraphy. He secured a job as a telegrapher and began tinkering with electricity. Soon, tinkering gave way to invention, and by the end of his life, this unschooled, practically deaf man from America's hinterlands had some three thousand patents to his name, for inventions affecting virtually every aspect of American life. The stock ticker, the phonograph, vastly improved telegraph and telephone devices, electrical generation and distribution, motion pictures, even wax paper—all emerged from Edison's workshop.

For his greatest single invention, the electric light, Edison spent months of frustrating experimentation and failure, during which thousands of filament materials were tested, before he finally succeeded. On December 31, 1879, he offered a public demonstration of the lamp and was granted a patent the next month. The first commercial installation of electric lights was made in a steamship, the *Columbia*, belonging to the Oregon Railroad and Navigation Company. By 1881 Edison had built the world's first central electric power plant, the Pearl Street Station in Manhattan, and in a remarkably short time, all of the urban

United States was being wired for electricity. Rural areas soon followed, and the nation and world entered a new technological epoch.

Booker T. Washington Founds Tuskegee Institute (1881)

The event: Born to a slave and a white father, Booker T. Washington attended school while working as a laborer and went on to found the Tuskegee Institute in Alabama, a pioneering industrial and agricultural school for African-American students, in 1881.

BOOKER TALIAFERRO WASHINGTON worked in a salt furnace and a coal mine in Malden, West Virginia, while attending school. After he made a name for himself as an educator, the Alabama legislature chose him as principal of Tuskegee Institute, the black industrial and agricultural school it had established. Under Washington's leadership, the school quickly became the best-known and best-supported black school in the country.

From its early emphasis on agriculture, Tuskegee Institute moved toward professional and business education in the 1920s. A college department was added in 1927, a graduate program in 1943. In addition, the institute began a school of veterinary medicine in 1945 and a school of nursing in 1953. During World War II it became home to the Tuskegee Army Air Field, where African-Americans were trained as pilots in a program segregated from other Army Air Force training schools.

Tuskegee faculty and alumni have included many influential figures, including Professor George Washington Carver, whose work with the peanut brought a measure of prosperity to southern farmers, both black and white, and student Ralph Ellison, author of the highly acclaimed novel *Invisible Man*. While Booker T. Washington gained widespread support among northern white philanthropists and acclaim among many blacks, he emphasized the achievement of economic self-determination rather than political and civil rights. "In all things that are purely social," he declared, "we can be as separate as the fingers, yet one as the hand in all things essential to mutual progress." The NAACP (National Association for the Advancement of Colored People) and other organizations were formed in opposition to Washington's pragmatic policy of racial accommodation and compromise.

Whatever Booker T. Washington's philosophical and political leanings, the school he created endured and has grown in stature, becoming, in 1983, a full-fledged university with a student body of 3,500.

Clara Barton Founds the American Red Cross (1881)

The event: Clara Barton, who had earned the respect and gratitude of the nation through her tireless work as a volunteer nurse during the Civil War, founded the American Red Cross in 1881.

A FORMER SCHOOLTEACHER and clerk in the U.S. Patent Office, Clara Barton was struck during the Civil War by the urgent need for an organization that could distribute food and medical supplies to troops. Believing the War Department and the U.S. Sanitary Commission, the two federal agencies in charge of such work, to be incapable of achieving efficiency, Barton worked as a volunteer with the Army, nursing the wounded and sick—often in the thick of battle—and soliciting and distributing supplies. Soldiers adored her, calling her the "angel of the battlefield."

After the war, Barton established an office to help families locate prisoners of war, missing men, and the dead buried in unmarked graves. Overwork and physical and emotional exhaustion threatened her health, prompting her to travel to Europe for a rest cure. She found in Europe precisely the kind of agency she had advocated during the Civil War: the International Committee of the Red Cross. Returning to the United States, Barton began a vigorous campaign to gain American acceptance for the Red Cross. In 1882, after years of work, the U.S. Senate ratified the Geneva Convention, which included an enabling provision for the American Association of the Red Cross.

Barton served as the organization's first president, but her administrative role did not keep her from personally visiting disaster areas and battlefields. Victims of the Johnstown, Pennsylvania, flood in 1889 and the 1893 hurricanes in the Georgia Sea Islands benefited from her direct assistance. During the Spanish-American War, Barton traveled to Cuba, but her work there brought to the forefront a problem with the Red Cross she herself had created. Those in Red Cross supervisory roles followed her example of reluctance to delegate authority and share responsibility. The result was a crippling administrative inefficiency, which finally compelled Barton to step down as president in 1904. She nevertheless continued to work in the aid of disaster and war victims until her death in 1912 at the age of ninety-one, and her shortcomings as an administrator paled beside the inestimable legacy of comfort, relief, and humanity she bequeathed to the nation's victims, civil and military.

The Brooklyn Bridge Is Completed (1883)

The event: Thousands celebrated on May 24, 1883, the official opening of the East River Bridge, better known as the Brooklyn Bridge—a magnificent structure that represented the summation of nineteenth-century technology and the ultimate expression of American will and know-how.

THE BRIDGE HAD its origin in the mind of John Augustus Roebling, a civil engineer trained in his native Germany who immigrated to the United States in 1831. After a series of ventures, Roebling became the nation's first manufacturer of wire rope (1841), which he used to build a suspension bridge over the Monongahela River at Pittsburgh (1846). Other bridges followed, including a spectacular span at Niagara Falls (1851-55). Then, in 1857, Roebling suggested building a suspension bridge across the East River, to join Manhattan with Brooklyn. A charter for the project was granted, and Roebling was appointed chief engineer. His plans for the structure were approved in 1869, but on June 28 of that year Roebling suffered a leg injury at the construction site, developed tetanus, and died the next month. His son, Washington Augustus Roebling, took over supervision of construction.

Building the structure was an epic struggle with men, materials, and the elements. Special watertight caissons had to be developed to make the underwater construction of the two great towers possible, and workers were menaced by cave-ins, blow-outs, and "the bends"—an agonizing, crippling, and potentially lethal condition caused by nitrogen bubbles in the blood resulting from too rapid a return from the high pressure of underwater work to the normal atmospheric pressure of the surface. Roebling himself was terribly disabled by the disease and was forced to oversee much of the construction from a bed in a Brooklyn Heights apartment overlooking the site while his wife Emily acted as his go-between and on-site representative. The bridge was also plagued by corruption, with a supplier of steel cable furnishing inferior wire. Yet all obstacles, natural and manmade, were overcome in this great American treasure of engineering, architecture, and art.

The opening of the bridge was celebrated not only in Manhattan and Brooklyn but across the nation. As Americans understood, the bridge was more than a link between two cities (Brooklyn did not become a borough of New York City until 1898). Here at last the scientific and industrial technology that had produced for the most part the grim artifacts and dismal living conditions of the Industrial Revolution had created an object with all the spiritual power and grace of a great gothic cathedral. It inspired awe in the nineteenth century, and in the twentieth century it inspired painters, poets, and writers. A New York landmark, it is certainly among the most beautiful architectural and engineering creations of mankind.

Mark Twain Publishes *Adventures of Huckleberry Finn* (1884)

The event: In 1884, Mark Twain—the most beloved man of letters in American history—published *Adventures of Huckleberry Finn*, a seminal work in American literature.

ERNEST HEMINGWAY OBSERVED, "All modern American literature comes from one book by Mark Twain called *Huckleberry Finn* . . . it's the best book we've had. . . . There was nothing before. There has been nothing so good since." Few books have enjoyed more of the admiration and love of readers young and old, of critics, of scholars, and of other writers.

The novel is an artistic masterpiece, maintaining throughout the beautifully controlled point of view of its semiliterate boy hero, evoking a masterful range of American dialects, balancing episodes of nostalgic romanticism, unflinching realism, moving pathos, and outrageous comedy—all set within the mythically powerful framework of a journey down the Mississippi. Beyond demonstrating what a great American writer could do with great American subject matter, *Adventures of Huckleberry Finn* shaped the world's view of America and America's view of itself. One of the most popular books of all time—having sold at least thirteen million copies in virtually every language on the planet—Twain's novel, a kind of national biography, was in every sense a breakthrough achievement.

Samuel Langhorne Clemens was a most unlikely candidate for literary greatness. Born in 1835, he spent his childhood in Hannibal, Missouri, where he witnessed frontier life at its most idyllic and its most brutal. He realized his boyhood ambition to become a Mississippi riverboat pilot and derived his pen name from the Mississippi lead man's call, *mark twain!* indicating a depth of two fathoms. The advent of the Civil War brought an end to Twain's riverboat days, and he became a miner, lecturer, and journalist, traveling to California, where he wrote his first popular work in 1865, a sketch entitled "Jim Smiley and His Jumping Frog" but better known as "The Celebrated Jumping Frog of Calaveras

County." It launched his career.

Although *Adventures of Huckleberry Finn* was Twain's masterpiece, many of his other books endure as monuments of American literature, including *Innocents Abroad* (1869), *Roughing It* (1872), *The Gilded Age* (1873), *The Adventures of Tom Sawyer* (1876), *Life on the Mississippi* (1883), *A Connecticut Yankee in King Arthur's Court* (1889), and *Pudd'nhead Wilson* (1894).

Geronimo Surrenders to General Nelson A. Miles (1886)

The event: On September 4, 1886, Apache chief Geronimo surrendered to General Nelson A. Miles in a canyon just north of the Mexican border, marking the final surrender of the native Americans to the white invasion of the West.

BORN ALONG ARIZONA'S upper Gila River in 1829, Geronimo grew to manhood under Mexican rule. Mexican soldiers killed his mother, his wife, and his three children, and Geronimo's hatred of them was implacable. Even Geronimo's fellow Apaches, the most feared of all the Indians of the Southwest, considered him—as one warrior put it—"a true wild man." When Mexico ceded much of the Southwest to the United States in 1848, the Americans, too, became the object of Apache bellicosity as the new intruders disrupted established Apache ways with their mines and ranches and dusty small towns.

After the U.S. conducted sustained campaigns against the Apaches during 1860-1865 and 1871-1873, most reported dejectedly to reservations. The first reservation established for Geronimo's Chiricahuas in 1872 at least included portions of their traditional lands. Disgruntlement with reservation life turned to seething anger in 1876, however, when the Anglo-American government gathered up all the various Apache bands and forced them onto a single reservation at San Carlos, Arizona. For the next decade, Geronimo and his followers again and again broke out of what they considered their imprisonment. And once free of the reservation, they were extremely hard to find among the canyons and arroyos of south Arizona and nearby Mexico.

Geronimo's escapes repeatedly embarrassed the politicians and army officers of the American Southwest, and the mention of his name soon evoked terror in the area's settlers as local newspapers continually blared his name across their front pages. General William Tecumseh Sherman, commanding the armies of the West, grew determined to stop Geronimo once and for all. Twice General George Crook, a man who respected and understood Indian methods of combat, captured Geronimo, and twice he escaped. Crook, limited tactically by his superiors' demands that Geronimo surrender unconditionally, exhausted and discouraged by the chase itself, and questioning the very morality of what he was being asked to do, gave up his command. He was replaced by General Nelson A. Miles, a highly skilled Indian fighter who stopped at nothing in his quest to capture Geronimo, not even the sovereignty of a foreign country—penetrating at one point two hundred miles into Mexican territory. He finally ran Geronimo to ground in Skeleton Canyon, Arizona.

Geronimo and his band were taken to Fort Bowie, then shipped off to Florida. Eventually, the Chiricahuas and Warm Spring Apaches would be permitted to return to the West, but only as far as a reservation in Oklahoma. When Geronimo died, aged eighty, at Fort Sill, Oklahoma, in 1909, he had been a legend among both Indians and whites for more than a generation.

Walter Camp Becomes Yale's Football Coach (1888)

The event: In 1888, Walter Camp became the coach of the Yale football team, the beginning of a career in which Camp led his team to undefeated seasons between 1888 and 1898, suggested most of the major innovations that came to define modern football, literally wrote the game's rule book, and for many years named every candidate to the "All American" teams.

AMERICAN FOOTBALL DESCENDS from a medieval game in which villagers kicked, threw, or carried a ball across fields to another village. The medieval sport evolved into soccer and rugby, and these two nineteenth-century sports gave birth to football. Many adaptations have been made to the game over the years. Downs and measured yardage were incorporated in 1882. The forward pass came to football in the early 20th century.

By the end of the 19th century, under ardent supporter and innovator Walter Camp's tutelage, intercollegiate football was fiercely competitive and highly popular, spreading to the Midwest and the West Coast. The annual Yale-Harvard game, held on Thanksgiving Day, was the social event of the season on the eastern seaboard, with the wealthy and the powerful coming from far and wide to be seen at the game's round of balls, parades, and parties.

Brutality and violence marred the competition, however, and a rising number of sudden deaths led some colleges in the early twentieth century to consider abandoning the sport. It was saved by the formation in 1906 of the National Collegiate Athletic Association (NCAA) an organization spearheaded by New York University's president, Henry MacCracken. The NCAA established rules that reduced the violence on the field, but the organization was unable to solve problems linked to unethical recruiting.

In the 1890s, professional football was established, but it was not until the 1920 founding of the National Football League that it attracted a widespread following. In its early days, professional football was segregated, but in 1946 Kenny Washington and Woody Strode were signed by the Los Angeles Rams and the color line was broken. Professional football received a major boost after World War II with the beginning of televised "Monday Night Football," and in 1967 with the broadcast of the first "Super Bowl," professional football's championship game became an annual national event.

The Oklahoma Land Rush Begins (1889)

The event: On April 22, 1889, the federal government officially opened an unsettled region of Indian Territory to homesteaders, setting off the first of three major land rushes to claim western homesteads and beginning the transformation of Indian Territory into the present state of Oklahoma.

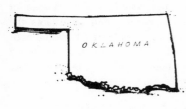

FROM 1828 TO 1846, the territory of Oklahoma became home to the people of the Five Civilized Tribes—the Cherokees, Choctaws, Chickasaws, Creeks, and Seminoles—who had been removed from their eastern homelands and set upon what the Cherokees called the "Trail of Tears" to a western land promised them in perpetuity. These tribes of Native Americans settled in Indian Territory in distinct "nations" and, through hunting and farming, began slowly to prosper.

In the late 1870s, land-hungry whites learned that a large section of land deep within Indian Territory had yet to be settled. Called "Unassigned Lands" or the "Oklahoma Lands" by western newspapers, the region had been ceded to the United States by the Creeks and Seminoles after the Civil War. The papers stated that the "Oklahoma Lands" could be claimed by homesteaders, whereupon settlers, called "Boomers," moved into the region. At first the federal government removed the settlers, declaring that only Native Americans could occupy the area. But with the illegal entry of cattlemen and the building of the Atchison, Topeka, and Santa Fe Railroad line through this country, there was little the government could do to enforce its policy. Unable to prevent settlement, it sanctioned it, dividing the land into the 160-acre parcels that had been specified in the Homestead Act of 1862 for the creation of homesteads on public lands.

At noon on April 22, 1889, signal guns were fired, and hundreds of settlers swarmed across the border of Indian Territory to claim homesteads. Over the next few years the government rescinded other agreements to protect Native American lands from white encroachment. The Sac and Fox, the Iowa, and the

Shawnee-Potawatomi reservations were opened to white settlement in 1891, unleashing another wave of migration. In 1893, the biggest land rush of all occurred with the purchase and opening of the Cherokee Outlet.

When Oklahoma gained territorial status, civic leaders demanded that the United States government abandon its treaties with the Five Civilized Tribes. Congress created the Dawes Commission in 1893 to negotiate an end to the sovereign status of the Native American nations. After more than a dozen years of work, appropriating the tribal lands and carving them into individual plots, the Dawes Commission completed its mission, and the people of Oklahoma petitioned Congress for statehood. At the time statehood was granted, Oklahoma had a population of 1.4 million, of whom only about seventy-five thousand were Native Americans.

Jacob Riis Publishes *How the Other Half Lives* (1890)

The event: In 1890 Jacob August Riis published *How the Other Half Lives*, a work of social conscience that shocked a nation with its exposé of the atrocious living conditions in New York's slums.

RIIS IMMIGRATED TO New York City from Denmark in 1870 and spent the next seven years drifting in semipoverty until, in 1877, he became a police reporter, first for the *New York Tribune* and then the *Evening Sun*. His office, on lower Manhattan's Mulberry Street, was across from police headquarters and in the middle of the city's Lower East Side immigrant slums. Riis habitually walked the streets of this district between two and four in the morning to see the slum "off its guard," touring Bandits' Roost, Bottle Alley, Bone Alley, Thieves' Alley, and Kerosene Row. Working in the ferment of America's Progressive Movement at a time when many reformers were engaged in exposing the ills of society, he declared of the slum that "it was not fit for Christian men and women, let alone innocent children, to live in, and therefore it had to go."

His instruments of choice for excising the cancer of slum life were the camera and the pen. With the eye of an experienced reporter, the thoroughness of a sociologist, and the zeal of a reformer, he set about documenting the neighborhood in which he had labored for almost two decades. *How the Other Half Lives* struck, in the words of Theodore Roosevelt, as "an enlightenment and an inspiration." It not only exposed slum conditions in New York but alerted the nation to such conditions elsewhere. No one who read the book and looked at its photographs could innocently turn a blind eye to the misery of "the other half." The effect of *How the Other Half Lives* was simple and immediate. Before 1890 there had been no real effort to clear the slums. After 1890, there was.

Louis Sullivan Pioneers the Development of the Skyscraper (1890)

The event: In 1890, the Chicago architectural firm of Sullivan and Adler designed and began construction of the Wainright Building in St. Louis, the first skyscraper to be built by the pioneer of the modern cityscape, Louis H. Sullivan.

IN THE EARLY years of the twentieth century, the most prominent distinguishing feature of the American city was the skyscraper, this country's single most important contribution to world architecture. It was made possible technologically by the development of steel-cage construction, which allowed for much greater height than traditional masonry construction. The Home Insurance Company Building in Chicago (1883-1885), designed by William LeBaron Jenney, is generally considered the first skyscraper. However, the major exponent of the new skyscraper technology was Louis Sullivan (1856-1924), who, in 1879, formed a highly successful and innovative partnership with Dankmar Adler. Their practice was based in Chicago, an ideal place for architects at the time, since the city had been devastated by the Great Fire of 1871 and was in need, quite literally, of rebuilding.

Sullivan and Adler's 1890-1891 Wainwright Building was distinguished not only by its majestic height but by the beauty of a "vertical aesthetic" Sullivan had developed especially to suit this new and unprecedented style of building. For Sullivan advocated an architecture beholden to no buildings of the past. The form of a building was to be determined not by traditions and historical examples but by the building's function. The result was an architecture of great strength, practicality, honesty, and grace, which, in giving the skyscraper aesthetic validity, transformed first the American urban landscape and then that of the world.

Congress Passes the Sherman Antitrust Act (1890)

The event: The 1890 Sherman Antitrust Act outlawed trusts—conspiracies that restrained interstate or foreign trade—and declared that individuals engaged in monopolizing such trade were guilty of misdemeanors. Individuals or businesses harmed by the operation of trusts were entitled to sue in federal courts for triple damages.

IN THE LAST half of the nineteenth century, the nation's most powerful businessmen had developed unified trusts capable of handling supplies, transportation, marketing, and financing. In the competitive economic times that followed the Civil War, businessmen used the giant trusts they had formed to force competitors out of the market. Thus freed from the need to price products competitively, the trusts inflated prices to raise huge profits.

The Sherman Antitrust Law was welcomed in principle, but many regarded it as vague, and the courts had difficulty applying the law. Businesses continued to form monopolies, so that by the turn of the century three hundred corporations claimed assets of more than $10 million; scarcely a decade earlier, only ten or eleven companies were that large. President Theodore Roosevelt put the law to work in 1902, however, asking his attorney general, Philander C.

Knox, to file suit against the Northern Securities Company, a railway trust. When the case was taken to the Supreme Court, the justices ruled that the trust was illegal and ordered it dismantled. Throughout his presidency, Roosevelt continued to press for the breakup of trusts—Standard Oil Trust, the American Tobacco Company, and others—and the next president, William Taft, continued that work.

Inadequate though it was, the Sherman Antitrust Law remained the government's only control over the formation of monopolies until Woodrow Wilson pushed Congress to authorize the Federal Trade Commission and pass the Clayton Antitrust Act. The new law banned pricing agreements designed to restrain trade, overlapping corporate directorates, and the acquisition of stock in competitors' companies. The commission and the Clayton Antitrust Act were largely ineffective, however, and trusts continued to operate. Thurman Arnold, under President Franklin Roosevelt, revived the trust issue, which remained a government priority until the presidency of Ronald Reagan, under whose administration very few antitrust suits were filed.

Products of an age of reform, the antitrust laws remain on the books whether they are fully applied or not. They stand as a warning to businesses and a reminder of the need for healthy competition in a democratic state.

The U.S. Army Massacres Indians at Wounded Knee (1890)

The event: On December 28, 1890, the U.S. 7th Cavalry, in a tragic sequence of events, surrounded and killed perhaps 300 Sioux led by ailing chief Big Foot and camped at a creek called Wounded Knee.

BY THE CLOSING decade of the nineteenth century, the United States contained 187 reservations—181,000 square miles of land—domiciling 243,000 Indians. For all practical purposes, some four hundred years of Indian-white warfare in the New World had come to an end. Indian suffering had not ceased, however, and, as it turned out, neither had the killing.

Driven from their lands, vast numbers of Indians were consigned to a federal reservation system run with a heartbreaking mixture of corruption, indifference, and inefficiency. There arose from this misery a prophet, a Paiute shaman's son named Wovoka. Having spent part of his youth with a white rancher's family, he imbibed Indian as well as white Christian religious traditions. He preached to the reservation Indians of a new world coming, one in which only Indians dwelt and in which buffalo were again plentiful. To hasten this millennium, Wovoka counseled, all Indians must dance the Ghost Dance and, most important, must "do no harm to anyone."

Soon, Ghost Dancing swept many of the western reservations. Among the Teton Sioux, however, Wovoka's commandment to do no harm was suppressed. Calamitously, Short Bull and Kicking Bear—Teton apostles of the Ghost Dance religion—urged hastening the day of deliverance by a campaign to obliterate the white man. They even fashioned a "ghost shirt," which, they said, was infallible armor against white men's bullets.

Some of the white Indian agents in charge of the reservations panicked and summoned Army reinforcements. In a sinister atmosphere of fear and distrust, the influential Hunkpapa Sioux chief Sitting Bull now began actively to espouse the Ghost Dance religion. The agent in charge of Sitting Bull's reservation dispatched reservation police officers—who were Indians—to arrest the chief before a full-scale uprising developed. A near-riot did ensue and, in the scuffle, either deliberately or accidentally, Sitting Bull was slain. His death brought the reservations to a fever pitch.

Of status comparable to that of Sitting Bull was the Miniconjou Sioux chief Big Foot. Unlike Sitting Bull, however, Big Foot renounced the Ghost Dance religion as so much futile desperation. Following Sitting Bull's death, the most militant chiefs and warriors took a stand in a part of the Pine Ridge Reservation called the Stronghold and prepared for a fight. Chief Red Cloud, a Pine Ridge leader friendly to the whites, asked Big Foot to come to the reservation and use his influence to persuade the Stronghold party to surrender. Tragically, the Army commander in the region, General Nelson A. Miles, knew nothing of this. What he did know is that the Sioux were near rebellion and that Big Foot, a prominent Sioux leader, was on his way to meet with the leaders of that rebellion. Miles ordered his troops to pursue and intercept any and all Miniconjous—in particular, Big Foot.

On December 28, 1890, a squadron of the 7th Cavalry located the chief and about 350 followers camped near a stream called Wounded Knee Creek. Big Foot huddled miserably in his wagon, desperately ill with pneumonia. During the night, more troops moved into the area, so that by morning five hundred soldiers, under Colonel James W. Forsyth, surrounded Big Foot's camp. Outraged, a medicine man named Yellow Bird began dancing, urging his people to fight. The ghost shirts they wore, he said, would protect them. At some point, a shot was fired, and the soldiers opened up on the camp with deadly Hotchkiss guns, firing almost a shell a second, indiscriminately: at men, at women, at children. In less than an hour Big Foot and 153 other Miniconjous were known to have been killed. So many others staggered, limped, or crawled away that it is impossible to determine how many finally died. Most estimates put the number of slain at 300 of the 350 who had been camped at Wounded Knee Creek. The 7th Cavalry lost 25 killed and 39 wounded, mostly from their own stray rounds.

Neither Nelson A. Miles nor the nation was proud of Wounded Knee. Miles summarily relieved Forsyth of command and ordered a court of inquiry—which, to Miles's consternation, exonerated the 7th's colonel. In the meantime, "hostile" and formerly "friendly" Sioux factions united in a December 30 ambush of the 7th Cavalry near the Pine Ridge Agency. Elements of the 9th Cavalry came to the rescue, and General Miles subsequently marshaled 3,500 troops (out of a total force of 5,000) around the angry Sioux who had assembled fifteen miles north of the Pine Ridge Agency along White Clay Creek. Exercising patient restraint, Miles contracted the ring of troops around the Indians, all the while pledging good treatment. At last, even the most determined Sioux saw the hopelessness of the situation.

The formal surrender took place on January 15, 1891.

James Naismith Invents Basketball (1891)

The event: In the winter of 1891, Dr. James A. Naismith, an instructor at the YMCA's International Training School in Springfield, Massachusetts, invented an indoor sport using a round ball and two peach baskets as a ploy to improve YMCA attendance during cold weather, giving birth to the "all-American" game of basketball.

THE MAYANS AND possibly the Olmec, from whose culture the Mayans adopted their calendar, played a game with some similarities to basketball, throwing a ball through a basket with a vertical-facing hoop attached to a wall. It is the only precedent for the game Naismith invented when he was approached by the head of the YMCA's physical training staff Dr. Luther H. Gulick, who was worried about the drop in winter attendance at his clubs and had concluded that the dearth of competitive sports during the season was at fault. Naismith probably knew nothing about the Mayans, and he was less concerned with history than with the fact that the game he was to create had to be played indoors. It had to have a ball, because all games did; since it was indoors, its players shouldn't be allowed to run with the ball, as they did in football, or kick it, or tackle other players, or knock them down. Naismith settled on a rounded goal, rather than uprights as in football, to keep players from charging at it, and stuck it above their heads to keep defenses from clustering around it. He found his peach baskets, threw in a soccer ball to play with, came up with half a dozen simple rules, and *voilà!*

Because it was simple, easy to learn, and did not require an army of specialists, the game caught on quickly. Beginning with seven players per team, which grew to nine, shrank to eight, and finally settled at five, in 1894 the game was being administered by the Amateur Athletic Union as well as the YMCA. A professional league, with teams in Brooklyn, Philadelphia, New Jersey, and New York, formed in 1898 but lasted only a couple of seasons. An exhibition game was played at the 1904 Olympics, and after several pioneering seasons played by Yale and Penn, the National Collegiate Athletic Association established its rules officially in 1908. Soon basketball was attracting crowds in high schools and colleges around the country.

The original Celtics, out of New York City, began as a semi-pro team and dominated the American Basketball League formed in 1925, but after they won 109 games and lost only 11 in a single season, they were tossed out of the league for being too talented. They took their show on the road, drawing crowds of 20,000 or so wherever they played and popularizing the game immensely before they got so good nobody would play them. About the time they disbanded in 1928, the Harlem Globetrotters—dreamchild of Abe Saperstein—dribbled onto the scene. Saperstein hired five extremely talented black players, bought a road map, stuffed them in his car, and went looking for crowds. The Globetrotters have been on the road ever since. By 1937, a new National Basketball League began showcasing basketball's better players, and in 1946 a rival Basketball Association of America opened competition. When the two merged as the National Basketball Association in 1949, professional basketball was truly under way.

In 1934, sportswriter Ned Irish, talking about the huge crowds colleges were attracting, persuaded promoters at Madison Square Garden to invite Notre Dame, NYU, Westminster, and St. John's to play a doubleheader, which evolved four years later into the National Invitational Tournament. Though the NCAA offered its first tournament the following year, it was passed from city to city and did not draw the stable crowds commanded by the Garden. The NIT dominated post-season play for decades, until the advent of big-time television coverage made the site of the tournament irrelevant. Television, too, and the money it promised, brought to the college game a persistent corruption.

Scandals plagued college ball even before television. In 1951, thirty of the best college players from City College, Long Island University, NYU, Manhattan College, Kentucky, Bradley, and Toledo were indicted for shaving points in fifty games. A point shaving scandal in the late 1950s proved that the influence of gamblers had not been an anomaly. In later decades, point shaving, recruitment bribes, endorsement payoffs, grade-fixing—you name it—became ubiquitous among NCAA teams.

Despite the scandals, however, basketball's popularity continued to grow.

Individual players sometimes came up with exciting innovations. In the 1930s, Stanford University's Hank Lusetti invented the jump shot, and scores—which previously had often been in the teens—soared into the 60s and 70s. In later years, two big men—Bill Russell and Wilt Chamberlain—demonstrated that the sport could be played "above the rim," ushering in the age of the slam dunk perfected by Kareem Abdul-Jabbar.

At first, the sport introduced rule changes to prevent "easy scoring," a code phrase for restraining individual play that carried the whiff of racism. The three-second zone, a six-foot-wide "lane" between the goal and the foul line in which no player was allowed to remain beyond three seconds, was introduced to keep tall players from parking underneath the basket. When Russell and Chamberlain came along the zone was extended to twelve feet in an ill-fated attempt to deny them the huge scores with which they were dominating college basketball. Similarly, the dunk shot was outlawed in college play in the false hope of stopping Jabbar, still a second-year college player named Lew Alcindor, from leading UCLA to yet another NCAA championship.

Ultimately, however, the sport realized that fans loved to see the high scores and outstanding individual effort and one-on-one play of an Elvin Hayes, a Pistol Pete Maravich, and an Oscar Robertson. The fans wanted fast-paced, quick-scoring games, but more than that, they wanted "stars." Recent rules changes have been intended to speed up the game and enhance individual play—introducing a twenty-four second shot clock, creating a three-point line, outlawing zone defenses, expanding the number of personal fouls allowed from five to six per game. Now the Larry Birds, Magic Johnsons, and Michael Jordans regularly score more than entire teams once did, while teams routinely pass 100 points per game.

Ellis Island Opens (1892)

The event: Inundated with masses of immigrants, the United States Immigration Bureau opened, on January 1, 1892, a large facility on Ellis Island in upper New York Bay for the reception of newcomers. For the next sixty-two years, Ellis Island would serve not only as the main point of entry for America's immigrants but as a symbol of the hopes, fears, and disappointments of all those who entered the country from foreign lands.

ONCE A PICNIC ground for the early Dutch settlers, the island, about a mile off the tip of lower Manhattan, was named for Samuel Ellis, who owned it in the 1770s. It was purchased by federal authorities from New York State in 1808 for use as a government arsenal and fort. After the creation of the Immigration Bureau in 1891, the immigration station was moved from inadequate facilities at Castle Garden—the former fortress at Battery Park on the extreme southern tip of Manhattan—to Ellis Island.

Officials saw the island as a *cordon sanitaire*, where masses of immigrants could be received, examined for disease, and quarantined, admitted to the mainland, or deported. For millions, Ellis Island was either the portal to the New World or the locked gate from which they were turned away.

At the height of its activity early in the twentieth century, Ellis Island processed, in its flag-draped Great Hall, a million people a year, twelve million passing through the place between 1895 and 1924. It was the principal immigrant processing station for the United States from 1892 to 1943. Since 1965 Ellis Island has been part of the Statue of Liberty National Monument, though it was allowed to fall into decay. After an extensive restoration project, the facility reopened as the Ellis Island Immigration Museum in 1990.

Not every generation of Americans would have erected a monument to immigration. While Americans have always enjoyed thinking of their country as a refuge of peace, liberty, and opportunity, immigrants have frequently been subjected to hatred and prejudice, and immigration has been periodically reduced by restrictive legislation and quotas. The United States, of course, began as a nation of immigrants in the seventeenth century, the vast majority English speakers who became farmers and espoused the Protestant religions. The next century saw waves of German immigration, which made many native-born Americans nervous about the capacity of American society to absorb foreign-speaking new-comers. The next "assault" on Americans' perceived cultural identity came in the nineteenth century as large numbers of Irish-Catholics fled to these shores in an effort to escape famine and political oppression. This time, many Americans worried that their essentially Anglo-Protestant culture would disintegrate, and the Irish were subjected to a good deal of prejudice and abuse, some of it sanctioned by law.

Balancing the nation's fears were the needs of industry, which sought cheap immigrant labor in ever-increasing numbers by about 1880. This period saw the greatest influx of Italians, Greeks, Turks, Russians, Slavs, and Jews, sparking new fears about the possibility of "assimilating" so many and diverse peoples into an American culture. The Chinese Exclusion Act of 1882 barred Chinese immigration into the United States for a period of ten years and was regularly renewed until 1920. In 1917 immigrants were subjected to a literacy test, and in 1924 legislation put sharp limits on the number of immigrants permitted to come to the United States (154,000 annually, plus the wives and minor children of U.S. citizens). The 1924 act established national origin quotas aimed at sharply reducing immigration from southern and eastern European countries on the xenophobic grounds that these immigrants were less likely to make good Americans than those from northern and western Europe.

Following the horrors and devastation of World War II, some restrictive legislation was lifted to admit wartime refugees. In 1965, as the result of a growing sensitivity to civil rights issues, amendments to the Immigration and Nationality Act repealed quotas based on national origin. But the World War II refugees were usually the white Europeans always favored by nativist sentiment, and the 1965 amendements left enough restrictions to allow the government, in recent years, to use immigration policy as a means of rewarding political client states—welcoming, for example, pro-American South Vietnamese and anti-Sandinista Nicaraguans, while denying entry to Salvadoran refugees.

Given traditional biases, Congress's ham-handed attempt to address the problem of the massive illegal alien population in the Southwest in the 1980s came as no surprise. Passing a law aimed at providing legal status and official protection to long-standing illegal residents and temporary workers, most of whom were Mexican, Congress only made matters worse by punishing employers for failing to keep track of the proper papers, which led them to discriminate against anyone with a foreign-sounding name.

The refusal of the government to accept Haitian refugees in the 1990s, excused on the grounds that Haitians had already overrun the temporary camps set up to process their applications for immigrant status, only underlined the historical consistency of American immigration policy. No one could reasonably imagine white Europeans huddled into barbed wire enclosures as authorities debated whether the military regime they fled was brutal enough to qualify them to become Americans.

John Muir Founds the Sierra Club (1892)

The event: On June 4, 1892, the great pioneering naturalist John Muir merged a citizens' group, which he had organized to protect the Sierra Nevada from exploitation, with the Alpine Club, a small group of mountain-loving University of California, Berkeley, students, to form the Sierra Club, the nation's first group of environmental activists.

MUIR REASONED THAT those who enjoy the wilderness would also fight to protect it; therefore, the charter of the new club proclaimed a dedication to "exploring, enjoying, and rendering accessible the mountain regions of the Pacific Coast" as well as a commitment to enlist "the support and cooperation of the people and the government in preserving the forests and other features of the Sierra Nevada."

The Sierra Club's first major political action was to arrange the transfer of the Yosemite Valley from state to federal jurisdiction in 1906. Next the club did legal battle with the city of San Francisco, which proposed to convert Yosemite National Park's Hetch Hetchy Valley to a reservoir. The club lost in 1913, and a year later, Muir died.

After Muir, William E. Colby became the club's director. During the period between the world wars, the Sierra Club campaigned successfully to enlarge Sequoia National Park, establish Kings Canyon National Park, and block logging in Washington's Olympic National Park.

Beginning in 1901, the Sierra Club sponsored annual High Trips in the mountains. The trips became increasingly popular, so that club guides were eventually leading approximately five thousand persons on almost five hundred trips annually. By the 1950s, however, the charter mandate to render the mountains "accessible" came into conflict with the aim of preserving the wilderness. During that decade the Sierra Club was increasingly critical of national policy with regard to outdoor recreation and successfully campaigned for the Outdoor Recreation Resources Review Act of 1958, which compelled public and private agencies to catalog park, wilderness, and wildlife resources and their recreational potential with an eye toward curbing overuse. In concert with the Wilderness Society, the Sierra Club campaigned for the National Wilderness Act of 1964, which established a National Wilderness Preservation System.

The 1950s also saw the expansion of the club from an association of independent local chapters to a centrally directed national organization. David R. Brower, the first executive director of the newly constituted club, led a campaign to preserve Dinosaur National Monument against a Bureau of Reclamation dam project in 1952; between 1952 and 1954, Brower established Atlantic and Pacific Northwest club chapters. Beginning with the 1960 publication of naturalist-photographer Ansel Adams's *This Is the American Earth*, the club began the highly acclaimed and profitable Exhibit Format book series. The 1960s saw a steady increase in membership and political influence until 1966, when, as a direct result of its lobbying, the organization lost its tax-exempt status. The later sixties were marked by financial problems and dissension within the organization, a trend that was gradually reversed by the 1970s, when the Sierra Club again assumed a leadership role in battles over Alaskan lands and worldwide environmental issues. Today, the Sierra Club has some three hundred thousand members in fifty-three chapters throughout the United States and Canada.

The Homestead Strike Erupts (1892)

The event: In 1892, ten thousand workers belonging to the strongest labor union in the country struck the Carnegie Steel Company in Homestead, Pennsylvania, and the town erupted into a pitched battle between labor and management that shocked the nation.

FROM JULY 6 to November 20, 1892, the Amalgamated Association of Iron and Steel Workers waged class warfare against the Carnegie Steel Company. Three years earlier the union had gained a favorable contract, but in 1892 Andrew Carnegie was in no mood to cater to its demands again. He ordered his plant manager, Henry Clay Frick, to increase production demands. When the union members refused to accept the new conditions, Frick locked them out of the plant. On July 2 he fired all union members. These totaled less than a fifth of the 3,800-strong workforce, but many nonmembers soon vowed to support the union. When the strikers took over the town, Frick hired three hundred Pinkerton guards, who arrived on July 6. A full-scale battle ensued. At the end of the day nine strikers and seven guards were dead, and the Pinkertons surrendered.

On July 12 the governor of Pennsylvania, Robert E. Pattison, sent eight thousand militiamen to Homestead. Gradually they were able to get control of the situation, and strikebreakers went to work for the company. Over the next four months the company made formal complaints against about a hundred strikers, many of whom were arrested for murder. Although most were released, the union bled its coffers dry on legal defense. On November 20 the strike was declared over. Carnegie Steel had won the showdown, and its managers quickly slapped the workers with longer work hours and lower wages.

Although the Homestead strikers inspired many union members, the strike itself only underscored the dangers and difficulties any union faced in trying to match the combined power of the corporation and the government.

John L. Sullivan and Jim Corbett Fight a Heavyweight Championship Bout (1892)

The event: On September 7, 1892, James J. "Gentleman Jim" Corbett defeated John L. Sullivan in the first heavyweight championship boxing match to be fought by Marquis of Queensberry rules, initiating what remains the most controversial American spectator sport.

BOXING GOT OFF to a slow start in America during the early 1800s. By mid-century, British boxers were touring the country and taking on all comers. During one such bout, the amateur Paddy Ryan upset the English heavyweight titleholder, Joe Goss, and became the first American champion, losing his title to John L. Sullivan in a bare-knuckle bout at Mississippi City in 1882. With the $5,000 in prize money, Sullivan—like the English before him—toured the country and took on all comers, insisting on the use of gloves to attract more than a crowd of barroom rowdies. He knocked forty-nine of fifty opponents out cold, until Gentleman Jim Corbett took the crown in twenty-one brutal rounds in New Orleans. Though outlawed in most states, boxing continued to grow over the next quarter-century, producing a great number of box-office attractions—Bob Fitzsimmons, Tommy Burns, Jack Johnson, George Dixon, Joe Gans—before New York legalized the sport in 1920 and set up a boxing commission.

The 1920s became the golden age of boxing—and many other spectator sports—when the flowering of the entertainment business, a cult of celebrity, and leisure-oriented consumerism resulted from the widespread popularity of the new motion-picture industry and the introduction of commercial radio. Tex Rickard, who had built Madison Square Garden, made his arena part of boxing's vocabulary with bouts that reached a national audience stitched together by broadcasters and sportswriters. Boxing passed the million-dollar gate mark in 1920 when Jack Dempsey fought Frenchman Georges Carpentier, the first fight to go "on the air," and gate receipts only went up as championship fights became world "events" on the radio and in the papers. The *New York Times* ran over a dozen pages on the 1923 Dempsey bout against Gene Tunney.

Boxing had become big business, and sportswriters and gamblers—the public and private face of almost all American professional sports—bought "pieces" of a fighter. Boxing became the most gangster-ridden of all spectator sports, and hardly a major match in its history has passed without at least the suspicion that it was fixed. When television came along in the 1950s and made the "Friday Night Fights" an institution, boxing as a sport took a nosedive, since TV was interested in only the "stars." Small clubs, which had produced great fighters in the past, could no longer attract crowds. Heavyweight champions like Floyd Patterson fought rarely, and then usually only against "bums." The game was almost ruined when Sonny Liston knocked out Patterson twice in early rounds before a theater-television audience whose members had paid five dollars minimum to see the fiascoes.

The flamboyant Cassius Clay, probably the best heavyweight of all time, revived interest in the fight-game in the 1960s. When Clay converted to the Black Muslim faith, changed his name to Muhammad Ali, and refused to be drafted into the armed services, he was banned from boxing during the prime years of his career, only to stage two incredible comebacks. By then, however, boxing had become a series of extravagantly staged entertainments, the province of the very rich and a few shady promoters, who made tens of millions from the media exposure of their "clients" in carefully controlled mismatches or endlessly negotiated title bouts.

Professor Turner Announces the Closing of the Frontier (1893)

The event: On July 12, 1893, an obscure history professor from the University of Wisconsin rose to deliver a paper at the Art Institute of Chicago as part of the World Columbian Exposition. Based on his reading of the 1890 census, in which the United States Bureau of the Census had decided that it could no longer designate the boundaries of a western frontier by means of population statistics, Frederick Jackson Turner announced that the frontier, the source of so much of

America's distinctive identity, was now, in effect, "closed." Turner's "frontier thesis" not only made him America's foremost historian, it profoundly influenced the way most Americans would think about themselves and their past ever afterward.

IN REACTION TO the New England-dominated academic history of his day, which seemed at times to blithely ignore any event that had occurred south or west of Harvard Square, Turner brought his remarks to this conclusion: "What the Mediterranean Sea was to the Greeks, breaking the bond of custom, offering new experiences, calling out new institutions and activities, that, and more, the ever retreating frontier has been to the United States." No one in the hot, stuffy auditorium stirred from their lethargy as he went on to say, "And now, four centuries from the discovery of America, at the end of a hundred years of life under the Constitution, the frontier has gone, and with its going has closed the first period of American history."

In the course of the speech, Turner had argued that the expansive character of American life—"that restless, nervous energy; that dominant individualism . . . that buoyancy and exuberance which comes from freedom"—created by the frontier would not end with its closing. Instead, he argued, "American energy will continue to demand a wider field of exercise." The closing of the frontier was to be mourned because the subduing of the American wilderness had made its conquerors superior people—and now their greatness might vanish with the conditions of its birth.

Turner used the closing of the frontier to invoke an American equivalent of the Greek Golden Age. For him the frontier curiously retreats rather than advances, since not civilization but the wilderness has become definitive for the American character. On the frontier, he argued, that character was formed. Even if the frontier experience was morally ugly, it had made the Americans a unique people, a people whose virtues could be celebrated even as their horrifying excesses could be dismissed as peculiar to conditions now in the past. Finally, Turner went on, because the frontier had closed, America's "safety valve" was shut off. Without the limitless West in which to escape, Americans would be impelled to undertake imperialist ventures overseas.

The immense influence Turner's theory would have was certainly not evident the night he first gave his "frontier-thesis" speech. No questions were asked in the discussion session that followed, and except for a brief mention in a single Chicago newspaper, his thesis was pretty much ignored until his friend Woodrow Wilson—the president of Princeton University, himself destined for a higher calling—borrowed and adapted Turner's ideas for his own use. As a result, other academics and a few editors gradually saw the revolutionary potential of the theory, and soon the *Atlantic Monthly* published an article about it. As Turner's views spread, they changed utterly the teaching of history, as professor after professor, high school teacher after high school teacher, politician after politician took up and exaggerated the new theory.

Recent historians have questioned whether the frontier ever existed, much less whether it closed in 1890. Yet the fact remains that, before 1900, virtually no space was given to the West in the standard textbook histories, whereas the vast majority of those published since the turn of the century have trumpeted the frontier as a major force in America's development as a nation. Turner, who eventually took a job at Harvard, could boast that his frontier thesis not only explained American history, but defined it for decades.

William Jennings Bryan Delivers His "Cross of Gold Speech" (1896)

The event: In 1896, the brilliant young orator William Jennings Bryan electrified the Democratic National Convention with his famous "Cross of Gold" speech, winning the presidential nomination for himself and a prominent place on the national agenda for the Populist cause he represented.

THROUGHOUT THE 1880s and the early 1890s, halls of governments around the country rang with the farmers' complaints. If sometimes their protests seemed disjointed, they were certainly understandable, given the changes that had swept over American agriculture after the Civil War. Postwar industrialists had stolen from the farmers the very words with which they had once defined themselves, appropriating for use by big capital the slogan traditionally belonging to Jeffersonian and Jacksonian radicals. "Laissez faire," gussied up in a top hat and frock coat, now meant allowing men with economic power to have everything their own way. Under an imperious capitalism, Jefferson's basic philosophical and ethical concepts—democracy, liberty, equality, opportunity, individualism—had suffered a strange political transformation. Rather than the popular watchwords of good government, Jefferson's hoary terms had become the clarion calls of the new industrialists for virtually no government at all.

Nor was it merely a matter of words. New machinery—sulky plows with wheels and a driver's seat, corn planters, end-gate seeders, spring tooth rakes, binders, threshing machines, hay balers, hoisting forks, corn shellers—had helped farmers in the South recover from the devastation of the war, and those in the North and West vastly to improve their productivity. Self-sufficiency had once been the rule; now the farmer produced for the market, and the increased yields, combined with a revolution in communications and transportation, broke his isolation forever. The farmer now had to compete in a world-wide market without protection or control over production, and found himself tied to the swings and fortunes of business and price cycle.

The farmer could not see the huge abstract market itself, but he could see his productivity increase while the prices for his commodity dropped. And he could feel the unfairness of it all: the more he grew, the less he earned; the poorer he became, the higher his expenses mounted. With the gap between income and expenses constantly widening, farmers found themselves forced to mortgage their land or borrow money to cover debts. Pushed beyond their old Jeffersonian vocabulary by the historic trap of their economic situation, farmers felt, to quote Georgia's Thomas E. Watson, later the head of the Populist Party, "like victims of some horrid nightmare."

Farmers around the country began forming unions and alliances that went by a number of different names, starting with the old People's Party created by the Grangers in 1874. From 1876 to 1878 they called themselves the Greenback Party, then the Greenback Labor Party in 1880, 1882, and 1884, then the Union Labor Party in 1888, and then the Farmers' and Laborers' Union in 1890. Whatever the name, as a group they proposed some of the most radical economic and political changes of the late nineteenth century: government ownership of the railroads and utilities, a graduated income tax, the secret ballot, women's suffrage, Prohibition, and most of all the creation of inflation through manipulation of the money system, or, as they called it, "the free coinage of silver."

They were the first to insist that laissez-faire economics was not the final solution to all industrial problems, that the government had some responsibility for its citizens' social well-being. They scared the hell out of people—especially eastern capitalists.

On February 22, 1892, at a huge meeting of the Congress of Industrial Organizations in St. Louis, the National Farmers Alliance took control of the floor over delegates from assorted reform groups—the Knights of Labor, the Nationalists, Single-Taxers, Greenbackers, Prohibitionists, and a dozen others—and declared the formation of a new political party, the new People's Party, which became better known as the Populist Party—the most radical third party in American history. The new party called for a national convention to nominate a candidate for president in 1892, which it did in Omaha on July the Fourth.

The Populist candidate, James B. Weaver, promptly lost the election, as did the Republicans, to the Democratic nominee, Grover Cleveland. But that hardly mattered. The Populists' main service was to usher in a long-delayed period of reform. They bridged the gaps between parties, sections, races, and classes that had kept reformers apart in the past, reviving the old agrarian alliance between the South and the West and creating a new one between farmers and labor.

Their best chance at national power came in 1896, when they were able to steal the Democratic nomination from Cleveland for Bryan. What gave them the edge was the worst depression yet. The Panic of 1893 began when the Philadelphia and Reading Railroad went bankrupt, shaking the New York Stock Exchange into the biggest selling spree on record. Banks called their loans. Credit dried up. The Erie, the Northern Pacific, the Union Pacific, and the Santa Fe all failed, one after another. Mills, factories, furnaces, and mines everywhere shut down. By the time it was over, five hundred banks and fifteen hundred firms went down in bankruptcy. What had once seemed like wild rhetoric suddenly appeared more reasonable, and the outlandish Populist demands, from an income tax to the franchise for women, seemed if not entirely acceptable, at least *thinkable*. Masses poured into the party. The Democrats, with an eye on those votes, threw out the conservatives, President Cleveland among them, and struck a deal with the Populists.

Going from "The Boy Orator of the Platte" to "The Great Commoner," William Jennings Bryan would capture not only the nomination for the Populists but the Democratic Party itself, of which he would be the undisputed leader for two decades. Though the joint Populist-Democratic ticket was soundly trounced by McKinley, whose war with Spain and empire building would spell the end of Populism, its reforms were on the national agenda. In a few short years an assassin's bullet would make Teddy Roosevelt president, and the process of writing into law the Populists' demands, gussied up in the middle-class garb of Progressive "moral uplift," would get under way. But though the Democrats would nominate Bryan again and again for president, and though he would become Woodrow Wilson's secretary of state (only to resign when Wilson went to war), he would never achieve the political significance he achieved the day he told America that it was crucifying its farmers on a cross of gold.

America Declares War on Spain (1898)

The event: On February 15, 1898, the U.S. Navy battleship *Maine* exploded while at anchor in Havana Harbor, galvanizing war fever in the United States and catapulting the nation into armed conflict with Spain.

IN FEBRUARY 1896, General Valeriano Weyler of Spain arrived in Havana to assume the office of governor of the Spanish colony of Cuba. Foremost among his new duties was the task of routing rebel forces which had been fighting against Spanish rule for a year. One of his first actions was to round up Cuban citizens and place them in "reconcentration" camps, in order to keep them from secretly supplying the rebels. This outrage only strengthened Cuban resistance efforts, and Americans, who saw the struggle as a fight against Spanish imperialism, openly sided with the rebels.

President Grover Cleveland recoiled from the notion of engaging America in the Cuban-Spanish conflict, and his successor, William McKinley, elected in 1896, continued Cleveland's policy. Across the country, however, debate intensified over whether the United States should intervene on behalf of the Cuban rebels. One manifestation of that popular debate was found in the press, particularly in Joseph Pulitzer's *New York World* and William Randolph Hearst's *New York Journal*, bitter rivals in a war of their own—a circulation war. The rivals eagerly fed their readers sensational stories of the atrocities carried out by Cuba's Spanish rulers, heating up circulation as well as war fever.

Despite Spain's efforts to end the rebellion, fighting and rioting in Cuba continued. In January 1898, President McKinley ordered the battleship *Maine* to Havana Harbor in order to protect American citizens; for the United States had considerable investments in Cuba, especially in its sugar plantations, and many Americans were living on the island. When the *Maine* blew up, killing 266 crewmen, Americans who supported intervention blamed the Spanish for the disaster and called for American retaliation. Although it is now generally believed that an explosion in one of the ship's powder magazines caused the disaster, a naval court of inquiry convened at the time found that the battleship had exploded after hitting a submarine mine. That was enough to rouse the American public to cries of "Remember the *Maine*!"—a battle slogan that consciously recalled the "Remember the Alamo!" of the Texas Rebellion and the Mexican War.

President McKinley continued to attempt a neutral course but soon realized that Congress, heavily influenced by the American public, was on the verge of declaring war on its own, thereby discrediting his administration. In April, the reluctant president asked Congress for authority to send armed forces to Cuba. Congress eagerly agreed and also resolved to recognize Cuba's independence from Spain, declaring that the United States had intentions of annexing it as a territory. On April 24, in response to its military threat, Spain declared war on the United States.

The first American action in the war took place not in Cuba but in the Spanish-occupied Philippine Islands. Admiral George Dewey, after learning of the declaration of war, took his Asiatic Squadron from Hong Kong to Manila Bay. On May 1 he fired on the Spanish fleet, destroying all ten ships in the bay. President McKinley sent eleven thousand troops to the Philippines, and that force, along with Filipino irregulars commanded by Emilio Aguinaldo, defeated Spanish forces in Manila on August 13.

Military action in Cuba was equally quick and decisive. On May 29 the American fleet blockaded the Spanish fleet at Santiago Harbor on the eastern end of Cuba. The following month, seventeen thousand troops invaded the island at Daiquiri and moved toward Santiago. The American troops, including Lieutenant Colonel Theodore Roosevelt's Rough Riders, stormed and captured San Juan Hill on July 1. Spanish Admiral Pascual Cervera, under fire from American troops on land and bottled up by the American fleet in the harbor, decided that the only way out was to run the blockade. In a four-hour engagement, the American fleet, sustaining only minor damage and the loss of a single sailor, completely destroyed the Spanish ships. On August 12 Spain agreed to withdraw from Cuba and to cede Puerto Rico and Guam, an island in the Marianas, to the United States. Formal peace negotiations in Paris resulted in Spain's also selling the Philippine Islands to the United States for $20 million, though nationalist guerillas in the Philippines plagued the American occupiers until 1901.

The United States set up a territorial government in Puerto Rico with little difficulty, but the problems surrounding the American-Cuban relationship were more knotty. In 1898 President McKinley installed a military government that was quickly in conflict with Cuban leaders. Because of the precarious state of Cuba's economy and its overall political instability, some Americans and even some Europeans advocated the U.S. annexation of Cuba to protect American investments there. In May 1902, however, the United States finally and completely abandoned any plans for annexation. Cuban leaders had drafted a new constitution, which gained American approval after the addition of clauses establishing American military bases on the island and guaranteeing the right of the United States to intervene in Cuban affairs in order to "preserve" the island's independence.

In large part as a result of the popularity he gained during what John Hay had called "that splendid little war," McKinley's vice-president, Theodore Roosevelt, who had assumed office following McKinley's assassination, was elected president in 1904. He established a policy toward the Caribbean islands and Latin America that determined American action in the region for decades to come. Known as the Roosevelt Corollary to the Monroe Doctrine, the policy called for the United States to act as an international police force in the region. In this way, and for better or worse, the United States moved away from the isolationism that had dominated its policies ever since George Washington had warned against "foreign entanglements," and closer to assuming a position as a *world* power.

The Film *The Great Train Robbery* Is Released (1903)

The event: In 1903, Edwin S. Porter created *The Great Train Robbery*, a "flicker" based on the chases and gunfights of the turn-of-the-century "Wild West" shows. It revolutionized the making of motion pictures through the use of "cuts" to show parallel and overlapping action leading up to a climax, turning a vaudeville curiosity into a new popular art form.

A FRENCHMAN NAMED Georges Méliès, a former professional magician, anticipated Porter's narrative film in witty, inventive productions filled with frenetic activity and a lot of imagination, but he was driven out of business by sharp operators who "duped" his films and sold them at discount to vaudeville houses. By 1905

 a few entrepreneurs, inspired by the popularity of the bootlegged Méliès productions and Porter's immense success with *The Great Train Robbery*, began opening "nickelodeons," crude theaters set up in the backs of stores and warehouses that charged customers a nickel to watch minute-long shorts, produced as fillers between vaudeville acts, and the new ten-minute one-reelers.

Porter's film established the single reel, which took up precisely the same amount of time as the traditional vaudeville "turn," or act, as the standard length for American movies. It also set the fashion and the pattern for the long-lived American "Western" and encouraged others—like the creative genius D.W. Griffith—to follow his lead in exploring the implications of disjunctive editing, which took liberties with space and time. Soon nickelodeons sprang up in almost every neighborhood in the cities, and outright purchase gave way to rentals. New "exchanges"—middlemen buying prints from studios and renting them to exhibitors—served some eight thousand nickelodeons by 1908, and the little theaters—immediately and immensely profitable—attracted more than twenty-five million viewers a week. The audience was mostly urban working-class, people who could watch the "flickers" and enjoy them no matter what language they spoke, what country they came from, or which tenement they lived in. The movies became the poor man's theater.

The Wright Brothers Fly Their First Plane (1903)

The event: On December 17, 1903, at Kitty Hawk beach on the North Carolina Outer Banks, Orville Wright made the first piloted, powered, sustained, and controlled flight in the history of mankind.

ORVILLE AND WILBUR WRIGHT, sons of Bishop Milton Wright of the United Brethren in Christ, had little formal schooling, but they were hard workers with great intellectual curiosity. In 1892 they opened a bicycle shop in their hometown of Dayton, Ohio, from which they made enough money to finance their

 unique hobby: aeronautics. Their interest in the subject began in 1896, when they read a newspaper story about the death of Otto Lilienthal, a German aeronautical experimenter killed in a glider crash. The brothers bought every book and periodical they could find on the subject and built a biplane kite in 1899. Over the next three years they built three man-carrying gliders and tested them at Kitty Hawk. When the first two gliders failed to perform well, the brothers invented the world's first wind tunnel in the fall of 1901, making it practical to test a wide variety of designs safely.

Armed with the results of the Kitty Hawk glider flights and the wind tunnel tests, the brothers built a craft. It was a weighty 750 pounds, equipped with a 170-pound, twelve-horsepower gasoline engine. The first manned flight at Kitty Hawk remained aloft for twelve seconds over a distance of about 120 feet. The Wright brothers made three more flights that day, Wilbur remaining aloft just shy of a full minute over a distance of 852 feet.

The modest, unassuming brothers did not immediately publicize their achievement but returned to Dayton, where they continued their experiments in a local cow pasture. By 1905 they had achieved a flight of thirty-eight minutes' duration over a distance of twenty-four miles. With their invention now largely perfected, they received a patent on May 22, 1906, and during 1908-1909 toured with the plane throughout England, France, and Italy. In 1909 the brothers demonstrated the aircraft for the U.S. Army, which accepted their design on August 2 of that year, and the Wright brothers organized the Wright Company to begin large-scale manufacture.

The U.S. Senate Approves the Panama Canal Treaty (1904)

The event: In 1904, at the urging of President Theodore Roosevelt, Congress ratified the Panama Canal Treaty, clearing the way for the emerging world power to flex its muscles and demonstrate its technological and financial might.

THE BUILDING OF the Panama Canal required over-coming enormous obstacles of geography, climate, and politics. The origin of the project lay in the 1840s, when westward-bound settlers were looking for alternatives to the arduous overland routes. The United States negotiated an agreement with New Granada (a nation consisting of present-day Panama and Colombia) for rights of transit across the Isthmus of Panama, which separates the Caribbean Sea from the Pacific Ocean. Crossing the dense and disease-ridden isthmus jungle was preferable to making the long sea journey all the way down one side of the South American continent and up the other, and the 1849 California gold rush prompted the United States to fund the Panama Railroad across the isthmus. The ultimate goal, of the United States as well as Great Britain, was to build a *canal* across the isthmus. The two nations concluded the Clayton-Bulwer Treaty (1850), agreeing that neither would assert exclusive control over the canal.

Of course, there was no canal. In 1881 a French firm under the direction of Ferdinand de Lesseps began construction of a canal but went bankrupt in short order. Twenty years later, in the flush of imperialist fervor brought by victory in the Spanish-American War and encouraged by an expansionist president, Theodore Roosevelt, the United States persuaded Great Britain to relinquish its claim to joint control of a Central American canal. In 1901 an American commission recommended building the canal not in Panama but in Nicaragua; however, the New Panama Canal Company, successors to de Lesseps's defunct firm, persuaded Roosevelt to build the canal through Panama when it offered its rights to the canal route not for its original asking price of $109 million, but for $40 million. Congress authorized construction early in 1902, and the next year ratified the Hay-Herrán Treaty, granting the U.S. a ten-mile-wide strip of land across the isthmus in return for a $10 million-dollar cash payment and an annuity. When the Colombian senate held out for a higher figure, however, the United States helped engineer an uprising in Panama, by means of which Panama became an independent republic. A new treaty was concluded with the new government on the same terms that had been offered to New Granada.

Construction through the Panamanian jungle was a logistical nightmare. Climate and terrain presented tremendous difficulties, of course, but it was disease—yellow fever and malaria—that threatened to wreck the project before it had fairly begun. Colonel William Gorgas waged an all-out war against mosquito-breeding swamps and improved sanitation practices. By 1906 his efforts had largely eradicated the two jungle plagues, and it was now up to Colonel George Washington Goethals, of the U.S. Army Corps of Engineers, to build the forty-mile-long channel, replete with a complex system of locks. Eight years, $300 million dollars, and 240 million cubic yards of earth later, in 1914, the Panama Canal was opened to shipping. The formal dedication took place on July 12, 1920. The United States had succeeded in changing the political—and physical—geography of the planet.

"Big Bill" Haywood Founds the IWW (1905)

The event: In 1905, William "Big Bill" Haywood presided at the founding convention of the Industrial Workers of the World, or Wobblies, the most radical labor union in American history.

FROM RUDE BEGINNINGS in Salt Lake City, Utah, a fatherless Haywood went to work in the mines at age fifteen, working his way up through the ranks of the Western Federation of Miners, the era's preeminent radical labor union. Haywood was with the WFM in Colorado between 1903 and 1905, when its conflict with mining and smelting corporations flared into class warfare that pitted miners against state militia in one of the most bitter and violent labor disputes in the country's history. Convinced by his experience in Colorado that American workers needed to organize into "one big union," Haywood, in company with Socialist Party leader Eugene V. Debs, Daniel de Leon, and seventy-five-year-old United Mine Workers organizer Mary Harris "Mother" Jones, founded the IWW.

Though half a century of right-wing red-baiting has permanently scarred the face of American socialism, in the early twentieth century it was a real political force, especially among the working class, who saw it as a method of distributing social wealth through government control rather than private enterprise. For all the Wobblies' revolutionary rhetoric and their reputation for violence, they were the only ones at the time organizing women, blacks, the newer immigrants, and all unskilled, semiskilled, and migrant laborers, groups the American Federation of Labor craft unions wouldn't touch. They struck mines in the Rocky Mountain states, lumber camps in the Pacific Northwest and across the South, and the textile mills of the Northeast—and for their trouble were jailed, beaten, and sometimes, as in the case of the legendary Joe Hill, framed and executed. Attacked by both vigilantes and federal agents, who prosecuted them under any law they could find—espionage, sedition, even criminal conspiracy—the Wobblies were swept away by the Red Scare just as the Communists, inspired by the Russian Revolution, began vying with them for the allegiance of American radicals.

Haywood himself, after being acquitted of conspiracy in the murder of former Colorado governor Frank Steunenburg, did a stint with the avowedly passivist Socialist Party before returning to the Wobblies, whose taste for direct mass action more closely fit his temperament. Caught up in the net of espionage indictments in 1918, Haywood was tried and convicted in Chicago along with a hundred other IWW leaders. Alcoholic now, and racked by diabetes, Haywood jumped bail when his appeal was rejected by the Supreme Court and fled to Russia, where he died in Moscow, alone and alien.

Upton Sinclair Publishes *The Jungle* (1906)

The event: In 1906, Upton Sinclair published a novel entitled *The Jungle* that created a storm of indignation from the American public against the meat packing industry for its arrogant disregard of basic health standards and that led to government regulation of food and drugs.

SINCLAIR'S NOVEL TOLD the story of Jurgis Rudkus, a Lithuanian immigrant who worked in a meat-packing plant. An instant success, the now-classic work of

American muckraking captured the plight of millions of immigrants, who—unable to speak English—made good targets for exploitation by employers, policemen, and others with power. *The Jungle* described in nauseating detail the horrors of the meat-packing business, which sanctioned, among other things, the use of tubercular beef and the grinding up of rats. Six months after its publication Congress passed the Pure Food and Drug Act and a Meat Inspection Act.

Sinclair was part of a literary tradition that captivated American readers in the early twentieth century. President Theodore Roosevelt gave the movement its name—"muckraking." He had adopted the word from John Bunyan's *Pilgrim's Progress*, which portrayed a man armed with a "muck-rake" to sweep up the filth around him while he remained unaware of the celestial glory above his head. Muckraking was born from the historical marriage of the Progressive movement and the professionalization of journalism. Sinclair, Ida Tarbell, Lincoln Steffens, and others considered themselves dispassionate observers of the American scene. Their job was to report what they saw, and their works fed the progressive spirit that called for reform.

Among the many concerns the muckrakers targeted for exposure were business corruption, political skullduggery, child labor, slum conditions, racial discrimination, prostitution, sweatshop labor, insurance fraud, and illegal stock manipulations. The magazines *McClure's*, *The Atlantic Monthly*, and *Collier's*, in particular, took pride in the scandals and injustices exposed by their muckrakers, and took heart in the increased circulation the popular journalism brought to the magazines. In 1902, *McClure's* serialized Ida Tarbell's landmark exposé of a dangerous monopoly, *History of Standard Oil*, and ran a series by Lincoln Steffens about urban corruption and political machines, collected in the book *The Shame of the Cities*.

The muckrakers created real change in American society. Their writings coalesced a diverse collection of progressive-minded individuals into a national movement, and their influence stretched into the late twentieth century, as magazines, like the *Nation* and the *New Republic* picked up the muckraking mantle even after the death of the Progressive movement proper.

William James Publishes *Pragmatism* (1907)

The event: In 1907, William James published *Pragmatism*, perhaps the single most significant American contribution to philosophy.

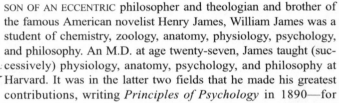

SON OF AN ECCENTRIC philosopher and theologian and brother of the famous American novelist Henry James, William James was a student of chemistry, zoology, anatomy, physiology, psychology, and philosophy. An M.D. at age twenty-seven, James taught (successively) physiology, anatomy, psychology, and philosophy at Harvard. It was in the latter two fields that he made his greatest contributions, writing *Principles of Psychology* in 1890—for many years the most widely used text in the field—*The Varieties of Religious Experience* (1902), a scientific study of the psychology of religion, and, of course, *Pragmatism* (1907).

In *Pragmatism* James developed ideas first expressed by the American philosopher Charles Sanders Peirce in 1878 into America's only true home-grown philosophy. Peirce's work, a series of lectures published in book form, was conceived as a means of reconciling, or at least moderating, conflicts between religious and scientific viewpoints. "The pragmatic method is primarily a method of settling metaphysical disputes that otherwise might be interminable," James wrote. How? By cultivating "the attitude of looking away from first things, principles, 'categories,' supposed necessities; and of looking towards last things, fruits, consequences, facts."

It is this approach—evaluating ideas not by origins but by psychological, aesthetic, and moral consequences—that made pragmatism far more than a means of settling disputes between scientists and theologians. Generations of American thinkers following James saw pragmatism as a philosophy vital enough to meet the intellectual needs of America's fast-moving, hard-headed democracy, inherently concerned less with origins than with ends. In America it mattered not if a man was born the son of a king or a laborer; what counted was the sum and consequence of his own life. By narrowing the gulf between airy speculation and heedless activity, pragmatism provided a method of thinking through to the consequences of an act without causing paralysis on the one hand or thoughtless action on the other.

The philosophy of pragmatism was central to the work of later American philosophers and social thinkers, including John Dewey and Bertrand Russell, and American authors and artists, including William Carlos Williams, Ernest Hemingway, and Jackson Pollock.

Henry Ford Introduces the Model T (1908)

The event: In 1908 Henry Ford introduced the Model T, the first mass-produced automobile, intending to make the new internal combustion engine vehicles affordable for the average working American.

A DEARBORN, MICHIGAN, farm boy (born July 30, 1863) with an aptitude for machinery, Henry Ford was a machinery shop apprentice, a traveling repairman for a farm machinery company, a sawmill operator, and chief engineer for the new Edison Illuminating Company in Detroit before he became interested in a novelty invention known as the "horseless carriage," or automobile. Ford built his first car in 1896, completing it in his shed at two a.m. on June 4. After working for a manufacturer of custom-made automobiles, Ford built his first racing car (the "999") and then organized the Ford Motor Company in 1903.

The company was profitable from the start but became even more so in 1908, when Ford introduced the Model T. Up to this point, all manufacturers, including Ford himself, had seen the automobile as a custom-made luxury item for the wealthy. To manufacture the Model T, Ford began to develop the principle of the assembly line. The first Model T sold for $850, cheaper than a custom-made vehicle but still beyond the reach of the average American. By 1913, however, Ford had thoroughly developed the assembly line throughout his plant. In 1908 he turned out 10,607 cars. In 1916, he turned out 730,041, priced at $360 each. By 1927, the last year the model was made, Ford had produced fifteen million

Model Ts.

The Model T, sturdy, reliable, and generic product of the early perfection of mass production, changed not only America but civilization itself. It fostered a consumer-driven society; it bestowed upon virtually all economic classes equal and unprecedented mobility; it began the unification of the nation through a vast network of roads; it began the suburbanization of the country; it dramatically changed the relation of labor and management; and it changed the nature of labor itself forever.

The NAACP Is Founded (1909)

The event: In 1909, the National Association for the Advancement of Colored People (NAACP) was founded to champion the rights of African-Americans. It became the most influential black organization in American history.

THE NAACP WAS founded by a group of intellectuals—both black and white—in New York City, who conceived of it as a response to the theory of gradualism advocated by Booker T. Washington. Not willing to wait for the white majority to recognize racial equality, the leaders of the NAACP instituted an aggressive program of speaking engagements, lobbying, and publishing. Its magazine, *The Crisis*, was edited for many years by W. E. B. Du Bois, a writer, sociologist, and historian. Du Bois was the country's first African-American Ph.D., with degrees from Fisk University, Harvard, and the University of Berlin, and was the foremost African-American intellectual of the twentieth century.

In addition to its public programs, the organization devoted efforts to testing discriminatory legislation in the courts. Among the first laws to fall to the NAACP's attack was the grandfather clause used in Southern states to prevent blacks from voting. By 1920 the NAACP claimed ninety thousand members, nearly half of whom were southerners. As the civil rights movement gained momentum in the South, the organization quickly became a leader in the fight against Jim Crow laws and lynching.

The relationship between Du Bois and the other NAACP leaders was always testy. One of its founders, Du Bois resigned from the organization in 1934 in a dispute over policy and direction. The Great Depression, Du Bois believed, meant that the organization should shift from what he saw as its narrow focus on legal rights and integration to concentrate on black economic advancement, even if it meant temporarily accommodating segregation. After several years of teaching, Du Bois returned to the NAACP in 1944 to guide its research efforts, only to be fired in yet another dispute four years later.

Perhaps the most famous NAACP court case was *Brown v. Board of Education of Topeka*. In this case, the Supreme Court ruled that "separate but equal" facilities were no longer acceptable and that the nation's public school systems must be desegregated. Since the heyday of civil rights action in the 1960s and early 1970s, the NAACP has directed its attention beyond the borders of the United States to address the problem of attaining equal rights in countries around the world.

Fire Breaks Out at the Triangle Shirtwaist Company (1911)

The event: At the end of the workday on March 25, 1911, one of the five hundred employees of the Triangle Shirtwaist factory noticed that a rag bin near her eighth-floor work station was on fire. Within minutes, the factory—a fire trap typical of the period's working conditions—was engulfed in flame, killing 146 workers, mostly immigrant women.

WHEN THE FIRE was discovered, workers immediately set about trying to extinguish the blaze. Their efforts proved fruitless, as piles of fabric ignited all over the eighth floor. The manager of the factory, Samuel Bernstein, ordered his employees to unroll the fire extinguisher hose, but they found it rotted and useless.

Only three avenues of escape were open to the factory workers, who occupied the top three floors of the ten-story Asch Building in New York City. They could use the freight elevators, the fire escape, or the stairways.

Some of the workers rushed to the single, inadequately constructed fire escape, which descended from the tenth floor to the second, stopping at a small courtyard. Some of the young women who used it fell from one landing to the next; one of the male employees fell from the eighth floor to the courtyard.

Other employees ran to the stairways. Those on the eighth floor found that the door to the stairway on one side of the building had been locked. When they rushed over to the other stairway, they found it completely clogged with workers fleeing from the ninth and tenth floors. The freight elevators were all that remained open to the workers on the eighth floor, and several of the cutters risked their lives by taking turns at operating the elevator to carry their coworkers to safety.

The seventy employees who worked on the tenth floor escaped by way of the staircases or climbed onto the roof, where students from New York University, located across the street, stretched ladders across to the Asch Building.

The 260 workers on the ninth floor suffered the worst fate of all. The warning telephone call from the eighth floor workers did not reach them, so that by the time they found out about the fire, their avenues of escape were mostly blocked. Some managed to climb down the cables of the freight elevator after they found it jammed full of employees from the tenth floor. Others crammed their way into the narrow staircase. Still others climbed onto the fire escape. But that spindly structure could not support the weight of hundreds of people, and it separated from the wall, falling to splinters on the ground and carrying many people with it.

Other ninth-floor workers fled to the window ledges. Firemen stretched a net about a hundred feet below on the street, and the workers began jumping off the ledge. Some of the young women were so frightened that they held hands and jumped in pairs. The weight was too much for the net, which split as bodies ripped through it.

To combat the blaze, the New York Fire Department sent thirty-five pieces of equipment, including a hook and ladder. The young women on the ninth-floor window ledge watched in horror as the ladder, fully raised, stopped short at the sixth floor.

Officials set up a temporary morgue on 26th Street, and over the next few days streams of survivors filed through the building to identify the 146 dead.

The fire brought a public outcry for laws to regulate the safety of working conditions. The New York Factory Investigating Commission was formed to examine and approve the working conditions in factories throughout the state. The commission's report, compiled during two-and-a-half years of research, brought sweeping changes to existing laws and introduced many new regulations. The fire had occurred early in an era of reform that was beginning to sweep the nation, as people decided that government had a responsibility to see to it that private industry protected the welfare of the laboring public.

Frederick Taylor Publishes *Principles of Scientific Management* (1911)

The event: In 1911 Frederick Taylor published *The Principles of Scientific Management*, which introduced the system of rationalizing the production process named after him and which profoundly affected the American workplace.

WHILE TAYLOR WAS a foreman at the Midvale Steel Company during the 1880s, he observed that, despite the growing mechanization of the plant, the rate of production was still largely dependent on the pace and methods set by the more skilled workers. This, Taylor reasoned, would always result in an excessive idiosyncracy that must ultimately retard the rate of production. To maximize productivity, Taylor decided, managers, not workers, must take control of the process, prescribing methods and setting the pace. Moreover, they must do this scientifically, based on meticulous observation and analysis of each manufacturing step—indeed, of each and every movement made by each and every worker. Collation of these observations would allow managers to determine the best method for getting a particular job done. It was a step toward making human workers as efficient as machines.

Taylor became a pioneer management consultant, and his method, which soon became known as Taylorism, caused great controversy in the American workplace. Taylor's methods did increase productivity, helping to make America an industrial giant. Owners and their managers argued that it also improved the lot of unskilled labor. Anyone could be trained to do the repetitive tasks assembly-line work demanded, they pointed out, and thus more jobs were made available to the growing numbers of unskilled laborers immigrating into the country during the early twentieth century. Moreover, Taylorism prescribed a system of "scaled piecework rates" as an incentive for workers to move faster and achieve higher output. For management this meant that productive workers were rewarded or that less productive workers were penalized. For the workers, however, Taylorism dehumanized the workplace, depriving them of most of their autonomy, and alienating them from motives of craftsmanship. Taylorism, widening the gulf between labor and management, was instrumental in creating the character of twentieth-century American industrial life, with consequences that could be viewed as both positive and sinister.

Robert M. La Follette Founds the Progressive Party (1912)

The event: In 1912 a U.S. senator from Wisconsin, Robert M. La Follette, led a group of Republican insurgents calling themselves Progressives and challenging conservative party regulars in an attempt to take the presidential nomination away from William Taft. The group would draft a longtime ally and former president—the very willing Teddy Roosevelt—to be their champion in the most important third-party movement in American history.

THE PROGRESSIVES, WHO came to power at the dawn of the twentieth century, were part of a national political movement that transcended party but not class. Born of the decay of Populism, the sensational writings of muckraking journalists, and the involvement of America's churches in social issues, Progressives re-

acted to the growing power of organized labor, the revolutionary demands of America's new intellectual radicals, and the changing racial and ethnic composition of America's cities with a moral "uplift" program of reform intended to check the excesses of capitalism while preserving it.

The Progressives spoke largely for upper- and middle-class reformers and developers, business and religious leaders, and the more successful newspapers. Interested in economic growth and clean government, they talked in lofty terms of "progress," "civic reform," and "modernization." They attacked mere politicians—particularly those elected officials more interested in patronage than patriotism, in political power than honest government, in vote-getting than moral decay. Their crusade for "good government" called for the initiative and referendum, public control of the railroad and utilities, a certain amount of trust-busting, primary elections, the popular election of senators, women's suffrage, and Prohibition.

They did not, however, speak for the urban poor, or racial and ethnic minorities, or labor radicals, all of whom they tended to view as morally decadent at best, and viciously criminal at worst. These views were reflected in the nativist pandering of American newspapers to these middle-class sentiments. From their country clubs, comfortable homes, and smug Protestant churches, they reached out to destroy the saloons and brothels where the workingman relaxed and talked politics. They acquiesced in the great "Red Scare" to purge from American society the intellectuals who took up the cause of the oppressed. They used World War I as an opportunity to attack ethnic cultures and homogenize America's white population, while the merit system with which they hoped to replace the spoils system routinely excluded blacks and other ethnic minorities from local, state, and federal government.

Progressivism began amid great promise in the fall of 1889 with the founding of Hull House by Jane Addams and Ellen Gates Starr. Their dedicated and pioneering social work made them role models for young men and women around the country and soon attracted the likes of John Dewey and George Herbert Mead, who developed a pragmatic philosophy based on that work to solve the problems of democracy. A new breed of journalists, derisively labeled "muckrakers," not only subscribed to the philosophy but also, by publicizing the social problems it addressed, helped to create a network of social workers, intellectuals, and reporters that could be loosely called a "movement." The movement captured the imagination of two charismatic young men—New York's Teddy Roosevelt and Wisconsin's Robert La Follette—and its political fortunes were made. When La Follette became governor of Wisconsin, he instituted the full range of Progressive reforms, including public administration by nonpartisan civil servants mostly drawn from the University of Wisconsin faculty. With the progressive press touting his "Wisconsin Idea," La Follette was elected to the U.S. Senate in 1905, where he would remain until his death in 1925. And when TR was inaugurated as president in 1901, the movement had in the nation's "bully pulpit" a national hero capable of reforming the entire country—on those days when he was willing.

Out of the movement, in fact, came three presidents, Roosevelt, Taft, and Wilson, whose achievements constitute the main legacy of Progressivism. TR, however truculently, moved against the trusts and backed government regulation of the railroads, got a pure food and drug law enacted, and championed the conservation of natural resources. Taft, despite his backsliding on tariff law and conservation, did his share of trust-busting and strengthened both the Interstate Commerce Commission and the court system. And Wilson lowered tariffs, introduced the graduated income tax and the Federal Reserve, and entered into World War I on what sounded suspiciously like yet another Progressive crusade—to make the entire world safe for democracy *and then* impose on it "good government."

La Follette was almost booted out of the Senate when he broke with Wilson, whose domestic policies he supported, over entering the war, becoming the leader of the isolationist opposition. Never much trusting Teddy Roosevelt's progressive credentials, he got the opportunity to prove his own when he ran as a third-party candidate against Coolidge in 1924. Garnering only 6 percent of the thirty million votes cast, La Follette was buried under a Coolidge electorial landslide, carrying only his home state. By then Progressivism was little more than a bitter memory, lost amid the rubble of Wilson's foreign policy.

In the long run, Progressive reform didn't seem to matter much. Prohibition was a disaster, creating a nation of lawbreakers rather than sober, civic-minded do-gooders. Women used their new vote to help elect throwbacks like Warren G. Harding, whose administration was wrecked with good old-fashioned Gilded Age scandals, and Calvin Coolidge, who folded his hands and smiled as the biggest wave of mergers and monopolizing yet marched the country and the world toward a massive depression. The initiative, the referendum, the recall, and the popular election of Senators had little impact on the way the country conducted its business. Only the Federal Reserve and the income tax remained.

Franklin Roosevelt revived some of the spirit of the best progressive reform, his New Deal being in many ways an extension of the social work from which Progressivism sprang. As for the Progressive party, its last candidate was Henry A. Wallace, in 1948, who—tainted by accusations of communist support—won only 2 percent of the popular and none of the electoral vote.

The Sixteenth Amendment Is Ratified (1913)

The event: In February, 1913, the Sixteenth Amendment, duly ratified by the states, became the law of the land, granting the federal government the right to collect taxes based on personal income.

INCOME TAXES ARE as old as the Bible, which documents the collection of a tithe payable in commodities. It was, however, the British who introduced the modern income tax during the Napoleonic Wars. The U.S. Treasury picked up on the idea, considering the possibility of introducing an income tax at the time of the War of 1812, but not until the Civil War did the federal government actually manage to levy one, with rates ranging from three to five percent. Though income taxes were phased out after the war, the Bureau of Internal Revenue established in 1862 lived on. In 1894 the growing anger among farmers and industrial workers over America's lopsided income distribution led Congress to bring income taxes back, but the act was declared unconstitutional by a conservative Supreme Court that saw even in its ungraduated tax a "communistic threat."

Progressive reformers whipped up sentiment for a graduated income tax after the turn of the century, and in 1909 President William Howard Taft suggested turning to a constitutional amendment as a way of avoiding the recalcitrant Court. A coalition of progressives alarmed by the rapid concentration of wealth in the hands of a few industrialists and conservatives looking for a reliable way to raise money for national emergencies made ratification possible.

The first rates imposed by the new law claimed one percent on taxable income above $3,000 for individuals or $4,000 for married couples and rose to a maximum of seven percent on incomes over $500,000. During World War I rates shot straight up from there, reaching by war's end 77 percent. They were scaled back in the prosperous and mostly Republican twenties, but began rising again with the huge Treasury deficits caused by the Great Depression. During World War II, when revenue was again tied to national survival, the top rate reached 91 percent. The war effort got a big boost in 1943 when Congress imposed an automatic withholding system on taxpayers, doubling the amount collected in its first year. At the same time, exemptions were lowered to broaden the tax base, turning what had been in effect a class tax into a mass levy. After the war, the government reduced rates moderately, only to raise them again when the Korean War broke out. Lyndon Johnson's Great Society, seeking equality of sacrifice as well as of opportunity, sharply increased the progressiveness of the income tax.

In fact, from the day the Sixteenth Amendment was ratified both major political parties had accepted the need for the tax to be progressive, though just *how* progressive was often a matter of passionate debate. Over time, the attempt to accommodate conflicting special interests led to a bewildering thicket of sometimes logic-defying deductions, credits, subsidies, and exemptions, all patched into a Tax Code that grew to some two thousand pages. Filled with a vast accumulation of precedents, administrative rulings, and case law, the code seemed to please no one but the Internal Revenue Service.

Charged with collecting the income tax since 1953 when it was created in a sweeping reorganization of the scandal-ridden old Bureau of Internal Revenue, the IRS liked the code's complexity because it served to check the machinations of clever tax lawyers, many of them IRS alumni, who by the 1980s helped nearly 40 percent of all those filing taxes to avoid paying any more than was absolutely necessary to keep out of jail. For most citizens—the 60 percent who could not afford professional help or chose to file their own returns—the byzantine provisions of the Tax Code only enhanced the authoritarian image of the IRS. While simplification remained a vague, reluctant, but official—if laughably unobtainable—agency goal, taxpayers lived out their working lives in abject fear of the IRS and its apparently monolithic powers.

The Tax Reform Act of 1986 was supposed to help by closing up loopholes and reducing the number of exemptions while lowering overall rates, but it proved much better at curtailing the progressive features of the income tax system than at simplifying individual tax returns. The idea that the wealthy should be taxed not at the same rate as the poor, but according to their ability to pay, seemed almost intuitive to most taxpayers. Even as Congress introduced the tax amendment, however, conservative economists and high-income taxpayers argued the notion that the general welfare was better served when the rich were lightly taxed and encouraged instead to save and invest. Seven decades after a "trickle down" theory had first been articulated before the House Ways and Means Committee, where all revenue bills begin, right-wing Republicans kept the idea alive. But it took a tax revolt by the middle class in the early 1980s to get the theory embodied in tax law.

Reality proved to be somewhat different than the theory. While the rich got richer, neither investment nor saving seemed much increased. What *did* increase was the federal deficit. When shrinking income proved inadequate to cover the cost of running the government, the federal government borrowed the money to pay for politically sacred entitlement and defense programs, instead of turning to the taxpayer as it had done historically. As the government plunged ever deeper into debt, Congress passed laws that set spending limits it then ignored, and political candidates made promises about not raising taxes they simply could not keep.

The truth of the matter is that nobody has ever liked paying taxes of any kind, as the American Revolution amply demonstrated. Income taxes, especially, are odious to the modern taxpayer since they are so immediate, as close as the next paycheck. At the same time, income taxes have become the chief source of revenue for every major industrialized nation in the world. Unable to do without an income tax, the real questions for such nations are simple: how much do their citizens have to pay and what do they get for their money? If they are satisfied with the answer to the latter question, they are apt to live with the answer to the former.

W.C. Handy Writes "The St. Louis Blues" (1914)

The event: In 1914, W.C. Handy, unable to find a white music publisher for his "St. Louis Blues," put out the song himself. Still popular today, it created the first significant demand for what we call "jazz."

LIKE MANY OTHER NATIONS, the United States has produced a rich heritage of folk music. More than most nations, it has produced an extraordinary variety of popular commercial music. But until the late 20th century, when it came to so-called "classical" music, America seemed to defer to Europe, producing, as many have noted, surprisingly few originals, with the exception of the radically innovative Charles Ives. Veteran jazz composer, performer, and musicologist Billy Taylor sees the nation's musical heritage differently, however, calling jazz "America's classical music." Jazz combines African-American folk roots with elements of popular commercial music and European classical traditions in a varied musical idiom that is uniquely American and wonderfully complex, one that strikes any thoughtful listener as much more than the sum of its parts.

The origins of jazz are as richly textured as the music itself, and no single event can claim to be the "birth" of this form of expression—in part, because "jazz" is a term that really covers many different kinds of music. When an admiring socialite asked Louis Armstrong to tell her what jazz is, he replied, "Lady, if you got to ask what it is, you'll never know." Nevertheless, two land-mark events early in this century ushered jazz into the mainstream of American culture and, in popularizing it, contributed to its ongoing development.

Toward the end of the nineteenth century, African-Americans began per-forming the music that soon became known as "the blues." Its origins lay in the work songs and "hollers" of slavery days, and if whites took notice of it at all, it was to acknowledge it as a quaint species of folk music. Within the African-American community, however, the blues had evolved, by the beginning of the twentieth century, into popular commercial music. Then, in 1911, W. C. Handy (born in 1873 in Florence, Alabama), a black orchestra leader, wrote the "Mem-phis Blues" as a campaign song for Memphis mayor Edward H. "Boss" Crump. Adapting the down-home African-American idiom to white (that is, European) conventions of orchestration and harmony, Handy produced a more-than-local hit that attracted some notice, but his real breakthrough came three years later with the publication of "The St. Louis Blues." The song became tremendously influential among African-Americans as well as whites, and Handy's style of music soon became famous under the label of "jazz."

As no single event can be called the birth of jazz, no single place can be credited with having engendered it; for early jazz and proto-jazz musicians were active in many cities and towns throughout the southern United States. And yet New Orleans, with its long tradition of fostering popular African-American music, was home to a great many acknowledged "fathers" of jazz, in-cluding Jelly Roll Morton, King Oliver, Alphonse Picou, Sidney Bechet, Kid Ory, and Louis Armstrong, many of whom performed in the brothels of the city's Storyville district. This colorful area was created not by accident but by a city ordinance, proposed by alderman Sidney Story and enacted in 1898. It was intended, in effect, to "zone" prostitution by granting it semilegal status within a strictly defined area. For the next two decades, madams and musicians flour-ished, the latter creating some of the greatest early examples of jazz.

Then came World War I, and with it the United States Navy, which had set up a base in New Orleans to protect the Gulf of Mexico and the mouth of the

Mississippi. The sailors were, of course, delighted with the pleasures of Storyville, but the secretary of the navy, Josephus Daniels, was not. On November 14,
1917, he issued an order prohibiting open prostitution within five miles of any
U.S. Navy base. On that date Storyville was effectively closed down, and from
that date onward, the musicians of the district joined the general northward migration of African-Americans. The first great *national* mecca of jazz became
Chicago, through which the music entered the mainstream and even bestowed
its name on the decade of the 1920s. In closing the doors of Storyville, Secretary
Daniels had thrown open to jazz the doors of America and the world.

Charlie Chaplin and Mary Pickford Become World-famous (1917)

The event: In 1917, at the age of twenty-seven, Charlie Chaplin signed a contract with the First National film company to deliver eight films in eighteen
months for a million dollars, joining "America's Sweetheart" Mary Pickford,
who made just under a million dollars annually, as a world-famous celebrity.
The two were called "stars" by the motion-picture industry.

IN 1908, THOMAS EDISON and others who had
been engaged in extended litigation over patent rights to produce the "flickers" of the
rapidly growing film industry, buried the
hatchet and formed the Motion Picture Patents Company, which independent film producers called through clenched teeth, "the
Trust." The Trust, controlling all the important patents related to motion picture mak-
ing, attempted to monopolize the infant business through vigorous lawsuits,
questionable business practice, and, when all else failed, brutal strong-arm tactics. It was, in part, an attempt to escape the Trust's enforcers, as well as a search
for reliably good weather and cheap real estate, that led a bunch of street-wise
Jewish entrepreneurs from New York to open up shop selling dreams to the poor

and lonely in a little backwater suburb of Los Angeles called Hollywood.

One of the more odious of the Trust's prohibitions was a ban on giving credit to those playing in its nickelodeon dramas. Prior to 1910, the movie-going public had no idea who they were seeing up on the screen, and as audiences developed favorites they began to refer to them by the names they used in the pictures. Petite, golden-haired Gladys Smith was called "Little Mary" long before she adopted the stage name Mary Pickford, while cowboy star G.M. Anderson was known simply as "Bronco Billy." Some actors were known only by their studios—"The Biograph Girl," "The Vitagraph Girl," "The Imp Girl." It fell to independent filmmaker Carl Laemmle to break the hold of the Trust over its actors when he seduced Florence Lawrence, the popular "Biograph Girl," away from the studio with promises of more money and—for the first time in movie history—her name up in lights. Laemmle quickly discovered that Lawrence's devoted fans could be counted on to show up in sufficient numbers at the box office to justify increased rental fees for his pictures. Thus was born not only a star but also the star system that has dominated Hollywood ever since.

Vitagraph became the first Patent Company to follow suit and break the Trust ban, making stars of the good-looking Maurice Costello and "The Vitagraph Girl" herself, Florence Turner. The studio's globular John Bunny became the first movie comedian known by name to the public, and its Arthur Johnson the first "matinee idol." But for sheer popularity, none of these could hold a candle to Mary Pickford, whom Laemmle made a star when he swooped down on Biograph again to carry off both her and her hard-drinking husband, Owen Moore; nor could they hope to match the public's adoration of the Little Tramp, Charlie Chaplin, who worked his way to stardom from the ranks of the slapstick players in Mark Sennett's Keystone comedies.

The attention paid Pickford and Chaplin was part of a general cult of celebrity that arose from the new consumer-goods culture of the 1920s and continued to flourish in the decades that followed. Three-quarters of a century later, an ability to appeal to media audiences itself became a qualification for high political office in America.

The United States Enters World War I (1917)

The event: On April 2, 1917, President Woodrow Wilson asked the U.S. Congress to exercise its constitutional power and declare war on Germany, bringing America into the European conflagration known as World War I.

EUROPE, IN THE opening fifteen years of the twentieth century, was held together by a complex network of alliances and pulled apart by an equally complex network of enmities. When an assassin's bullets struck down the Austro-Hungarian Archduke Francis Ferdinand and his wife Sophie in the then-obscure Balkan capital of Sarajevo on June 28, 1914, it was as if a switch had been thrown. One by one, the nations of the European network declared war on one another and embarked on a course of mindless self-destruction unparalleled in the experience of the world. With a sense of mingled relief and complacent superiority, the United States observed the horror, happy to be well out of the action.

World War I began, in 1914, with a spectacular German drive deep into France. It seemed as if the whole thing would be over quickly, but the Germans dug in some thirty miles outside of Paris, and for the next three years the war's Western Front was a complex of wretched trenches, with much death and destruction on both sides but little movement. Europe had machine-gunned and gassed itself to a standstill.

Into this "Great War" Woodrow Wilson decided to drag his anxious and still wary people, trying desperately to convince himself, his ethnic minorities, and his embittered intellectuals that he had the best of intentions, the holiest of purposes. Most of the country still favored neutrality, though some factions advocated entry on one side or the other. Throughout his first term of office, Wilson had navigated a course that avoided involvement in the war and had campaigned for his second presidential term on the slogan "He Kept Us Out of War," which made it difficult for him to face the isolationists in Congress once he changed his mind.

Events would come to his aid. As the war ground on, and news of German atrocities in Belgium and elsewhere filtered out of Europe, American sentiment turned increasingly against Germany. On May 7, 1915, German U-boats torpedoed and sank the British steamer *Lusitania*, with the loss of 1,198 lives, including 124 Americans. In the meantime, evidence of German espionage and sabotage in the United States began to mount, culminating in the infamous Zimmerman Telegram of January 19, 1917. It was a coded message sent by Germany's foreign secretary, Alfred Zimmerman, to the German ambassador in Mexico, proposing a Mexican-German alliance against the United States. The public disclosure of the Zimmerman Telegram, on March 1, came only one month after Germany resumed unrestricted submarine warfare against all manner of shipping. On February 3, 1917, the *U.S.S. Housatonic* was sunk without warning, and the United States severed diplomatic relations with Germany. Throughout February and March, the nation began arming its merchant fleet. At last, on April 2, 1917, Woodrow Wilson convened a special session of Congress and called for a declaration of a war to end all wars. The measure passed after eighteen hours of debate on April 6.

The United States entered the war at a relative low point for the Allies. Shipping losses were at an unprecedented high, major French land offensives had failed (leading to mutinies throughout the French army), and the British offensive in Flanders had been largely inconclusive and very costly. At the same time, on the Eastern Front, the Russians were suffering terrible defeats and, on the eve of revolution, were moving inexorably toward a "separate peace" with Germany, which would release masses of German troops for combat on the Western Front. The prospect of the Americans' arrival did much to offset flagging Allied morale.

At the time of the war declaration, the U.S. Army numbered about two hundred thousand men. During the war, the number swelled to four million, including 2,800,000 draftees. About half the army served in the American Expeditionary Force (A.E.F.), which was sent to France. Of forty-two infantry divisions sent overseas, twenty-nine took part in active combat. The A.E.F. ground forces were commanded by General John J. ("Black Jack") Pershing, who had fought Indians in the American West and Pancho Villa on the Mexican border, while naval forces were under the direction of Admiral William S. Sims. Pershing arrived in Paris on June 14, 1917, his first troops following on the twenty-sixth, but no units were committed to the front until October 21, and it was not until the spring and summer of 1918 that massive numbers of American soldiers entered into the fighting. Pershing's own first battle was with the Allied high command, however, who insisted that the U.S. forces be placed under joint Allied authority. Pershing demanded control of his own troops, and with the full support of Wilson at last prevailed.

Back home the isolationists suspended their public opposition for the duration of the hostilities. They could hardly have done otherwise in the face of the hysterical patriotism Wilson whipped up with his powerful propoganda machine, called the Committee on Public Information. Headed by Denver newspaperman George Creel, the committee's task was to foment war fever with pamphlets, posters, newspaper reports, and silent movies. Creel supposedly documented atrocities committed by the dreaded Hun and patriotic sacrifices made by American troops at the front and ordinary citizens in the American hinterland. As Creel freely admitted later, most of the stories were fabricated, but they were nevertheless quite effective. Not surprisingly, many of the Creel committee's writers and artists went into the booming advertising business after the war.

In addition, the administration censored, intimidated, or incarcerated critics of the war—sundry intellectuals, socialist workingmen, conscientious objectors, and of course communists—and turned a blind eye to the mistreatment of German-American citizens. In the Midwest especially, efforts were made to discourage the use of the German language in ethnic newspapers and in public; Iowa actually passed a law banning its use everywhere, including over the telephone. In cities like St. Louis and Chicago there was talk of segregating the German-American population entirely. German-Americans learned to fear their neighbors, who spied on them, threatened them, forced them to buy Liberty Bonds to prove their loyalty, and sometimes physically attacked them.

None of this had much bearing on a war fought an ocean away. The

A.E.F. saw its first heavy action in the early spring of 1918, when the Germans launched a series of desperate offensives along the Western Front from March through June. From June 6 through July 1, U.S. forces in sizable numbers—some 27,500—recaptured Vaux, Bouresches, and Belleau Wood from the Germans. An equal number of Americans held the town of Cantigny against a massive German offensive threatening Paris during June 9-15. Then, between July 18 and August 6, some eighty-five thousand American troops crushed the last major German offensive at the Second Battle of the Marne. It was the turning point of the war, as the Allies were now in a position to take the offensive. American troops figured importantly in the Somme, Oise-Aisne, and Ypres-Lys offensives of August 1918, and executed independently of the other Allies an offensive against the St. Mihiel Salient (September 12-16). From the end of September through the day of the Armistice, all available U.S. forces were concentrated along a sector between the Meuse River and the Argonne Forest. The campaign, aimed at cutting the Germans' principal line of supply, involved 1,200,000 American troops, who suffered a heavy 10 percent casualty rate. The success of this offensive brought about the capitulation of Germany. An armistice was declared on November 11, 1918, and the Treaty of Versailles concluded on June 28, 1919.

Although the United States had entered the war late, its armed forces suffered deaths numbering 112,432 (about half from an influenza-pneumonia pandemic), and wounded numbering 230,074. In money, the war had cost more than twenty billion dollars. President Wilson was determined that the war—and especially his nation's participation in it—should not have been in vain. Accordingly, as early as January 8, 1918, he announced to Congress "Fourteen Points . . . as the only possible program" for peace, as far as the interests of the United States were concerned. The Fourteen Points included provisions for open covenants of peace (no secret treaties and alliances such as those that led to war in the first place), freedom of the seas, withdrawal of invading armies and restoration of occupied territories, adjustment of borders, and, most significantly, the establishment of a general association of the world's nations for the purpose of ensuring the political independence and territorial integrity of states great and small.

But America's isolationist faction, quiescent during the war, would have none of it. The battle for ratifications of the Treaty was a mean and bitter one, and it broke Wilson's health. He tried to appeal over the heads of Congress directly to the American people. But they reacted badly to what sounded suspiciously like yet another Progressive crusade, this time to provide the entire world with "good government." Coming out of its war stupor as if awakening from a bad dream, America rejected Wilson's idealistic hopes for a peaceful future guaranteed by a League of Nations.

The Eighteenth Amendment Is Ratified (1919)

The event: In 1919, the Eighteenth Amendment was ratified by a sufficient number of state legislatures to become the law of the land, plunging the country into what Herbert Hoover called a "noble experiment" but that American citizens came to consider simply "Prohibition."

FROM JANUARY 1920 to April 1933, the federal government forbade, under the Volstead Act (passed to provide for enforcement of the recently ratified amendment), the manufacture, transport, and sale of alcoholic beverages anywhere in the United States. Prohibition signaled a triumph of the fundamentalist movement that had been slowly taking command of the rural parts of the country since before the Civil War. Throughout the nineteenth century, the Temperance Movement was its chief beneficiary. By 1855, the manufacture and sale of alcoholic beverages had been outlawed in thirteen of the thirty-one states. During the Civil War and Reconstruction period, however, the Republican Party was reluctant to take a stance on prohibition, fearing that to do so would weaken its control of government at both the state and federal levels. In the 1870s, groups of women mobilized against alcohol consumption and formed the Woman's Christian Temperance Union, and in 1895, members of the newly created Anti-Saloon League were successful in influencing state and local elections in favor of "dry" candidates. By 1916, twenty-one state legislatures outlawed saloons, and voters in Congressional elections that year sent a "dry" majority to Congress. These Congressmen secured the passage of the Eighteenth Amendment, which was submitted to the states for ratification in December 1917. Once the states ratified the amendment, the Prohibition Bureau went into operation. With between fifteen hundred and three thousand agents, the Bureau was responsible for finding and bringing to trial those who engaged in the illegal liquor trade.

From the moment the Eighteenth Amendment passed, America became a nation of lawbreakers. The big city ethnic neighborhoods, unlike the rural-dominated state legislatures, had, for a generation, overwhelmingly voted against various prohibition referendums. Folks in those neighborhoods began immediately to brew and bootleg bathtub gin and moonshine, often with the encouragement of their friends and neighbors. Contemptuous of a law they hated, determined themselves to continue drinking, and looking to make a buck, these neighborhood bootleggers had the support of their local grocers, who supplied the necessary raw materials, and of their local former saloon keepers, restaurant owners, and ice cream and soft drink parlor operators, who helped distribute their products. Neighborhood policemen looked the other way. Friends warned one another about raids.

But the business was risky. Raids did occur. People were punished. Some even lost their citizenship. And lured by the chance for big profits, the underworld moved in. The gangsters, like those they preyed on, were immigrants. Crime simply offered a convenient, alluring, and quick way up the ladder of success, and bright, ruthless, upwardly mobile immigrant youths, convinced that other means to wealth and the pursuit of happiness were cut off to them, turned to it as a profession. Such men tended to be at home with violence, and neighborhood bootlegging looked like a good, easy mark.

The mobsters began terrorizing the illegal traffic in liquor, extorting protection money and brutalizing the uncooperative. Gangs, their members often no more than teenagers, battled each other for control, using sawed-off shotguns and Thompson machine guns to make their points and establish their monopolies. The mainstream press, pandering to its nativist, middle-class audience, tried to make an ethnic issue out of the crime wave Prohibition created in the major American cities. Almost weekly, headlines announced still another Sicilian gang war or the discovery of yet another illegal warehouse in one Little Italy or another. But the first well-known mobster in New York was an Englishmen, Owney Madden, the second a Jew, Arnold Rothstein, and the Irish and Germans, too, had their gangs in every city. Protected by their big city politicos, mobsters poured their profits into clubs to play jazz over the machine-gun rat-tat-tat in the background. The Jazz Age was born in the speakeasies of Prohibition.

U.S. Attorney General A. Mitchell Palmer Launches the Red Scare (1920)

The event: On the evening of January 2, 1919, agents of the U.S. Department of Justice, operating under direct orders from the attorney general, descended on the headquarters of radical organizations in twelve different cities and illegally detained some 6,000 American citizens and immigrants they believed sympathetic to the Communist movement in what became known as the "Red Scare."

AFTER THE RUSSIAN Revolution of 1917, America's ruling class became almost obsessed with Communism, and a series of bombings at the homes of prominent men in 1919 helped the establishment bring that fear home to the middle classes in the great "Red Scare." Little distinction was made between working-class Communists and the anarchists suspected of targeting for elimination Attorney General A. Mitchell Palmer, robber barons John D. Rockefeller and J. P. Morgan, the right-wing former U.S. senator from Georgia Thomas Hardwick, and more than thirty others. The anarchists mailed bombs to these men through the U.S. postal system, but many of the packages were held by the Post Office because of insufficient postage.

After the bombing of his own home on June 2, Palmer set out to catch the anarchists. He believed there was a full-scale conspiracy of Communists operating in the United States. Foreigners and labor union members were his prime suspects. To combat the Reds, Palmer created the General Intelligence Division headed by J. Edgar Hoover in the Justice Department. Over the next three months, Hoover organized a massive card index system that included the names of 150,000 radical leaders, organizations, and publications. Using the geographical cross-reference he created, he could pull out the names of all the radicals in or near a particular city. He also amassed comprehensive files on more than 60,000 people, groups, and periodicals.

Circulating the names compiled by Hoover, Palmer sent directives to his undercover agents instructing them to investigate all foreign anarchists, Bolsheviks, and other radicals. These investigations were to lead to possible deportation of the foreigners. Also targeted for investigation, however, were American citizens who belonged to radical organizations. Palmer told his operatives that cases should be developed against these citizens so that when the United States Congress passed laws against the kinds of activities they engaged in, the Justice Department would be ready to prosecute them.

In the meantime, Palmer's campaign received a boost when the convention of the Socialist Party splintered into the Communist Labor party and the Communist Party of America. Capitalizing on this event, the attorney general circulated hundreds of press releases and other anti-Communist propaganda. Hoover wrote two legal briefs on Communism, and these documents were used as justification for the department's scheduled Communist round-up and as evidence in the subsequent deportation hearings.

The round-ups planned by Palmer involved the Department of Labor as well as the Department of Justice. The heads of the two government agencies agreed that the Justice Department would provide the Labor Department with a list of names and arrest warrants. The Labor Department would then issue the warrants, and Justice would make the arrests. Then the Labor Department would handle deportation hearings using the deportation provisions of the 1918 Immigration Act as a basis on which to act.

In Manhattan, the target was the Russian People's House, where 183 men were initially arrested. Of these, thirty-three were detained and sent to Ellis Island. The arrests were particularly brutal. Some people were hurled down the stairs of the Russian People's House. Others were beaten. Drunk with the success of the raid, Palmer went to Congress a week later to ask that a peacetime sedition act be passed. Although the congressmen turned down that request, they cheered Palmer in the halls of the Capitol.

Palmer's massive round-up on the evening of January 2, 1920, in thirty-three cities ensnared six thousand people in all, with the largest concentrations in Detroit, New York City, and Boston. During the subsequent hearings, the Labor Department ruled that membership in a Communist organization was sufficient ground for the deportation of aliens. Only 556 people, however, were deported.

After the January round-ups, Palmer told a wide-eyed American public that a huge Communist demonstration was scheduled for May Day 1920. Police across the country prepared for the revolt, but nothing materialized. A few days later, the Labor Department ruled on some important deportation hearings. It found that since the Communist Labor Party accepted the possibility of change through parliamentary action, it could not be considered to be an advocate of violent revolution. Therefore, the members of the party arrested in the round-up could not be deported. Thus discredited, Palmer ceased his round-ups. The country, however, did not abandon its xenophobia. In 1921 Congress passed an immigration act that restricted the numbers of immigrants from southern and eastern Europe, and three years later, that law was made even more prohibitive.

And there were, of course, the lessons learned by J. Edgar Hoover, which he put to use when he became head of the FBI. Under his lifetime tenure as director, the "Bureau" became America's secret police organization, spying on American citizens, blackmailing the country's elected officials, and grabbing as much political power for its leader as any man outside the presidency has ever held.

The Nineteenth Amendment is Ratified (1920)

The event: After decades of struggle, American women were granted the right to vote when the states ratified the Nineteenth Amendment in 1920.

AFTER THE REVOLUTIONARY WAR, which the American colonists had fought to secure political rights, voting privileges were withheld from more than half the

population of the United States. Women, slaves, indentured servants, men without property, and, in many states, free blacks were denied voting rights. The only state that allowed women to vote was New Jersey, which inadvertently drafted its voting laws in such a way as to allow all *individuals* worth 50 pounds or more to vote. In 1777, women who met that criterion went to the polls, but the loophole was quickly closed up.

In 1848, what would become a long struggle to secure women's suffrage in the United States began at the Seneca Falls Convention, where 240 women and men met to draw up a list of grievances and a set of resolutions for action. Organized by Elizabeth Cady Stanton and Lucretia Mott, both active in the abolition movement, the meeting was reconvened in this New York town annually. After the Civil War, women active in the suffrage movement were divided over whether to tie the campaign for women's rights to the campaign to enfranchise former slaves. Stanton and Susan B. Anthony fought strenuously for constitutional amendments that would enfranchise both blacks and women, and Mott was elected chair of the Equal Rights Association. When the Fourteenth and Fifteenth Amendments, extending the vote to black men, failed to address women's rights, Stanton and Anthony broke with Mott's group to form the National Woman Suffrage Association, which opposed the Fifteenth Amendment and accepted only women as members. Another splinter group, the American Woman Suffrage Association, supported the Fifteenth Amendment as a necessary first step in the broadening of voting rights.

These national groups were joined in the later years of the nineteenth century by federations of women's clubs, which, since the late 1860s, had devoted much attention to women's issues. Members of the Woman's Christian Temperance Union also joined the crusade for women's suffrage. In 1890 the two rival women's rights organizations, the National Woman Suffrage Association and the American Woman Suffrage Association, merged under the leadership of Anna Howard Shaw and Carrie Chapman Catt to become the National American Woman Suffrage Association. From 1900 to 1920, this organization led a massive propaganda campaign for suffrage and, with the notable exception of the Congressional Union's National Woman's Party, enjoyed a unity that had eluded the movement in earlier years. The Congressional Union, organized by Alice Paul, was more militant in its campaign. Its members participated in pickets, hunger strikes, and other forms of civil disobedience in an attempt to gain a constitutional amendment granting women equal rights with men.

In 1919 Congress and President Woodrow Wilson approved the briefly worded Nineteenth Amendment, giving women the vote, and it was ratified by the states in August 1920. The realization of this hard-won goal did not end the women's movement, however. Congressional Union suffrage reformers formed the National Woman's Party to push for laws for total equality for women. In 1923 it began a campaign for an Equal Rights Amendment. The National American Woman Suffrage Association was re-formed into the League of Women Voters, an organization that works to educate voters on political issues while maintaining a nonpartisan stance. The effectiveness of these organizations was diminished, however, in the 1930s, 1940s, and 1950s. Women did not vote as a bloc, nor did they support female political candidates. Although they gained a measure of employment equality during World War II, filling many of the jobs left vacant by men joining the military, when the soldiers returned to their jobs after the war, women returned to their domestic life, and feminism took on a cast of deviance. This changed yet again in the 1960s, a decade of heightened activism, when the cause of women's social and economic equality became part of the ongoing struggle for civil rights.

The U.S. Senate Rejects the League of Nations (1920)

The event: Between 1919 and 1921, in the course of protracted and acrimonious debate, Congress rejected the League of Nations, a move that contributed to the postwar climate that made World War II inevitable.

AS THE HOSTILITIES of World War I came to an end, President Woodrow Wilson made plans to attend the peace conference in Paris in January 1919. He arrived

in Paris armed with a plan for building a lasting peace among the world's nations. He first hinted at the existence of this plan in his "Fourteen Points" speech to Congress in January 1918. Among the points he had outlined was an association of nations that would mutually guarantee the political independence and territorial boundaries of all the world's countries.

As the European and American delegates to the peace conference set to work, power quickly became concentrated in the hands of the Big Four—England, the United States, France, and Italy. While the terms of the peace they negotiated were far from satisfactory to those desiring a lasting world peace, the Versailles Treaty did incorporate the establishment of the League of Nations. Wilson was disappointed with the treaty, which did not call for the freedom of the seas, for disarmament, or for a reduction of tariffs, and which seemed to punish Germany too heavily for the war. Still, he remained certain that the League of Nations, once in operation, would mandate freedom of the seas and disarmament. Designed to arbitrate disagreements between countries, the League would serve as a register of treaties and would be empowered to use both military and economic sanctions against aggressors.

Wilson returned home to present the Versailles Treaty and the League of Nations to the Senate and the American public. While most Americans probably supported the League, the members of the Senate were another matter. Thirty-seven senators had already voiced their opposition to the League as early as March 1919, and others were angry that Wilson had not involved them in drafting the proposal. Some Republicans argued that the United States would lose its sovereignty by membership in an organization that had the authority to arbitrate international conflicts. Some opposed the League simply because they disliked Wilson.

Wilson needed a two-thirds majority to achieve ratification of the treaty and the League in the Senate. He could count on the Democrats, but he needed the support of many Republicans as well. Leading the Republican opposition was Senator Henry Cabot Lodge of Massachusetts, who insisted on protecting American sovereignty. In a set of proposals called the Lodge Reservations, he declared that Congress, based on its constitutional treaty-making authority, should have the authority to decide when to abide and when not to abide by any decision made by the League. In addition, he declared that Congress could vote to ignore the League's commitment to the political independence and territorial integrity of the signatories. Lodge campaigned among the Republican senators to gather support for his Reservations, and Wilson, partly because of his hatred of Lodge and partly because of his own failing health, stubbornly refused to compromise the principles of the League in any way. It would be all or nothing.

Wilson took the case for the League of Nations to the American people, beginning a 9,500-mile tour of the nation on September 4, 1919. On September 25 he collapsed in Pueblo, Colorado, and was rushed back to Washington, where he suffered a stroke on October 2. Though incapacitated, Wilson still insisted that his followers settle for nothing less than unconditional acceptance of the treaty and the League. As a result, congressional debate dragged on until July 2, 1921, when Congress resolved that war with Germany and its allies was indeed concluded, but declined to ratify U.S. participation in the League. Wilson, too ill to run for reelection himself, nevertheless urged his party to make acceptance of the League part of its platform. The Republicans, for their part, straddled the issue, but when Republican Warren G. Harding defeated Democrat James M. Cox, he declared in his inaugural address, "We seek no part in directing the destinies of the world." Later he addressed Congress, stating that the League "is not for us." Woodrow Wilson, crippled, sick, and near death, having committed so much of the national treasure and its young manhood to winning a "war to end all wars," could only watch in bitterness as his hopes for a world governed by reason rather than force crumbled and dissolved.

Alfred P. Sloan, Jr. Introduces Planned Obsolescence (1920)

The event: In the decade of the 1920s, faced with a need to broaden a limited market for automobiles, General Motors chairman Alfred P. Sloan, Jr., formulated a controversial but soon universally accepted concept of production and marketing. It was called planned obsolescence.

AS THE 1920s roared on, the automobile industry began to find that its market was no longer growing. Automakers had instituted installment sales in 1916 in an attempt to broaden the market, but by the 1920s, they could expect no further saturation. To increase the need for his products, Alfred P. Sloan, Jr., head of General Motors, formulated a strategy of planned obsolescence. Whereas the cars of the 1920s differed little in substance from the original Model T, Sloan planned minor stylistic alterations for each year's models and major overhauls every three years in an attempt to make owners dissatisfied with their cars. Owners, Sloan theorized, would then trade in their cars on the new, more expensive models.

By 1927, Sloan was reaping the harvest of his plan. Chevrolet dominated the low-price field, a position it had captured from Ford. GM claimed a 43-percent market share by 1936 and continued to lead in annual profits until 1986, when Ford once again regained top position. For half a century, as it became apparent that "Sloanism" did, in fact, create a greater demand for cars, American automakers followed GM's lead, producing annual cosmetic changes and manufacturing progressively heavier, longer, more powerful cars that were equipped with more and more new gadgets—and that were increasingly expensive. Slighted in this process was basic engineering, which failed to keep pace with the superficial developments.

After dominating the automobile industry for so many years, Sloan's planned obsolescence was dealt crippling blows by federal safety, pollution, and energy-consumption standards in the 1960s and 1970s. In addition, Japanese and German cars penetrated American markets, demonstrating that the public could also be attracted by innovative and sound engineering. Regulation and foreign competition finally forced GM, other American automakers, and American industry in general to shake off encrusted complacency and rethink their philosophies of design, production, and marketing.

Pittsburgh's KDKA Broadcasts Election Results (1920)

The event: On November 2, 1920, radio station KDKA in Pittsburgh broadcast the results of the presidential election, inaugurating a new industry and a new system of entertainment and communication that was to reshape the country's politics, its economy, and its culture.

IN 1899, WHEN the Irish-Italian inventor Guglielmo Marconi demonstrated to a group of Americans how his wireless telegraph might be used by the press to cover the America's Cup, he was thinking not about broadcasting but about rapid communication. His American competitors, however, hoped to use Marconi's invention to broadcast much more than coded messages of sports scores and business statistics. On Christmas Eve, 1906, Reginald Fessenden, who had developed the high-frequency alternator, the first workable radio transmitter, sent out a program that included music and voice. The inventor of the radio tube, Lee de Forest, made attempts to broadcast opera in New York between 1907 and 1909, and within a decade amateur operators in a dozen cities were regularly transmitting music, speech, and coded communications before World War I put an end to their activities. After the war they picked up where they'd left off, and radio boomed.

Within three years of the first commercial broadcast, the number of radio stations had shot up to 556. The explosion of stations created chaos on the airwaves, and nobody could figure out how to pay for the programs. Seeking to reduce competition and maximize profits, station owners organized into networks that broadcast the same show at the same time and fiddled around with on-the-air advertising. Many objected to the ads, calling them an invasion of privacy that forced the marketplace into the listeners' homes, and radio made do for a while with "indirect" advertising in which singing groups, comedians, and bands adopted a company's name without ever mentioning a product's merit, price, or point of purchase. Advertisers were attracted to the new networks—the

National Broadcasting Company (NBC), the Columbia Broadcasting System (CBS), and the Mutual Broadcasting System (MBS)—that had stitched together a national audience.

In 1912 the federal government got into the act, licensing stations and introducing a crude wavelength-allocation system, though broadcasting was still a haphazard and amateurish affair without commercial interest. Congress expanded the Radio Act of 1912 in 1927 after broadcasting became an industry and revamped it in 1934, setting up the Federal Communications Commission (FCC) to consider license applications and renewals. Fearing the power of the new medium, the FCC insisted that every three years stations demonstrate they were serving the public interest. The FCC also issued guidelines on obscenity and fraudulent advertising. At the same time the commission allocated most of the broadcast spectrum and all of the best wavelengths to those with the most powerful transmitters, a policy that automatically favored business interests over the less well-heeled groups establishing educational stations.

By the late 1930s radio was an inextricable part of American life, broadcasting everything from heavyweight championships to old vaudeville routines. The millions who listened in private increasingly relied on the radio for all their news, which they had, on occasion, difficulty distinguishing from radio dramas. (Orson Welles's 1938 Halloween broadcast of "War of the Worlds" sent thousands fleeing their homes and clogging local highways in fear of an invasion from Mars.) The coming of World War II made broadcast journalism into a serious competitor for newspapers, as Edward R. Murrow, Eric Sevareid, Howard K. Smith, Charles Collingwood, and others brought the conflict into America's living rooms with an eloquence and courage more powerful than anything print news could hope to achieve.

Television, whose appearance coincided with the post-war consumer boom, developed along the lines of the radio, and together the two broadcast media had a more immediate if not more profound impact on American lives than any of the other major inventions of the twentieth century.

George Washington Carver Invents Peanut Butter (1921)

The event: In 1921, George Washington Carver appeared before Congress to promote the virtues of the humble peanut. In so doing he helped secure a measure of prosperity for African-American farmers and southern agriculture generally.

BORN IN 1864 in Diamond, Missouri, to a slave mother, George Washington Carver was raised by his mother's masters after she disappeared during a Civil War raid. Barred from attending the segregated local schools, Carver traveled around the Midwest, supporting himself by cooking, washing clothes, and homesteading before enrolling at Simpson College in Indianola, Iowa, in 1890. Carver graduated from college with a degree in art, but his interest soon turned to agriculture. He enrolled in Iowa State College, earned a master's degree in agriculture in 1896, and accepted a teaching position at the Tuskegee Institute in Alabama.

Carver used his Tuskegee appointment to conduct research aimed at finding an agricultural solution to the debt and poverty plaguing black farmers. He demonstrated scientific agricultural methods, published bulletins, and devised new uses for easily and inexpensively grown crops: cow peas, sweet potatoes, and, most spectacularly, peanuts.

The humble peanut greatly intrigued Carver. A food source rich in protein, the peanut (Carver believed) could replace cotton (notorious for depleting soil) as the staple crop of farmers—if the market for it could be developed. To that end, Carver testified before Congress in 1921 on behalf of the National Association of Peanut Growers. Carver personally developed more than a hundred products from the peanut and the sweet potato, including plastics, lubricants, dyes, pharmaceuticals, ink, wood stains, facial creams, tapioca, and molasses. Although he had spent most of his career looking for alternatives to the one-crop agricultural dependence on cotton, he also developed "Carver's Hybrid," a sturdy cross between short-stalk and long-stalk cotton.

Carver was an extraordinary scientist whose work immediately bridged the gap between "pure" and "applied" science. His work significantly improved the lot not only of African-American farmers but of southern farmers generally. His career exploded stereotypes about the "natural inferiority" of blacks, and he served as something of an intellectual icon in a period when racist ideologies were sweeping the globe. In 1940, three years before his death, he gave his life savings to establish the Carver Foundation "for research in creative chemistry."

Congress Restricts Immigration (1924)

The event: In 1924 Congress passed the Johnson-Reed Act, which severely re-stricted immigration into a country whose Statue of Liberty proclaimed its pride in being a haven for the huddled masses.

SEVERAL MOVEMENTS COALESCED in the early 1920s to make possible the passage of laws stemming the flood of immigrants from Europe, Ireland, and Asia, a flood that had been transforming America's big cities since before the Civil War. Emerging from a costly world war, many Americans feared that the millions of new immigrants would take jobs from the native-born. America's capitalists had long been blaming the labor unrest of previous decades on radical dissidents among the immigrants, and now—with the Russian Revolution constantly in the press—middle-class Americans were ready to believe that the new wave of labor unrest that broke out after the war was inspired by the immigrant-spawned Communist parties, which had about a hundred thousand members in America. It was also during the post-war period that a few prominent Americans, including John D. Rocke-feller, Oliver Wendell Holmes, Jr., and A. Mitchell Palmer were attacked by would-be assassins, all immigrants. Americans seemed to be willing to trans-form their war-time fear of the Germans to a post-war fear of the Italian, Jewish, or Slavic immigrant industrial worker.

The first manifestation of this general xenophobia was the Red Scare of

1919 and 1920. The next manifestation was more lasting. In 1920 Congress passed the Immigration Act, setting for the first time national quotas on the number of immigrants allowed. Gone were the pre-World War I days of virtually unlimited admission; four years later, the Johnson-Reed Act reduced further the number of immigrants to be admitted to a mere 150,000, divided by quotas so that almost 90 percent of even that small number had to come from northwestern Europe. The life blood of the American city's ethnic neighborhoods dwindled to a trickle, as the so-called "new immigrants" from southern and eastern Europe were for the most part denied entry.

America had slammed the doors of the New World shut on the Old World's tired, its poor, its disaffected masses yearning to breathe free. A nativist strain, though fainter in some periods than others, would ever afterward run through American immigration policy, betraying the very idea of America as a land of opportunity even while seeking to preserve it for those who had already arrived.

Thomas Watson Founds IBM (1924)

The event: In 1924, Thomas Watson took over the Computing Tabulating Recording Company (CTR) and out of it created IBM, a company destined to become not only one of the nation's largest but, with its role in the invention of the computer, one of the world's most historically significant corporations.

THE 1880 U.S. census took eight years to count. Worried experts estimated that the upcoming 1890 census would be counted by 1902, with the lag becoming greater with each succeeding census. John Shaw Billings, an Army surgeon in charge of vital statistics at the Census Bureau, had the idea of using punch-hole cards to record and then process census information, and he gave the project to Herman Hollerith, who developed the cards and an electric machine to read them. The 1890 census was completed in less than three years. In 1911, Hollerith joined CTR (the Computing Tabulating Recording Company), which, in

February 1924, became International Business Machines.

Under the leadership of Thomas Watson, IBM became the nation's leading manufacturer of "business machines"—electro-mechanical calculators, collators, sorters, typewriters, and the like. Though precursors of the modern computer, neither these "business machines" nor the 1890 census machine were computers in the truest sense: general-purpose devices that can be programmed to solve any specific, solvable problem. The theoretical breakthroughs in true computer science came earlier, with Englishman Charles Babbage's and Lady Lovelace's "analytical engine" of 1837, and later, with the work of another Englishman, the mathematician Alan Turing, who most fully developed the theory of the modern computer in 1935 with his concept of the "Turing machine."

In 1940, IBM joined with a development team at Harvard University to create the Mark I, an advanced electro-mechanical device generally acknowledged to be the first truly modern programmable computer and a prelude to the fully electronic computer "ENIAC," which was unveiled at the University of Pennsylvania in 1946. The Mark I was successfully demonstrated in January 1943 and was immediately pressed into war service, calculating complex mathematical tables used mainly to determine the speed and trajectory of artillery shells. This was no simple task, for the gunners of World War II were asked not merely to aim at stationary targets or slow-moving warships but at high-speed aircraft and other fast-moving objects. Both the Mark I and ENIAC were enormous devices; Mark I was fifty feet long and eight feet high; ENIAC, which occupied a large room, was three thousand cubic feet in volume, weighed thirty tons, and used 18,000 vacuum tubes.

Over the next fifty years, as electronic technology rapidly developed and the vacuum tube gave way to the transistor and the transistor to the integrated circuit ("chip"), computers became progressively smaller, less expensive, more powerful, and, finally, ubiquitous, finding their way beyond government and military agencies to academia, business, industry, and the home, and transforming each of them in the process.

The Scopes Trial Begins in Tennessee (1925)

The event: In 1925, when he taught Darwin's theory of evolution to his Dayton, Tennessee, biology class, teacher John T. Scopes was arrested and tried for violating a new Tennessee law banning the teaching of any theory that conflicted with the story of creation presented in the Bible.

FAMED LAWYER Clarence Darrow and perennial Populist presidential candidate William Jennings Bryan went head to head in a trial that captured the nation's attention in the summer of 1925. The American Civil Liberties Union financed Scopes's defense, hiring Darrow for the job in an effort to challenge the constitutionality of a law that violated free speech and the separation of church and state.

Thousands of spectators descended on the small town of Dayton, transforming the sleepy hamlet into a carnival, with vendors selling Bibles, toy monkeys, and assorted souvenirs and refreshments. For those who could not travel to Dayton, the trial was broadcast live over the radio.

Judge John Raulston presided over the trial in anything but an unbiased fashion. Each day he opened the proceedings with a prayer, and he refused to admit expert testimony on evolution. Deprived of his experts, Darrow called a single witness: prosecutor William Jennings Bryan. By leading Bryan through a series of biblical stories, Darrow discredited the prosecution by pointing out the illogic and contradictions inherent in the fundamentalists' belief in the literal truth of the Bible. The jury, nevertheless, found Scopes guilty, and Judge Raulston fined him $100. Bryan, the hero of fundamentalists and rural conservatives, was broken by the humiliation he had suffered at the hands of Darrow and died a few days after the trial. Scopes moved away from Dayton. Judge Raulston failed to win his bid for re-election to the bench. The Tennessee Supreme Court later overturned the Dayton court's decision on a technicality, and the case was never reviewed by the U.S. Supreme Court. The trial served, however, to dramatize before a national audience the virtues and vices of the American judicial system, forcing a confrontation between parochial, regional values and more cosmopolitan views and raising important issues of religious freedom, the separation of church and state, and freedom of speech.

F. Scott Fitzgerald Publishes *The Great Gatsby* (1925)

The event: In 1925 the young, glamorous American writer whose first works had defined the 1920s as America's "Jazz Age" published his masterpiece of individual passion and national destiny, *The Great Gatsby*.

FRANCIS SCOTT KEY FITZGERALD, named after the ancestor who wrote the words to "The Star-Spangled Banner," was born in Saint Paul, Minnesota, on September 24, 1896. The son of a financially faltering father and a socially pretentious mother, Fitzgerald was sent east to a Catholic prep school in 1911. Impressed with the sophistication of the East Coast, he nevertheless always retained the feeling of being an outsider, a provincial coming into a more worldly society. Fitzgerald went on to Princeton University in 1913 but left in his junior year, mainly because of low grades resulting from a lack of serious interest in his studies. In 1917, eager for the adventure promised by the Great War, he entered the army as a second lieutenant but saw no action.

Fitzgerald's Princeton years were by no means wasted, as they exposed him to the world of literature. In 1920 he published his first novel, a vivid picture of "Jazz Age" youth called *This Side of Paradise*, which enjoyed immediate success and launched its author's career. Almost immediately after the publication of the novel, Fitzgerald married the wildly glamorous Zelda Sayre, a beautiful Alabama girl who became, directly or indirectly, the focus of much that he wrote during the early 1920s, including short stories and his second novel, *The Beautiful and Damned* (1922), which presents a glittering, rather desperate couple clearly based on the Fitzgeralds themselves.

Fitzgerald's life and work mirrored the frenzy of the Jazz Age, but the ceaseless drinking, party-going, and wild spending had already begun to take a toll on the couple's emotional life, Fitzgerald's health, and, paramountly, his work.

Yet *The Great Gatsby* of 1925, written in Europe, is a graceful, lyrical work of tortured genius. In it Fitzgerald explored the nature not of merely personal romance but the ageless romantic quest. The story of the shadowy Gatsby, part innocent knight and part criminal, is inextricably associated with the story of America itself, from its discovery as a New World of limitless possibility through its development as a land of promise in conflict with corruption and materialism. *The Great Gatsby* is a great romantic novel, a monument of American English prose, a vivid picture of the 1920s, and a compact myth-legend-allegory of the entire American experience.

Tragically, as the Jazz Age decade roared on, the author's drinking became frank alcoholism, while Zelda, always an eccentric, lapsed into schizophrenia. As the 1920s came to a crashing end with the stock market collapse that ushered in the Great Depression, Fitzgerald, too, declined. With great effort, he struggled to find structure for his next masterpiece, *Tender Is the Night* (1934), suffering a nervous breakdown the year after its publication.

Fitzgerald tried to carve out a living as a screenwriter and worked fitfully at a novel about Hollywood, *The Last Tycoon* (1941), which was left unfinished at his death, from a heart attack, on December 21, 1940.

Radio Station WSM Broadcasts the First Grand Ole Opry (1927)

The event: In November 1925, WSM Radio in Nashville, Tennessee, after scarcely a month in business, broadcast a live performance called the "WSM Barn Dance," which it renamed a year and a half later as "The Grand Ole Opry."

FIFTEEN MONTHS AFTER its first broadcast under the new name, the immediately and immensely popular Grand Ole Opry was the best-known country music show on radio. It remains today the longest-running radio show in history and is still broadcast by WSM, now located in Nashville's Opryland USA complex, where the show itself is performed live. Originally staged at the old Ryman Auditorium in downtown Nashville, the Opry was the center of Country and Western music, whose writers, singers, and stars tended to move to the city—which in turn created a large and lucrative recording industry and led Nashville to bill itself as "Music City, USA."

From its beginnings as the voice of the National Life and Accident Insurance Company, the Opry grew from an informal barn dance broadcast over a 1,000-watt radio station to a highly polished but seemingly off-the-cuff performance. By 1932, WSM radio had completed its new radio tower, and the show reached most of the country with its fifty-thousand-watt clear-channel signal. In 1939, the program gained national network affiliation on NBC.

As more and more people across the country became Opry fans, the emphasis on southern and country or folk themes and settings gave way to a western or cowboy focus. Among the early stars who emerged through their participation on the Grand Ole Opry shows were the Carter Family, a Virginia family who sang folk songs in three-part harmony, and Jimmie Rodgers, a former railroad brakeman whose "blue yodel" style perfectly fitted his repertoire of blues, train, hobo, and love songs. During World War II, Roy Acuff first came to the country's attention through roadshows all across the country, and for years he was considered the Opry's major performer. The post-war period was dominated by Eddy Arnold, Kitty Wells, and, most important, Hank Williams, whose songs were being picked up by pop singers at the time of his death in 1953. During the 1950s and 1960s, country music suffered a decline in popularity as the nation's baby boomers tuned their radios to the rock-and-roll that had been born of a marriage between white country music and black rhythm-and-blues in the Memphis studios of Sun Records. But with the dawning of the 1990s, country music was more popular than ever, playing on more radio stations than any other form of music.

Charles A. Lindbergh Flies the Atlantic (1927)

The event: At 7:52 on the rainy morning of May 20, 1927, *The Spirit of St. Louis*, heavily laden with fuel, took off from muddy Roosevelt Field in Nassau County, Long Island. Thirty-three-and-a-half hours later, Charles A. Lindbergh touched down at Le Bourget Field, just northeast of Paris.

BORN IN 1902, the year before the Wright brothers' first flight at Kitty Hawk, Lindbergh grew up during the formative years of aviation. During the second half of his sophomore year at the University of Wisconsin, he announced to his father, a Minnesota congressman, that he wanted to drop out in order to learn to fly. He made his first flight in 1922 and earned a precarious living as a "barnstormer," an itinerant stunt flier who also gave passengers thrill rides at five dollars a pop. After two years of this life, Lindbergh decided to join the Army, where he would receive the best flight training then available. After graduating from flight school, Lindbergh was commissioned a second lieutenant in the Army Air Service Reserve in March 1925, but did not see active service. Instead, he became an air mail pilot. During this time he conceived the idea of flying solo from New York to Paris.

It was no mere stunt. Lindbergh obtained the backing of a group of St. Louis businessmen and worked with the Ryan Aviation Corporation to custom-build a plane—it was to be called *The Spirit of St. Louis*—for the journey. The flight would further aeronautical technology and, equally important, win public acceptance of aviation. If a Lone Eagle—as Lindbergh was called—could make it across the ocean safely, the future seemed bright for commercial aviation.

Both in France and in America, Lindbergh was riotously hailed as a hero. His feat had put him in a position from which he could encourage the development of aeronautical technology and commercial aviation. Lindbergh became a key adviser to aircraft manufacturers and airlines. Although he was an outspoken pacifist and isolationist, he served as a consultant to the military when World War II erupted and even flew fifty secret combat missions in the Far East. During the last four years of his life, Lindbergh became a vigorous environmentalist, opposing the development of the supersonic transport (SST) on environmental grounds.

Sacco and Vanzetti Are Executed (1927)

The event: In 1927, two anarchists, Nicola Sacco and Bartolomeo Vanzetti, were executed for a 1920 Massachusetts robbery in which two men were killed.

THE CELEBRATED CASE of Sacco and Vanzetti captured America's attention throughout the 1920s. The self-proclaimed anarchists were arrested for murdering the paymaster and guard of a shoe company in South Braintree. Despite the testimony of Sacco and corroborating witnesses that he was at the Italian consulate in Boston on the day of the murder, the two hapless Italian immigrants were convicted. The court's ruling was upheld in subsequent appeals, and Sacco and Vanzetti were sentenced to death in 1927.

Throughout the country and even abroad, demonstrators took to the streets to protest the impending execution. Well-known authors wrote the governor to plead for clemency. None of these efforts succeeded. The two radicals went to the electric chair on August 23, 1927.

Yet another example of the rampant xenophobia sweeping the country, the trial was a case study in the fate of the lower class in a country whose courts catered to the monied and whose middle-class had been conditioned to live in fear of radical politics. In the 1970s an underworld informant revealed that the crime had actually been committed by the notorious Morelli gang, five mafioso brothers who had moved to New England from Brooklyn during World War I.

The Great Depression Begins (1929)

The event: On October 29, 1929, the bottom fell out of the stock market. "Black Tuesday," a harbinger of the Great Depression to come, was the worst single day in the history of the New York Stock Exchange up to that point.

THROUGHOUT THE LATE 1920s, Americans speculated on Wall Street in record numbers. Not content to spend their discretionary income on stock purchases, they also poured in their savings and borrowed money as well. At the beginning

 of 1929, the market was climbing steadily higher and higher. In September, though, the first signs of trouble were seen. The market wavered wildly up and down, with the average prices decreasing. On October 24, a selling spree put almost 13 million shares up for sale. The crisis came to a head five days later, when the market crashed and stocks lost an average of forty points.

Although thousands of Americans lost everything they owned on Black Tuesday, the stock market crash was less the cause of the Great Depression that followed than its messenger boy. At the root of the depression lay the rapid industrialization of America. Over the past century, as the country had become increasingly industrialized, much of its wealth had become concentrated in the hands of a few. While production soared with technological advances and infusions of money into industry, the market for new products was shrinking. American consumers simply did not have enough money to buy all the products industry made. Thus the cycle of economic collapse began and was perpetuated: workers lost their jobs because of industry cutbacks; industries could not hire workers because there was no market for their goods; there was no market for their goods because the workers had no money; the workers had no money because industries could not hire them.

As industries shut their plants and workers lost their jobs, banks across the country failed. In 1930, the first full year of the depression, 1,300 banks closed their doors. Over the next two years another 3,700 followed suit. The bank failures fed into the cycle of collapse by denying people access to funds, which in turn kept those people from pumping funds into the economy.

No sector of the economy escaped the Great Depression. Even agriculture suffered when out-of-work individuals were forced to cut down on their food consumption. People, as well as markets, simply starved without money.

President Herbert Hoover was determined to check the downward spiral and restore public confidence. Claiming that prosperity was "just around the corner," he devised a program for action by federal, state, and local government contrary to the advice of his secretary of the treasury, who declared that the economy should be left alone to hit bottom and then to rebuild slowly. Between

1929 and 1932 Hoover called on businessmen to maintain prices and wages; proposed a cut in federal taxes and in interest rates; designed public works programs and cooperative farming plans; asked states and localities to institute relief programs for the unemployed; and proposed a plan of federal aid to homeowners who could not meet their mortgage payments. Nothing he proposed, however, worked to check the downslide, and matters soon grew worse.

Many of Hoover's programs relied on state and local governments, but these were already unable to meet the demands being placed on them. The president could not see that the federal government needed to shoulder responsibility during the national emergency. In addition, he refused to allow federal funds to be spent directly on relief for individuals. He believed that individual relief was the responsibility of private charities and city agencies, funds for which had already disappeared.

Americans stood in bread lines for what little public and private relief was available. When they lost their homes, they moved to disease-infested slums with "houses" constructed of packing crates and sheet metal, which they called, with grim humor, "Hoovervilles." When the bread lines ran out of free food, they lived on scraps of food scavenged from garbage cans. In the summer of 1932, twenty thousand out-of-work veterans marched to Washington to demand the bonuses that had been promised to them. Nearly two thousand veterans remained in the capital even after Congress refused to dole out the bonuses. Living in shacks and tents at Anacostia Flats, the "Bonus Army" settled in with their families to wait for the congressmen to change their minds. Hoover claimed that most of the men in the "Bonus Army" were criminals, a calumny against the unfortunate poor, and he sent federal troops to clear out Anacostia Flats with bayonets, tear gas, and tanks.

The vision of the Army pursuing unarmed Americans, coupled with the dire economic and social conditions, put an end to the Republicans' hopes for victory in the presidential election of 1932. Meanwhile, across the country traveled a buoyant, optimistic, energized Franklin Delano Roosevelt, promising everybody he talked to a "New Deal." With nothing to lose, the American people began listening to the Democratic candidate—and to hope.

The Scottsboro Boys Are Convicted of Rape (1931)

The event: On March 25, 1931, nine black men, ranging in age from thirteen to twenty-one, were taken off a freight train in Alabama and arrested for raping two white women who were riding in the same boxcar. Within two weeks the young men were convicted and sentenced to die in the electric chair. Their case become the focus of national attention, a rallying point for various reform and radical groups, and a landmark in civil rights law.

THE INTERNATIONAL LABOR Defense, an organization backed by Communists, took up the case of the "Scottsboro Boys" and presented their appeal to the Alabama Supreme Court. In the meantime, the National Association for the Advancement of Colored People tried to convince the defendants to use its team of lawyers instead. The young men, however, were all committed to the ILD.

The ILD was not successful in Alabama—the state Supreme Court upheld the convictions—but the United States Supreme Court overturned the convictions and ordered a new trial for the Scottsboro Boys on the grounds that they had not been afforded adequate legal defense in their original trial.

A full two years after their arrest, the Scottsboro Boys were again brought before the court. Their new ILD lawyer, Samuel Liebowitz, was no more successful in the Alabama courts than his predecessor had been in the defendants' first trial. The young men were convicted again, and again the United States Supreme Court overturned the convictions, this time on the important grounds that the defendants had been tried before all-white juries—Alabama law prohibited blacks from serving on juries—and were therefore denied due process of law. A third trial of five of the defendants resulted in a third set of convictions; the charges against the other four defendants were dropped. The third trial did not result in death sentences for the five men, who were instead handed long prison terms.

Franklin Delano Roosevelt Announces the New Deal (1933)

The event: In 1932 Franklin Delano Roosevelt was elected the thirty-second president of the United States and immediately announced the "New Deal" he had promised during his campaign.

THE GREAT DEPRESSION'S dire social conditions made a Democratic victory in 1932 a sure bet. President Herbert Hoover, despite a grand scheme for action by the federal government, had refused to consider direct relief to desperate individuals, constructing most of his program to provide infusions of cash to failing businesses and industries. Meanwhile, Americans went hungry and homeless. To oppose Hoover, the Democrats selected a governor of New York who had pioneered a model relief program and who had engineered other social programs such as old-age pensions, unemployment insurance, and public power programs.

Roosevelt traveled across the country in a strenuous campaign schedule despite a crippling encounter with polio he'd endured in 1921. Although he was generally confined to a wheelchair, the American public saw him upright, with leg braces locked, and took to heart his promise of a "New Deal." In November they gave him 22.8 million votes to Hoover's 15.8 million, and Roosevelt carried the Electoral College 472 to 59.

During the first months of his administration, called "The Hundred Days," Roosevelt introduced sweeping legislation to Congress to deal with the national emergency. In Congress's first session it established the Federal Deposit Insurance Corporation to guarantee bank deposits, expanded the powers of the Federal Reserve Board, established the Home Owners Loan Corporation, and enacted a Federal Securities Act, which required companies to disclose fully financial information on new stock issues. To combat unemployment, Roosevelt called on Congress to appropriate $500 million for relief programs and to create jobs programs, including the Civilian Conservation Corps.

To stimulate industry, the president directed Congress to pass the National Industrial Recovery Act. Though industry itself at first resisted strenuously, Roosevelt had his way in the end. The act established the Public Works Administration and forced industrial leaders to enact codes of fair practices, allowing them in turn to set prices without fear of antitrust prosecution. Minimum wages and maximum work hours were set under the law, and workers were given the right to bargain collectively. In addition the law established the National Recovery Administration, led by General Hugh Johnson. The bureau was responsible for drafting business codes, and through it the federal government could accomplish such progressive reforms as the regulation of child labor in the textile and other industries. At the same time, labor unions used the legislation to garner more power and attract more members.

Roosevelt was much concerned about the desperate plight of American farmers, and he created with Congress the Agricultural Adjustment Administration in May 1933. This program of production limits and federal subsidies had as its goal the raising of agricultural prices to "parity" with the prices farmers had enjoyed when agriculture was economically in its best years.

The Hundred Days also witnessed the birth of the Tennessee Valley Authority, an agency responsible for broad social programs within the Tennessee River Valley region. Hydroelectric plants, nitrate manufacturing for fertilizers, soil conservation, flood control, and reforestation were all part of the program, headed by a board of three men and covering parts of seven states.

The American people adored Roosevelt for what he was trying to do in the New Deal. Even though nine million people were still out of work in 1934, the Democrats succeeded in gaining even larger majorities in both houses of Congress. Jobless Americans were loyal to the Roosevelt administration because they could point to decisive and dramatic actions. Four million of them had found jobs through the Federal Emergency Relief Administration, and many more had received relief funds. Although congressional leaders and the president himself were dismayed over the cost of the FERA jobs program of the Civil Works Administration, they could see the need for the program. Roosevelt abolished it in 1934, but the following year he called on Congress to establish the

Works Progress Administration. From 1935 to 1943, when the program was disbanded, it spent $11 billion and put 8.5 million people to work. Among the many components of the WPA were public works programs, the Federal Theater Project, the Federal Writers' Program, the Federal Art Project, and the National Youth Administration.

Despite all the money pumped into the economy through these federal programs, the Great Depression continued. Beginning in 1936, Roosevelt launched a "Second New Deal," and Congress went to work during the second Hundred Days enacting many more programs: The National Labor Relations Act, known as the Wagner Act, to increase labor union power; the Social Security Act, to create old-age pensions through payroll and wage taxes; the Public Utility Holding Company Act, which restricted the control of electric and gas companies; the Rural Electrification Administration, which brought electricity to nine out of ten farms in America by 1950; and the Wealth Tax Act, which increased the rate of taxes on incomes over $50,000 to 75 percent.

But before the second hundred days came the 1936 presidential election, and it was a landslide: Roosevelt carried every state except Maine and Vermont and defeated his opponent, Alfred M. Landon, by more than ten million votes. When—despite the rash of new programs—the economy failed to improve, and in fact worsened in mid-1937, Roosevelt asked Congress to pass a $3.75 billion public works bill. Previously committed to maintaining a budget that was close to being balanced, Roosevelt shifted to deficit-spending, thereby alienating even those conservatives who did not already despise him. Though the wealthy and big business in general considered Roosevelt something of a class traitor, the common folk adored him, and made this abundantly clear when he decided to run for a unprecedented third term. For all the entrenched interests' grousing about FDR's "democratic dictatorship," American voters returned him to office not just for a third, but a fourth term as well.

While the country was battling the Depression, events across the globe were gaining dangerous momentum. In Italy, Mussolini established a program of universal military training and invaded Ethiopia in 1935. General Francisco Franco amassed a force of rebels and began fighting against the Spanish government. In July 1937, Japan invaded China yet again. In March 1938, Hilter's Germany invaded and annexed Austria. Though isolationist sentiment was strong in America, when war broke out worldwide, Roosevelt grew determined to come to the aid of England and Western Europe. A surprise attack by Japan on Pearl Harbor gave him the pretext he needed, and America entered World War II led by the most popular and longest-serving president in its history.

World War II would do what the New Deal could not: end the Great Depression. Yet the New Deal had fulfilled much of the progressive agenda of reform that had been developing support for over a century. As much as anything else, the New Deal, with its Social Security and entitlement programs, shaped the America of the twentieth century.

Vladimir Zworykin Demonstrates the "Iconoscope" (1933)

The event: In 1933, Vladimir Zworykin broadcast a television picture over a radio-wave relay between New York and Philadelphia—the first such broadcast in history.

THE STORY OF the development of television is complex, involves the work of many people, and is not yet over. But two very different men can be singled out as indispensable in having brought it into being.

Vladimir Zworykin, born in Mourom, Russia, in 1889 and trained as an electrical engineer at the Petrograd Institute of Technology, came to the United States in 1916 and was naturalized in 1924. From 1920 to 1929 he served as a research engineer with Westinghouse, where he developed and patented the "iconoscope" in 1925. This was the basis of the television camera and the most direct ancestor of modern television. As director of electronic research for RCA (1929-1942) and associate director, then director of the RCA Laboratories (1942-1947), he further refined his invention. It was first used in a 1933 experimental broadcast. (Zworykin, incidentally, was also instrumental in the development of the electron microscope, today regarded as a basic tool of medical scientific research.)

Despite Zworykin's breakthrough, television did not explode upon the American scene. The first genuinely public broadcast took place in 1939, when NBC aired live video of Franklin D. Roosevelt at the New York World's Fair, but regularly scheduled programs were not broadcast until 1944—and these to a very small number of New York-area subscribers. Early television sets were costly, cumbersome, and finicky. Attractive full-scale programming required a large "user base" to attract advertisers, but the public was reluctant to invest in an expensive appliance to view a limited schedule of boxing matches, game shows, and old movies. What the fledgling television networks needed to find was a *reason* for the public to purchase TV sets.

That reason came in the form of Milton Berle (born Milton Berlinger in New York City on July 12, 1908). After a relatively undistinguished comedic career in vaudeville, the New York stage, and a few films, NBC tapped him in 1948 as the comic star of a show originally titled "The Texaco Star Theater," which premiered on September 21. The nation fell in love with the show and with Berle, who was affectionately christened "Uncle Miltie" and, more accurately, "Mr. Television." Berle utterly dominated the medium from 1948 to 1956. Families routinely interrupted dinner—or took their plates with them to the TV—to watch the hour-long program every Tuesday evening. Attendance at motion-picture theaters plummeted as people stayed home to watch. And those who didn't own televisions soon went out and bought them. An industry was launched; a nation—and the world—transformed.

John L. Lewis Founds the C.I.O. (1935)

The event: In 1935, the fiery labor leader John L. Lewis founded the Committee for Industrial Organization, which soon broke with the American Federation of Labor to become the most radical labor organization in the country.

JOHN L. LEWIS, the son of Welsh immigrants in Lucas, Iowa, went to work for the interests of labor in 1907. Over the next six decades he consolidated power and became recognized as a national labor leader. His first work was at the coal mines in Panama, Illinois, where he built a base of power among immigrant coal

miners. In 1909 he went to work as a national organizer for the American Federation of Labor. In 1917 he returned to the United Mine Workers, where he worked as a statistician and editor before becoming president of the union. During the 1920s and early 1930s, Lewis became recognized as a creative labor leader. Membership in the union increased from 150,000 to 500,000, and companies in nonunionized regions of the company began recognizing the union. In the 1930s, with membership in all unions increasing at a dramatic rate, Lewis became determined to develop a previously untapped resource. He encouraged the AFL to accept unions of unskilled mass production workers, and when the AFL did not respond, he resigned his position as vice-president of the AFL and created the CIO. Disregarding craft distinctions, Lewis's organization sought to enroll workers into unions created according to industry type. The AFL expelled these unions, but the newly renamed organization, the Congress of Industrial Organization, was off and running. By 1940 the organization claimed more than 2.6 million members and was successfully negotiating on behalf of its members.

Membership in the CIO leveled off in the early 1950s at about five million. AFL membership reached about 7.1 million; the organization had, over the years, accepted industrial unions as members. With the passage of the Taft-Hartley Act, the rival organizations had a common enemy. Passed over president Harry S Truman's veto by a Republican-controlled Congress, the act outlawed closed shops and allowed the states to enact "right-to-work" laws, which drove the two organizations to merge in order better to fight for the gains labor had made during the New Deal and that were now under attack by the new law. In 1955, the AFL-CIO was formed with George Meany as president. The combined membership rolls totaled sixteen million.

Eugene O'Neill Accepts the Nobel Prize (1936)

The event: In 1936, Eugene O'Neill, America's foremost dramatist, accepted the Nobel Prize for Literature.

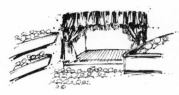

AT 4:39 ON A Friday afternoon, November 27, 1953, Eugene O'Neill, the only American playwright to win a Nobel Prize, died in a Boston hotel room after a lifelong battle with tuberculosis. His last words were, "Born in a hotel room—and God damn it—died in a hotel room!"

He was the son of a popular actor, and was, in fact, born in a Broadway hotel on October 16, 1888. A prank got him bounced from Princeton University in 1907, and he set out on a gold-prospecting voyage to Honduras and then, as a merchant seaman, to Buenos Aires. Returning to the United States, he acted briefly, wrote for a newspaper, then suffered the first attack of the tuberculosis that would plague his life. During five months in a sanatorium and a year of convalescence afterward, he read the great ground-breaking playwrights Wedekind, Strindberg, and Ibsen, as well as the political philosophy of Marx and Kropotkin. He also searched his own soul. In 1916, O'Neill was living in Provincetown, Massachusetts, when a vacationing group of Greenwich Village intellectuals, having learned that the young man had begun scribbling plays, invited him to submit a work to be performed in the playhouse they had improvised chiefly for their own amusement. The play, a one-act melodrama entitled *Bound East for Cardiff*, became the first of his works to be given publicly when it was performed that autumn in Greenwich Village at the tiny Provincetown Playhouse, which the group had just opened.

From this almost casual beginning O'Neill's career skyrocketed. His first major play, *The Emperor Jones*, opened in 1920 to great acclaim—"an avalanche of applause," as one witness recalled—and earned O'Neill a Pulitzer Prize. Like the almost fifty plays that followed it, *The Emperor Jones* was daring and experimental, reaching far beyond the limits of conventional theater. A psychologically symbolic mood play about terror and suspicion, it featured as its central character a black Pullman porter, Brutus Jones, who flees to a tropical island after killing a man. There he sets himself up as the despotic Emperor Jones until his "subjects" revolt and he attempts to escape through the jungle. In the end, his own fears trap him, and he is murdered.

Among the greatest productions of O'Neill's restless imagination, each one a daring innovation in drama, are *The Hairy Ape* (1921), *The Iceman Cometh* (1922), *Desire Under the Elms* (1924), *Mourning Becomes Electra* (1931), and his most profound masterwork, *Long Day's Journey Into Night* (produced posthumously in 1956). While America had produced many important literary figures before O'Neill, none were playwrights. O'Neill's work made the world look to the American stage and opened the way for the likes of Clifford Odets, Arthur Miller, Tennessee Williams, and Edward Albee.

World War II Begins with a Sneak Attack on Pearl Harbor (1941)

The event: On December 7, 1941, despite Franklin Roosevelt's appeal to Emperor Hirohito to use his position to avert a war, the Japanese—fearing that war with the United States was inevitable in any case—launched a surprise attack on the American fleet anchored at Pearl Harbor in Hawaii, killing 2,403 Americans, destroying nineteen ships and 150 planes, and providing the American president with the excuse he needed to go to war, with the consent of Congress, against the fascist governments of Europe and Asia. The century's second worldwide conflict was under way.

WORLD WAR II was the great, central, cataclysmic event of the twentieth century. When Japan struck Pearl Harbor, the United States was as prepared as it had ever been for war. It was openly providing supplies and equipment to the Allies. Armaments were pouring out of the country's factories. The year before, Congress had passed the first peace-time draft in the nation's history. The armed forces were rapidly expanding their training courses and their manpower. And for weeks the government had been waging an undeclared war against Germany in the Atlantic. And yet, the American public remained deeply divided over the drift of U.S. policy toward a declared war. The surprise attack ended the debate for good.

America entered the war more unified than perhaps it ever had been or ever would be again. Congress granted the president unprecedented powers to wage intercontinental battle, and Roosevelt used them to launch an immense mobilization and to build a massive war machine.

Despite the clear indications that war lay on the horizon, however, for the vast majority of Americans World War II struck suddenly, creating incredible fear and anger. Thousands rushed to enlist, and the U.S. government conscripted millions more. As a result, most of the sixteen million men and women who served in the U.S. armed forces during World War II were not professional soldiers but ordinary citizens torn from their homes, their jobs, and their families and thrust into a huge bureaucratic machine fighting a global conflict in the far-flung reaches of strange lands. Such changes happened quickly, before those enlisting or being drafted had any real understanding of the realities of war, its indifference to individual life, its terrible logic of destruction, or its absolute dedication to victory at any cost.

Overnight, boys hardly old enough to shave or to drive a car, much less vote, were dropping bombs on centuries-old centers of Western culture or dodging bullets in some of the most Godforsaken spots on earth. Quickly trained, hastily assigned enlisted personnel were expected to repair, supply, and operate the most sophisticated machinery produced by the modern world under impossible conditions ruled by a complex bureaucratic apparatus that regulated their every hour—and their very fate. Whether they carried out routine duties behind enemy lines or endured the most extreme conditions of heavy combat, they fought boredom, isolation, loneliness, homesickness, and debilitating fear. They contracted exotic diseases, manned bleak outposts, and ran short of supplies—in the middle of deserts, surrounded by jungles, on tiny islands, or amid the rubble of war-torn civilizations. Living in drafty Nissen huts, dank caves, and moldy tents, and eating food they detested, they strove to find ways to pass the time when they weren't fighting the enemy. They gambled and drank to excess, read old magazines, comic books, and paperback novels, watched sappy movies, listened to Frank Sinatra and Glenn Miller on the radio when they could get them, Tokyo Rose and Lord Haw Haw when they couldn't, took weekend passes and attended USO shows, or tried to pick up strangers for quick, desperate sex. Mostly they lived for mail call and longed for home.

Back home those Americans who did not march off to war found themselves caught up in the conflict nevertheless, for World War II touched almost every aspect of American life. The government regulated automobile tires, cars, shoes, farm machines, gasoline, sugar, and meat, among other commodities. It established a point system, allowing only fifty points per month for canned goods. A can of tomatoes cost twenty points. When almost no one could afford steak or pork chops, butchers offered unrationed shark meat at forty-five cents a pound. For those who could afford more, black markets sprang up everywhere dealing in everything from nylons to new tires.

All over the country, in vacant lots and backyards, Americans planted "victory gardens" to supplement their diets. Since the government had set a 35-mph speed limit to conserve gas and tires, highway patriots honked their horns at speeders—three short blasts and a long one, Morse code for "V." Salesmen joined car pools. Women went to work in factories and found the resulting economic freedom exhilarating. Grandparents volunteered for the Civilian Defense. And many a neglected teenager turned to vandalism and sexual delinquency. Farmers found themselves short of labor, since not only had many volunteered or been drafted, thousands had left for the well-paying war plant jobs and the inflated wages of the big cities. They would never come back. As a result, farmers improved their productivity by improving their habits—using commercial fertilizers, proper crop rotation, and hybrid seeds. The war stimulated America's sluggish industry with its demands for munitions, explosives, prefabricated railway bridges, blasting machines, airplanes, gliders, uniforms, boots, helmets, guns, beef, vegetables, and exotic new chemicals for use in everything from rocket propellant to plastic pins and synthetic rubber tires.

At home and overseas, Americans closely followed the progress of the war. Though it had started in the Pacific, the United States took as its first priority the salvation of Europe and the defeat of Nazi Germany. The official war aims, however, did not match the mood of the American public, which supported the war primarily as a means of taking revenge on Japan. Not only had the Japanese caught the United States unawares in Hawaii, but within two hours of dropping the first bombs on Pearl Harbor they had also struck Clark Field, the main U.S. base in the Philippines, trapping General Douglas MacArthur's Far East air force on the ground and destroying about half of it. In short order, Japan ran the American command out of the islands, captured massive numbers of American troops who were fighting a last-ditch effort on the Bataan Peninsula, and soundly defeated the British in Singapore to take control of the Pacific.

The first counterstrike against Japan came in an action that spoke more for the desperate needs of American morale than of sound strategic thinking. On April 18, 1942, Lieutenant Colonel James Doolittle led sixteen Army Air Force B-25s, launched from the U.S. Navy aircraft carrier *Hornet*, in a spectacular low-level surprise attack against Tokyo that wrought only minor damage and ended in the loss of all aircraft in bad weather over China. Most of the crews were saved, however, Americans felt better, and the shocked Japanese kept four fighter groups home as they moved against the remainder of the American Pacific Fleet at Midway Island, where the Navy, under Admiral Chester Nimitz, was waiting for them. The Japanese lost their first major battle in the war, America took control of the Pacific, and the U.S. could turn its attention to its primary goals on the other side of the world.

Anxious to engage the enemy, America enlisted in the North Africa campaign when British leaders, veterans of the bloodletting of World War I, refused a hasty, ill-prepared American plan to invade the European continent. At that point Germany's eastern front was stagnant and Field Marshal Erwin Rommel was not quite ready for a new desert offensive. Hitler had already invaded Russia, and still determined to crush the Soviets, he ordered a drive into the Caucasus, only to be held back by rains till June. Encouraged by his earlier successes, Hitler decided to mount a major attack on Stalingrad as well as the Caucasus when the rains let up. By fall, victory seemed certain. Then the Russians struck back. In North Africa, after wrangling among themselves, the Allied forces had finally decided on a strategy and taken control of the air over the

Mediterranean, cutting off Rommel from resupply. After fighting a brilliant campaign, the "Desert Fox's" Afrika Korps simply ran out of gas. Despite Hitler's order not to retreat "one inch," Rommel recognized a rout when he saw one and withdrew. Back in Stalingrad, in a tremendous counterstrike, the Soviets had encircled Hitler's Sixth Army, and more than two hundred thousand German troops simply *vanished*. By the end of the year it was clear that Germany had all but lost the war in the East.

All through the summer of 1942, MacArthur had been slogging his way across New Guinea toward his lost command on the Philippines, while Nimitz's amphibious forces leapfrogged from island to island up the Pacific. The Japanese put up a tremendous resistance, fighting for five deadly months at Guadalcanal before Japan evacuated the survivors. The Allies in the West commenced a terribly costly strategic bombing campaign against Europe, in which the average life of an 8th Air Force B-17 and its crew was fifteen missions, while the assigned tour of duty was twenty-five. "Skipper," one navigator told his pilot, "mathematically there just ain't any way we're gonna live through this thing." The controversial strategic bombing campaign achieved few of its objectives, though it continued even after the Allied invasion of Europe, as the AAF set the very atmosphere above German centers of culture aflame in a campaign of civilian terror.

The much-delayed invasion itself came on June 6, 1944, when the most massive armada in history struck the beaches of Normandy. Directed by General Dwight D. Eisenhower, the invasion took Hitler by surprise and cleared the way for General George Patton's Third Army tanks to dash across Europe. On July 20 worried German generals almost succeeded in assassinating Hitler. On August 25 the Allied forces liberated Paris. By the fall they had driven the Germans back to the Fatherland. Faced with disaster, Hitler ignored the advice of his general staff and attempted one last, desperate counteroffensive. At the Battle of the Bulge on December 15, 1944, the U.S. troops retreated for eight days before regrouping and routing the Nazis. Two weeks later the Red Army crossed the Vistula. As Germany was crushed from both sides, Hitler shot himself rather than surrender. The war in Europe was at an end.

As the Allies invaded Europe, Nimitz's island-hopping had brought U.S. troops face to face with the Japanese at Saipan, the main bastion protecting the Empire's homeland. In a savage air battle on June 19, 1944, Japan lost 346 planes while shooting down only 50 Americans, and its navy was fatally crippled. Saipan's civilians committed mass suicide, and its 40,000-strong garrison died fighting to the last man, but a month later the U.S. had a base for launching massive B-29 bombing raids on Japan, directed by a Curtis LeMay fresh from burning down Europe. MacArthur, who arrived on Leyte in October 1944, had cleared the island by mid-January of 1945, just as the marines took Iwo Jima. Six months of hard fighting later, Okinawa was occupied and Japan's fate was sealed. President Roosevelt had died in 1944, and Harry S Truman, convinced that a direct attack on the homeland would be too costly, ordered the dropping of atomic bombs on Hiroshima and Nagasaki, virtually the only targets of any significance Curtis LeMay had left.

Whether the Americans fighting in World War II had spent the war in combat, facing death, injury, or capture daily, or in backwater bases worrying that the war was passing them by, they no longer looked at the world or life through the same eyes when it was over. Young, inexperienced, unaccustomed to the rigors of military life, innocent of war itself, they had learned to fight a modern war of almost unimaginable destructiveness and returned home to a world as transformed by the last four years as they were.

The U.S. Government Interns Japanese-American Citizens (1942)

The event: In 1942, responding to deep-seated nativist fears unleashed by war hysteria, the U.S. began evacuating Japanese-Americans from their homes on the West Coast, placing them in "internment" camps for the duration of World War II.

WHEN JAPAN BOMBED Pearl Harbor on December 7, 1941, about one hundred twenty thousand Japanese were living in the United States. Nearly eighty thousand of them had been born in the United States and were American citizens. As rumors spread across the country of a Japanese plot to sabotage war industries

and invade the west coast, Americans demanded that something be done about the Japanese living among them. Many of the demands came from farmers and politicians on the west coast, where most of the Japanese-Americans lived. The farmers were seeking to eliminate competition by the Japanese; the politicians were playing on the public's fears to gain popularity.

The federal government gave in to these demands, and on February 19, 1942, President Franklin D. Roosevelt signed Executive Order 9066 requiring all Japanese-Americans, both citizens and non-citizens, living within two hundred miles of the Pacific Coast to evacuate their homes. More than a hundred thousand Japanese-Americans were moved to ten internment camps located in California, Idaho, Utah, Arizona, Wyoming, Colorado, and Arkansas. Some young men won release from the camps by joining the U.S. Army. The remainder, however, were forced to stay in the camps until President Roosevelt rescinded the evacuation order and closed the camps in 1945.

The Japanese-Americans, forced to leave behind their land, their homes, and most of their belongings, brought suit against the United States government, but the Supreme Court upheld the government's actions in *Hirabayashi v. United States* and *Korematsu v. United States*. In 1968, however, the government reimbursed many of those who had been relocated for lost property, and in 1988 Congress appropriated funds to pay $20,000 to each of the sixty thousand surviving internees.

Congress Passes the G.I. Bill (1944)

The event: In 1944, Congress passed the Servicemen's Readjustment Act, better known as the "G.I. Bill," a benefits package for returning World War II veterans that helped kick off a post-war boom in housing and babies.

THE G.I. BILL officially established veterans' hospitals, provided for vocational rehabilitation, made low-interest mortgages available, and granted stipends cover-

ing tuition and living expenses for veterans attending college or trade schools. Unofficially it was part of a new world in the making. That world lived under the threat of instant destruction, but it was also one transformed by new forms of popular travel, entertainment, and industry, and supported by the longest curve of sustained economic growth in memory. Post-war Americans saw the largest real estate boom in history, a boom fueled by their need not only to return to normality but to create the "good life" they had dreamed about during the war. It was a world that seemed to need the skills and training of the masses of new veterans, and also one willing to offer them the kind of education they could never have hoped for before the war. As they poured back onto America's soil, filling its classrooms, its new tract homes, and its burgeoning airlines, aerospace, automobile, communications, plastics, steel, and service industries, the years of separation, hardship, and fear seemed to have given birth to new hope, and the veterans in turn gave birth to a new generation, the largest in history, in what Americans came to know as the Baby Boom.

The United Nations is Chartered (1945)

The event: In June 1945, delegates from fifty nations met in San Francisco to draft the charter of the United Nations, an attempt to stabilize world politics by bringing together the nations of the planet into a single, cooperative, deliberative forum for the peaceful resolution of disputes.

THE MEETING HAD been scheduled during the 1945 Yalta Conference in the Crimea, where British Prime Minister Winston Churchill, United States President Franklin D. Roosevelt, and Russian President Josef Stalin met to discuss the postwar division of Europe and the final Allied assault on Germany. The three leaders had before them the example of a continent destroyed in part as a result of similar discussions at the end of the last world war. That war, too, had ended with the call for a world-wide organization of nations, and the results had not been particularly encouraging. The League of Nations had failed, but in the shadow of potential annihilation, the world was ready to try again.

At the San Francisco convention, the delegates devised a charter that called for a General Assembly, composed of delegates from each member country, and a Security Council, made up of delegates from five permanent member nations and six other members elected for two-year terms. The permanent members of the council—the United States, the Soviet Union, Great Britain, France, and China—were given responsibility for maintaining world peace and could use a variety of diplomatic, economic, and military measures to achieve that end. To ensure that no coalition or alliance within the Security Council wrested control, the five permanent members had to agree unanimously on any action. Since such unanimity was rare, the United Nations became, in practice, a forum for international discussion rather than an organization that relied on military or diplomatic action.

The General Assembly of the new organization first met in London in 1946, but later assemblies met at the permanent headquarters in New York City. At the London meeting, bitter debate surrounded Russia's continued occupation of the Azerbaijan region of Iran and Great Britain's continued occupation of Greece. Another early debate centered on the control of atomic energy. The Atomic Energy Commission, created by the General Assembly in 1946, explored the issue of atomic control, and in June of that year devised a plan whereby all atomic weapons would be outlawed. The commission called for inspectors appointed by the United Nations to travel across the globe to ensure that no country was secretly making atomic bombs and to supervise the destruction of existing weapons. In addition, the plan called for the commission, not the Security Council, to hold ultimate responsibility for the atomic issue. The debate ended with a Soviet veto of the plan: the Soviet Union refused to allow inspectors inside its borders and chose not to relinquish its veto power over atomic matters in the Security Council.

The failure to eradicate the nuclear threat was a major setback for the

United Nations, one that doomed the world to almost five decades of Cold War. As the atomic superpowers engaged in ideolgical chess, using a map of the world as a game board, the United Nations became not much more than a debating society for so-called "Third World" countries. When the Cold War began to wind down, however, the usefulness of the United Nations suddenly became clear again, and the organization played a strategically central political role in the Gulf War and the policing of the defeated but still renegade Iraq in its aftermath—an intimation at least that it might one day function as originally imagined.

America Drops an Atomic Bomb on Hiroshima and Nagasaki (1945)

The event: On August 6, 1945, the United States dropped the first atomic bomb on the Japanese city of Hiroshima, and three days later dropped a second bomb on Nagasaki, ending the war with Japan and ushering in the age of potential mutual destruction called the Cold War.

THE POSSIBILITY OF nuclear fission was discovered in Germany in 1938, but not until 1943 did British scientists come up with a realistic plan for building an atomic bomb within a few years. Heeding a warning by no less prominent a scientist than Albert Einstein, Franklin Roosevelt established the Manhattan Project and charged its military head, General Leslie R. Groves, with developing a working bomb before the Nazis did, since everyone mistakenly assumed that Germany had a head start in what became the first nuclear arms race. A group of scientists directed by Robert Oppenheimer spent months locked on a base at Los Alamos, New Mexico, feverishly experimenting with the "gadget," as they called it—ultimately conducting a successful test in the desert at Alamogordo shortly after Roosevelt's death—and after the defeat of Germany in World War II.

Although, during the war, a small group of scientists proposed steps that could be taken to avoid a nuclear arms race in the future, Roosevelt—and Harry

S Truman after him—became enamored of the advantages he and Winston Churchill imagined would result from an American-British nuclear monopoly. Faced with the choice of dropping the bomb on Japan, Truman made the fateful decision to go ahead because the Japanese, fearing for the life of their emperor, continued to resist the Allied demand for unconditional surrender even with their cities already in large part reduced to rubble by the massive fire-bombings of the American air forces. Fearful that Japan's truculence would give Stalin time to enter the war against the Japanese and claim his share of the spoils of victory as he had in Europe, Truman ordered the only nuclear attacks in world history, killing over two hundred thousand Japanese civilians in explosions of unimaginable ferocity and horror.

Nuclear saber-rattling from the U.S. began almost immediately. At the Potsdam meeting of Churchill, Stalin, and Truman, the Soviet dictator had less cause to be worried than the western leaders assumed. Karl Fuchs, working on the Manhattan project, had passed atomic secrets to the Soviets, and Stalin knew all about the bomb—he just hadn't built one yet. Within a few years both the USSR and the United States had thousands upon thousands of nuclear weapons and could launch them from almost anywhere on land, at sea, or in the air. Prisoners of their own technology, the two Superpowers spent forty years locked in a Cold War dance of death that neither could control or bring to a good end.

George C. Marshall Announces a Plan for European Recovery (1947)

The event: In a commencement address at Harvard University on June 5, 1947, George C. Marshall, Secretary of State and former army chief of staff during World War II, outlined a plan whereby the United States would give economic assistance to the European nations attempting to rebuild their countries.

EUROPE AFTER WORLD WAR II was in dire need of assistance. France, England, and the other European Allies were economically devastated by the war, and the United States feared that, in such a debilitated condition the European nations would be easy prey for communism. Marshall claimed that the American policy

of economic aid would restore "normal economic health in the world, without which there can be no political stability and no assured peace." He attempted to assuage the fears of the Soviets by stating that the policy was not aimed "against any country or doctrine but against hunger, poverty, desperation, and chaos."

Great Britain and France spearheaded the formation of a Committee for European Economic Cooperation, made up of delegates from sixteen nations, and the committee officially requested $22.4 billion from the United States. Congress appropriated the funds to be dispersed through the Marshall Plan, and more than $13 billion poured into Europe. In addition the program created a Displaced Persons Plan, through which nearly three hundred thousand Europeans, including many survivors of the Holocaust, became American citizens. Europe got back on its feet and formed new alliances, which resulted in the formation of a West German Republic out of the western sector of divided Germany. Outraged by this, the Soviets, who governed the eastern sector, blockaded Berlin (squarely in the eastern sector, but divided into western and eastern zones) in June 1948. During the blockade, the United States airlifted supplies for nearly a year to residents of West Berlin.

The aid given to the European nations by the United States laid the foundation for a military alliance, the North Atlantic Treaty, signed in April 1949. The actions on the part of the Western Allies—the Marshall Plan and the creation of NATO—fed Soviet fears that the West would not be satisfied until Communism and the Soviet nation were obliterated. In retaliation against the West's actions, the Soviet Union, in addition to blockading Berlin, seized Czechoslovakia in February 1948 and created a military alliance of Communist-controlled countries, the Warsaw Pact. The Cold War, which would dominate world politics for four decades, was in full swing by the beginning of the 1950s.

Jackie Robinson Gets a Contract with the Brooklyn Dodgers (1947)

The event: In 1947, Jackie Robinson became the first African-American to play professional baseball in the major leagues during the twentieth century, a breakthrough in race relations not only for the "national pastime" but for American society as a whole.

A HANDFUL OF blacks played major league ball before the 1880s, when Jim Crow laws led to strict segregation in the South and the hardening of the color line throughout the country. Blacks, forced out of the white leagues, formed their own loosely structured touring teams, which in the 1920s grew into the Negro Leagues. Segregation kept many of the finest ball players out of the major leagues, as anyone who knew baseball well realized. Certainly Brooklyn Dodger president and general manager Branch Rickey knew of the immense waste of black talent, and in 1947— greatly influenced by the writing on race of a Columbia University history professor named Frank Tannebaum, among others—the inventor of baseball's farm system decided to breach the all-white barrier in professional baseball.

Rickey selected and groomed an outstanding college player from UCLA named Jackie Robinson, who was immensely proud of his talents and of the color of his skin. Robinson had fought racism since childhood, throughout his college career, and in the army, where he faced a court-martial for challenging the illegal segregation he encountered on an army bus. Jackie Robinson spent a year on Rickey's farm team and then was hired by the Brooklyn Dodgers.

Robinson's imposing talent, combined with Rickey's public relations skill, made his name a household word. Many white fans, however, did not immediately accept the new player. Rickey forced Robinson to promise that he would silently endure any abuse he might receive, and for two years Robinson, biting back his tongue, took the jeers, insults, threats, and hate mail. More ominously, there were a number of death threats on the new Dodger's life. Robinson played anyway, and played spectacularly. Then in 1949 he broke his agreement and spoke out against racial discrimination, Jim Crow laws, and the slowness of integration within professional baseball.

Retiring in 1957, Robinson could claim many legacies. Though the National Football League had actually been integrated the year before Robinson became a Dodger, it was his play and his personality that captured the imagination of the nation and ensured the abandonment of the color line on the professional playing fields and courts of America. More importantly, Robinson spurred thousands of blacks to see that the policy of "separate but equal" had no place anywhere in American society.

Levittown Is Developed (1947)

The event: From 1947 to 1951, Levitt and Sons, a construction company, built a suburban development in Hempstead, New York, consisting of 17,450 homes for 75,000 people, using crews who followed a precise twenty-seven-step process working with prefabricated materials.

MORE THAN THIRTY homes a day were completed at the peak of production, and middle-class families poured into the new community with the help of Levitt's easy credit terms, made possible by funds from the Federal Housing Administration and the Veterans Administration.

Levitt and Sons first experimented with mass production during World War II under contract from the government to build housing for war workers. The company innovated prefabricated materials and an assembly-line process that cut costs and saved time. After the war, Levitt and Sons translated these advances to the private home-building industry with great success, creating "instant" suburbs for the legions of men and women who were creating the postwar "Baby Boom."

The second Levittown was built in the 1950s near Philadelphia. The last was built in New Jersey in the 1960s. Other building companies adopted the

Levitts' advances in mass production, and the increase in housing precipitated a move to the suburbs that profoundly changed the appearance of the American landscape. By 1990, 45 percent of the American population lived in suburban areas, and 66 percent of American families owned their own homes.

Congress Passes the National Security Act (1947)

The event: In 1947, Congress passed the National Security Act, reorganizing the Department of Defense and creating the Central Intelligence Agency.

THE YEAR THE CIA was born, President Harry S Truman announced his new "doctrine" in the face of a threatened Communist takeover of Greece and Turkey. The Truman Doctrine was based on the theory of containment put forward by the State Department's George F. Kennan under the pseudonym "X" in the influential journal *Foreign Affairs*. In one of the most important essays in the history of the twentieth century, Kennan held that the way to combat Communism was to contain its spread, which meant confronting the Soviet Union with all means at the United States' disposal, including force if necessary, wherever in the world it sought to expand its influence. The Cold War had begun in earnest, and minute attention to the workings of a single foreign power became central to the government's concept of national security. The immediate result was a renewed "red scare" inside the United States, and a vast expansion of "covert action"—basically foreign policy initiatives that the government wished to keep hidden from the American public.

In this atmosphere, the CIA—an outgrowth of America's World War II espionage organization, the Office of Strategic Services—expanded rapidly in size and power, becoming something of a shadow government as the cold warriors who ran it took advantage of statutes providing the agency great leeway and secrecy in its operations. At the expense of its information gathering function, the CIA mounted covert actions that often proved not only unsuccessful but counterproductive, while producing analyses that were politically skewed when they weren't simply wrong. Its operation of U-2 spy planes over Russia led to an aborted summit conference when the Soviet Union shot Gary Powers's plane down in May of 1960. And its planned invasion of Cuba ended in disaster at the Bay of Pigs, leading President John F. Kennedy to threaten to dismantle the agency.

Invoking the rubric "National Security," the CIA managed not only to circumvent legitimate congressional oversight but to hide all but the most blatant of its failures and excesses from the public. That changed, however, when the chicanery of the Watergate era led to congressional investigation. The revelations of Senator Frank Church's committee, among others, shocked Americans, who learned that the CIA had planned and helped conduct secret invasions and overthrows of Central and Latin American countries, assassinated foreign heads of state, conducted a mass murder campaign in Vietnam (code named "Phoenix"), spied on American citizens, trafficked in drugs to support its "dummy" corporations, and sought constantly to subvert the legal oversight power of the Congress that had created it. While the findings resulted in a cutback of some funds and closer scrutiny by Congress, they did not prevent the agency, under Reagan-appointed Director William Casey, from attempting to finance illegal covert operations in Nicaragua through the sale of arms to Iran in exchange for American hostages held throughout the Mideast—yet another CIA secret action at odds with the public policy of the United States.

The United States Launches the Berlin Airlift (1948)

The event: On June 24, 1948, a little over two weeks after the announcement by the United States and other western nations of their intention to create the republic of West Germany, the Soviet Union blockaded Berlin, the divided city in the eastern sector of the divided nation. In response, the United States risked war with the Soviets by airlifting supplies to the beleaguered city.

IN LATE MARCH 1948, increasingly wary of the strong alliances being formed by the western nations and concerned over the growing commitment on the part of the Western allies to establish a separate capitalist state of West Germany, the Soviets began detaining troop trains bound for West Berlin. On June 7 the western nations officially announced their intention to create West Germany, and little more than two weeks later, the Soviets blockaded West Berlin, arguing that Berlin, located deep within Soviet-occupied East Germany, could not serve as the capital of West Germany.

President Harry S Truman acted swiftly. Believing that the loss of West Berlin would ultimately mean the loss of all of Germany, he ordered an airlift. Over most of the next year, some 321 days, the Allies made more than 272,000 flights over Soviet-occupied territory to provide West Berlin with thousands of tons of supplies each day. The airlift was a logistical and political triumph. On May 12, 1949, the Soviets at last conceded that the blockade had failed and reopened Berlin to Western traffic. East and West Germany were formally created as separate nations later in the month.

The Allies' success in forcing the Soviet Union to abandon the blockade was a boost to the morale of European nations still struggling to recover from World War II and hovering in the shadow of the looming Soviet giant. In addition, the airlift seemed to validate the Western European and American policy of containing Communism, a policy that carried the force of a military alliance when the North Atlantic Treaty Organization was formed in April 1949.

Joseph McCarthy Claims to Know of 205 Card-carrying Communists (1950)

The event: On February 9, 1950, Senator Joseph R. McCarthy of Wisconsin electrified his audience at the Women's Republican Club in Wheeling, West Virginia, by announcing that he was holding in his hand a list of 205 communists in the State Department.

FOLLOWING THE WHEELING speech a massive "witch hunt" got under way, as, over the next four years, McCarthy and his followers, looking to carve out political futures for themselves, exploited America's fear of Communism by making reckless, usually groundless accusations wherever they went.

Two early victims of McCarthy's savage escapades were Owen Lattimore, a China expert and professor at Johns Hopkins University, and John S. Service of the state department. At Senate hearings chaired by Millard Tydings of Maryland, no evidence was offered to support McCarthy's claims that these men were Communist spies. Yet the accusations themselves were sufficient to instill lingering suspicions about these men and others, whose "soft" stance on Communism, according to McCarthy, had contributed to the "loss" of China after the war.

The senator from Wisconsin was undaunted by the Senate's failure to brand Lattimore and Service communists. He gained chairmanship of the Senate Subcommittee on Governmental Operations, from which he launched investigations of the Voice of America and the U.S. Army Signal Corps. Astoundingly, he pointed an accusing finger at General George C. Marshall. McCarthy and his aides, most notably a young and highly opportunistic lawyer named Roy Cohn, launched investigations of prominent celebrities, including Hollywood stars, writers, and producers. The Hollywood witch hunt and similar campaigns undertaken against other industries were especially destructive because the mere accusation of communist affiliation or sympathies was sufficient to ruin the career of the accused.

As his strident campaign wore on, McCarthy became increasingly oblivious to the changing realities around him. Even after his own Republican party won control of the White House and Congress in the 1952 elections, the Senator continued to attack the government, which he claimed was "infested" with Communists. In the spring of 1954 he took on a quite formidable opponent when he accused the entire U.S. Army of being infiltrated with Communists.

Dwight D. Eisenhower, a former army general and now president of the United States, did not take these accusations lying down. He discovered that McCarthy had tried to coerce army officials into granting preferred treatment for a former aide, Private G. David Schine. Armed with this information, Eisenhower encouraged Congress to form a committee to investigate McCarthy's manipulations. The so-called "Army-McCarthy" hearings were televised between April and June 1954, and the nation was stunned to see the "crusading" McCarthy for the desperately blustering bully he really was. Discredited before the public, McCarthy was censured by the Senate later in the year. Always a hard-drinking man, he retreated deeper into the bottle and died within three years, a pathetic figure who had nevertheless tyrannized the nation for four grim years, undermining its citizens' most basic rights.

Harry S Truman Begins the "Police Action" Against Korea (1950-1953)

The event: On June 25, 1950, Communist-backed forces from North Korea crossed the thirty-eighth parallel into South Korea, prompting the United States to call for a United Nations sanction against the invasion and, finally, propelling the nation into war.

GENERAL DOUGLAS MACARTHUR, hero of the Pacific theater in World War II, was named head of the U.N. Command on July 7. MacArthur was already in charge of the American Far East Command, based in Japan and including four army divisions, the Fifth Air Force, and parts of the Seventh Fleet. MacArthur would remain in command of the U.N. forces until April 1951. From July 1950 until the time of his replacement by General Matthew Ridgway, MacArthur concentrated first on holding the southeastern portion of the Korean peninsula. His ground troops were aided by American air power that effectively crippled the North Korean supply lines. From September to November 1950, the U.N. forces made an amphibious assault at

Inchon and progressed toward the Yalu River. The assault was at first highly successful, until masses of Communist Chinese troops reinforced North Korean forces, pushing MacArthur's troops once again below the thirty-eighth parallel. The U.S. Eighth Army, under the command of Ridgway, then pushed the North Koreans and Chinese north of the thirty-eighth parallel in a massive counter-offensive from January to April 1951.

From April 1951 until the end of the conflict, fighting continued to concentrate near the thirty-eighth parallel, particularly in the "Iron Triangle" and the "Punch Bowl" regions immediately north of the line. The U.N. forces engaged in massive battles at Heartbreak Ridge in September and October 1951 and at Pork Chop Hill in April 1953, where they were successful in driving back the Communists, but at great cost.

Negotiations for peace began in July 1951, but the war ground on for a full two years more, until July 27, 1953, when an armistice was signed. The cease-fire satisfied no one, not the United Nations, not the United States, not South Korea, not North Korea. The Korean peninsula remained tensely divided along a line near the thirty-eighth parallel.

In addition to substantial costs in men and materiel—of 1.8 million Americans serving in Korea, 54,200 were killed and 103,300 wounded, with 8,200 classified as missing in action—the war had significant consequences in the United States. First, it occasioned the desegregation of the army, a major step forward for African-Americans in the military. Second, it brought a popular president, Harry S Truman, into direct conflict with a popular war hero, Douglas MacArthur. (When MacArthur wanted to bomb bridges over the Yalu River, which would have meant attacking Red China directly, Truman and others warned against spreading the conflict. MacArthur protested, loudly and publicly, the strictures imposed upon him, leading Truman to relieve MacArthur of command.) Third, because the inconclusive and costly war lasted much longer than had been anticipated, the Democratic Party lost the White House to Dwight D. Eisenhower, who was elected president in 1952. Finally, the Korean War heightened the anti-Communist hysteria of the McCarthy era, threatening basic American freedoms, including the guarantee of due process and the presumption of innocence until proven guilty.

In foreign relations, the Korean conflict prompted the United States to commit more of its military budget to NATO (the North Atlantic Treaty Organization). The United States also formed another alliance along the lines of NATO, SEATO (the Southeast Asia Treaty Organization), which included the United States, Great Britain, France, Australia, New Zealand, the Philippine Republic, Thailand, and Pakistan. During the Korean hostilities the United States also stepped up its military assistance to South Vietnam—another step in the American Cold War policy that called for the containment of Communism. Inexorably, this military aid would escalate into another full-scale—and tragically inconclusive—war.

William Faulkner Wins the Nobel Prize (1950)

The event: In 1950, William Faulkner—the most important writer of the twentieth-century Southern Literary Renaissance—received the Nobel Prize in literature.

BORN IN SEPTEMBER 1897, Faulkner grew up in Oxford, Mississippi, during a time of rapid change in the South. Though still transfixed by memories of the Civil War, the South was becoming increasingly industrial and urban in character. Faulkner was fascinated by the disappearance of the basically rural heritage of the so-called Old South.

Faulkner's first novel, *Soldier's Pay*, appeared in 1926; his second, *Mosquitoes*, in 1927. After these, the two least-read of Faulkner's works, failed to attract an audience, he turned his attention to the creation of the mythical Yoknapatawpha County in Mississippi, a rural region peopled by unforgettable characters named Snopes, Compson, Burden, and McCaslin—a hodge-podge of people who faced problems distinctly southern yet decidedly universal.

Among his most well-known works are *The Sound and the Fury* (1929), *As I Lay Dying* (1930), *Sanctuary* (1931), *Light in August* (1932), *Absalom, Ab-*

salom! (1936), *Go Down Moses* (1942), and *The Reivers* (1962). Because commercial success came to Faulkner with only a few of his works, he turned to writing screenplays for the motion picture industry and short stories for popular magazines to earn a living. He began to make better money from his writing after Malcolm Cowley published *The Portable Faulkner* in 1946, which brought about a re-release of many Faulkner titles that had been out of print. With the Nobel Prize came the recognition Faulkner deserved.

Although perhaps the best-known southern writer of the twentieth century, Faulkner was by no means the only voice emanating from a culture undergoing rapid change. A Southern Literary Renaissance emerged during the 1920s and 1930s, as the works of authors like Thomas Wolfe, Richard Wright, Robert Penn Warren, and others appeared in print. The renaissance was in part the result of a new literary magazine, *The Fugitive*, first published in 1922 by a group of Vanderbilt University professors and students. In its pages appeared the poetry and stories of John Crowe Ransom, Allen Tate, Robert Penn Warren, and Donald Davidson. With *The Fugitive*'s last issue in 1925, these four writers began to explore agrarianism as an answer to the South's major problems. Arguing for the need to resist modern technological change and to embrace the traditional agrarian heritage, these writers—and others recruited to their cause—published their manifesto, *I'll Take My Stand*, in 1930, a book that has became pivotal in the contemporary debate over the relative value of science versus humanism.

During the 1930s and 1940s, southern fiction writers continued their prolific outpouring of works. The two decades saw the appearance of such notable writers as Katherine Anne Porter, Carson McCullers, James Agee, Eudora Welty, Andrew Lytle, Jean Toomer, and Stark Young. After World War II a second wave of southern writers emerged: Flannery O'Connor, William Styron, Truman Capote, Harper Lee, Ralph Ellison, Walker Percy, and James Dickey.

The combined talent and works of the Southern Renaissance writers are matched only by the writers who came to prominence during the American Renaissance of the early nineteenth century, when Herman Melville, Nathaniel Hawthorne, Washington Irving, James Fenimore Cooper, Henry Wadsworth Longfellow, and others began to create literature with a new and distinctly American voice.

Jackson Pollock Establishes the "New York School" (1950)

The event: Around 1950, American artist Jackson Pollock established the "New York school" of abstract expressionists, one of the most revolutionary and controversial styles in the history of art.

THE UNITED STATES had produced many great visual artists in the nineteenth and early twentieth centuries, but during the first 150 or so years of the nation's existence, Americans persisted in deferring to Old World traditions and arbiters of taste in matters of art and "high culture." All that changed after World War II. With Europe in physical shambles and spiritual disarray, the world now looked to America for direction in the arts.

The most exciting movement in the postwar years took place in New York City, among a group of extraordinary painters who came to be known as abstract expressionists or, collectively, as the "New York school." The group was diverse, as the works of its most famous exponents—Willem de Kooning, Robert Motherwell, Franz Kline, Mark Rothko, Barnett Newman, Adolph Gottlieb, Arshile Gorky, and Jackson Pollock—attest. But the artists were united by their lofty metaphysical ambition, to create in a postwar world of discredited traditions, shattered illusions, and heartbreaking realities a new truth in art. Rather than attempt to imitate ("represent") the world beyond the painting, these artists used the elements of art itself—form, line, and color—to convey emotion, myth, and symbol purely and directly.

Jackson Pollock (1912-1956) was certainly the most famous and perhaps the most daring of the abstract expressionists. He took the idea of direct expression to its extreme form in what critics called "action painting." By the late 1940s and early 1950s, Pollock set aside pallette, brush, and easel, laid his huge, unprimed canvases flat on the floor, and dripped, poured, and splattered paint on them without contacting the surface. The result was not random accident but a graphic record of action, of human movement, emotion, passion, and rhythm, unfettered by limits, externally imposed regulations, or even conscious thought.

As pioneering American religious reformers like Roger Williams and Anne Hutchinson had challenged accepted theology; as early American political thinkers had challenged the limits of traditional government; as nineteenth-century writers like Herman Melville, Walt Whitman, and Emily Dickinson had challenged the limits of conventional literature; as philosophers like Charles Sanders Peirce and William James had challenged the priorities of intellectual systems long taken for granted; as architects like Louis Sullivan and Frank Lloyd Wright had challenged historical precedents in building; so Pollock and the other members of the New York school challenged the centuries-old assumptions of visual art. More than any other single painter, Jackson Pollock freed expression from artificial, thoughtless limits and regulation. His work taught the world to create and even to see in new and liberating ways.

Estes Kefauver Opens Hearings on Organized Crime (1950)

The event: In 1950 and 1951, the Senate Subcommittee to Investigate Crime in Interstate Commerce, known popularly as the "Kefauver Committee," began to look into the dealings of urban gangsters, claiming it had uncovered a vast conspiracy of organized criminals who cost the nation billions of dollars each year, corrupted governments in almost every section of the country, and reached into the highest ranks of American society.

IN 1929, GANGSTERS grown wealthy off the illegal proceeds from the sale of prohibited alcohol organized under the leadership of Sicilian-born Charles "Lucky" Luciano and a Polish-born Jew named Meyer Lansky at a "conference" held in Atlantic City. The idea of an underworld "syndicate" that would apportion geographical regions and areas of criminal activity to various gangs and Mafia families was something new under the sun. The previous century had been plagued by gangs, loosely bound ethnic organizations that fought among themselves, robbed a few honest citizens, looted the waterfronts of various cities, held-up banks now and then, owned a gambling establishment here and there, fielded an army of prostitutes, and turned for protection to the political machines and their bosses in exchange for delivering votes from their neighborhoods. With the coming of Prohibition, turf wars between rival gangs became endemic, and waves of public outrage and reform occasionally threatened the gangs' existence and livelihood. Lucky Luciano and Meyer Lansky hoped to change all that.

Though the loose organization they put together included elements of the old Italian Mafia imported from Sicily, it was not synonymous with it. In fact, it sought to avoid the intense loyalties that characterize all gangs, but particularly the "family" values of the Italian gangsters, in favor of strictly business relationships based on a more-or-less rational partition of criminal markets. While the organization they put together was never so monolithic as it was later portrayed, resembling more a chamber-of-commerce than a corporate approach to crime, it nevertheless provided a forum for the underworld to get together and air its grievances. And it was ubiquitous enough to hold national conferences from time to time. Now and again such conferences accidentally received the kind of publicity that was anathema to the organization, as at Havana in 1946, when the popular young Italian-American singer Frank Sinatra's presence created an unwanted stir, and at the so-called Appalachian Convention in 1956 when the New York State police discovered the meeting and staged an impromptu raid.

When a Senate committee headed by Tennessee Democrat Estes Kefauver began parading the leading lights of the underworld before national television audiences in the 1950s, Kefauver had no doubt that organized crime existed, a fact long disputed by FBI Director J. Edgar Hoover, who contented himself with tracking down, to great fanfare, the petty bankrobbers and individual psychopaths who comprised his "Public Enemies" list. In the Senate hearings, which traveled from city to city exposing local corruption from New York to New Orleans, from Chicago to Los Angeles, Americans saw not only minor hoods and major mobsters but crooked policemen, mayors, even governors in the sway of the mob. Racketeer after racketeer refused to testify, invoking the

Constitution's protection against self-incrimination under the Fifth Amendment and making "taking the Fifth" part of the American vocabulary. Frank Costello, Joe Adonis, Longy Zwillman and a dozen others gave weight to Kefauver's grandiose accusations with their silence, and at least one of the gangsters—Willie Moretti—was later executed by his associates for having too loose a tongue.

Kefauver's hearings catapulted him into national prominence and forced J. Edgar Hoover to take face-saving measures to compensate for his strangely stubborn refusal to accept the existence of organized crime in the past. By the end of the decade the FBI was in an all-out war with the underworld, a war that continued through the series of investigations and committee hearings launched by Congress in the following decades. A federal witness protection program was established that brought in testimony from any number of insiders and left little doubt that organized crime, whether it was called the Mafia, La Cosa Nostra, or simply the Mob, not only existed but exercised much power and influence over local governments and police forces, the labor unions, and a growing number of "legitimate" industries. Under the Kennedy administration, Attorney General Robert Kennedy gave the Justice Department the task of eliminating organized crime entirely, but it failed to do so. Presidential commissions and congressional committees investigating organized crime in later decades revealed ties between the Mob and the FBI and CIA, implicating it in official World War II operations along the New York waterfront and during the invasion of Italy, in aborted attempts to murder Cuban dictator Fidel Castro, and possibly in a conspiracy to assassinate John F. Kennedy.

The Rosenbergs Are Executed for Espionage (1953)

The event: On June 19, 1953, after the U.S. Supreme Court, meeting in special session, refused to overturn their convictions, Julius and Ethel Rosenberg, accused of passing atomic secrets to the Soviet Union, were executed.

AMERICANS DID NOT have long to glory in the triumph over fascism that had ended World War II. In addition to the Korean War, the postwar years were en-

 gulfed in a "Cold War" with the Soviet Union, its allies, and satellite nations. In the 1920s, following the 1917 Russian Revolution, the United States had been gripped by a "red scare." In the 1950s another, even more intense red scare swept the nation as a Soviet "Iron Curtain" (Winston Churchill's memorable phrase) descended on eastern Europe and Red China menaced Asia. As the series of congressional hearings spearheaded by Senator Joseph McCarthy demonstrated, Americans could be made to fear the existence of Communist spies at every level of government and in every walk of life. What lay behind that fear was not merely concern over foreign agents pilfering this or that government document, but the terrible anxieties generated by the awesome destructiveness of the new weapon produced by World War II—the atomic bomb. It was the loss of the technological secrets associated with the bomb that shocked Americans into modern-day witch hunting.

Early in 1950, federal agents arrested David Greenglass, who had been a soldier stationed near the atomic testing site at Los Alamos, New Mexico during World War II. British authorities had already arrested Karl Fuchs, a British atomic scientist who confessed to having leaked atomic and hydrogen bomb secrets to the Soviets. He implicated as his accomplice Harry Gold, an American chemist whom Greenglass had supplied with information from Los Alamos. Greenglass claimed that his brother-in-law, a machine-shop owner named Julius Rosenberg, acted as a go-between in these clandestine exchanges, and on July 17, 1950, U.S. agents arrested Rosenberg and his wife Ethel.

The Rosenbergs had a history of Communist affiliation, a fact they did not deny, but they pleaded innocent to the charges of having conspired to obtain national defense information for the Soviet Union. Though Julius was probably guilty of at least dabbling in espionage, the fact that they were liberal intellectuals and Jews hurt them as much or more than the evidence presented in support of the charges. Greenglass's testimony against the couple was self-serving. He was sentenced to a fifteen-year prison term (of which he served ten), but the Rosenbergs were sentenced to death. The sentence was appealed to the Supreme

Court, which refused to overturn the conviction, but, in June 1953, Justice William O. Douglas granted a stay of execution on the grounds of doubt about whether Justice Irving Kaufman, who had presided over the Rosenbergs' trial, had the power to issue a death sentence. In special session, the Supreme Court then voted 6-3 (Douglas, Hugo Black, and Felix Frankfurter dissenting) to allow the execution.

The Rosenberg case deeply divided the country. Many believed the couple innocent, and even many others who thought them guilty felt that the sentence was unjust and unwarranted—especially as the couple's two small children were frequently seen on newsreels and in newspaper photographs visiting their parents in prison. Many saw the trial—or, at least, the sentence—as the product of antisemitism and Cold War, McCarthy-inspired hysteria. There is little, if any, good to be seen in the tragedy of the Rosenbergs, except that it did move many Americans to think beyond the prevailing hysteria of what one historian has called "the politics of fear."

The Supreme Court Rules on *Brown v. Board of Education* (1954)

The event: On May 17, 1954, the United States Supreme Court declared racial segregation illegal in its landmark decision in the case of *Brown v. Board of Education of Topeka*.

FOR MORE THAN half a century, since its 1896 ruling in *Plessy v. Ferguson*, the high court had upheld as constitutional all "separate but equal" accommodations and facilities for blacks. Schools, conveyances, restaurants, hotels, and other public facilities were rigidly segregated throughout much of the country, especially the South. Beginning in the mid-1930s, the National Association for the Advancement of Colored People brought a series of suits against segregated school districts. In these early cases the Supreme Court ruled that because the "tangible" aspects of schools for blacks and those for whites were equal, the laws providing for segregated schools were constitutional. In the case of *Brown v. Board of Education*, however, the NAACP lawyers, among them Thurgood Marshall, presented expert testimony on the debilitating effects of segregation—testimony that proved to be extremely important in the court's ruling, which this time held that segregated school systems were inherently unequal because of *intangible* factors. In 1956 the Supreme Court issued guidelines to be used in desegregating the nation's school districts.

The success achieved by the NAACP in *Brown v. Board of Education* spurred thousands of blacks, especially in the South, to rise up against other laws and traditions that violated their civil rights, and the modern civil rights movement was born.

Jonas Salk's Vaccine for Polio Receives Government Approval (1955)

The event: In 1955, as American parents dreaded another summer with its ever-present threat of epidemic polio, Jonas Salk's vaccine against the disease won government approval.

JONAS SALK FIRST became interested in vaccines while a student at New York University's Medical School. After graduating, he took up research on immunology under Dr. Thomas Francis at the University of Michigan, where scientists produced the first killed-virus vaccine against influenza. Before the influenza vaccine was developed, medical theory held that vaccines prepared from dead bacteria were effective in immunizing against bacterial infections, but that immunization against viruses required often-dangerous live-virus vaccines. The work at Michigan proved that theory wrong.

Armed with the new evidence that killed-virus vaccines could be effective, Salk became head of a viral research laboratory at the University of Pittsburgh. Of primary interest to him was developing a vaccine against polio, and his research in that area was supported by the March of Dimes Foundation. In 1954 he began testing a killed-virus vaccine for polio, and the following year Food and Drug Administration authorities declared it safe and effective.

The polio vaccine was used universally throughout the United States until 1962, when Dr. Albert Sabin persuaded much of the medical community to switch to his live-virus vaccine, which is administered orally rather than by injection. It was Salk's pioneering work, however, that rid the nation and the world of one of its most terrifying scourges, a disease that had resulted in the deaths or massive disability of thousands of children annually. Salk is one in a long line of scientists, including Jenner, Lister, Pasteur, Koch, and others, who have led the public—with considerable justice—to expect miracles from modern medicine. Since the early 1980s, Salk has engaged in research to develop a vaccine for another, more recent plague, AIDS.

Rosa Parks Initiates the Montgomery Bus Boycott (1955)

The event: On December 1, 1955, Rosa Parks, a black resident of Montgomery, Alabama, boarded a bus to return home from her job. Tired from her day's work, she sat in the forward section of the bus, the section traditionally reserved for white passengers. When she refused to give up her seat to a white person, she was arrested and jailed.

THROUGHOUT THE CITY, civil rights activists called for blacks to boycott the city's buses. Some took advantage of car pools organized to take them to work. Others walked wherever they needed to go. Despite hardship, the boycott lasted for more than a year, demonstrating the effectiveness of organized, nonviolent activity in the civil rights movement.

It was during the Montgomery boycott that the Reverend Martin Luther King, Jr., emerged as a leader. Advocating nonviolent means to attain racial equality, in 1957 King was elected president of the Southern Christian Leadership Conference, an organization that was to become increasingly active in the civil rights struggle. Over the next decade, the movement gave birth to other organizations equally intent on nonviolence. The Student Non-Violent Coordinating Committee, founded in 1960, concentrated its activities in rural areas of the Deep South, and the Congress of Racial Equality and the Mississippi Freedom Democratic Party worked in Mississippi to enlist rural blacks in the civil rights struggle. While violence occasionally broke out during the early protests, it was not until the 1965 march on Selma, the founding of the Black Panthers during the late 1960s, and the deaths by assassination of Malcolm X and King himself that black civil rights protesters turned away from nonviolent gestures epitomized by Rosa Parks on that Montgomery city bus.

Congress Passes the Interstate Highway Act of 1956

The event: In 1956 Congress passed the Interstate Highway Act, the highwater mark of a half-century of frenzied road building at government expense and the largest public works program in history.

THE UNITED STATES Post Office's decision to operate a system of rural free delivery at the close of the last century made the development of hard-surface roads, passable in all kinds of weather and in the gloom of night, essential, but the move to pave highways would have come anyway. The automobile was every American's ticket to freedom, and two-lane blacktops, like the railways before them, seemed capable of making or breaking a community. Good roads became a passion in the twenties. The construction of streets and highways was one of the largest items of government expenditure, often at great cost to everything else, including education.

Led by Ford's assembly-line Model Ts, automobiles became the backbone of a new consumer goods-oriented society. American car registrations shot up from one million in 1913 to ten million in 1923. Kansas alone had more cars than either France or Germany, and automobile sales in Michigan outdistanced those in Great Britain and Ireland combined. By the mid-1920s automobiles ranked first among products valued by consumers, and by 1927 Americans were driving some twenty-six million of them, one car for every five people in a country where Detroit built about 85 percent of the world's motorized vehicles.

At the same time, radio stations began commercial broadcasting in 1920, and within a few years almost every American hamlet had at least one, usually two, motion picture theaters. Broadcast radio and the movies added to the immense changes automobiles brought about in the lives of the individual farmer and small-town resident, breaking down the isolation of rural life and dispelling the claustrophobic atmosphere of Main Street culture. Through the radio, the siren call of the saxophone beckoned the young in the back parlors and the local cafes to jump in their roadsters and head for a speakeasy, or "blind pig," in the big city, stopping perhaps at a roadhouse on the way for fuel. On the silver screen, Gloria Swanson, Clara Bow, Rudolph Valentino, and Douglas Fairbanks showed them how to act once they got there. In doing so, they accelerated trends already under way—the decline of the small towns and the depopulation of the rural countryside.

In 1920 the U.S. Census had revealed that for the first time more people lived in cities than on farms, and increasingly they left the one and reached the other via automobile. The growth of roads and the automobile industry fired the economy, making cars the lifeblood of the petroleum industry and a major customer of the steel factories. They also drove expansions in outdoor recreation and tourism and their related industries, service stations, roadside restaurants, and motels. After the war the automobile industry boomed to new heights, and new roads now led out of the city to the suburbs, where two-car families transported 2.5 children to de facto segregated schools and to shopping malls that sprang up like mushrooms. The Interstate Highway System, a network of federally subsidized highways connecting major urban centers (justified, like almost everything else in the 1950s, as a national defense measure), stretched American mobility to new distances, making two-hour commutes, immense traffic jams, polluted cities, and Disneyland standard features of American life.

The triumph of private transportation was ensured by the federal government. The United States, unlike Europe, treated public transportation like a private business, allowing a few tycoons to grow rich on the poor service they offered the urban masses while treating the mostly middle-class motorcar as an object worthy of tremendous public subsidies. Between 1945 and 1980, 75 percent of federal funds for transportation were spent on highways, while a scant one percent went to buses, trolleys, or subways. Years before the Interstate Highway system got under construction, the American bias was clear—which is why America by the 1990s had the world's best road system and very nearly its worst public transit system.

Elvis Presley Appears on the *Ed Sullivan Show* (1956)

The event: In 1956, Elvis Presley, the most revolutionary figure in the history of popular music, appeared on the immensely successful television variety program the *Ed Sullivan Show*, shaking his hips and twisting his knees in a display of raw, unruly power that shattered the bland suburban world tuned in to Sunday night's family entertainment.

AS OUTRAGED ADULTS and the mainstream media they patronized fumed and complained about Presley's "vulgarity," deriding him as "Elvis the Pelvis," "Melvin Pelvin," and the like, he came to embody the "rock 'n 'roll" rebel, initiating a cultural revolution among young people against an adult world they saw as conservative and trivial. When Sullivan, on subsequent programs, broadcast Presley's performance only from the waist up, his original performance—with its powerful fusion of adolescent exuberance and the pounding sexuality of rhythm and blues—became the founding moment of a generation that would march under the banner of "sex, drugs, and rock 'n 'roll" to stop a war and escape for a time the conformity of their parents' prosperous world.

Presley had been born in rude circumstances, the brother of a dead twin, to a family of Tupelo, Mississippi, sharecroppers in 1935. Working briefly after high school as a truck driver, he haunted the studios of Sun Records, an independent label created by Sam Phillips to produce the music of black country blues singers experimenting with the sounds of the new "race" music at clubs lining the famous Beale Street in Memphis, Tennessee. Phillips, who thought the black singers were the only performers creating something new at the time, had mused that if he could find "a white man who had the Negro sound and the Negro feel" he could make a fortune. When Phillips received a demo tape from a Nashville studio with an exciting "new" sound, he immediately called the studio. The singer, he was informed, was a young black man who had simply walked in off the street. The studio had no idea who he was or where to find him. It was at that point that his secretary suggested he give "the kid with the sideburns" who had been hanging around, a chance at recording the song. Presley never could reproduce the quality of the unknown singer, but in the process of trying he recorded a version of bluesman Bill "Big Boy" Crudup's "That's All Right Momma" in an incredible up-tempo beat marked by his exuberant and unrestrained style. Sam Phillips had found the white man—and the sound—he was after.

There followed the release of four other singles, recorded at Sun Records between 1953 and 1955 and regarded by many critics as his best work, while Presley played a few Beale Street clubs and toured the local countryside, singing at shopping malls and fairs and discovering his power to drive pubescent females into a frenzy. Each record had a country side and a blues side, a Sam Phillips formula for the new "rockabilly" singers—Carl Perkins, Jerry Lee Lewis, Johnny Cash—he had begun to collect for Sun. In Presley's case, the country songs expressed a genuine affection for the tradition of poor white southerners, while his blues cuts thundered rebellion and defiance against those same traditions. The conflict gave his early music both emotional complexity and power. Presley soon attracted the major labels, and Phillips sold his contract to RCA for around $20,000, which was considered a phenomenal sum in the industry at the time. Beginning with "Heartbreak Hotel," Presley had a string of hits with RCA between 1956 and 1959 that was unparalled in rock music and perhaps only matched at that point by Frank Sinatra.

After his Sullivan appearance made him a household word, Presley was drafted into the army in 1958. When he returned from Germany and mustered out in 1960, his career began a steady decline. Under the thumb of his domineering manager, Colonel Tom Parker, Presley retreated from rock 'n 'roll to star in dozens of very popular but generally awful movies, issuing soundtracks that made a mockery of everything he had come to represent. A stunning comeback in a 1968 television Christmas special, in which Presley appeared dressed from head to toe in black leather and performed with a small combo, recaptured, even surpassed, the passion and intensity of his early work, but the live performances he returned to in its wake again led to singing that was careless at best. Miserable in his private life, living in the rococo cocoon of his Memphis home (called "Graceland" after his mother), Presley was consumed by drugs and died suddenly of an overdose in 1977. In death, his popularity revived as he reached legendary status. Graceland became a de facto national shrine, attracting many thousands more annually than Mount Vernon. They came to pay respect to an American success story: the country boy made good, whose pursuit of happiness brought him a freedom most can only fantasize about—but left him a burned-out shell.

The United States Confronts the USSR over Missiles in Cuba (1962)

The event: On October 22, 1962, President John Fitzgerald Kennedy announced in a special television broadcast that, contrary to its assurances, the U.S.S.R. had been building bomber and nuclear missile bases in Cuba. The president declared a naval blockade of the island, and the world suddenly found itself perched on the edge of thermonuclear war.

UNITED STATES-CUBAN relations had been uneasy since the Spanish-American War. With the passage of the Platt Amendment in 1902, the United States had

pledged itself to maintain Cuba's independence. That agreement remained in force until 1934, when the United States ended all formal controls over the country. At the outset of the Cold War, Cuba became the setting for Soviet-U.S. confrontations. Fidel Castro had come to power in 1959 and had instituted a leftist regime in Cuba. Over the next two years the dictator allied himself closely with the Soviet Union.

The Central Intelligence Agency then devised a plan to overthrow Castro. Amassing a force of Cuban exiles, the CIA directed an invasion at the Bay of Pigs on April 17, 1961. The invasion was a fiasco. The Cuban people did not rise up to join the invaders, nor did the promised air support from the United States materialize. Within three days the invasion was over, and the United States was discredited for its role in the failed attack, which drove Castro farther into the Soviet camp. Certain that the United States would again attempt to invade his country, he agreed to allow the Soviet Union to construct missile bases on Cuba. In October 1962, an American spy plane photographed the bases under construction. President Kennedy demanded the immediate withdrawal of the Soviet missiles and the closing of the bases, ordering a naval blockade on October 24. With each passing day an armed confrontation between American and Soviet vessels seemed more likely.

The stalemate was broken on October 28 when Soviet premier Nikita Krushchev offered to remove the missiles under United Nations supervision. On the following day President Kennedy suspended the blockade, and by November 2 the missile bases were being dismantled. The showdown was a triumph for the young American president and did much to redress the humiliation of the Bay of Pigs invasion. While the episode must be counted as a major American victory in the Cold War, it was also the closest brush with a nuclear Armageddon the world has yet experienced.

John Fitzgerald Kennedy Is Assassinated (1963)

The event: On November 22, 1963, John F. Kennedy, the youngest elected president in the nation's history, was assassinated while riding in a motorcade on a campaign trip in Dallas, Texas.

KENNEDY WAS ELECTED thirty-fifth president of the United States in 1960, at the age of forty-three. Remembered for several pioneering programs and bold actions—the establishment of the Peace Corps, the strengthening of the American space program, his handling of the Cuban missile crisis, and his establishment of the Alliance for Progress with Latin American countries—Kennedy was also held responsible by many at the time for bungling the Bay of Pigs invasion, the fiasco that encouraged the Soviet Union to send nuclear missles to Cuba in the first place. Some accused him of escalating the fighting in Vietnam by first overcommitting himself to President Ngo Dinh Diem and then becoming an accomplice in his overthrow. Known for his wit, vigor, and style during his presidency, his reputation subsequently suffered from revelations of incessant womanizing. Though adored by the national communications media and quite popular with the nation's youth and the intelligentsia, Kennedy could never garner much support in Congress, whose members thwarted his efforts to improve the civil rights record in the United States, increase governmental spending on education, and provide a program of medical care for the elderly.

Kennedy's sudden martyrdom changed all that, quickly becoming the inspiration for Lyndon Johnson's Great Society social reforms. That, and the romantic overtones of his death—a young, attractive man cut down in his prime—gave birth to the Kennedy legend of a demonstrably great president frustrated by the short-sightedness of his political enemies, destroyed just as he was about to make his mark on world history. For millions he became the almost mythic embodiment of the ideal American president.

On the day he was shot, a suspected assassin named Lee Harvey Oswald was arrested by the Dallas Police, only to be himself assassinated on national television by local night-club owner and shady mob fringe figure Jack Ruby. The shocking turn of events prompted President Johnson to appoint a commission, headed by Chief Justice Earl Warren, to investigate the assassination. The Warren Commission report, based on a ten-month investigation, found Lee Harvey Oswald to be the lone assassin, though certain eyewitness reports and forensic evidence contradicted that conclusion and led many to brand the findings a "whitewash."

Fueled by an aborted conspiracy trial in New Orleans, by the secrecy surrounding the original investigation, by countless conspiracy theories advanced over the years in popular books and the media, Congress produced startling new revelations about the CIA and FBI when the U.S. House of Representatives appointed a special committee to reopen the investigation in 1976. The House committee found a conspiracy likely, a conclusion long held by the majority of the American public but summarily dismissed by most government officials and establishment spokesman since the publication of the Warren Commission findings.

Betty Friedan Publishes *The Feminine Mystique* (1963)

The event: The publication of Betty Friedan's *The Feminine Mystique* in 1963 heralded a new wave of feminism, challenging the prevailing domesticity that had characterized middle- and upper-class women's lives since they were forced out of the workplace by soldiers returning from World War II.

AN IMMEDIATE BEST-SELLER, the book coincided with—and helped foster—the return of women to the job market, a market that offered new opportunities in the service industries that were beginning to dominate the American economy by the 1960s. The 1960s also brought a wave of consumerism that propelled women into the workplace in order to earn additional income for their families. More and more women were graduating from college in the 1960s, and with the availability of the birth-control pill, many went to work instead of to the nursery.

A keen observer of the emerging social scene, Friedan, a graduate of Smith College and a free-lance magazine writer, compiled data for her book by sending a questionnaire to members of her own graduating class. From their descriptions of their lives since college and from additional research, Friedan hypothesized that middle- and upper-class women were not satisfied with their roles as wives and mothers. She identified as the "feminine mystique" the pervasive notion that women could gain satisfaction only through marriage and children, a myth her book handily punctured.

In 1966 Friedan helped to found the National Organization for Women, serving as its first president. The group began a campaign for full equality for women and worked for liberalized abortion laws and for the passage of the Equal Rights Amendment. The proposed amendment, in fact, created much divisiveness within the women's movement. Some argued that its passage would invalidate many state and federal laws designed to protect women. Others argued that without it women would never achieve total equality. Despite the disagreements, the membership of NOW continued to grow. By 1982 it claimed more than 210,000 members. An Equal Rights Amendment has yet to be ratified by the states.

The success of *The Feminine Mystique* and the widespread acceptance of NOW among college-educated, liberal women gave rise to another manifestation of the campaign for equality in the 1970s. The popular *Ms.* magazine, edited by Gloria Steinem from 1972 to 1987, was a primary vehicle for the spread of the feminist message. As the magazine grew more successful, however, advertisers demanded greater control over its content and threatened to co-opt it. The magazine was sold, and in 1990 a new version of *Ms.* appeared—without advertising and with Steinem in the role of consulting editor.

As NOW became more politically powerful and *Ms.* spread the doctrines of feminism, various strains of the women's movement could be discerned. The work carried out by NOW came to be characterized as liberal feminism. The organization began lobbying not only for women's rights but also for the rights of gays and lesbians. Most of its attention focused on reform through the electoral process, lobbying, and legislation. Distinct from the NOW movement were women who doubted that reform could be achieved by conventional political means. Most of these women had previously been involved in the civil rights movement and in the New Left where they, as women, had been accorded little power. Meeting first in small support and discussion groups, these more radically inclined women began to define *all* their relationships with men—in the workplace and in the home—as political. Labeled "women's liberationists," these activists found NOW lacking in its failure to address women's subordination to men in the family and the workplace. In-depth studies by Shulamith Firestone, Kate Millett, Ti-Grace Atkinson, and others analyzed the debilitating effects of male supremacy on women. By the mid-1970s, however, the women's liberationists and the members of NOW found themselves working against a common threat—antifeminists of the reactionary right who claimed that feminism would lead to a society in which men behaved irresponsibly toward women and children.

Despite the differences that have plagued—or enriched—the women's movement since Friedan's publication of *The Feminine Mystique*, women have made substantial gains in American society. In state legislatures the number of women elected to office doubled between 1975 and 1988. By 1987 forty states had implemented policies to ensure that women received comparable pay for comparable work. In addition, laws protecting female victims of rape have been strengthened in many states. Still, few women hold national political office or sit in the nation's boardrooms. Rape and domestic violence remain rampant in American society. And recent highly publicized cases of sexual harrassment in government and the military indicate the deeply rooted antagonisms among many, not only male Americans, to female equality and freedom.

Congress Passes the Civil Rights Act of 1964

The event: On July 2, 1964, President Lyndon Johnson signed into law the Civil Rights Act, banning racial discrimination in all public places—hotels, theaters, and restaurants—outlawing racial discrimination by employers and unions, and withdrawing federal funds from state programs that discriminated against blacks.

WITH THE RETURN of soldiers from World War II, racial unrest racked America, especially in the big cities. President Harry S Truman, reluctant to propose civil rights for political reasons, argued in public that no federal law could, by itself, achieve racial equality. During the Eisenhower administration, the Supreme Court ordered the nation's schools desegregated in its *Brown v. the Board of Education of Topeka* decision. Blacks across the country drew inspiration from that decision and began testing racial barriers. The Montgomery bus boycott led to a Supreme Court decision that barred segregation in public transportation systems and pushed the Reverend Martin Luther King, Jr., to the forefront of the civil rights movement. More than seventy thousand people participated in sit-ins in 112 southern cities in 1961 to press for the desegregation of restaurants. Others tested the desegregation of interstate transportation in freedom rides throughout the segregated South. In August 1963, more than two hundred thousand people marched on Washington and demanded immediate racial equality.

The passage of the Civil Rights Act of 1964, in many ways the culmination of the legal struggle for equality, did not immediately provide true social equality to the nation's blacks. Severe repression by state and local governments and certain institutions, such as the FBI, within the federal government, the assassinations of Malcolm X and Martin Luther King, and the heated infighting among black militants caused a decline in social protest as the volatile 1960s drew to a close.

Nevertheless, the changes wrought by the struggles, court decisions, protests, and legislation of the decade did leave a lasting mark on American culture and society. The more overt forms of racial discrimination, the social acceptance of expressed bigotry, and the official segregation of public establishments, schools, and facilities all came to an end. Black politicians ran for office, and won, in communities where once blacks could not even vote. Colleges and universities, even those in the South, recruited black students instead of banning them. Racial violence in the South declined. Commercial television began featuring black actors and black family dramas and situation comedies. And many employers, especially governmental bodies and non-profit organizations that depended on the largess of the federal government, instituted affirmative action programs.

But even as de jure (law-based) segregation disappeared, de facto (end-results) segregation remained as strong as ever—North as well as South—in the public school systems, the housing market, and elsewhere. Despite the civil rights gains of the 1960s, despite the clear intent of the Civil Rights Act of 1964, despite Johnson's War on Poverty and King's Poor People's Campaign, racial bigotry and repression continued to play a significant role in American life. Greater inequalities in wealth and income than ever before appeared in the 1970s and 1980s as the trickle-down economic policies worked their magic, increasing black unemployment at alarming rates and cutting the entitlement programs once aimed at correcting long-term inequalities. For the most part, in fact, civil rights leaders have felt that their energies in recent decades have been spent holding onto the gains of the past rather than working toward the complete social and economic equality imagined by the framers of the Great Society.

Lyndon Johnson Launches the "Great Society" (1964)

The event: During the 1964 presidential campaign, Lyndon Baines Johnson called on America to build a "Great Society," a society that "rests on abundance and liberty for all." The phrase became the blanket term for a series of laws passed in Johnson's second term that in many ways transformed American society.

AFTER HIS VICTORY over Republican Barry Goldwater, the president and Congress embarked on a period of social legislation matched only by Franklin Roosevelt's New Deal.

Civil rights was a major part of Johnson's Great Society. In 1964 Congress passed a Civil Rights Act that desegregated public accommodations like restaurants, hotels, and theaters, and banned job discrimination on the basis of race. The following year a Voting Rights Acts guaranteed blacks their right to vote in elections at all levels. In 1968 another civil rights act outlawed housing discrimination.

While blacks were enormously affected by Johnson's civil rights programs, it was the social welfare laws that typified Great Society legislation. In 1965, Congress passed a law creating the Medicare program, which aided all Americans over the age of sixty-five, regardless of need, in paying for medical treatment. The following year, medical coverage was expanded to include welfare recipients in a program called Medicaid.

Great Society legislation also profoundly affected American education. The 1965 Elementary and Secondary Education Act provided federal funds to poor school districts across the country. The Higher Education Act of 1965 gave tuition assistance to college and university students, ensuring that millions who before could not afford to attend could now earn a college degree, the traditional American ticket into the middle class.

Great Society legislation also created the Department of Housing and Urban Development, the Department of Transportation, the National Endowments for the Humanities and the Arts, and the Corporation for Public Broadcasting. The environmental field was immensely affected as well, with the passage of the National Wilderness Preservation System and the Land and Water Conservation Act in 1964 and the National Trails System and the National Wild and Scenic Rivers System in 1968.

Most dramatic among the various Great Society laws were those passed as a result of Johnson's declared War on Poverty. In 1964 Congress passed the Economic Opportunity Act, which created the Office of Economic Opportunity to oversee the numerous commmunity programs, including the Job Corps, the Volunteers in Service to America (VISTA), the Model Cities Program, Upward Bound, the Food Stamps program, and Project Head Start.

Most of the programs of Johnson's Great Society were inadequately funded, mainly as a result of America's deepening involvement in the Vietnam War. Many were discontinued after the Republicans captured the White House in 1968, and Johnson's record as a megalomaniacal and dissembling commander-in-chief—rather than his compassionate and inclusive domestic initiatives—became the measure by which his presidency was judged. The War on Poverty may have been as wrongheaded as the war in Vietnam, although in the end all that can be said is that both were lost for the same reasons: funds were cut and the U.S. government backed out. (Aid to dependent children and unemployment compensation, the two main programs that make up the "welfare system" against which conservatives so often rail, were part of the *New Deal's* social security legislation. The two Great Society programs that still thrive—Medicare and Medicaid—are the only form of health care provided its older and poorer citizens by a country that, alone among industrialized nations, offers no national health insurance.) For the most part, the social policy experiments of the 1960s died along with American soldiers in the rice paddies of Southeast Asia.

Congress Passes the Gulf of Tonkin Resolution (1964)

The event: On August 7, 1964, the U.S. Senate passed the Gulf of Tonkin Resolution after the U.S. destroyer *Maddox*, conducting electronic espionage in the gulf in support of a clandestine South Vietnamese raid on the coast, was fired upon by North Vietnamese torpedo boats. Giving President Lyndon Johnson a free hand to prevent further "aggression" by North Vietnam, the resolution was looked upon as providing broad congressional approval for expanding the war in Southeast Asia.

IN THE WAKE of World War II, the Vietnamese—led by the Communist Ho Chi Minh—had fought French colonizers to a standstill. This resulted in a 1954 Geneva peace conference that divided Vietnam into North and South, pending free elections two years later. President Dwight D. Eisenhower, admitting that "possibly 80 percent" of the Vietnamese would have voted for Ho Chi Minh, gave covert support and American approval to South Vietnamese President Ngo Dinh Diem when he aborted the election and viciously suppressed the opposition—an action that led to the expansion of already existing guerilla forces, a mixed bag of Buddhists, Nationalists, and Communists supported by North Vietnam and other Communist nations.

For five years South Vietnam engaged in civil war, with North Vietnam calling on the National Liberation Front, popularly known as the Viet Cong, to lead the struggle against Diem. Fearing a Communist takeover, President John F. Kennedy carelessly, covertly, and without Congress's consent sent combat troops to aid Diem, and by 1962 15,500 Americans were involved in an undeclared war against the Viet Cong justified only after the fact in 1966 by invoking the ambiguous SEATO treaty. In 1963 Kennedy implicated himself even further in Vietnam's fate by allowing the CIA to plot the murder of Diem in a military coup that led to years of instability, during which time South Vietnam had twelve governments, none—not even the last—popular enough to survive on its own. By 1965, twenty-five thousand South Vietnamese soldiers had died and another hundred thousand or so had deserted, leaving the South's army finished as a fighting force.

Even as the Gulf of Tonkin resolution was being passed, Lyndon Johnson assured the American public that its sons would not die fighting an Asian war. But scarcely was the 1964 presidential election over, when Johnson—faced with withdrawing from or escalating the conflict—sent 22,000 fresh troops. By 1965, 75,000 Americans were fighting in Vietnam; by 1966, 375,000; by the next election, over half a million.

As draft calls increased by 100 percent in 1965, young men flooded into American colleges to avoid the draft. Starting in February of that year, the U.S. would bomb the North, then stop to see Ho Chi Minh's response, which was usually to send more leaders, weapons, and troops to help the Viet Cong. Over the next eight years the American army in Vietnam would grow to a peak of 542,000 and the cost of the war shot up astronomically, derailing Johnson's Great Society at home in order to drop bombs and chemicals to destroy and defoliate the little country Johnson claimed he was "protecting."

By 1966, opposition to the war was mounting, as citizens and senators no longer consulted by an obsessed president or the seemingly independent military watched Vietnam turn into the fourth-bloodiest conflict in American history. The growing protests were fueled first by Defense Secretary Robert McNamara's 1967 admission that the bombing had not stopped North Vietnam's infiltration, then, in 1968, by the stunning massive and coordinated attack of the Viet Cong in the January Tet Offensive. In thirty-five cities all over South Vietnam, allied troops were surprised by the enemy's ferocity and determination. Though they suffered enormous casualties, the Viet Cong continued the attack for a month, penetrating the U.S. Embassy in Saigon and capturing the ancient capital of Hue, before being forced back into the countryside, where they destroyed hamlet after hamlet during their retreat. Abandoning the hamlets en masse, 350,000 refugees poured into the recently besieged towns, and on May 10, 1968, America forced its puppet-regime in South Vietnam to the peace table with the North in Paris. Lyndon Johnson, faced with bitter opposition to his policies at home, withdrew from the upcoming presidential election.

When Richard Nixon took the helm, he turned most of the fighting over to the less-than-willing South Vietnamese army and began massive illegal bombings of nearby Cambodia to buy time for American withdrawal. In the huge antiwar demonstrations that followed, the National Guard killed four students at Kent State University in Ohio. Responding to an American public outraged by the four deaths at home, the 750,000-odd deaths abroad on both sides, and the shocking revelations of the Pentagon Papers, Congress cut off funds for the war, leading Nixon and his negotiator Henry Kissinger to settle with the North Vietnamese, regardless of the consequences, in 1973. By 1975, North Vietnam had defeated the South and reunited a country that would have come under its leaders' control without additional bloodshed in 1956 if the United Nations had been allowed to conduct legitimate elections.

The Autobiography of Malcolm X **Is Published (1965)**

The event: In 1965 *The Autobiography of Malcolm X* was published following the assassination of its author, a controversial and highly influential black activist.

THE SON OF an Omaha, Nebraska, Baptist preacher, Malcolm X (born Malcolm Little) was influenced early in life by his father, who urged blacks to take control of their own lives. When Malcolm was six years old, his father was killed by a group of Black Legionnaires, a white racist organization akin to the Ku Klux Klan. Malcolm and some of his siblings were placed in foster homes.

Malcolm dropped out of school in Detroit after the eighth grade and joined a series of street gangs. At twenty-one he was convicted of burglary and sentenced to prison, where he first encountered the teachings and work of Elijah Muhammad, the leader of the Lost-Found Nation of Islam, popularly known as the Black Muslims. This organization spread the doctrine that African-Americans would be forever corrupted by contact with white men, viewed, quite literally, as incarnations of the devil. Renouncing his "slave name," Malcolm Little became Malcolm X, a man who adopted an ascetic life, studied the Black Muslim faith, and developed his own ideas on ways blacks could improve their lives.

After his release from prison, Malcolm X became a minister of Temple No. 7 in Harlem. From his pulpit, with an anger tempered by great eloquence, he condemned white crimes against blacks. Whites feared him and the potential for violence his rhetoric inspired. Yet Malcolm X was never himself a simpleminded racist. He gradually became dissatisfied with the Nation of Islam and with Elijah Muhammad in particular, whom he began to regard as corrupt and tyrannical.

In December 1963, Malcolm X was suspended by the Black Muslims. He then traveled to Mecca, where he studied the orthodox Islam religion and discovered that it taught equality of races. He abandoned his earlier belief in the utter corruption of whites and returned to America, now calling himself El-Hajj Malik El-Shabazz. Founding the Organization of Afro-American Unity in June 1964, he began leaning toward socialism as a cure for the corruption of American society. On February 21, 1965, he was assassinated by three Black Muslims while speaking in a Harlem auditorium. His autobiography, published posthumously, had a huge impact on American society and was the chief catalyst of the "black power movement" of the Student Non-Violent Coordinating Committee (SNCC).

Because of his untimely death, Malcolm X bequeathed to the cause of civil rights an incomplete legacy open to wide interpretation. Many whites saw his transformation from hatred and anger to a religiously inspired quest after racial equality as a hopeful sign in black-white relations. Militant blacks emphasized Malcolm X's earlier message that only blacks could free themselves, and the most extreme of them called for an end to the involvement of whites in the civil rights movement.

Riots Break Out in Watts (1965)

The event: On August 11, 1965, a white policeman patrolling the predominantly black Watts neighborhood of Los Angeles, California, stopped a young black man on suspicion of drunken driving. A crowd gathered at the scene, and rumors of police brutality spread throughout the community. Over the next six days, widespread rioting broke out.

DESPITE THE NONVIOLENT teachings of Civil Rights leader Martin Luther King, Jr., the 1960s brought unprecedented racial unrest. Medgar Evers, a leader of the National Association for the Advancement of Colored People, was assassinated in Jackson, Mississippi, in 1963. Four young girls died when white segregationists hurled a bomb into a black church in Birmingham, Alabama. Civil rights workers were killed in Mississippi while working to register black voters.

Malcolm X, first a leader of the Black Muslims and later the founder of the rival Organization of Afro-American Unity, was assassinated by Black Muslims in February 1965. Many black Americans, profoundly affected by the violence of the early 1960s, regarded King's message and methods as too passive, too conciliatory. Thousands turned away from King to more militant organizations, like the Congress for Racial Equality, organized by Floyd McKissick, and the Student Nonviolent Coordinating Committee, led by Stokely Carmichael, who called for "Black Power" and an end to white involvement in the civil rights movement. By the summer of 1965, the civil rights movement was badly split, and the atmosphere was primed for violence.

In Watts, as what should have been a simple arrest developed into a major confrontation, police reinforcements arrived. The crowd began throwing stones, concrete blocks, and glass bottles at the officers. The police responded by sealing off the neighborhood, but the violence was far from over. The next evening thousands of blacks roamed through the area, hurling Molotov cocktails and looting stores. The National Guard was called in to aid the Los Angeles police, but peace was not restored. The officers, the Guard, and the black rioters fought for six days. Thirty-five people were killed and more than a thousand injured. Property damage totaled approximately $200 million.

Watts signaled a shifting attitude among African-Americans. Rioting broke out in the summer of 1966 in New York and Chicago. In 1967 Newark and Detroit were the scenes of deadly riots, and in the spring of 1968, when Martin Luther King was assassinated in Memphis, more than a hundred cities across the nation erupted in violence. America's urban citizens began to speak in tones of dread of the approach of each year's "long, hot summer."

After the riots in Watts and elsewhere and the death of King, black civil rights organizations hardened themselves against white influence; some, like the Black Panthers, became even more militant. This resistance, in turn, compelled many whites, who had been at least somewhat sympathetic to the organizations' goals, to abandon the civil rights movement. Other whites began to resent federal and state programs aimed at improving the economic condition of blacks. Some whites turned to violence as the courts ordered desegregation of neighborhood schools through compulsory busing. By the late 1960s and early 1970s, American society was as polarized as it had ever been, despite the massive gains in civil rights won by black Americans. While the past two decades have seen a decline in black activism, distrust and violence continue to plague race relations in the United States. African-Americans continue to live in poorer, more dangerous neighborhoods than white Americans, are less well educated, and enjoy fewer of the opportunities and comforts American society offers.

Cesar Chavez Calls for a National Boycott of Table Grapes (1965)

The event: On September 6, 1965, Cesar Chavez led migrant farm workers in a strike against California grape growers, triggering a nationwide grape boycott that pressured the growers to recognize the United Farm Workers.

TO THE NATION'S poorest laborers, its migrant farm workers, the American dream had long seemed a closed door. Cesar Chavez, born near Yuma, Arizona, in 1927, was the son of a migrant family who experienced firsthand the squalor, uncertainties, and abuses of migrant life. In 1952, Father Donald McDonnell, an activist Catholic priest, and Fred Ross, an organizer with the Community Service Organization, introduced Chavez to labor organizing and recruited him into the Community Service Organization. He soon rose to become director of the CSO, which he left in 1962 to organize a farm workers' union.

His organization, the Farm Workers Association (renamed the United Farm Workers when it became part of the AFL-CIO), joined and sanctioned a strike begun in September 1965 by Filipino farm workers in the grape fields of Delano, California. Inspired by the rhetoric and tactics of the civil rights movement, then at its height, Chavez made the plight of these laborers, who had been virtually invisible, a national issue.

The grape boycott and the UFW did not magically transform the lives of migrant farm workers, but it did improve them by persuading growers to sign far more equitable contracts with the workers, and it dramatically demonstrated the power of moral passion, committment, and solidarity to bring about change in a democratic society.

The Supreme Court Rules on *Miranda v. State of Arizona* (1966)

The event: Civil libertarians won a major victory with the 1966 Supreme Court decision in *Miranda v. State of Arizona*, in which the court ruled that the Constitution's Fifth Amendment, which extends to an individual the right to refuse to testify in court against him- or herself, also applied to individuals in police custody.

IN 1963 A high school dropout named Ernesto Miranda kidnapped and raped a teenage girl. After he was arrested and identified during a police lineup, he made a written confession, which included a statement that he had been informed of his rights. During his trial, Miranda's attorney argued that the defendant had not been told by the arresting officers of his right to have legal counsel present during interrogations. When Miranda was convicted, his case was adopted by the American Civil Liberties Union, whose lawyers presented it before the Supreme Court. The court voted five to four to reverse his conviction, ruling that Miranda had incriminated himself because he had been improperly advised of his rights.

The Miranda decision requires law enforcement officers to inform individuals in their custody that they have the right to remain silent, that anything they say can be used against them, that they have the right to have an attorney present, and that if they cannot afford an attorney, the court will appoint one to represent them before any questioning takes place. The court held that any statement provided by an individual in police custody before being "Mirandized"— that is, advised of his rights—is inadmissible in court. Also barred from court testimony is the fact that a defendant has chosen to remain silent when accused of a crime.

The Supreme Court based its ruling in part on a thorough examination of police practices. Finding that physical abuse and deception were sometimes used to obtain confessions, the justices maintained that "custodial interrogation exacts a heavy toll on individual liberty and trades on the weakness of individuals." The Miranda decision is only one of many restrictions law enforcement officers must work under in a democratic society, which, following English common law, regards an accused person as innocent until proven guilty and which would rather allow a guilty person to go free than risk punishing the innocent. As for Ernesto Miranda himself, he was subsequently retried on new evidence and convicted.

Martin Luther King Is Assassinated (1968)

The event: On April 4, 1968, the Reverend Martin Luther King, Jr. was assassinated, a tragic event that shocked the nation and intensified the alienation of America's youth and minorities, who were growing increasingly militant in their protests against the Vietnam War in Southeast Asia and social injustice at home.

1968 WAS A year already marked by intense racial unrest and massive protests over the Vietnam War. When Martin Luther King, Jr.—leader of the civil rights movement since his participation in the 1955 Montgomery bus boycott—was gunned down in April on the balcony of a Memphis motel by James Earl Ray, it became a year like no other.

The Communist Tet Offensive kicked off the year. A massive and coordinated attack on American positions throughout Vietnam on January 31, Tet indicated the Vietcong's ability to strike at will and decimated the optimistic propaganda of American military leaders. A month later, on February 29, Defense Secretary Robert McNamara resigned after concluding the war was unwinnable. That same day Los Angeles blacks rioted and Watts went up in flames. Two weeks later, on March 12, Senator Eugene McCarthy, an outspoken opponent of the war, nearly defeated President Lyndon Johnson in the New Hampshire primary, prompting Robert Kennedy to declare his candidacy for the Democratic nomination four days later on March 16. Before the month was out, Johnson stunned America by withdrawing from the race on March 31. Within the week, Martin Luther King lay dead.

King had gone to Memphis to address the city's striking sanitation workers. The night before his death, he had delivered his famous "I've been to the mountaintop" address. In more than a hundred cities across the country, shocked and enraged blacks expressed their despair and anger by setting ablaze the ghettos and slums in which America had confined them.

Strongly influenced by the teachings of Mahatma Gandhi, King had been an advocate of nonviolence, the leader of the Southern Christian Leadership Conference, and the dramatic and impassioned voice of the civil rights movement. He had led the March on Washington in 1963 and had stirred the nation with his "I have a dream" speech. He won the Nobel Peace Prize in 1964, but his leadership of the movement had come under attack by more militant blacks. Malcolm X's calls for black nationalism and Stokely Carmichael's calls for Black Power were direct challenges both to King's nonviolent message and to his role as spokesman for the African-American polity. Before his death, King had grown more radical, publicly demonstrating his support of the anti-Vietnam War protest movement and planning a massive "Poor People's March," at which some who knew him suspected he intended to call a general strike. He never, however, eschewed non-violence, and he remained a strong symbol of the movement even after his death. An incomparable leader and a great American whose contributions to his people and to his country, King richly deserved to have his birthday declared a national holiday, as indeed it was some years later.

At the time, King's death was a powerful symbol to disaffected African-Americans of the broken promise of America. In the wake of his assassination—and of Robert Kennedy's two months later—the turmoil in American society grew to dangerous proportions. The Chicago police riots, the increasingly larger anti-war demonstrations (resulting in mass internments), an aloof and imperial presidency conducting war in isolated secrecy, the rise of white underground organizations and black paramilitary groups, the exposure of the American atrocity at My Lai, the illegal and brutal bombing of Cambodia, the gunning down of four college students by

National Guardsmen—all these made it seem as if Martin Luther King's dream for America had been replaced after his death by a nightmare.

Robert F. Kennedy Is Assassinated (1968)

The event: On June 6, 1968, following his victory in the California presidential primary, Robert F. Kennedy was assassinated by a self-professed Arab nationalist named Sirhan Sirhan.

KENNEDY SERVED AS attorney general of the United States during the presidency of his brother, John, and briefly held the same post under Lyndon Johnson. As attorney general, Kennedy was a strong proponent of the civil rights movements and had pushed for a sweeping new voting rights bill, enacted during the Johnson administration as the Civil Rights Act of 1964. The Kennedy Justice Department also mounted a major legal campaign to arrest, convict, and imprison the leading members of organized crime and the Mafia. Kennedy's appeal to the youth of America as a voice of idealism was enormous, and his sensitivity to the needs of the poor and the desires of minorities was remarkable, but he had a harsh authoritarian side that made him many enemies, FBI Director J. Edgar Hoover among them. His dogged attempts to convict controversial Teamster Union President Jimmy Hoffa amounted almost to a vendetta—and led Hoffa to say of *John* Kennedy's assassination, "Bobby Kennedy is just another lawyer now."

There was little love lost between President Johnson and Robert Kennedy even before the latter's resignation as attorney general, but as it became obvious that Kennedy was searching for a way to run against the incumbent president of his own party their enmity swelled into loathing, especially after Kennedy embraced the anti-war movement. When Gene McCarthy showed strongly in the democratic primary in New Hampshire, demonstrating that a mainstream presidential campaign opposing the Vietnam war was viable, Kennedy entered the ring, winning both the Indiana and Nebraska primaries.

Johnson's worst fears were realized. The press despised him; the voters did not trust him; his approval ratings were the lowest in history; the 1968 election was obviously turning into a referendum on America's involvement in Indochina; and the hated Bobby Kennedy would likely humiliate him by stealing the nomination of the Democratic Party for president. Surprising almost everyone in the world, Johnson went on national television before the California primary and announced he would not seek a second term, throwing the election wide open.

Under such circumstances, Kennedy's death poses one of the most intriguing "what if" questions in the entire history of American politics. What if Richard Nixon had faced a resurgent heir to the martyred hero JFK had become for the American public who opposed the Vietnam War? What if, in other words, the 1968 election had indeed been what Lyndon Johnson so feared it would become that he ended his political career—a referendum on the war? What if, in short, Americans had settled the issue at the ballot box, pro or con, five years before the 1973 withdrawal of U.S. troops? Robert Kennedy was clearly working toward that end, trying to mold the anti-war constituency into a true Democratic coalition, even going so far as to endorse sending blood to wounded Viet Cong fighters before he encountered a public backlash and backed away from the idiotic and politically suicidal position.

Without doubt, part of the enduring tragedy of the Vietnam experience is that the American public never got the chance to make that yes-or-no choice at a national level until McGovern's laughably weak campaign of 1972. By removing the opportunity to resolve a critical national debate, and perhaps even form a meaningful national consensus on Vietnam, Sirhan Sirhan took more than an individual man's life, and destroyed more than one man's vision of how the nation's problems should be solved. He took away the American middle class's chance to embrace the anti-war movement politically, which it did wholesale a few years later. The delay left scars, bad ones.

For it is worth remembering that the Yippie organizers of the anti-war movement did not finalize their plans to march on the Democratic National Convention in Chicago until after it was clear that Hubert Humphrey, whom they saw as LBJ's proxy, was going to be the nominee. By November, large numbers of young voters had simply turned their backs on the election, convinced that all politics had to offer was Richard Daley and Humphrey, two men they detested because they associated them with the police beatings in Chicago and the carnage in Vietnam, respectively. While disaffected older Democrats turned to segregationist George Wallace, younger ones considered writing in a hog rather than choose either the Republican or Democratic candidate for president.

The point is not that Robert Kennedy would have made a good president, nor even that he would have beaten Nixon, neither of which we can ever know. The point is that his murder turned a disorienting, violent, and chaotic year into a brutally incomprehensible one, virtually ensuring that the United States would be politically incapable of avoiding profound, dangerous divisions in the body politic more serious than any since the Civil War.

The Chicago Police Riot at the Democratic Convention (1968)

The event: During August 26-29, 1968, thousands of Civil Rights and anti-Vietnam War protestors clashed with Chicago police during the Democratic National Convention, focusing national attention on the war, the protest movement against it, the radical left, and the failings of Chicago mayor Richard J. Daley and his police force.

TEN THOUSAND ANTI-WAR and Civil Rights protestors descended on the city of Chicago when the Democratic National Convention met to select its candidate for the 1968 presidential election. For the better part of a week, the protestors and police clashed so violently—and in many instances, one sidedly—that broadcast commentators and eyewitnesses described the event as a "police riot."

Hundreds of demonstrators were arrested; the convention was disrupted, although not stopped; and Mayor Daley, hitherto absolute boss of Chicago machine politics and a major figure in the Democratic Party, was embarrassed—even, as many saw it, disgraced. But it was the trial of the protest leaders that captured the most enduring national attention. David Dellinger of the National Mobilization against the War, Tom Hayden and Rennie Davis of the Students for a Democratic Society (SDS), Abbie Hoffman and Jerry Rubin of the Youth International Party (YIPPIEs), John Froines and Lee Weiner, leaders of the Chicago protestors, and Bobby Seale of the Black Panthers were charged with conspiring to incite riots. During the five-month trial, defense attorney William Kunstler, representing all the defendants except Seale, who defended himself, argued that the violence that occurred in the streets of Chicago was due not to plans laid by the defendants but instead to the overreaction on the part of the police.

Although five of the seven Kunstler defended were found guilty, their convictions were later overturned on appeal, based on procedural errors and hostility toward the defendants manifested by Judge Julius Hoffman.

The Chicago convention riots epitomized the 1960s as the decade of protest. To many who witnessed the clashes between demonstrators and the police in the city's Grant and Lincoln parks, the nation seemed to be on the verge of revolution. So polarized was public opinion that many greeted the prospect of revolt with a sense of joy and liberation, while others looked on in dread and horror.

The United States Puts a Man on the Moon (1969)

The event: On July 20, 1969, at 4:17 p.m. Eastern Daylight Time, two American astronauts landed on the moon.

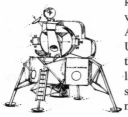

REBOUNDING FROM A serious setback in early 1967, when three astronauts were killed in a fire on board an Apollo command module during a ground test, the United States' space program made great strides over the next two and a half years, culminating in the lunar landing of 1969, when Apollo 11 astronauts Neil Armstrong and Edwin ("Buzz") Aldrin became the first human beings to walk on the moon.

The American space program began in 1958

with the creation of the National Aeronautics and Space Administration (NASA). Almost immediately the new federal agency found itself the underdog in a fierce competition with the Soviet Union's space program. The year before NASA was created the Soviets had launched the first successful artificial satellite, Sputnik I, and four years later launched the first manned satellite, carrying Cosmonaut Yuri Gagarin.

Less than a month after Gagarin's flight, NASA's Project Mercury sent Alan B. Shepard into space for a fifteen-minute suborbital flight on May 5, 1961, and about nine months later John Glenn became the first American to orbit the globe.

Project Mercury was succeeded by Project Gemini, a series of manned missions that provided NASA with valuable experience leading toward a lunar landing. Gemini astronauts took the first "walks" in space, practiced in-space docking procedures, and undertook flights that were much longer than the Mercury missions.

After astronauts Armstrong, Aldrin, and Michael Collins (who flew the Apollo spacecraft's "command module," which orbited but did not land on the moon) returned from their triumphal lunar mission, NASA sent six more flights to the moon before the end of the lunar exploration phase of the Apollo program in December 1972. Thereafter NASA worked on the development and launching of Skylab, an orbiting space station, in 1973; the Apollo-Soyuz Test Project, a joint American-Soviet endeavor in 1975; and the space shuttle program.

Whereas the previous space vehicles had been designed to fly one mission only, the *Columbia* shuttle was a reusable vehicle capable of carrying equipment and scientific teams to space and returning to earth, landing on a runway, like an airplane, rather than splashing down in the ocean, as all earlier spacecraft had done. *Columbia* was first launched on April 12, 1981, and other flights followed. But the shuttle program met with disaster on January 28, 1986, when the *Columbia*'s sister craft, *Challenger*, exploded during take-off, killing its crew of astronauts and civilian mission specialists. For the next two and a half years NASA modified several design components on the shuttle, and in September 1988 resumed shuttle flights with the launch of *Discovery*.

In addition to manned space flights, NASA has launched numerous unmanned satellites and planetary space probes. Pictures transmitted back to earth from the Explorer satellites and the Ranger, Surveyor, Lunar Orbiter, Mariner, and Voyager probes have provided extremely valuable information about the earth, other planets, the solar system, and the universe. In 1990 NASA launched the Hubble Space Telescope, which promises unprecedented views of the solar system and beyond, although preliminary results have called several design elements of the equipment into question.

Four Students Are Killed at Kent State University (1970)

The event: On May 4, 1970, twenty-eight National Guardsmen fired into a crowd of Kent State University students protesting the war in Vietnam. Four were killed, nine wounded.

AMERICAN INVOLVEMENT IN the Vietnam War escalated during the 1960s under the administrations of John F. Kennedy and Lyndon B. Johnson. Richard M. Nixon continued the grim process, announcing in April 1970 the U. S. invasion of Cambodia. Across the country, students poured onto the grounds of colleges and universities to protest. At Kent State University in Ohio, protesters set fire to the ROTC building. In response, the governor called out nine hundred National Guardsmen, most of them inexperienced "weekend warriors." In the heat of the confrontation, they "overreacted" (a word much used during this period), with tragic results. A photograph of a bewildered and grief-stricken young woman kneeling beside the body of a slain student, which appeared in *Life* magazine, seemed to sum up the tragedy of the protest in a single, horrific image. It was as if the war in Vietnam had come home.

Although the President's Commission on Campus Unrest investigated the shootings and issued a report calling them "unnecessary, unwarranted, and inexcusable," no legal action was taken against the Guardsmen. As for the anti-war protests, they continued to escalate in proportion to the war itself until they finally convinced President Nixon to conclude the Paris Peace Agreement with North Vietnam in January 1973, agreeing to the withdrawal of American forces from Vietnam.

The New York Times Publishes the Pentagon Papers (1971)

The event: In June of 1971 *The New York Times* launched a series of articles on a government study known collectively as "The Pentagon Papers," which revealed that for three decades the United States government had not only bungled its handling of Vietnam but had, intentionally and as a matter of course, deceived the American people about its foreign policy.

OFFICIALLY ENTITLED *The History of the U.S. Decision Making Process in Vietnam*, the "secret" study had been ordered by Secretary of Defense Robert McNamara, a Kennedy appointee, before his resignation from the Johnson administration in 1968. Daniel Ellsberg, a professor at MIT, leaked the massive two-million-word document to *Times* reporter Neil Sheehan. One of the Rand Corporation team collecting and analyzing the thousands of documents, telegraphs, memos, and position papers that made up the study, Ellsberg had—like McNamara—lost his former enthusiasm for the Vietnam conflict. Like McNamara, he quit his job. Unlike McNamara, the conscience-striken former "hawk" decided to go public with what he knew, becoming one of the most famous and effective "whistle-blowers" in history.

The Pentagon Papers traced a tale of confusion, conflict, and covert action in the policy making of every administration from Harry S Truman to Lyndon Johnson. Americans learned for the first time that their government had helped plan the ouster and execution of another country's head of state—South

Vietnam's Prime Minister Diem. They discovered that the Gulf of Tonkin resolution, supposedly a response to North Vietnam's attack on the U.S. destroyer *Maddox*, had been drafted months in advance of the attack. And they learned that one of their presidents, Lyndon Johnson, had been clearly lying to them in his public pronouncements that he had no long-range strategy for Vietnam. The Pentagon Papers were official confirmation of what the most radical anti-war activists had been claiming for years.

President Richard Nixon, at first delighted to see past—Democratic—administrations come under attack, soon realized that to let the leaking of classified documents go unchallenged established a dangerous precedent. He sent Attorney General John Mitchell to threaten the *Times* with charges of espionage, and when that failed, got a temporary injunction from the federal courts blocking further publication. By this time, *The Washington Post* and *The Boston Globe* had also begun publishing the papers, and they, too, were restrained until June 30, 1971, when the Supreme Court ruled six to three in favor of freedom of the press under the First Amendment. The action reinforced the "bunker mentality" of the Nixon White House, and Nixon's response was to have Ellsberg investigated with hopes of discrediting him personally. He set up a special "unit" run directly from the White House by a former CIA special agent, E. Howard Hunt, and an ex-FBI agent, G. Gordon Liddy under the tutelage of Special Counsel Charles Colson. The unit was called the "Plumbers" because it was supposed to plug leaks.

Starting with the burglary of Ellsberg's psychiatrist's office, the Plumbers would go on to bug Democratic Party headquarters at the Watergate apartment complex, engendering there the scandal that would lead to Nixon's resignation.

The publication of the Pentagon Papers destroyed America's security credibility and severely damaged its intelligence operations, while immensely strengthening First Amendment guarantees to the press and providing the Vietnam protest movement with respectability and new vigor. At the cost of public disillusionment with the government, Ellsberg's act of conscience hastened the end of a war that had for nearly a decade bitterly divided the country.

J. Edgar Hoover Dies (1972)

The event: On May 2, 1972, J. Edgar Hoover died in his sleep. For almost fifty years director of the FBI and perhaps the most publicly respected (and privately hated) man in the nation's history, Hoover left a mixed legacy of effective public service tempered with an egomaniacal lust for power, a combination that had allowed him to build a weak and obscure federal agency into a famous and all too often unaccountable American secret police force.

BORN IN 1895, the son of a low-level bureaucrat in Washington, D.C., Hoover's first job out of George Washington University's law school 1917 was with the Justice Department, monitoring radical activities as an assistant in the alien registration section. Quickly promoted to head of the General Intelligence Division in 1919, Hoover was instrumental in planning the series of raids that became known as the "red scare," the abuses of which wrecked the career of Hoover's boss, Attorney General A. Mitchell Palmer. Because Palmer became the focus of the misuse-of-power scandal, Hoover emerged unscathed, and his real administrative genius, coupled with fanatical diligence, won him promotion under a new president, Warren G. Harding, and a new attorney general, Harlan Stone. In 1920, he became assistant director of the Bureau of Investigation.

The agency Hoover joined had been created in 1908 by then attorney general Charles J. Bonaparte, the American-born grandnephew of Napoleon, over the initial opposition of a Congress who feared its potential for the political abuse of power. A "bureaucratic bastard," as one congressman called it at the time, it became a dumping ground for political hacks under its first director, William J. Burns, a former spy turned private detective who went prematurely, if—for Hoover at least—providentially senile.

During World War I, the Bureau shifted its focus from investigating crime to chasing draft resisters, suspected spies, and alien radicals. After the war, with Hoover on board, those activities expanded to investigation of individuals somehow considered to be domestic security threats, a group including the likes of social-reformer Jane Addams and future Mayor of New York Fiorello La Guardia. Just as Congress had suspected, the Bureau abused its power, and the result was a reorganization in 1924 under which the agency was ordered to cease all wiretapping and stop all investigation of the political activities of individuals. Once again, Hoover's boss took the fall; once again Hoover was promoted, this time to director.

He had learned an important lesson. Publicly opposing the creation of a national police force and declaiming the limit of his agency's responsibilities, Hoover ostentatiously professionalized the organization and touted the development of new crime-fighting techniques. In the late 1920s and early 1930s, he made a few hapless bank robbers and a hopeless psychotic or two famous by labeling them "public enemies" and plastering mug shots of them in post offices around the country on a "Ten Most Wanted" list, after which he sent his agents out to gun them down with much attendant press coverage. Responding to the apparent crime wave, the public came to accept the need for the federal government to play a role in law enforcement. In 1935 the bureau was renamed the Federal Bureau of Investigation, and Hoover was entrenched in the power bureaucracy.

World War II and the Cold War prompted an expansion of security investigations, despite the still-extant ban on political surveillance, and under the guise of national security, Hoover's FBI truly came into its own. He willingly put the agency at the service of Franklin Delano Roosevelt for political use and policy enforcement, as he would for every president thereafter up to and including, most infamously, Richard Nixon. Using his undeniable administrative genius, Hoover invented complex recording procedures that hid his authorization of illegal break-ins, wiretaps, and bugs to gather and accumulate damaging information on the private lives not merely of subversives, but of anyone Hoover disliked or thought powerful enough to hurt him.

Hoover's FBI became an autonomous agency operating independently of executive, congressional, or judicial oversight. During his tenure at the FBI, Hoover blocked all demands for independent investigations of the bureau's conduct and his administration. He won a strong constituency with his keen understanding of public relations, his careful cultivation of the press during the early days, his pandering of information to powerful members of Congress, civic leaders, and conservative groups in later years. It was virtually impossible for presidents to fire him, even had they wanted to do so. In 1968, Congress—closing the proverbial barn door—passed a law requiring Senate confirmation of future FBI directors and limiting their service to ten years. But only after Hoover died did Congress truly try to rein in the "bureaucratic bastard" it had given birth to half a century before.

Nixon's "Plumbers" Are Caught Burglarizing the Watergate (1972)

The event: On June 17, 1972, during a presidential campaign, Washington, D.C., police officers—alerted by a security guard at the Watergate apartment complex—arrested five employees of the Nixon campaign's Committee to Re-elect the President as they were breaking into the Democratic National Committee's headquarters, located in the building. The arrest led to a scandal that forced the first resignation of a president in American history.

THE FIVE WATERGATE burglars were attempting to "bug" the telephones of Democratic leaders and obtain political documents outlining the Democratic campaign strategy. They were members of the "Plumbers," a unit the Nixon White House had organized to plug leaks in the wake of the Pentagon Papers brouhaha, which included anti-Castro Cuban refugees (veterans of the Bay of Pigs), former FBI agents, and a former CIA agent who had helped plan the Bay of Pigs. One of the former FBI agents, G. Gordon Liddy—a rabid right-winger with a penchant for quoting untranslated Nietzsche—and the former CIA man, E. Howard Hunt—a "spook" (secret agent) who had authored any number of second-rate spy novels—were in charge of the group. Both of them worked for CREEP, as Nixon's campaign committee was affectionately called, and both had been on the White House payroll.

As Nixon won the election and assumed his second term, details of the scandal appeared in the *Washington Post*, and the news stories led the Senate to form a select committee to investigate the scandal in special televised hearings. During the Watergate hearings it became painfully clear to the millions of Americans who remained glued to their television sets that not only had Nixon, his aides, and his reelection committee conspired to sabotage the Democratic challenger's campaigns—now the White House was trying to impede the Watergate investigation itself, a criminal offense known as obstruction of justice.

In May 1973, mounting public outrage over the scandal forced Nixon to appoint a special prosecutor for the case. The well-known Harvard professor and legal authority Archibald Cox, working with a federal grand jury presided over by Judge John Sirica, subpoenaed secret tapes of presidental meetings and phone conversations. These the ever-more embattled Nixon refused to produce, citing national security as his defense and invoking the doctrine of executive privilege as his authority. In October 1973 the president ordered Attorney General Elliott Richardson to fire Cox, but Richardson resigned rather than carry out the order, as did his second-in-command. Nixon finally found a Justice Department employee who would obey his orders, but public indignation over the firing of Cox forced Nixon immediately to appoint a new prosecutor, Leon Jaworski, who renewed the legal battle for the tapes.

By July of the following year, Jaworski's grand jury had named Nixon as an unindicted co-conspirator in the obstruction of justice, and the House Judiciary Committee adopted three articles of impeachment on the similar charges. The Supreme Court rejected Nixon's claim of executive privilege, and Judge Sirica once again ordered the tapes produced. Nixon, who was now hardly functioning as president in any meaningful sense, finally released eight transcripts of the tapes, portions of which had apparently been intentionally erased, but all to no avail: the tapes proved that Nixon was lying. He knew about the cover-up. He had violated the law. Rather than face an impeachment trial, Nixon resigned on August 9, 1974, and was pardoned the following month by his successor, Gerald Ford, for all offenses he had or might have committed during his presidency.

All of the Watergate conspirators, save Nixon, were convicted, and all of them, save Nixon, went to jail. In the decades following the scandal Nixon attempted to gloss over his criminal activities and claim that Watergate, in the words of his White House spokesman at the time, was nothing but a "third-rate burglary," which he did not plan and did not order, and for which he was hounded from office by his political enemies. As the memory of the televised hearings, the shocking revelations in the press, and Nixon's obdurate refusal to obey the legal rulings of the legitimate branches of government, including his own Justice Department, receded, Nixon managed partially to rehabilitate his public image. Historically, however, the Watergate break-in and even Nixon's desperate obstruction of justice were only moments in a pattern of illegality—domestic spying, misuse of campaign funds and government agencies, abuse of power—that, as president, Nixon cloaked under a blanket of national security. In corrupting the legitimate electoral process, in seeking to expand the power of the presidency beyond its constitutional limits, and in undermining the American legal system itself lay Nixon's historical high crimes and misdemeanors.

The Supreme Court Rules on *Roe v. Wade* (1973)

The event: In 1973, in the case of *Roe v. Wade*, the U. S. Supreme Court ruled that a woman's constitutional right to privacy includes the right to abort a fetus during the first trimester of pregnancy. The decision, among the high court's most controversial ever, held profound moral and legal implications.

IN A SEVEN-TO-TWO VOTE, the Court determined not only that women have a constitutional right to abortion during the first three months of pregnancy, but that beyond three months the fetus is "viable" and the state, therefore, has the responsibility of protecting it.

The case was first filed by Norma McCorvey, who sued the state of Texas for denying her the right to an abortion. When the case reached the Supreme Court, few people expected the justices to overturn the Texas law. The court had become increasingly conservative with the appointments by President Richard

Nixon of Chief Justice Warren Burger and Justices Harry Blackmun, Lewis Powell, and William Rehnquist; the retirement of Chief Justice Earl Warren; and the deaths of Hugo Black and John Marshall Harlan II, all judicial liberals.

Justice Blackmun wrote the court's majority opinion, which extended the "right to privacy" implied in the First and Ninth Amendments. Dissenting from the majority ruling were Justices Rehnquist and Byron White. The ruling, one of the most controversial in the Supreme Court's history, barred the states from prohibiting abortion in the first trimester. The ruling gave rise to opposing movements, one to preserve women's right to have abortions ("pro-choice") and the other to limit or deny that right ("right-to-life"). Beginning in the early 1980s, the right-to-life movement called for a constitutional amendment to ban abortions except in cases of rape, incest, or threat to the mother's life. Taking on the defense of the *Roe v. Wade* decision, the National Organization of Women (NOW) has supported pro-choice candidates for public office. *Roe v. Wade* was challenged in 1976 by the Hyde Amendment, which prohibited federal funding for abortions, and in 1989 by *Webster v. Reproductive Health Services*. In that ruling the Supreme Court upheld its fundamental decision in *Roe v. Wade*, but urged the states to seek new solutions to the problems engendered by abortion policy. Few right-to-life supporters—or pro-lifers, as the anti-abortion forces are sometimes called—found anything useful in the Webster ruling.

The legal status of abortion has gone through various changes since the American Revolution. Under colonial and early American law, abortion was legal, provided that it was carried out before movements of the fetus could be felt—generally about midway through a pregnancy. In the 1830s abortion was widespread as a method of birth control; newspapers and magazines carried advertisements of abortionists, and women freely discussed the topic with their doctors. By the 1860s, doctors estimated that women had abortions at the rate of one for every four live births.

In the 1860s, the newly created American Medical Association—for professional, ethical, and hygienic reasons—began a campaign to outlaw abortions, except when deemed necessary by doctors themselves. A wave of legislative reform followed, though most of it was wrapped up with regulations concerning the licensing and qualifications of medical practitioners. These new laws sent abortionists underground, but substantial numbers of women continued to have abortions throughout the nineteenth century and into the twentieth. The movement to repeal state laws banning abortions was begun in the 1950s, in a context of concern over the postwar "population explosion," by activists armed with data indicating that abortions undertaken in the first trimester of pregnancy were actually safer than birth. New supporters of the movement included a more powerful women's constituency; individuals fighting against the inequality that existed between wealthy women, who could afford safe abortions, and poor women, who could not; and physicians, 87 percent of whom favored liberalized abortion laws in 1967. Opposed to such liberalization were the Roman Catholic Church and various fundamentalist and evangelical Protestant groups. But the Supreme Court's *Roe v. Wade* ruling meant that all states were directed to lift their bans on abortions, though many resisted actually doing so.

Roe v. Wade, important in itself, also raised issues concerning the degree to which the federal government could legislate the most private and fundamental issues of life and death, including the question of when life begins, a question continually debated by scientists, moralists, and theologians, and one that has proved to be political dynamite.

OPEC Embargoes Oil to the West (1973)

The event: On October 17, 1973, the Organization of Petroleum Exporting Countries (OPEC) declared an embargo on oil exports to nations that had supported Israel in its war with Egypt.

FROM THE TIME that Henry Ford turned out his first Model T at the beginning of the century, Americans have been in love with the automobile. In the years following World War II, automobile ownership and use had come to seem a right almost synonymous with citizenship, and between 1950 and 1974, American oil consumption doubled. The U.S. claimed a mere 6 percent of the world's population, but it consumed fully one-third of the world's energy. What of it? Life was good, people were mobile, and gas was cheap.

Then came the Arab oil embargo. Gasoline prices, which had been (on average) 38.5 cents in May 1973, shot up to 55.1 cents in June 1974. Although Americans cut their consumption of oil by some 7 percent, shortages and long, long lines at filling stations were the norm for several months. In some cases, factories requiring large quantities of fuel oil had to curtail operations.

Severe as the short-term effects of the OPEC oil crisis were, it is the long-term consequences, still felt today, that have most affected American life. For the first time since the Great Depression, average Americans had a taste of what it was like to *want*, to *do without*. They came to realize that, at the threshold of the last quarter of the twentieth century, the United States—and, indeed, the world—faced an "energy crisis." A nation of energy consumers had to come to grips with the realization that energy is a finite resource. While this new awareness is, in the main, a positive result of the OPEC embargo, the crisis produced another, more dangerous result. Since 1973-1974, the United States had adopted a policy of responding to any threat to its supply of oil as a threat to national security. This has played a role in repeated brushes with armed conflict—and, in the case of Saddam Hussein's Iraq, one full-fledged war—involving oil-producing nations of the volatile Middle East.

An Accident Occurs at the Three Mile Island Nuclear Facility (1979)

The event: On March 28, 1979, the nuclear reactor at the Three Mile Island electric power plant near Harrisburg, Pennsylvania, approached meltdown. Although disaster was avoided, Americans were forced to rethink their assumptions about energy, big business, and government regulation.

IT BEGAN AT four in the morning when a turbine driven by steam generated by the heat of a nuclear reactor shutdown. Finding water seeping onto the floor of the reactor containment building about two hours later, engineers at the Three Mile Island facility determined that the loop circulating coolant water to the re-

 actor's radioactive core had been damaged. With temperatures exceeding the critical 600° (Fahrenheit) mark, a partial meltdown of the core had occurred, releasing radioactive gases into the atmosphere. After some delay, plant officials notified Pennsylvania governor Richard Thornburgh, who issued a warning to people living near the plant to stay indoors and called for pregnant women to evacuate the area.

Although the Nuclear Regulatory Commission later found that the amount of radioactivity released into the atmosphere was insufficient to pose a serious health risk, anti-nuclear activists demonstrated in cities across the country. One such rally in New York City attracted more than two hundred thousand demonstrators. The near-total meltdown at Three Mile Island fed the growing controversy over the safety of nuclear power, and over the next five years numerous nuclear projects were canceled and no new ones were planned. The episode brought to the fore long-standing conflicts between big business interests and the public welfare and raised questions about the federal government's role in resolving such conflicts. It also challenged the nation's consistent tendency to embrace high technology avidly and without thought.

Iran Takes Ninety Americans Hostage (1979)

The event: On November 4, 1979, five hundred Iranians stormed the American embassy in Tehran and took ninety American diplomats hostage, igniting a crisis that ended Jimmy Carter's political career and set the stage for the major scandal of the Reagan Administration.

AS AN ACT of revenge for President Carter's support of the Shah of Iran, the Khomeini-inspired hostage taking proved effective. Not only were Carter's ability to govern effectively and his chances of reelection eventually destroyed, his inability to free the hostages and his much-publicized abortive rescue mission came to symbolize American powerlessness to such an extent that the taking of

 hostages became a popular tactic in the Middle East's domestic politics.

While the "Iran Hostage Crisis" ended on the day Ronald Reagan became president, when Khomeini—much to Reagan's political benefit—released the embassy hostages, another round of kidnappings inspired by the crisis was soon to take place in the war-torn, anarchy-ridden Lebanon. Most of the new hostages were to remain in captivity, their whereabouts unknown, their kidnappers unidentified, throughout the Reagan presidency, their fates and the plights of their families a source of torment and outrage for American authorities and citizens alike. The president and his men were especially worried about hostage William Buckley, since his captors knew that Buckley was the CIA's head of station in Beirut. Because of what had happened to Jimmy Carter, however, President Reagan declared that he would not negotiate with terrorists for hostages, since negotiation only encouraged more hostage-taking.

In 1985 a group of Israelis broached the subject of the American hostages in Lebanon with National Security Advisor Robert MacFarlane. The Israelis claimed that a rather shady Iranian arms dealer could win the release of the hostages if the U.S. was willing to swap a few hundred antitank missiles, which Iran desperately needed for its long war of attrition with Iraq, in exchange for Tehran's promise to use its influence over the kidnapers. McFarlane later testified that the deal interested him because it offered not only a chance to free the hostages but to make contact with "moderates" inside the Iranian government. When McFarlane outlined the arms-for-hostages plan at a meeting of the president with his key advisors, however, both Secretary of State George Schultz and Secretary of Defense Caspar Weinberger voiced strong opposition and left the meeting thinking they had killed the idea.

Instead, according to MacFarlane, the president told him to go ahead with the deal. This he did, managing to get one arms shipment through and one hostage released, though not the one he wanted most—William Buckley, whom the Iranians had already tortured to death, a fact the shady Iranian middleman carefully concealed from MacFarlane. MacFarlane turned the second shipment over to one of his Security Council deputies, Colonel Oliver North, who became the central figure in the Iran-Contra scandal that erupted around the secret hostage negotiations.

North, a Vietnam veteran and right-wing zealot, was—as he told it—the darling of CIA Director William Casey for his handling of a plan to funnel money secretly and illegally to the anti-Sandinista rebels, the "Contras," in Nicaragua. When Congress, controlled by Democrats, passed an amendment outlawing the use of U.S. funds to support the rebels, Reagan decided to sidestep the law by raising money for the Contras from foreign governments friendly to the U.S.—despite warnings from White House staff that sending such funds might be an impeachable offense. The job was then turned over to North, who began recruiting former CIA and American military men to help him. It was North who came up with the idea of using the money from the sale of arms to Iran to fund the Contras. Under the enthusiastic guidance of CIA director Casey, the ambitious North expanded his assignments into the building of what he and Casey called a permanent, off-the-shelf covert enterprise for use in circumventing legitimate congressional oversight of secret CIA operations.

Under North's handling, the second shipment of arms-for-hostages went awry, and before he could mount a third, an obscure Middle Eastern magazine broke the story that would lead to the unraveling of the Iran-Contra plans. Within days of finding out that North and MacFarlane had been to Iran, U.S. papers ran stories about the affair. As in the Watergate scandal, the White House issued conflicting statements, and Reagan held press conferences that the day's news immediately contradicted. Perhaps to distinguish himself from Richard Nixon, Reagan appointed a presidential commission headed by Senator John Tower, but its report was a scathing indictment of the president. As in Watergate, Congress formed a special committee to investigate, and as in Watergate, a special prosecutor was appointed. And as in Watergate, the administration used the excuse of "national security" to withhold vast amounts of evidence. Unlike Watergate, it worked.

A charismatic Oliver North, under a congressional grant of immunity, freely admitted at least those of his lies, deceptions, and illegal activities covered by the grant, in all of which he implicated his superiors, including the president. But CIA director Casey, the one man North fingered as behind the entire operation, had died, and North's superiors remained steadfast in their denials of or loss of memory about the events to which North testified. Eventually escaping conviction on all the more serious Iran-Contra-related charges, North was given a suspended sentence on the number of counts on which he was found guilty by a sympathetic judge who called North a "fall guy." MacFarlane, whose testimony and integrity North challenged on the witness stand, attempted suicide early in the scandal (he survived).

Though Ronald Reagan came out of Iran-Contra legally unscathed, the scandal crippled the final days of his administration, and in 1992 Weinberger was anticlimatically indicted for lying to Congress. Never taking the scandal as seriously as Watergate, the public seemed more worried about the image of a doddering president, out of touch with reality, than about a fanatical junior officer running major illegal foreign-policy initiatives unchecked by any elected authority, or about arrogant spies making secret CIA plans yet again to sidestep Congress and subvert the legitimate functioning of the American democracy.

The Cold War Ends (1989-1991)

The event: In the fall of 1989, the most visible symbol of the Cold War—the Berlin Wall—was chipped away piece by piece by a joyous German population determined to end the politically enforced partition of their country that began after World War II and reached its apotheosis with the building of the wall in 1961.

DURING THE YALTA CONFERENCE in 1945 the Allied powers agreed to divide Germany and its capital, Berlin, into two sectors in order to weaken forever the national juggernaut that had started two world wars. One sector would be controlled by the United States, Great Britain, and France; the other, by the Soviet Union. The division made life difficult for residents of West Berlin, located deep within Soviet-occupied East Germany. In the ensuing Cold War, actions by the Soviet Union included an alliance with Cuba to provide economic subsidies

and military training and aid, the formation of the Warsaw Pact, and the construction of the Berlin Wall—a tangible reminder of the ongoing and potentially apocalyptic competition between the superpowers.

The concrete and barbed wire structure had been built ostensibly to keep East Berliners from crossing the border into the west, but was actually more in the nature of a double-dare by Soviet Premier Nikita Khrushchev to the young American President John F. Kennedy. It was not his only such gambit. Even as Kennedy traveled to West Berlin to announce, "Ich bin ein Berliner," Khrushchev was arranging the insertion of nuclear-armed Soviet missiles into Castro's Cuba.

By 1989, the building of the wall seemed an empty gesture, one that, mainly due to the reforms of the Soviet system introduced by Mikhail Gorbachev, had outlived its usefulness. The Cold War, sometimes quietly, sometimes overtly waged, was coming to an end with the deterioration of Communist control in Eastern Europe and in the Soviet Union itself. In 1991, a KGB-led coup inspired by the remaining hardline Communists, in the course of which Gorbachev was arrested and held captive, failed when junior officers in the Red Army refused to follow orders. Pressured by reform-minded Russian President Boris Yeltsin, Gorbachev first disbanded the Communist Party created by Lenin and Trotsky during the 1917 Russian Revolution, then abdicated his position as head of the U.S.S.R. The once mighty Soviet Empire, like its Tsarist predecessor, simply vanished overnight, replaced by a loose federation of former Soviet States under the now irrepressible Yeltsin.

The Cold War ended. The reckless national security system it engendered, in which two superpowers, armed with weapons capable of destroying the planet many times over, divided the world into hostile camps, vied for influence over unaligned Third World countries, and held each other in check at tremendous costs to their own people in dollars and freedom, seemed superfluous at best.

In its wake the Cold War left an America no longer quite sure of its place, feeling on the one hand it had somehow "won," but on the other that perhaps the winner after all had been Japan. Massively in debt, its inner cities deeply troubled, saddled with a huge defense budget it didn't need and a powerful national security apparatus it didn't know what to do with, America was ambivalent. At least it had not collapsed (as had its erstwhile foe the Soviet Union), which meant there was still time for its traditionally restless people to do what they probably did best—improvise.

AFTERWORD

The 201st Event

While books end, events keep occurring. Choosing two hundred events to struc-ture a historical narrative seems no more arbitrary than breaking it into themati-cally titled chapters, but isolating events as we have done almost naturally invites the question: "What about the 201st event?"

Historians have traditionally avoided the treatment of current events, since there is no way to tell if what now seems earth-shattering will count for much in ten or one hundred years. While events do shape and even change our lives, unlike religious conversions their significance is not always immediately clear. Significant events are more often like good wines; they age well and taste better later.

An embattled George Bush, trying desperately to hold onto the presi-dency for a second term, might well have argued during the eerie presidential campaign of 1992 that the 201st event was the Gulf War; American women might just as well have argued that the Senate confirmation of Clarence Thomas for a seat on the Supreme Court or the William Kennedy Smith rape-trial verdict were events so portentous as to qualify; a cynic might have suggested Johnny Carson's retirement as host of the *Tonight Show* actually affected more lives than either of these events.

Our guess is that the brutal beating of Rodney King by four Los Angeles policemen, the incredible not-guilty verdict in the subsequent trial of the police-men, and the extremely violent Los Angeles riot the verdict engendered will prove in the long run the most significant choice for a 201st event.

Even at close remove from the Rodney King "incident," to adopt one of history's more pleasant euphemisms, several aspects of its historical significance seem clear. The role of television, for example. Without the video technology spawned by Vladimir Zworykin's invention, the vicious attack on Rodney King would never have become an "incident" in the first place. After all, most moderately informed citizens are not unaware of the brutality with which America's traditionally white police forces have, almost as a matter of course, treated black men. But being aware of routine police brutality and racism and seeing it in action are two different things.

Network news, despite the constant criticism by the politicians upon whom it spends so much of its coverage, is not very effective at capturing unstaged events, especially those like police brutality, commonly hidden from the light of public scrutiny. Traditionally, only when an event, or, more usually, its consequences, have forced the networks to suspend the normal time and content controls they exercise over tightly produced and artificially compressed "segments" of their nightly news programs have they had true historical impact. Examples include television's coverage during wars, riots, or politically charged public hearings.

Television did not, for instance, uncover the Watergate scandal, whose clandestine operations and secret White House plottings took place out of the normal range of the network's huge and cumbersome news-gathering apparatus. But when the diligent and dogged work of individual print reporters forced the scandal into the public arena, television *was* quite effective in bringing the extremely complicated story of the cover-up before the American people by simply giving over its time to the Watergate hearings. Similarly, John Kennedy's assassination was an event powerful enough to disrupt network scheduling, with the unexpected result that Americans saw Jack Ruby murder Lee Harvey Oswald on live TV, probably the medium's single most unforgettable moment of raw news coverage. Yet the advent of cable television and the proliferation of video equipment among the citizenry have changed the rules, and "real-life" coverage of significant events once beyond the reach of cameras has become more common.

Another historically significant aspect of the event may be the collapse of the law-and-order consensus that has ruled American politics for the last two decades. Based on the tacit approval of a quiescent middle class, both black and white, in the abandonment of the inner-city poor, the law-and-order establishment managed to make of electorial politics a morality play in which tough but underfunded cops battled evil, rich and ubiquitous drug-lords and youth gangs in a never-ending conflict of clear moral extremes. At risk were the souls of our children, confused innocents bewitched beyond our control by the all-powerful appeal of drugs. What was required was not attention to the social ills of poverty and unemployment, but the sacrifice of certain safeguards of individual liberty, superfluous to the morally upright in any case. What was necessary was not money for education and social welfare programs, but money for law enforcement and prisons; not a better future, but a more secure present.

Daryl Gates's crypto-fascist LAPD, with its "command presence" and its policing by fear and intimidation, was a part of that consensus, and if black males complained before Rodney King of arbitrary stop-and-search procedures and unnecessarily rough treatment at the hands of the Los Angeles police, those complaints were conjured away as necessary for cops staggeringly outnumbered by the Crips and Bloods. The videotape of Rodney King's beating unmasked the reality behind such posturing and created a "credibility gap" for Gates just as suppertime coverage of the Vietnam War had for Lyndon Johnson.

George Bush, too, who had won election by pandering to the fears behind that consensus with the now-infamous "Willie Horton" ad in 1988, found his credibility severely challenged by the incident. Sputtering that the riots had been caused by the very Great Society programs law-and-order administrations had been gutting for twenty years seemed, to most observers, not only absurd on the face of it, but almost beside the point. Blaming the outbreak of violence in L.A. on the breakdown of family values, even if true, had the same kind of effect that Jimmy Carter's lecturing the public on its general "malaise" had once had. The breakdown, to the extent that it was not code-language for the historically fatherless black family unit, went well beyond the ghetto, and the millions of divorced, remarried, or single-parent voters in the country certainly did not feel personally responsible for the riot.

Two things in particular undercut the law-and-order consensus. First, that the riot had happened at all was profoundly troubling to many Americans. After all, the reason Americans voted for law-and-order candidates was to prevent, for whatever reason, the kind of civil violence that had racked America in the 1960s, and the appearance of inaction by the Bush administration spoke more eloquently than its search for explanations or scapegoats. Second, for the first time in almost twenty years, the American public as a whole got a good look at the inner city itself, and it saw, in addition to gang members, drug dealers, and looters, normal people trying to get along against a background of poverty and decay. The networks were forced for the first time in decades to interview ghetto dwellers in depth about issues other than drugs and gang violence. What came through was the inescapable sense that they had been abandoned by America.

The changing nature of the inner city, then, was also made clear by the Rodney King incident. The flight by the black middle class had long been documented, but its replacement by Koreans and other Asians was less well known. The creation of a permanent underclass of blacks and Hispanics, and their frustration with the economic success of recent arrivers, received eloquent if horrifying display in the wide-open gun battles between blacks and Asian store owners. As more and more citizens described the scene to roving reporters as resembling more the street warfare of Beirut than an American city, and as the news media and political pundits described the riot more and more as a class conflict rather than a racial one, it became clear that the "us against them" drama of the law-and-order establishment was itself in trouble.

Americans want to "fix" problems. They came to believe twenty years ago that the social programs of the Great Society had, for whatever reasons, not fixed the tendency to violence of the inner city; now they knew that the law-and-order policies of those who attacked those programs had failed as well.

And finally there is the immediate cause of the riots, the Rodney King verdict itself. King's case is not unique. The American judicial system, it will come as no surprise, favors the rich. But we tend to think of that as a result of the ability to hire expensive lawyers, not a matter of institutionalized prejudice against the poor or those of another race. Even for the poor, even for minorities,

Americans want to believe, a "day in court" has meant a chance to make things right. The social activism of the Warren Supreme Court helped to bolster that legacy for the African-American population in general. But the King verdict, which defied the evidence of our very own eyes, flew in the face of such deep-seated beliefs, as if to illustrate just how deeply law-and-order concerns had corrupted the judicial system. It was as if "the law" would go to any lengths to protect the police. And, in fact, it was a white judge who granted a change of venue; it was another who quite narrowly instructed the jury. A different kind of "fix" seemed to be at work. Not just for black Americans, but for them especially, the verdict was an outrage, denying the very equality before the law upon which, in the last resort, the American pursuit of happiness depends.

In short, the Rodney King incident appears to us historically significant because so many of the salient events in American history served to shape this one. The constant struggle between social and economic equality and the lust for profit, the birth and rise of the electronic news media, the battle of African-Americans for true freedom and a piece of the American dream, the American demand for fairness and justice in political institutions—these themes have been with us for some time. And that they still trouble us is the best reason why knowing what those events were and what they mean is important in itself.

SELECT BIBLIOGRAPHY

Adair, James. *The History of the American Indians: Particularly Those Nations Adjoining to the Mississippi, East and West Florida, Georgia, South and North Carolina and Virginia; Containing an Account of their Origin, Language, Manners, Religious and Civil Customs, Laws, Form of Government, Punishments, Conduct in War and Domestic Life, Their Habits, Diet, Agriculture, Manufactures, Diseases and Methods of Cure, and Other Particulars, Sufficient to Render it a Complete Indian System* . . . . London: Edward and Charles Dilly, 1775; reprint ed., New York: Promontory Press, 1974.

Adams, Charles Francis. *Three Episodes of Massachusetts History: The Settlement of Boston Bay; The Antinomian Controversy; A Study of Church and Town Government.* Boston: Houghton Mifflin, 1892.

Adams, Ramon F. *Burs Under the Saddle: A Second Look at Books and Histories of the West.* Norman: University of Oklahoma Press, 1964.

Adams, Ramon F. *More Burs Under the Saddle: Books and Histories of the West.* Norman: University of Oklahoma Press, 1978.

Ambrose, Stephen E. *Crazy Horse and Custer: The Parallel Lives of Two American Warriors.* Garden City, New York: Doubleday, 1975.

Andrews, Charles M. *The Colonial Period of American History.* 1934-1938; reprint ed., New Haven: Yale University Press, 1964.

Andrist, Ralph K. *The Long Death: The Last Days of the Plains Indians.* New York: Macmillan, Collier Books, 1969.

Axelrod, Alan. *Art of the Golden West.* New York: Abbeville Press, 1990.

Axelrod, Alan. *A Chronicle of the Indian Wars from Colonial Times to Wounded Knee.* New York: Prentice Hall Press, 1992.

Bakeless, John. *Daniel Boone: Master of the Wilderness.* New York: William Morrow, 1939.

Barbour, Phillip L. *The Three Worlds of Captain John Smith.* Boston: Houghton Mifflin, 1964.

Bass, Althea. *Cherokee Messenger.* Norman: University of Oklahoma Press, 1936.

Beal, Merrill D. *"I Will Fight No More Forever": Chief Joseph and the Nez Percé War.* Seattle: University of Oklahoma Press, 1936.

Belz, Carl. *The Story of Rock.* New York: Oxford University Press, 1969.

Berry, Don. *A Majority of Scoundrels: An Informal History of the Rocky Mountain Fur Company.* New York: Harper's, 1961.

Billington, Ray Allen. *The Far Western Frontier 1830-1860.* New York: Harper & Brothers, 1956.

Bishop, Jim. *The Day Lincoln Was Shot*. New York: Harper and Brothers, 1955.

Black Hawk. *Black Hawk: An Autobiography*. Edited by Donald Jackson. Urbana: University of Illinois Press, 1955.

Blum, John M. et al. *The National Experience: A History of the United States Since 1865*, 2 vols. New York: Harcourt, Brace, and World, 1968.

Boatner, Mark M., III. *The Civil War Dictionary*. 1959; reprint ed., New York: Vintage, 1988.

Bowman, John S. *The World Almanac of the American West*. Edited by Samuel Eliot Morison. New York: Modern Library, 1967.

Brady, Cyrus Townsend. *Indian Fights and Fighters*. 1904; reprint ed., Lincoln: University of Nebraska Press, 1971.

Brandon, William. *Indians*. New York: American Heritage; Boston: Houghton Mifflin, 1985.

Brill, Charles J. *Conquest of the Southern Plains*. Oklahoma City: Privately printed, 1938.

Brodie, Fawn. *No Man Knows My History: The Life of Joseph Smith*. New York: Knopf, 1945; revised ed., 1971.

Browder, Nathaniel C. *The Cherokee Indians and Those Who Came After*. Hayesville, North Carolina: Browder, 1973.

Brown, Dee. *Bury My Heart at Wounded Knee: An Indian History of the American West*. New York: Holt, Rinehart & Winston, 1970.

Brown, Mark H. *The Plainsmen of the Yellowstone*. New York: Putnam's, 1961.

Catlin, George. *North American Indians*. Edited by Peter Matthiessen. New York: Viking Penguin, 1989. (Reprint ed. of *Letters and Notes on the Manners, Customs and Conditions of the North American Indians Written During Eight Years' Travel (1832-1839) Amongst the Wildest Tribes of Indians of North America*.)

Condon, Thomas. *New York Beginnings: The Commercial Origin of New Netherland*. New York: New York University Press, 1968.

Connell, Evan S. *Son of the Morning Star*. San Francisco: North Point Press, 1984.

Connor, Seymour V., and Jimmy W. Skaggs. *Broadcloth and Britches: The Santa Fe Trade*. College Station: Texas A & M University, 1977.

Cooper, James Fenimore. *The Deerslayer*. 1841; reprint ed., New York: Bantam, 1982.

Coupler, Charles J., ed. *Indian Treaties, 1778-1883*. New York: Interland, 1972.

Courlander, Harold. *Negro Folk Music: U.S.A.* New York: Columbia University Press, 1963.

Covey, Cyclone, tr. and ed. *Cabeze de Veca's Adventures in the Unknown Interior of America*. New York: Macmillan, 1967.

Craner, Verner. *The Southern Frontier, 1670-1732*. Ann Arbor: University of Michigan Press, 1929.

Davis, Kenneth C. *Don't Know Much About History: Everything You Need to Know About American History but Never Learned*. New York: Avon, 1990.

Debo, Angie. *A History of the Indians in the United States*. Norman: University of Oklahoma Press, 1977.

Dippie, Brian W. *The Vanishing American: White Attitudes and U.S. Indian Policy*. Middletown, Connecticut: Wesleyan University Press, 1982.

Dodge, Richard Irving. *The Plains of the Great West and Their Inhabitants, Being a Description of the Plains, Game, Indians of the Great North American Desert.*

Driver, Harold E. *Indians of North America.* 2nd ed., revised. Chicago: University of Chicago Press, 1969.

Dunning, William A. *Reconstruction, Political and Economic, 1865-1877.* New York: Harper and Row, 1962.

Dupuy, R. Ernest, and Trevor N. Dupuy. *The Encyclopedia of Military History.* New York: Harper and Row, 1986.

Eccles, W. J. *France in America.* New York: Harper and Row, 1972.

Editors at Time-Life, *The Expressmen.* Alexandria, Virginia: Time-Life Books, 1974.

Editors at Time-Life, *The Gunfighters.* Alexandria, Virginia: Time-Life Books, 1974.

Editors at Time-Life, *The Old West.* Alexandria, Virginia: Time-Life Books, 1976.

Editors at Time-Life, *The Spanish West.* Alexandria, Virginia: Time-Life Books, 1976.

Ehle, John. *Trail of Tears: The Rise and Fall of the Cherokee Nation.* New York: Doubleday, 1988.

Faust, Patricia L., ed. *Historical Times Illustrated Encyclopedia of the Civil War.* New York: Harper and Row, 1986.

Faust, Clarence H. and Thomas H. Johnson. *Jonathan Edwards.* New York: Hill and Wang, 1962.

Feather, Leonard. *The Book of Jazz from Then Till Now.* 1956; reprint ed., New York: Dell, 1976.

Feather, Leonard. *Inside Jazz.* 1949: reprint ed., New York: Da Capo, 1977.

Fahrenbach, T. R. *Lone Star: A History of Texas and the Texans.* New York: Macmillan, 1968.

Finger, John R. *The Eastern Band of Cherokees, 1819-1900.* Knoxville: University of Tennessee Press, 1984.

Fleischmann, Glen. *The Cherokee Removal, 1838.* New York: Franklin Watts, 1971.

Flint, Timothy. *Biographical Memoir of Daniel Boone.* 1833; reprint ed. edited by James K. Folsom. New Haven, Connecticut: College and University Press, 1967.

Floyd, Candace. *America's Great Disasters.* New York: Mallard, 1990.

Floyd, Candace. *The History of New England,* New York: Portland House, 1990.

Foley, William E. *A History of Missouri,* vol. 1. Columbia: University of Missouri Press, 1971.

Foner, Eric, et al. *The Reader's Companion to American History.* Boston: Houghton Mifflin, 1991.

Frost, Lawrence A. *The Custer Album: A Pictorial Biography of General George A. Custer.* Norman: University of Oklahoma Press, 1964.

Garruth, Gorton. *What Happened When: A Chronology of Lives and Events in America.* Signet, 1989.

Genovese, Eugene. *In Red and Black: Marxian Explorations in Southern and Afro-American History.* University of Tennessee, 1984.

Genovese, Eugene. *Roll, Jordan, Roll: The World the Slaves Made.* New York: Random House/Vintage, 1976.

Gentry, Curt. *J. Edgar Hoover: The Man and the Secrets*. New York: Norton, 1991.

Gibson, Charles. *Spain in America*. New York: Harper and Row, 1966.

Giedion, Siegfried. *Mechanization Takes Command: A Contribution to Anonymous History*. New York: Norton, 1969.

Gilbert, Bill. *God Gave Us This Country: Tekamthi and the First American Civil War*. New York: Anchor/Doubleday, 1989.

Goetzmann, William H. *Army Exploration in the American West, 1803-1863*. New Haven: Yale University Press, 1959.

Grun, Bernard. *The Timetables of History*. New York: Touchstone, 1963.

Hanchett, William. *The Lincoln Murder Conspiracies*. Urbana and Chicago: University of Illinois Press, 1983.

Hartley, William and Ellen. *Osceola: The Unconquered Indian*. New York: Hawthorn Books, 1973.

Hentoff, Nat, and Albert J. McCarthy, eds. *Jazz: New Perspectives on the History of Jazz*. New York: Da Capo, 1975.

Hodges, Andrew. *Alan Turing: Enigma*. New York: Simon and Schuster, 1983.

Hofstadter, Richard. *The American Political Tradition*. New York: Knopf, 1948.

Hollon, W. Eugene. *Frontier Violence: Another Look*. London, Oxford, and New York: Oxford University Press, 1974.

Hubbard, William. *The History of the Indian Wars in New England from the First Settlement to the Termination of the War with King Phillip, in 1677*. Facsimile of 1865 reprint of 1814 ed. New York: Kraus Reprint Co., 1969.

Jennings, Francis. *The Ambiguous Iroquois Empire: The Covenant Chain Confederation of Indian Tribes with English Colonies*. New York: W. W. Norton, 1984.

Jennings, Francis. *Empire of Fortune: Crowns, Colonies, and Tribes in the Seven Years' War in America*. New York: Norton, 1988.

Jones, Leroi. *Black Music*. New York: Morrow, 1967.

Jones, Leroi. *Blues People*. New York: Morrow, 1963.

Josephson, Matthew. *Edison*. New York: McGraw Hill, 1959.

Josephy, Alvin M., Jr. *The Civil War in the American West*. New York: Knopf, 1991.

Kaplan, Philip, and Rex Alan Smith. *One Last Look: A Sentimental Journey to the Eighth Air Force Heavy Bomber Bases of World War II in England*.

Keegan, John. *The Second World War*. New York: Viking, 1989.

Knight, Arthur. *The Liveliest Art: A Panoramic History of the American Movies*. New York: New American Library, 1957.

Kolko, Gabriel. *Anatomy of a War: Vietnam, the United States, and the Modern Historical Experience*. New York: Pantheon, 1985.

Kolko, Gabriel. *Triumph of Conservatism: A Reinterpretation of American History, 1900-1916*. New York: Free Press, 1977.

Lacey, Robert. *Ford: The Men and the Machine*. Boston: Little Brown, 1986.

Lamar, Howard R. *The Readers Encyclopedia of the American West.* New York: Crowell, 1977.

Lasch, Christopher. *The True and Only Heaven: Progress and Its Critics.* New York: Norton, 1991.

Lavender, David. *Bent's Fort.* Garden City, New York: Doubleday, 1954.

Lavender, David. *The Great West.* Boston: Houghton Mifflin, 1987.

Lavender, David. *Land of Giants: The Drive to the Pacific Northwest, 1750-1950.* Lincoln: University of Nebraska Press, 1958.

Lazarus, Edward. *Black Hills, White Justice.* New York: HarperCollins, 1991.

Limerick, Patricia. *The Legacy of Conquest: The Unbroken Past of the American West.*

Lyons, Len. *101 Best Jazz Albums.* New York: Morrow, 1980.

Malone, Michael P., and Richard W. Etulain. *The American West: A Twentieth-Century History.* Lincoln: University of Nebraska Press, 1989.

Marcus, Greil. *Dead Elvis: A Chronicle of a Cultural Obsession.* New York: Doubleday, 1991.

Marcus, Greil. *Mystery Train: Images of America in Rock and Roll Music.* New York: Plume, 1990.

Marshall, S. L. A. *Crimsoned Prairie: The Indian Wars.* New York: Da Capo, 1972.

McCandless, Perry. *A History of Missouri,* vol. 2. Columbia: University of Missouri Press, 1972.

McPherson, James M. *Battle Cry of Freedom: The Civil War Era.* New York: Ballantine, 1988.

Montgomery, David. *The Fall of the House of Labor.* New York: Cambridge University Press, 1989.

Morris, Richard B. *Encyclopedia of American History.* New York: Harper and Brothers, 1953.

Nash, Roderick. *Wilderness and the American Mind.* Revised ed. New Haven and London: Yale University Press, 1967.

Nye, Russell. *The Unembarrassed Muse: The Popular Arts in America.* New York: Dial Press, 1970.

Parker, Watson. *Gold in the Black Hills.* Norman: University of Oklahoma Press, 1966.

Parkman, Francis. *The Conspiracy of Pontiac and the Indian War after the Conquest of Canada.* Boston: Little, Brown, 1874.

Parkman, Francis. *France and England in North America: A Series of Historical Narratives.* 4 vols. Boston: Little, Brown, 1875.

Parrish, William. *A History of Missouri,* vol. 2. Columbia: University of Missouri Press, 1973.

Paul, Rodman W. *The Far West and the Great Plains in Transition, 1859-1900.* New York: Harper and Row, 1988.

Phillips, Charles, et al. "Empires Besieged," in *TimeFrame AD 200-600,* Alexandria, Virginia: Time-Life Books, 1988.

Phillips, Charles. *Heritage of the West.* New York: Crescent Books, 1992.

Phillips, Charles. *Missouri: Mother of the American West.* Chatsworth, California: Windsor, 1988.

Pratt, John Lowell, and Jim Benagh. *The Official Encyclopedia of Sports.* New York: Franklin Watts, 1964.

Prucha, Francis Paul. *The Great Father: The United States Government and the American Indian*. Lincoln: University of Nebraska Press, 1984.

Prucha, Francis Paul, ed. *Documents of United States Indian Policy*. 2nd ed., expanded. Lincoln: University of Nebraska Press, 1990.

Quinn, David B., ed. *North American Discovery Circa 1000-1612*. New York: Harper and Row, 1971.

Rawis, Walton. *Wake Up, America: World War I and the American Poster.* New York: Abbeville, 1988.

Reisner, Mark. *Cadillac Desert: The American West and Its Disappearing Water.* New York: Viking Penguin, 1987.

Rhodes, Richard. *The Making of the Atomic Bomb*. New York: Simon and Schuster, 1986.

Rice, Arnold S., et al. *United States History to 1877*. Harper and Row, 1977.

Rich, E. E. *The History of the Hudson's Bay Company, 1670-1870*. London: Hudson's Bay Record Society, 1958-59.

Riis, Jacob. *How the Other Half Lives*. 1890; reprint ed., New York: Hill and Wang, 1957.

Sauer, Carl Ortwin. *Sixteenth Century North America: The Land and the People as Seen by the Europeans*. Berkeley: University of California Press, 1971.

Sifakis, Carl. *The Mafia Encyclopedia*. New York: Facts On File, 1989.

Slotkin, Richard. *Regeneration through Violence: The Mythology of the American Frontier, 1600-1860*. Middletown, Connecticut: Wesleyan University Press, 1973.

Slotkin, Richard, and James K. Folsom, eds. *So Dreadfull a Judgment: Puritan Responses to King Phillip's War, 1676-1677*. Middletown, Connecticut: Wesleyan University Press, 1978.

Smelser, Marshal, and Joan R. Gundersen. *American History at a Glance*. New York: Harper and Row, 1978.

Smith, Page. *A New Age Begins: A People's History of the American Revolution*. 2 vols. New York: Viking Penguin, 19~6.

Smith, William, Jr. *The History of the Province of New York; Volume One: From the First Discovery to the Year 1732; Volume Two; A Continuation, 1732-1762*. 1757, 1830; reprinted., Cambridge: Harvard University Press, 1972.

Sobell, Robert. *IBM: Colossus in Transition*. New York: Times Books, 1981.

Stammp, Kenneth M. *The Peculiar Institution: Slavery in the Ante- bellum South*. New York: Random House/Vintage, 1956.

Steffens, Lincoln. *The Shame of the Cities*. 1904; reprint ed., New York: Hill and Wang, 1969.

Tiffts, Wilton S. *Ellis Island*. New York: Contemporary Books, 1990.

Tuchman, Barbara M. *The March of Folly: From Troy to Vietnam*. New York: Ballantine, 1984.

Turner, Thomas Reed. *Beware the People Weeping: Public Opinion and the Assassination of Abraham Lincoln*. Baton Rouge and London: Louisiana State University Press, 1982.

United States (archives and government documents). *War of the Rebellion: A Compilation of the Official Records of the Union and Confederate Armies*. Washington, D.C.: U.S. Government Printing Office, 1880-1901.

Utley, Robert M. *Billy the Kid*. Lincoln: University of Nebraska Press, 1989.

Utley, Robert M. *Frontier Regulars: The United States Army and the Indian, 1866-1890*. New York: Macmillan, 1973.

Utley, Robert M. and Wilcomb E. Washburn. *Indian Wars*. New York: American Heritage; Boston: Houghton Mifflin, 1977.

Vestal, Stanley. *Sitting Bull: Champion of the Sioux*. Boston: Houghton Mifflin, 1932.

Waldman, Carl. *The Atlas of the North American Indian*. New York: Facts on File, 1985.

Waldman, Carl. *Who Was Who in Native American History*. New York: Facts on File, 1990.

Washburn, Wilcomb. *The Indian in America*. New York: Harper and Row, 1975.

Williams. Juan. *Eyes on the Prize: America's Civil Rights Years, 1954-1965*. Penguin, 1987.

Woodward, C. Vann. *The Strange Career of Jim Crow*. New York: Oxford University Press, 1966.

INDEX